The Politics of
Race in Canada

Readings in Historical Perspectives, Contemporary Realities, and Future Possibilities

Edited by Maria Wallis
and Augie Fleras

OXFORD
UNIVERSITY PRESS

OXFORD

UNIVERSITY PRESS

8 Sampson Mews, Suite 204, Don Mills, Ontario M3C 0H5
www.oupcanada.com

Oxford University Press is a department of the University of Oxford.
It furthers the University's objective of excellence in research, scholarship,
and education by publishing worldwide in

Oxford   New York

Auckland   Cape Town   Dar es Salaam   Hong Kong   Karachi
Kuala Lumpur   Madrid   Melbourne   Mexico City   Nairobi
New Delhi   Shanghai   Taipei   Toronto

With offices in

Argentina   Austria   Brazil   Chile   Czech Republic   France   Greece
Guatemala   Hungary   Italy   Japan   Poland   Portugal   Singapore
South Korea   Switzerland   Thailand   Turkey   Ukraine   Vietnam

Oxford is a trade mark of Oxford University Press
in the UK and in certain other countries

Published in Canada
by Oxford University Press

Copyright © Oxford University Press Canada 2009

Library and Archives Canada Cataloguing in Publication

The politics of race in Canada: readings in historical perspectives,
contemporary realities, and future possibilities / edited by Maria Wallis
& Augie Fleras.

Includes bibliographical references and index.
ISBN 978-0-19-542805-6

1. Canada—Race relations—History. 2. Canada—Ethnic relations—
History. 3. Racism—Canada—History. I. Wallis, Maria A. (Maria
Antoinette), 1960– II. Fleras, Augie, 1947–

FC104.P66 2008   305.800971   C2008-906039-3

Cover image: Bjorn Rasmussen/iStockphoto

Printed and bound in Canada.

7 8 9 — 18 17 16

(Toronto: Canadian Scholars' Press Inc./ Women's Press, 2005), 51–76. Reprinted by permission of Canadian Scholars' Press Inc.

Lawrence, Bonita, and Enakshi Dua. 'Decolonizing Anti-racism', *Social Justice* 32, 4 (2005): 120–43. Reprinted by permission of *Social Justice*.

Levitt, Cyril, and William Shaffir. 'The Swastika as Dramatic Symbol: A Case-study of Ethnic Violence in Canada', in *The Jews in Canada*, eds Robert J. Brym, William Shaffir, and Morton Weinfeld (Toronto: Oxford University Press, 1993), 77–96. Reprinted by permission of the publisher and by permission of the authors.

Li, Peter S. 'Thorny Questions and Conceptual Biases', in *The Chinese in Canada*, 2nd edn (Toronto: Oxford University Press, 1998), 3–12. Copyright © 1998 Oxford University Press Canada. Reprinted by permission of the publisher.

Mahtani, Minelle. 'Tricking the Border Guards: Performing Race', *Environment and Planning D: Society and Space* (London: Pion Limited) 20 (2002): 425–40. Reprinted by permission. Minelle Mahtani is an Assistant Professor in the Department of Geography and Planning at the Program in Journalism at University of Toronto.

Ng, Roxana. 'Immigrant Women, Community Work, and Class Relations', in *The Politics of Community Services: Immigrant Women, Class and State* (Toronto: Garamond, 1988), 11–22.

Reprinted by permission of the publisher.

Razack, Sherene. 'Geopolitics, Culture Clash, and Gender after September 11', *Social Justice* 32, 4 (2005): 11–31. Reprinted by permission of *Social Justice*.

Stasiulis, Daiva K. 'Theorizing Connections: Gender, Race, Ethnicity, and Class', in *Race and Ethnic Relations in Canada*, 2nd edn, ed. Peter S. Li (Toronto: Oxford University Press, 1990), 269–305. Copyright © 1990 Oxford University Press Canada. Reprinted by permission of the publisher.

Tanovich, David M. 'What Is It?', in *The Colour of Justice: Policing Race in Canada* (Irwin Law, 2006), 9–30. Reprinted by permission of the publisher.

Walker, James St. G. '"Race" and the Law', in *'Race', Rights and the Law in the Supreme Court of Canada* (Toronto/Waterloo, ON: Wilfrid Laurier University Press for The Osgoode Society for Canadian Legal History, 1997), 12–32. Reprinted by permission.

Winks, Robin W. 'Negro School Segregation in Ontario and Nova Scotia', *Canadian Historical Review* 52, 2: 164–91. Copyright © 1969 Toronto University Press. Reprinted by permission of University of Toronto Press, Inc. <www.utpjournals.com>.

Woodsworth, James S. *Strangers within Our Gates, or Coming Canadians* (Toronto: F.C. Stephenson/Missionary Society of the Methodist Church, Canada, 1909), 190–227.

Introduction

Conceptualizing the Politics of Race: Taking Race Seriously

Re/Conceptualizing Race

A paradox haunts the politics of race in Canada. To one side is an awareness that race loomed large in the past (Walker 1997). The world's population was partitioned into bound and fixed categories of people whose distinctive assemblage of physical, mental, and moral attributes could be arranged in ascending/descending orders of superiority/inferiority. The application of this race logic proved disastrous to those negatively racialized. To the other side is a dismaying notion that race continues to matter for often similar reasons, namely, to justify the exclusion or exploitation of racialized others. Race matters not only as a predictor of success and failure but also as (1) a central organizing principle in constructing society, (2) deeply embedded in our thinking and acting, and (3) a core component of minority identities and patterns of resistance (Holdaway 1996; Young and Braziel 2006; Agnew 2007; Hier and Bolaria 2007). Yet another paradox prevails: Canadians may dismiss the salience of race as a cognitive category with any empirical legitimacy. But despite the myth of Canada as a raceless and colour-blind society (Backhouse 1999; Razack 2002; Das Gupta et al. 2007), people continue to act as if race is real, with often discriminatory consequences for racialized minority women and men—reaffirming yet again the all too prescient

postulate that phenomena do not have to be real to have real consequences.

Few would dispute the impact of race on contemporary Canada. Race exerts a pervasive influence at varying levels of expression—from where people live, to who they hire, to what they can expect from life. Public participation and political decision-making are influenced by prevailing stereotypes and racial prejudices. Social rewards are allocated on the basis of racial affiliation, with the result that race remains a key predictor in defining who gets what (Hier and Bolaria 2007). Racialized minorities bear the brunt of negative treatment, ranging from local snubs, to half-hearted service delivery, to blatant racism resulting in class-action race-discrimination lawsuits (Dei 2007; Hussain 2007). Race profiling remains a major problem in the policing of both young black and Aboriginal males (Wortley 2005; Tanovich 2006; Tator and Henry 2006; Engel 2008). People of colour continue to be employed as cheap and disposable labour in often menial tasks (Galabuzi 2006). Foreign-born racialized minorities tend to earn less than whites even when educational levels are held constant (Pendakur 2005; Teelucksingh and Galabuzi 2005). In that minority professionals in Canada and the United States can't escape the stigma of race in their daily lives, many find it difficult to get jobs consistent with their credentials (Roscigno et al. 2007). Even the emergence of race-conscious equity programs to ameliorate disadvantage are subject to criticism as reverse discrimination.

In other words, instead of being banished to the dustbin of history, as widely anticipated, the race concept has managed to do the improbable: not only to survive but also to flourish and inflame. Consider an article in the 15 April 2006 issue of *The Economist* that emphasized the growing importance of race for medical research ('Not a Black and White Question'), or the intensity of emotions kindled by playing the race card leading up to the election of the first black president of the United States, Barack Obama. And race rose to the fore during the 2008 Beijing Summer Olympics when Jamaican sprinters won four out of six gold medals in these events, while Ethiopian long distance runners earned three out of four gold medals, prompting questions of why and how. The salience of race as a lived reality/lived experience—not only in the language of the street but also in the idiom of identity (Pascal 2006)—is captured by Omi and Winant (1993: 5) when they write,

> Our society is so thoroughly racialized that to be without a racial identity is to be in danger of having no identity at all. To be raceless is akin to being genderless.

In citing Omi and Winant's argument about race as a historical process that is socially meaningful and politically consequential, Daniel Berardi (2008: xvi) reinforces the reality of race as a perceived difference that makes a difference:

> Race is conceived as both a social structure and a cultural discourse, susceptible to change, that informs how we see ourselves, how others see us, and how we represent each other. In this way, race is an identity that is simultaneously imposed on us and that we elect to assume. Anything but an illusion, race as identity is meaningful, even if not biological

or divinely determined, because it has [a] real impact on everyday life, on social practice, and the stuff of representation. Hence, while race and identity are often erroneously perceived as natural or divine, they are in fact historical and cultural processes fraught by oppression yet marked by resistance.

Such persistence and provocation raise an interesting if not perplexing question: If race originated when people didn't know better, why does it persist at present? After all, we live in a world of better-informed people, few dare to openly demonize minorities as racially inferior, and those who accentuate our differences are sharply rebuked for saying the unspeakable. In other words, accounting for the origins of race is one thing; explaining its persistence is something else (Cashmore and Jennings 2001).

Reactions to the politics of race are no less puzzling (Carter 2007). On the one hand are those who believe race is real and reflective of social reality (Sarich and Miele 2004). Consider the lingering popularity of racial evolutionary schemes that partitioned the world into races and then ranked these racialized groups according to their developmental levels (Rushton 1994). On the other hand are those who believe race should never dominate public discourse because it simply doesn't exist. What exists are relationships and activities that become racialized (i.e., defined along racial lines) by those in positions of power (Miles 1982). Accordingly, the concept of race must be rejected on grounds that its misguided use as bad science masks a hidden agenda. Others disagree: race is endorsed as a biologically grounded social construction that has proven politically significant in shaping everything from identities and relationships to opportunities and outcomes. Contradictions abound because of these varied responses. Race may reflect an accident of birth, yet profoundly shape a person's life or life chances; race may be skin deep, yet provide a quick indicator for judging the worth of an individual or group; race should never justify unequal treatment, yet may prove pivotal in reversing discrimination (Fernandez 1997); race constitutes a discourse in defence of dominant ideology, yet may be re-politicized into a discourse of resistance ('black is beautiful') that challenges and transforms.

Clearly, then, race is both 'more' and 'less' in defining who gets what, and why. Race may not be real in the conventional sense; nevertheless, as a social construct that explains and justifies, people perceive it to be real and act accordingly by denying or excluding. Insofar as a belief in race is tantamount to a self-fulfilling prophecy—if people are labelled in racial terms they are more likely to comply with this stigma—moves to dismiss its salience behind a self-righteous (if well-intentioned) facade of colour-blindness are short-sighted. To ignore race in a racialized society is tantamount to whitewashing the very situation that created the problem in the first place—that is, an acknowledgement that the legal principles and rule of law underpinning the foundational order of society are neither neutral nor passive, but racialized in Eurocentric ways that systemically privilege whiteness as the norm (Cose 1997; Doane 2007). This ambiguity is aptly conveyed by Constance Backhouse (1999: 274) when criticizing the banishment of race from modern discourses in the mistaken hope of fostering a colour-blind society:

But proponents of 'race-neutrality' neglect to recognize that our society is not a race-neutral one. It is built upon centuries of racial division and discrimination. The legacy of such bigotry infects all of our institutions, relationships, and legal frameworks. To advocate 'colour-blindness' as an ideal for the modern world is to adopt the false mythology of 'racelessness' that has plagued the Canadian legal system . . . and serve[s] to condone the continuation of white supremacy across Canadian society.

Another paradox informs the politics of race. The demise of race as a salient social category was long predicted and gradually embraced. Yet no matter how often discarded as intellectually dead, race manages to rebound as a politically charged but skilfully concealed marker of difference and discrimination. Or as succinctly put by Toni Morrison, the Nobel Prize–winning American author and professor, 'Race represents a metaphorical narrative'—that is, a way of referring to and disguising forces, classes, events, and expressions of social decay and economic division far more threatening to the body politic than biological 'race' ever was (cited in Young and Braziel 2006: 13).

Not surprisingly, reactions to race invariably invite scorn or criticism, regardless of the position taken. Those who endorse the race concept tend to be dismissed as the intellectual equivalents of 'knuckle-dragging Neanderthals'. Conversely, those who contemptuously dismiss race as fiction stand accused of trampling on a peoples' identity by ignoring their social history, group solidarity, or cultural aspirations. Those in between these poles confront a complexity of confusion, as Ken Wiwa (2001) concedes when reviewing Lawrence Hill's book *Black Berry, Sweet Juice: On Being Black and White in Canada*:

Race is just about the trickiest topic to write about with any measure of objectivity, and only brave men or fools should try. Anyone who wants to walk the minefield of race should invest in a thick skin with chameleon-like pigment . . . Because the trouble with race is that there are black and white and a kaleidoscope of shades in between.

In other words, the concept of 'race' can generate more debate and controversy than any other word in the English language, with some using it literally, others critically, still others preferring euphemisms like ethnicity, and yet others still squarely addressed. Just as racism continues to persist, albeit in more covert forms than in the past (Agnew 2007; Holdaway and O'Neill 2007), so too are the politics of race as salient today as then, albeit behind a smokescreen of denial or coded subtext (also Li 2007). But out of sight is not necessarily out of mind when it comes to race politics in Canada, and therein lies the challenge of addressing what many dismiss or deny. By bringing together selections that have informed debates and generated controversies from the nineteenth century onward, this unique collection confirms W.I. Thomas's prescient notion: when it comes to race, phenomena do not have to be empirically real to be existentially real and inexcusably destructive.

Acknowledgements

This book represents a reflection of my own life experiences in Canada since emigrating from Karachi, Pakistan, in 1975. On another level, it is also a reflection on, a critique of, and a hope for, the fields of race, social inequality, and feminist studies in Canada.

I want to express my profound gratitude to Peter Chambers, Developmental Editor, and Amanda Maurice, Assistant Editor, who were professional, constant in their enthusiasm and support, and very skilled in guiding this project through various stages. Euan White and others 'behind the scenes' have also been invaluable in this process. What an amazing team. I feel both privileged and honoured to have made this journey with you. Thank you. The work on this book has been an intense, exciting, and very enjoyable collaborative experience for me.

Thank you also to Lucia Alfonso, Augie Fleras, Siu-ming Kwok, Lisa Meschino, Lina Sunseri, and Esmeralda Wallis for their support and encouragement, specifically during 2006–8, a time of transition.

I dedicate this book to my daughter, Rose Mansi Wallis. This book hopes to contribute to a Canadian society that will be one of authentic racial equality and justice for her, her children, and the next seven generations.

Maria Wallis
wallismariarose@hotmail.com

Credits

Aylward, Carol A. 'Canadian Critical Race Litigation: Wedding Theory and Practice', in *Canadian Critical Race Theory: Racism and the Law* (Halifax, NS: Fernwood, 1999), 76–133. Reprinted by permission of the publisher.

Backhouse, Constance. 'Race Definition Run Amuck: "Slaying the Dragon of Eskimo Status" in *Re Eskimos*, 1939', in *Colour-coded: A Legal History of Racism in Canada 1900–1950* (Toronto: University of Toronto Press for The Osgoode Society for Canadian Legal History, 1999), 18–29. Reprinted by permission.

Boyd, Monica, Gustave Goldmann, and Pamela White. 'Race in the Canadian Census', in *Visible Minorities in Canada*, eds Leo Driedger and Shiva Halli (Montreal and Toronto: McGill-Queen's University Press, 2000), 33–54. Reprinted by permission.

Canadian Constitution Foundation. 'Japanese-Canadian Fishermen's Association: Seeking to Intervene before the Supreme Court of Canada in *R. v. Kapp*', available at <http://www.canadiancon stitutionfoundation.ca/files/pdf/JCFA%20back grounder%201%20October%202007[2].pdf> (2007). Reprinted by permission of the Canadian Constitution Foundation.

The Colour of Poverty Campaign. 'Fact Sheet #1: Understanding the Racialization of Poverty in Ontario: An Introduction in 2007', available at: <http://www.colourofpoverty.ca> (2007). Reprinted by permission of The Colour of Poverty Campaign.

Cooper, Afua. 'Acts of Resistance: Black Men and Women Engage Slavery in Upper Canada, 1793–1803', *Ontario History* 99, 1 (2007): 5–17. Reprinted by permission of the Ontario Historical Society.

Dei, George J. Sefa. 'Speaking Race: Silence, Salience, and the Politics of Anti-racist Scholarship', in *Race & Racism in 21st-century Canada: Continuity, Complexity, and Change*, eds Sean P. Hier and B. Singh Bolaria (Peterborough, ON: Broadview Press, 2007), 53–65. Copyright © 2007. Reprinted by permission of Broadview Press.

Foster, Cecil. *Where Race Does Not Matter: The New Spirit of Modernity* (Toronto: Penguin, 2005), 24–30. Copyright © 2005 Cecil Foster. Reprinted by permission of Penguin Group (Canada), a division of Pearson Canada, Inc., and by permission of the author.

Gibbon, John Murray. *Canadian Mosaic: The Making of a Northern Nation* (Toronto: McClelland & Stewart, 1938), v–xiii.

Henry, Frances, et al. 'The Ideology of Racism', in *The Colour of Democracy: Racism in Canadian Society*, 2nd edn (Toronto: Harcourt Canada, 2000), 15–33. Copyright © 2000 Nelson Education Ltd. Reproduced by permission <www.cengage.com/permissions>.

James, Carl E. 'Race and the Social/Cultural Worlds of Student Athletes', in *Race in Play*

Preface

The myth of racelessness in Canada never ceases to amaze. In contrast to the flagrant abuses of race that once prevailed in the United States, from slavery to the Ku Klux Klan—with Jim Crow laws in between—Canada is thought to have managed race differently. A supposedly kinder and gentler Canada not only rejected the relevance of race as grounds for managing diversity and social ordering but also upheld the ideals of colour-blindness as grounds for society-building (Vickers 2002). Canadians continue to be widely applauded for promoting achievement over skin colour as a basis for recognition, rewards, and relationships (Foster 2005). But like all powerful national dreams, this myth conceals more than it reveals, resulting in distortions that confuse or divide. Such a dilemma makes it doubly important to deconstruct these 'mythconceptions' by exposing those 'truths' that more accurately depict what 'really' happened.

This book of readings on the politics of race in Canada is predicated on a simple premise: race mattered in the past, race matters at present, and race will continue to matter in the future. Few once doubted the existence of race as a constituent unit of social reality. Many believed the world was divisible into fixed and bounded formations, each with its own unique assemblage of physical, cultural, and mental attributes that could be assembled into an ascending/descending hierarchy. Colonial regimes routinely introduced and sustained complex racial hierarchies to reinforce their exalted status over racialized others (Thobani 2007). The salience of race persists in the present—not in the historical sense of race as division and determination but because people believe it to be real and act accordingly. More perplexing still are signs that race as a social construct will matter in the future. Despite claims to race-neutrality as a preferred ideal, Canada constitutes a racialized society that is designed and organized to advance certain interests at the expense of others, with the result that race remains a key variable in influencing people's identities, experiences, and outcomes.

There is no point in denying the unavoidable. Race matters whether we like it or not, approve or disapprove, and it will continue to matter for as long as race underscores people's perceptions of others, influences their perceptions of themselves (how they see, think, experience, and relate to the world), and shapes their life chances with respect to predicting failure or success (Phillips 2007). Not surprisingly, debates over race generate some of the most bewildering dilemmas in contemporary politics. Quite possibly, more bad science has been conducted in the name of race than in any other area of scholarly endeavour, in large part because research is motivated by preconceived notions of superiority and inferiority (*The Economist* 2007). But instead of atrophying out of existence as many had predicted or hoped, race as a concept is experiencing a resurgence because of its association with genetics and genealogy (ancestry, descent, and belonging) (Carter 2007). The end result is a proliferation of polemics as diverse as 'playing the race card' and 'racial profiling' to those of 'race-based defence', 'critical race theory', 'race-neutral policies', and 'racial quotas'.

To say the politics of race are polarized is surely an understatement. Its politicization covers a lot of intellectual ground; for a few, race possesses a natural biological status; for many, race is a social construct without scientific merit; and for the rest, race represents an interplay of the social with the biological (Harding 2002). For some, Canada is by definition raceless; for others, race in Canada is real and must be addressed accordingly; for yet others, race is a fiction lacking any scientific validity that deserves to be ignored; and for still others, race is a biologically infused social construct that exerts a significant impact on the lives and life chances of racialized Canadians. Or consider the assertion that there is only a single race—the human race—albeit dominated by one group with the power to define what is normal and acceptable in society (Eisenstein 2007). Equally contested is its explanatory worth. To one side is the belief that race is key in explaining individual and group differences with respect to power and privilege; to the other side, gender, class, and ethnicity are as important as race for deciding outcomes; to yet another side, race cannot possibly explain anything because it no longer matters in a race-neutral ('colour-blind') Canada.

The conclusion seems inescapable: the concept of race is proving something of a 'floating signifier' that can mean everything—or nothing—depending on the context, criteria, or consequences. By utilizing a broad range of writing on race as a conceptual lens for analyzing and assessing inter-group relations in Canada, *The Politics of Race in Canada* provides a corpus of core readings that explore the principles, practices, and polemics of race both in the past and at present. If, as Paul Gilroy (2000: 11) once stated, we are living through a period of profound transformation in how the idea of race is understood and acted upon, including how racial differences are seen and identities constructed, the historical legacy behind this transformation and the continuation of race thinking needs to be explored. Previously published (and several unpublished) articles have been carefully selected to link the past with the present, and have been organized accordingly: (1) how the concept of race has been defined, utilized, and debated in modern society; (2) its long and complex history as an idea and mindset; (3) how race as an ideology continues to advance vested interests in political and economic arenas; (4) its continuing significance and changing meanings with respect to racialization, racism, and anti-racism; (5) its utilization for explaining, justifying, and maintaining group differences—sometimes openly, other times covertly; and (6) how the intersection of race with gender and class provides an analytical tool for understanding social equality (Cashmore and Jennings 2001; Dixson and Rousseau 2006). Theoretical articles are counterbalanced with substantive material that draws attention to specific events, emergent developments, and shifting contexts. Historical articles provide a framework for thinking about race while securing a much needed corrective for uncovering those mythologies that whitewash history. Recent selections are more probing and provocative by incorporating a range of perspectives and disciplines that attend to one of the perplexing dilemmas of our time—how to take seriously what shouldn't be taken seriously in a racialized Canada.

Clearly, then, a paradox informs the politics of race in Canada. On one side is an awareness that race shouldn't matter as it once did in the past. On the other side is a dismaying notion that race continues to matter even though it shouldn't, but because it does, the issue of race must be

Contents

with 'scare' quotes to warn the wary of unintended pitfalls (Das Gupta et al. 2007; Fleras 2008).

Let's not mince words: race matters even though it shouldn't, but because it does, its importance must be confronted squarely. Race shouldn't be taken seriously, but because it is, its status as an explanatory framework as well as identity marker and organizing principle should not be taken lightly. In rejecting the widely held perception of Canada as a colour-blind society, where race doesn't or shouldn't matter, the lived experiences and opportunity structures of racialized minorities suggests the exact opposite—proving yet again that when it comes to race politics, reality is no match for perceptions (Das Gupta et al. 2007). Why, then, does race persist? Why has a largely worthless fiction of minimal scientific/biological value exerted such a prolonged and punishing effect in shaping the course of human history? Why, indeed, does a largely discredited construct enjoy such staying power, even in those multicultural contexts that aspire to colour-blind principles? Why does race as a social construct possess extraordinary powers, including its own set of dynamics that can cut across class lines and internally divide classes (Omi and Winant 1994)? This paradox—that we must take seriously what should never have been taken seriously—is captured below:

> [race] . . . can be seen as nothing but a phantom invented to justify a myriad of power relationships but, on the other hand, is one of history's most instrumental agencies of social composition? How does one write about the most potent instrument of taxonomy ever imposed on humankind without giving added credence to the idea of race as a viable organizing tool? (Hall 2000: 120)

In short, race must be taken seriously as a powerful determinant (and key variable) in influencing thought and behaviour, but not too seriously lest the wrong kind of legitimacy become attached to a scientifically worthless concept. References to race must avoid dismissing it as purely an 'illusion', yet avoid the trap of reifying (i.e., 'essentializing') it as a fixed and objective essence that can be grasped independent of context. An intermediate position acknowledges the reality of race—not in the determinative sense of shaping behaviour but in the discursive sense that perception is reality. The implications of framing race as socially constructed rather than biologically real are profound. Race is defined as a politically infused process for negatively labelling people or activities ('racialization') rather than a thing with a corresponding set of traits (Chan and Mirchandani 2002). Framing race as a verb ('process') instead of a noun ('an object') provides a reminder that even if race is a fiction with no empirical validity or scientific reality it is a powerful fabrication with boundless implications.

In 1903, the sociologist W.E.B. DuBois predicted that the race ('colour-line') problem would be the quintessential American paradox of the twentieth century. Here we are in the twenty-first century, and it can still be written:

> Among the social paradoxes of the twenty-first century is race. In the United States, race is both central and submerged, both 'unimportant' and 'all consuming', a social fabrication and a material reality. While the presence of race exists as a familiar part of our social landscapes, the meanings of race remain conflicted and seemingly unrestrained by the demands of logic, proof, or coherence. (Pascale 2007: 23)

Let's extend that argument in time and space by re/conceptualizing race as a framework for understanding some of the most bewildering dilemmas pervading Canadian society (Hier and Bolaria 2007). In this book, a broad range of 'scholarly' contributions from the past and present are utilized to explore the politics of race as a discourse in defence of dominant ideology as well as a discursive framework that challenges and transforms. The central theme is fairly straightforward: if race constitutes a historically grounded social construction, dynamic and shifting as well as contradictory and ambiguous, it's never far from the thrust and parry of privilege and power (Morris and Cowlishaw 1997). In advancing the interlocking nature of race with inequality, difference, and power, the race concept is examined around the following topics: (1) meaning and content, (2) genesis and rationale, (3) impact and implications, and (4) validity and value. Discussed as well are those social forces that advanced and continue to advance the race concept as a misguided yet powerful explanatory tool. Conversely the micro-politics of race are shown to impact on the identities, experiences, and opportunities of racialized minorities (Mahtani 2002). Finally, attention is directed at the macro-politics of race when applied to the dynamics of racialization, evolving expressions of racism, and anti-racism initiatives. Our intent is unequivocal: we believe it both timely and relevant to re/conceptualize race by exploring the politics of race around historical perspectives, contemporary realities, and future possibilities. Doing so is critical not only for conceptual clarity but also for putting race to rest as a marker of inferiority.

Framing Race: Human Races or the Human Race?

Defining race has proven elusive and exasperating (Biddiss 1979; Winant 2002). There is much of value in Ellis Cose's (1997: 1) cogent dismissal of race 'as a strange and flexible concept, with an endless capacity to confound'. Part of the problem reflects the multi-dimensionality of race as a concept in a constant state of flux, both fluid and malleable, and sharply contested (Gallagher 2007). Its meaning is socially constructed from an array of arbitrary characteristics that society has defined as important, with the result that definitions tend to be highly politicized. The misapplication of the race concept to the human species compounds the difficulties. The biology of race alludes to the division of a species into subunits of breeding populations, resulting in a predominance of certain physical and genetic characteristics. Applied to humans, however, a different logic emerges. In that it entailed the classification of groups of individuals because of preconceived attributes, race embodied a modernist belief in all-encompassing ('totalizing') explanations, namely, that humanity could be divided into a limited number of fixed races, each of whom possessed a distinctive assemblage of physical characteristics that determined thought and behaviour. Not only were groups defined as different because of predetermined and determining properties, but a normative standard of evaluation was also evoked in which clusters of differences were ranked higher or lower than others along a cascading scale of worth.

How valid is the race concept? Most social scientists reject the validity of the race concept as germane to any understanding of human diversity (Brace 2005; but see Sarich and Miele 2004). References to race have been discredited as pseudo-science and dangerous politics, without any redeeming scientific value or empirical merit. Anti-race arguments are numerous, but most commonly include the following reason: discrete and distinct categories of racially pure people do not exist. The intermingling effect of migration with intermarriage has made it impossible to draw a definitive line around human populations, with certain characteristics on one side, but not on the other (Martin and Franklin 1973). High rates of internal variation indicate that differences within so-called racial groups are often as broad as differences between groups. The arbitrariness of dividing humans into groups on the basis of dubious criteria also reinforces the inadmissibility of race as reality or explanation. In other words, humans consist of a single intra-breeding species (the human race) whose variations are largely skin deep.

Human variation exists of course. Populations of people may possess a higher rate of certain bio-genetic features than other groups, while individual variation in biology and aptitude is well known. Social scientists do not reject the reality of differences between individuals or among groups (populations). Nor do they deny the validity of studying these differences in an objective and scholarly fashion. What comes under dispute is the framing of group and individual differences along race lines. Put bluntly, while differences exist, what doesn't exist are racially discrete populations with fixed inventories of innate characteristics for ranking along ascending and descending orders. Clusters of specific traits can be classified, to be sure, but particular races of people cannot because human populations are internally diverse, constantly moving, and gradually merging at borders. The dearth of any biological reality or scientific justification makes it abundantly clear (Brace 2005): race represents a physically based social construct involving vested interests rather than anything inherent about reality (Miles 1982; Macedo and Gounari 2006). Therein lies the logic behind Winant's (1998) definition of race as '*a concept that signifies and symbolizes socio-political conflicts and interests in reference to different types of human bodies*'.

Race in History: Race Mattered

There is in the world a hierarchy of races . . . [Some] will direct and rule the others, and the lower work of the world will tend in the long run to be done by the lower breeds of men. This much we of the ruling colour will no doubt accept as obvious. (Murray 1900; cited in Banton 1987: vii)

As the above quote implies, the concept of race and a global racial hierarchy were generally regarded as self-evident truths. It was commonly assumed in the Western world, including the literati, that non-white peoples were innately inferior. To think otherwise made as much sense as contesting the law of gravity as immoral or immaterial (cited in Backhouse 1999). Nevertheless, the actual term 'race' and its connotations are of relatively recent origins. The first mention of race in the English language with its connotation of kin–tribe–lineage appeared in the sixteenth century (Montagu 1965). References to race did not gain much traction until the nineteenth century when religious-based typologies gave way to race-based discourses involving innateness, immutability, and inferiority (Miles and Brown 2003). The racialization of human diversity reflected a growing biologism, namely, from an Enlightenment model of race as common history and shared lineage to the primacy of race as the defining characteristic of humanity (Stepan 1982; Hier 2007). With the publication of books like Robert Knox's *The Races of Man* in 1850, relations of inferiority/superiority were no longer aligned along the religious plane, but grounded in the terrestriality of racial hierarchies (Anderson 2007). Once racial types were assigned a fixed moral value—that is, prescribed by nature as superior or inferior and backed by the unquestioned authority of science—doctrines of racial superiority proliferated accordingly (Montagu 1965). The slew of twentieth-century genocides attests to the destructive power of these groundless ideas.

Justifying Imperialism and Colonialism

Any theorizing of race must go beyond simple cultural politics, but acknowledge the centrality of broader political and economic developments (Anderson 2007). Doctrines of racial superiority evolved in response to the needs of an expanding European empire (Winant 1998). The expansion of Europe into culturally diverse regions spawned a system of global stratification and international division of labour that assigned races to a specific hierarchical status based on (1) their physical appearance, (2) value of local resources, (3) levels of political development, (4) power to resist European imperialism, (5) geographical location, and (6) cultural proximity to Europe (Walker 1997). These hierarchies were intrinsically racist: they employed the authority of science to confirm the superiority of some groups over others, thereby legitimizing the right of ostensibly superior races to rule over the inferior stocks (Stepan 1982; Vickers 2002; Brattain 2007). Their impact proved devastating: despite the arbitrariness of the criteria or classification for justifying inequality or domination, the race doctrine ended up commodifying people as objects for exploitation or control, as targets of pity or contempt, or as passive victims of progress.

Many regard the nineteenth century as the age of imperialism. With imperialism, various European nations (as well as Russia and the United States) assumed an inalienable right to conquer, colonize, and exploit overseas territories (for discussion, see Fleras and Elliott 2007). An expanding capitalist system reflected a need for foreign markets, investment opportunities, cheap labour, and accessible resources. But this predatory approach toward global domination exposed a paradox. First, how could so-called civilized and Christian nations rationalize and justify the blatant exploitation of others? Second, how could colonialist exploitation be sustained without contradicting the image of Europeans as a sophisticated and enlightened people with a moral duty to civilize and convert? Answers to these awkward questions inspired an ideology that condoned the mistreatment of others as natural or normal—even necessary in light of the 'white man's burden'. The contradiction between Christian ideals and exploitative practices was masked and mediated by the racist conviction that lower-ranked races would benefit from servitude and

close supervision (Lerner 1997). And because racial differences were deemed to be ingrained and permanent, Europeans were absolved of any responsibility for improving the plight of the inferior or subhuman. Consciences salved, they were free to push around 'inferior stocks' with impunity and without remorse.

That race-based doctrines originated to condone the negative treatment of non-Western populations is beyond dispute. The classification of Indigenous peoples and immigrants into racialized 'others' secured a conveniently simple excuse to justify exploitation during the era of European exploration, capitalistic expansion, and imperialistic dispossession (McCalla and Satzewich 2002). As Goldberg (2002) and others note (Thobani 2007), the race concept proved integral to the emergence of the modern nation-state, resulting in a racial caste-like state, with whites occupying what virtually amounted to a racial dictatorship. To be sure, the race concept did not necessarily originate to control or dominate. Nor did a belief in race reflect a robust and self-serving view of white superiority. As Winston Churchill wrote in 1898 with seeming resignation to the relentless march of progress:

> I do not admit, for instance, that a great wrong has been done to the Red Indians of America or the black people of Australia. . . . by the fact that a stronger race, a higher grade race, a more world-wise race, to put it that way, has come and taken their place. (cited in Gilbert 2007)

However well-intentioned or inadvertent, the cumulative impact of racial doctrines exerted a controlling or dominating effect. When sanctioned by the unassailable troika of science, statistics, and measurements, these classifications made group differences appear more comprehensive, more entrenched, and more scientifically valid than scriptural alternatives (Stocking 1968; Stepan 1982). When harnessed to military prowess and technological advances, the effects of such categorization proved devastating. How ironic: the race concept may have proven a social fiction—a fabrication in defence of white domination—but its capacity to inflict and inflame was anything but fictional.

Reifying Race: Enlightenment, Exploration, and Explanation

The era of exploration proved no less conducive to fostering a race mindset. European imaginations were piqued by sustained contact with highly diverse populations whose appearance and culture stimulated an outpouring of amusement, fascination, and repulsion. Man or ape: one species or many? Questions regarding the origins and diversity of humankind fascinated eighteenth-century European science and Enlightenment thought. Increasingly precise systems of classification were formulated for assigning each variant of humanity into its proper space in the natural order of things—on the assumption that each life form occupied a distinctive place within the overall scheme, that each form embodied a specific ideal type, and that each part possessed a unique set of identifiable and fixed characteristics that differed from others (Ewan and Ewan 2006). There was no room for ambiguity in a world where reality revolved around a singular and defining essence.

The intellectual climate proved receptive to race thinking. Reference to race as lineage or kin converged with Enlightenment philosophies that extolled the virtues of human progress and individual perfectibility. These doctrines reflected the humanist thesis of humans as distinct from animals so that humanity entailed progressive advancement beyond nature by transcending its limitations (Anderson 2007). In creating a lens for looking distinctively at the world, the concept of race secured a 'common sense' explanatory framework for explaining civilizational differences beyond simple reference to climate or history

(Smedley 2007). Initial classifications tended to be descriptive in orientation (Gould 1994). For example, Carolus Linnaeus (1758) divided the species *Homo sapiens* by geography into a seemingly unranked order of Americanus (Native American), Europaeus, Asiaticus, and Afer (African). And while these four types were distinguished in terms of temperament, colour, and behaviour, with a decided bias toward Europeans (Ewan and Ewan 2006), later typologies proved much more discriminating in assigning virtue or vice. Relations of inferiority/superiority as innately fixed evolved from the eighteenth century onward, including Johann Friedrich Blumenbach's (1776) widely cited taxonomy of racial stratification consisting of a fivefold typology that visualized humanity as a pyramid and ranked it accordingly: Caucasoid, Negroid, Mongoloid, American ('Indian'), and Malayan (Polynesian, Melanesian, and Australian).

Far from being the product of irrationality or hate, the race concept reflected an Enlightenment ethos to classify, understand, and control the global diversity of plants, animals, and peoples. Collapsing human diversity into a single grand scheme not only secured order out of chaos but also achieved the modernist project of parsimoniously explaining the totality of the human experience (Goldberg 1993). Just as early anthropologists devised a host of unilinear evolutionary schemes to explain the coexistence of civilization with that of barbarism and savagery, so too did social theorists resort to race as a discursive framework for understanding human differences and similarities (Biddiss 1979). But no sooner did notions of progress and perfectibility take hold than the paradigm shifted. The thesis of human progress was reworked into a doctrine of irrevocable differences between groups of people, in part because Enlightenment doctrines of perfectibility through progress had met their match (or counter-example) with Australia's First Peoples (Anderson 2007). Under the sway of these dogmas that privileged whiteness while demonizing 'darkness', Europeans embarked on civilizing crusades that masked human rights violations behind a facade of moral righteousness (Ewan and Ewan 2006; Fleras and Elliott 2007).

Canada: Race Mattered

To say that race once mattered in Canada is a colossal understatement (Walker 1997; Backhouse 1999). Canadian history is informed by a perception of Canada as a 'white man's society'—a view reinforced by [Prime] Minister Robert Borden who declared the Conservative Party stood for a white Canada (cited in Taylor et al. 2007). In reflecting and reinforcing the whiteness of Canada, race played a key role in defining entitlements on the strength of people's proximity to the so-called superior European races. The designation of race by colour—red, black, white, and yellow—was ubiquitous, with a wide range of scientists undertaking the complex and convoluted task of delineating racial categories while endlessly speculating about minute distinctions and exacting measurements.

Canada's legal system was no less complicit in Canada's race history (Walker 1997). Legislators and judges endlessly manipulated classifications of race into rigid and congealed definitions under Canadian law, erected racial hierarchies, justified racial discrimination, denied racial groups the right to vote, and segregated minorities according to race. For example, the paternalistic and archaic Indian Act of 1876, which remains in effect at present as a blueprint for government–Aboriginal peoples' relations, constitutes possibly one of the world's few pieces of legislation designed for a particular 'race' of people. Put candidly, rather than a tool of justice or empowerment, Canada's legal apparatus deployed the race concept as an instrument of oppression that marginalized and exploited.

The implications of race went beyond mere intellectualizing over origins, classifications, and attributes. Immigration policy rested on racial classifications that restricted immigration from non-preferred sources like China (Thobani 2007). Perceptions of Aboriginal peoples as an inferior race simplified the task of divesting the original occupants of their land and resources. Racialized minorities like blacks were routinely denied and excluded, and forced into patterns of segregation every bit as isolating as those in the United States (Winks 1969). Constance Backhouse (1999: 6) acknowledged how race intersected with class to secure unequal group relations:

> Racial classifications functioned as the hand servant for many disparate groups as they sought to explain why they were entitled to hold inequitable resources, status, and power over others. The adoption of the notion of 'race' in aid of the institution of black slavery is well known. It is equally evident that 'racial' ideology was pressed into service as an excuse for the seizure of First Nations lands. 'Race' was offered as the definitive explanation for the punitive treatment of Asian immigrants in the late nineteenth century. 'Racial' terminology was also used to rationalize exploitation between whites. . . . Saxon, Celtic, Norman, Irish, Welsh, Scottish, and English communities. Immigrants from southern and eastern Europe, Syria, Armenia, Arabia, India, and the Philippines often found their claim to 'whiteness' contested in North America. The discriminatory treatment meted out to Canadian francophones, to individuals who practised religions other than Protestantism, and to groups who emigrated to Canada from eastern and southern Europe has also been ideologically fastened to notions of 'race'.

In addition, the intersection of gender with race also proved integral to the colonial process. In keeping with the notion of Canada as a white man's country and white women as 'mothers of the race', the ideals of racial purity played a pivotal role in the design and organization of colonization, including its power dynamics, social hierarchies, and legitimating tactics (Seuffert 2006; Agnew 2007). But while white women may have symbolized and served as the standard-bearers of civilization, they occupied an ambivalent status as civilizers and domesticators, wielding power at times yet subject to control at other times.

Nowhere were the politics of race more deeply etched than in debates over immigration. Immigration to Canada was informed by and organized around a historically based racialized hierarchy (Satzewich 2007). Immigrants were ranked in order from the preferred (from Britain and western Europe) to the non-preferred (eastern Europe), to the inadmissible (China and India). Once preferred sources dried up, admittance was reluctantly extended to eastern and southern Europeans. Those from Russia, the Austro-Hungarian empire, Italy, and Turkey were generally regarded as uncivilized races of questionable value to Canada-building. Prior to the American Civil War, the Irish were racialized as 'low browed and savage, grovelling and bestial, lazy and wild, simian and sensual' (Roediger 1991: 133). But the subsequent transformation of the once inferior Irish (and earlier the Germans and later Italians and other southern Europeans) into the status of honorary whites reinforced the socially constructed and historically shifting nature of race (Lopez 2006).

Less fortunate were the Chinese and Indian 'races'. Like peripheral Europeans they were deemed to be racially inferior, exposed to blatantly legal restriction before and after entry, and subject to prejudice and discrimination. But unlike their European counterparts, Chinese and Indian races were vilified as a barrier to Canada-building, perceived as incapable of assimilation into a white man's country, deemed unsuited to Canada's climate or its culture, and dismissed as inadmissible (except as guest workers in the building of Canada's railways). Canada was so fixated on racial purity and an insistence on a whiter than white immigration policy that immigrants from Asia were routinely demonized as backward, lazy and immoral, and a threat (see also Seuffert 2006). According to section 38 of the 1910 Immigration Act, Chinese nationals were restricted from normal entry into Canada, then virtually banned in 1923—a situation not rectified until 1947. Even then, the shift was qualified. Instead of framing races in the discourse of inferiority, the notion of compatibility—not inferiority—prevailed. According to William Lyon Mackenzie King, a selectivity of immigrants was critical for Canada's racial identity and future prosperity:

> That Canada should desire to restrict immigration from the Orient is regarded as natural, that Canada should remain *a white man's country* [emphasis mine] is believed to be not only desirable for economic and social reasons but highly necessary on political and national grounds. (cited in Hawkins 1972)

Later as prime minister, King continued to harbour the kind of reservations that served as the basis for Canada's immigration program until the early 1960s:

> The government is strongly of the view that our immigration policy should be devised in a positive sense, with the definite objective, as I have already stated, of enlarging the population of the country. . . . With regards to the selection of immigrants, much has been said about discrimination. I wish to make it quite clear that Canada is perfectly within her rights in selecting the persons whom we regard as desirable future citizens. . . . large-scale immigration from the Orient would change the fundamental composition of the population. (Canada, House of Commons 1947: 2645–6)

That race once 'mattered' in the historical past is beyond dispute. Individuals and groups were racialized as different and inferiorized based on their cultural or biological proximity to Europe. But the legitimacy of race as scientific orthodoxy and explanatory framework began to erode after the First World War, at least among intellectuals, thanks in part to the pioneering efforts of American social scientists like Franz Boas and Margaret Mead. American sociologist Robert Park argued that race was a ruse devised by the ruling class to preserve their privilege, while Swedish sociologist/economist Gunnar Myrdahl suggested there was nothing natural about race-determined behaviour except as the result of prolonged discrimination. Sir Julian Huxley wrote in 1935 that references to race may have justified political ambitions, economic ends, social bitterness, and class prejudice but 'human races don't biologically exist' (cited in Pascal 2006).

Opposition to race thinking after World War II gathered momentum because of civil rights and anti-racist movements as well as nationalist and anti-colonialist revolutions (Winant 2002). Postwar revulsion over Nazi Germany's advocacy of racial hygiene ('genocide') as a solution to its problems further eroded what little was left of race's legitimacy. So thoroughly discredited were the genocidal race politics of Nazi Germany that governments were compelled to distance themselves from race science, culminating in the virtual abandonment of race as basis for state policy (Thobani 2007). And when the UNESCO Statement on Race (see Appendices A and B) in 1950 asserted what was increasingly self-evident—that race was not a biological phenomenon but a social myth with staggering human costs—the demise of race was decided (Brattain 2007).

Canada also moved with the times. By the late 1940s, the term 'race' had lost its lustre in describing groups who differed physically or culturally from mainstream white Canadians (Wargon 2000; see also Dawson 1936). The term

'ethnicity' replaced 'race' in the 1946 census—a dramatic departure from the past when Canadian governments collected race-based census data (Callister et al. 2007). Enumerators for the 1901 census were instructed to designate races of men as white (only pure whites can be white; children of mixed relations would be classed as red, black, or yellow), red, black, or yellow. To avoid confusion over immediate colour distinctions, enumerators were issued with the following instructions when canvassing door to door:

> The whites are, of course, the Caucasian race, the reds are the American Indian, the blacks are the African or Negro, and the yellows are the Mongolian (Japanese and Chinese). But only pure whites will be classed as whites; the children begotten of marriages between whites and any of the other races will be classed as red, black, or yellow, as the case may be, irrespective of the colour. (cited in Backhouse 1999: 1)

And while Census Canada continues to use ethnicity and ethnic origins as the foundation for statistical collection, in 1996 it added the visible minority category (i.e., those persons other than Aboriginal who are non-white in colour and non-Caucasian in race)—a move that many critics slammed as a thinly veiled reference to race (Wargon 2000). Ironically, in March of 2007, the Geneva-based Committee on the Elimination of Racial Discrimination suggested that the term 'visible minorities' could be construed as implicitly racist, may violate the principles of the International Convention for the Elimination of All Forms of Racism which Canada ratified in 1970, and that the government should 'reflect further' on its continued use (Fleras 2008).

Equally important were political developments. Passage of the Citizenship Act in 1947 assigned equal rights and duties to all Canadians regardless of race or place of birth. The term 'race' was expunged from the 1952 Immigration

Act, while in 1962 references to national origin were removed as a criterion for entry into Canada, followed shortly thereafter by the introduction of the point system which further buried the salience of race from Canadian immigration. Discrimination based on race was increasingly viewed as an aberration. Changed were publicly posted 'whites only' signs, standard application forms requesting the race of the applicant, and title deeds on vacation property with covenants stating 'no sales to Jews or non-whites'. Passage of the Fair Practices Act in Ontario eliminated race as a legitimate reason to isolate people's rights and access to public facilities (Walker 1997). The combination of the Bill of Rights in 1960, the Human Rights Act of 1977, and the Charter of Rights and Freedoms in 1985 further cemented the inappropriateness of race to deny or exclude in the public domain. With the inception of an official Multiculturalism Policy in 1971 and passage of the Multiculturalism Act in 1988, it would appear that Canada was on the brink of becoming the world's first country where race did not matter (see Foster 2005).

Race Matters: Contemporary Perspectives on Conceptualizing Race

Does race matter at present? Canadians exult in the myth that they harbour a deep aversion to judging others by the colour of their skin (Thobani 2007). In a merit-based and achievement-oriented society like Canada's, references to race are thought to be odious and offensive, especially when equating the value of a person to their skin colour—a stigma beyond one's control but still a powerful predictor of job, status, and privilege. In a society that abides by the principles of multiculturalism, the race concept represents a tainted status that is deeply discrediting and shameful. Moreover, this concept chafes against core Canadian values; for example, according to the principle of liberal universalism,

our commonalities as rights-bearing individuals are more important for purposes of recognition or rewards than membership in racially distinct groups. In that differences are only skin deep, thus rendering the race concept expendable, references to race tend to be muted, often employing proxies such as visible minorities to defuse unnecessary provocations (Dei 2007; Li 2007).

And yet the more things changed, the more they stayed the same. Despite the impolitics of race and racial discrimination, white Canadians continued to think and act as if races were real, distinct, and differentiative of humans. While the Chinese in Canada were long despised as an unwelcome race, and their entry into Canada banned between 1923 and 1947, they are currently labelled as a model minority—a label that can hinder or help, depending on the context or criteria. And race certainly mattered and continues to matter in defining who gets what. Despite the effort of the Employment Equity, Multiculturalism, and Human Rights Acts, a racialized division of labour remains in effect, with racialized minorities serving as the hewers of wood and drawers of water (Galabuzzi 2006; Reitz and Banerjee 2007). Any taxi ride to an airport confirms the importance of race: who is working the ticket counters versus who constitutes the ground support staff, from drivers and cleaners to baggage handlers. Clearly, race matters because minority realities continue to be racialized—often against their best interests (Fernando 2006). Or as Kobayashi and Johnson (2007: 1) put it,

Canadian society is a landscape of negotiation, in which skin colour takes on multiple shades of meaning. As inhabitants of this landscape, we use culture, ethnicity, and physical characteristics to assign places and positions to one another, to fix identities. We do so every day by a simple word or gesture, an exchange over a service counter, or a glance across the room, so that the racialized body is constantly marked and its meaning reinforced. Such assignments of place can deepen or reduce the racial divides created by the meanings we attribute to identity.

Paradoxically, race theories survive in contemporary scholarship. Authors such as Herrnstein and Murray (1994) have reinvigorated classic race thinking by focusing on race as a biologically meaningful concept for categorizing and ranking (Schroer 2007). A professor of psychology from the University of Western Ontario, Philippe Rushton (1994) has also promulgated a theory of racialized evolution not altogether different from nineteenth-century antecedents. To account for human differences across a broad range of domains, Rushton argues that separate races, namely, 'Oriental', 'Caucasoid', and 'Negroid' (Rushton's terminology), evolved into a distinctive package of physical, social, and mental characteristics because of different reproductive strategies in diverse environments. High reproductive strategies (many offspring, low nurturing) evolved in tropical climates; low reproductive strategies (few offspring, intense nurturing) in temperate climates, resulting in a racial pecking order. 'Orientals' (Rushton's terminology) are superior to 'Caucasoids' in a range of sociobiological factors, who in turn are superior to 'Negroids' (also Rushton) along measurement lines involving skull size, intelligence, strength of sex drive and genital size, industriousness, sociability, and rule-following. For Rushton, 'Orientals' as a group have the biggest brains, smallest genitals, and least promiscuity; they are also more intelligent, family focused, and law-abiding than 'Negroids' who have the smallest brains, biggest genitals and most testosterone, lowest IQs, and highest crime rates. Caucasoids happily fall into the middle (for criticism, see Fleras and Elliott 2007).

That the race concept continues to matter at a time when we should know better is dismaying. Other seemingly persuasive nineteenth-century ideas like phlogiston or germ plasm have been consigned to the scrap heap of human history (Cashmore and Jennings 2001). Their banishment from the public domain culminated in new and improved ways of understanding the world, but not so with race. And while it is important to know why people accepted race thinking in the first place, more importantly, why does this antiquated concept persist? The fact that race 'matters' for possibly the same reasons as in the past—to explain or exclude or exploit—is more worrying still. Then as now, race matters not because groups of people are biologically inferior, as proclaimed by the narrow-minded, stubbornly obtuse, or politically inept, but because of perceptions and politics that differentiate and discriminate, either blatantly or subconsciously (BondGraham 2007). Consider how the relevance of race is played out at present:

- Race matters not because it's a real reflection of reality (i.e., the partition and ranking of humanity into fixed and determinative groups) but because people tend to act as if it's real, with very real consequences for those labelled as such ('racialized').
- Race matters not because it's a thing out there but because its existence is perceived as real and applied to reality, with the result that certain groups or activities are racialized or raced (become associated with race), with often negative consequences (Young and Braziel 2006).
- Race matters not because it determines the worth of an individual or group (although some believe it does) but because people attribute social significance to race as grounds for making sense of everyday social life.
- Race matters not because it reflects reality but because it reflects a socially constructed process by which the dominant group arbitrarily selects certain traits and attaches social, cultural, mental, and moral significance to them. Over time these socially

constructed meanings are tacitly assumed as natural and normal (Agnew 2007; Smedley 2007; Schroer 2007).

- Race matters not because people are inherently inferior or inherently unequal but because people are thought to be inferior, thus justifying unequal treatment. Race reflects a self-fulfilling prophecy that feeds into its own perpetuation; that is, identifying others as racial inferiors legitimates conditions that deny and exclude, thereby producing outcomes that reinforce the original perception (Cashmore and Jennings 2001).
- Race matters not because it compels people to see, think, or act in a given way but because the placement of people into a racial category will profoundly influence how they see, think, and relate to others (and vice versa), with corresponding negative impacts.
- Race matters not because it's about biology or genetics but because references to bio-genetic explanations are manipulated to justify who gets what and why by way of encoded terms so as not to violate cherished values and perceived collective images (Li 2007; Fleras 2008).
- Race matters not because of biological differences but because an exclusive preoccupation with biology detracts from scrutinizing those opportunity structures and racialized mindsets that generate unequal relations.
- Race matters not because it's real but because a very real racial divide persists between the haves and the have-nots with respect to income and poverty, access to social services, and incarceration rates (Gallagher 2007).
- Race matters because a commitment to a race-neutral (colour-blind) society, with a corresponding discrediting of race, may actually intensify interlocking patterns of racial stratification unless constructive policies are in place to actively engage with race

as a solution (Lopez 2006; Bonilla-Silva 1996; Doane 2007).

- Race matters because it remains a key predictor of success, not in the innate sense that race determines individual outcomes but because racialized minorities are more likely to be poor and powerless—in part because society is structured to favour some, not others; in part because they encounter discrimination rooted in perceptions of race (see Vickers 2002; Herring et al. 2004).
- Race matters because it says more about mainstream fears and fantasies than about minority realities—more about those doing the constructing ('racializing') rather than those being constructed ('racialized').
- Race matters because race as an identity is meaningful even if imposed because it informs how those who are racialized will see themselves, how they will see others, how others will see them, and how they will relate to each other (Berardi 2008).

Several themes can be gleaned from reading between the lines of this list. First, the politics of race are not always dismissive or oppressive. Race matters positively for whites, since their whiteness is the racialized norm that confers the pigmented privilege of being everything, yet nothing (Satzewich 2007). As many have noted (Frankenberg 1993; O'Connell 2007), whites are infrequently racialized since race is rarely acknowledged as part of the white experience. In contrast to its visibility in minority bodies and embodiments of the 'other', whiteness as a race is so obscured in public discourses that difficulties persist in capturing its elusive yet privileged reality (O'Connell 2007). In short, race matters for both whites and racialized minorities because people's social location, racially speaking, will profoundly racialize their expectations and opportunities.

Second, reference to race may be used to advance rewards and entitlements. Racially based distinctions that formerly stigmatized individuals as inferior or irrelevant are now invoked as a criterion for promotion or admission. The logic behind race-conscious programs such as employment equity is relatively straightforward: if race contributed to the problem of inequality and exploitation, then it must be included as part of the solution. Or as Justice Harry Blackman opined in defending affirmative action in *Bakke*: 'In order to get beyond racism, we must first take account of race. There is no other way' (cited in Lopez 2006). Nor should the transformative properties of race be ignored. Race serves as a distinguishing marker for those groups who are transforming the stigma of oppression into a mark of pride, identity, or resistance (Lerner 1997).

Third, rather than a monolithic discourse that is universally applied, the politics of race are historically variable, sharply contested, and socially (politically and economically) contextual (Miles and Brown 2003). Race constitutes a moving target that twists and bends across space and time—shifting in focus from race as biological classification to race as social construction (Blank et al. 2004; Backhouse 1999; Guess 2006). Whereas race was once defined as a 'thing' out there—a tangible object that could be isolated and measured as a fixed biological entity—it is increasingly conceptualized as a 'process' involving the imposition of racial meanings by the powerful on those less powerful. In shifting from race as a classification (a 'thing' or a 'noun') to race as a construction (a 'process' or a 'verb'), attention is moving from the physical attributes of minority groups toward the politics of power in imposing labels that deny or exclude (Chan and Mirchandani 2002). The shift from race as determination to race as discourse makes it doubly important to frame race within the discursive context of a sociology of knowledge:

Individuals and social institutions evaluate, rank, and ascribe behaviours to individuals on the basis of their presumed race . . . Sociologists are interested in explaining how and why social definitions of race persist and change. They also seek to explain the nature of power relationships between and among racial groups, and to understand more fully the nature of belief systems about race. (American Sociological Association 2003: 5)

In short, contemporary thinking rejects the notion of race relations as 'races' of people who stand in a relationship to another 'race'. In that the race concept has no empirical reality except in the discursive sense of socially constructed meanings, it is more accurate to speak of relationships that are 'racialized' instead of race relations (Bonilla-Silva 1996).

To the extent that race once mattered, that it continues to matter, and that in all probability it will continue to matter in the future (as argued in the concluding chapter to Part I), the power of an illusion has shown an astonishing staying power in human history—sometimes for better, often for worse. To be sure, race discourses from the past do not necessarily reflect the level of race talk at present (Brattain 2007). Contemporary race discourses are no longer about distinct groups in separate states of being who are slotted into pre-existing categories. References instead focus on the politics of relationships involving the placement of individuals into categories that are continually adjusted and re-evaluated within contexts of power and inequality. We anticipate that the following selection of articles will amply reveal that when it comes to theorizing race, there is much to be said for the expression 'words change things'.

Racing Canada:
Historical Perspectives

A commitment to racelessness is widely viewed as a cornerstone of Canada's identity. This commitment not only fosters a distinctive Canadian society but also distinguishes Canada's past from its present. Canadians tend to see themselves to be tolerant of racial and cultural diversity, to possess a history of equal treatment toward everyone, regardless of skin colour, and to be free of those blatant racisms that blighted black–white relations in the United States. Canada's embrace of racelessness as principle and practice is further rationalized by references to its non-violent history, respectful attitude toward diversity, endorsement of a colour-blind society, and dedication to the rule of law. And surely the policies and programs of Canada's official multiculturalism secures its crowning status as a society where race seemingly doesn't matter (Foster 2005).

Sadly, however, Canada's collective idealization is precisely that: a fictional aspiration that, while partly true, says more about mythology than reality (Backhouse 1999; Razack 2002; Tator and Henry 2006; Hier and Bolaria 2007). Injustices and restrictions based on racist perceptions underpinned the contours of Canadian history. Who got what and why was racially determined so that restrictions applied over access to schools and universities, voting and political office, and even employment opportunities. Barriers that denied or excluded were legally justified and permissible as long as they were intended to protect the most vulnerable members of racialized minorities, applied to all members of such a group, promoted national interests, and did not blatantly broach the protocols of international law. References to racial conflicts in the United States were frequently cited as a warning about the dangers (from lawlessness to conflict) of mixing different races. Admittedly, race in Canada often had less to do with skin colour and unfathomable inferiority and more to do with hostility to culture differences and the (in)capacity of minorities to assimilate (Guth 1997). Nevertheless, race and culture were so inextricably linked in the minds of most Canadians that any distinction would have been lost in public discourses.

Of course Canada did not invent the concept of race. The race concept was the product of a global paradigm that emerged from European expansion, conquest, and colonization (Walker 1997). As different peoples were assigned particular economic functions in an evolving global division of labour based on their usefulness to European interests, race-based typologies evolved in tandem with elaborate scientific doctrines to explain or exploit. Canadians, too, accepted the truth of race, race types, and racial typologies as so self-evident that neither examination nor proof was required. Race doctrines about civilized versus primitive cultures transformed policies, institutions, and laws into instruments that privileged Europeans over the 'lower orders'. And in a Canada that saw itself as a 'white man's country', races were (1) vilified as competitors for scarce resources, (2) deemed as unsuitable for Canada's climate, (3) rejected as participants in Canada's democratic government and social institutions, and (4) perceived as threats to sexual morality, not only to white women as guardians of Anglo-Saxon purity but also to the nation-state through race degeneration. These race politics did not necessarily reflect populist appeals, fear mongering, or racial baiting, as Walker (1997) observes, but were rooted in prevailing scientific opinions of the time. The fact that racial discrimination was embedded in law and reinforced by the courts did nothing to loosen its grip.

Part I provides a historical overview of the politics of race in Canada from the past to the present. Consisting of largely previously published but also original material, the articles have been selected to capture race-based thinking within Canadian history. The articles are arranged in a more or less chronological sequence to demonstrate shifts in race thought over time. As Michelle Brattain (2007) points out, what race *was* is not what it *is*, so that understanding its construction in the past is pivotal to understanding its current presence. Explicitly negative references to race are shown to have become more muted over time, and eventually lose their salience in public discourses. As Constance Backhouse (1999) observes, even while the scientific community endlessly measured and quantified the physical distinctions between the races, others challenged conventional wisdom by explaining differences on grounds of environment, social or historical circumstances, and situational adjustments. But discrediting the legitimacy of the race concept was one thing; discarding its persistence quite another. That is, race mattered in the past, yet it continues to matter in the present and in all likelihood will continue to do so into the future. Canada may endorse an official multiculturalism and Canadians may generally subscribe to a colour-blind ideology that rejects the reality of race and racism. Nevertheless, race remains pivotal in three ways: as a predictor of success and failure; as an explanatory framework to account for differences and inequities; and as a key variable in influencing people's identities, experiences, and outcomes. In that the race concept continues to matter at present in predicting success or failure—even when we should know better—demonstrates that when it comes to race in Canada, the more things change, the more they stay the same—as conveyed by the following readings.

The first article provides an ideal introduction for understanding the history of race in Canada. With its magisterial overview of how Canadian law functioned to reinforce racial distinctions and discriminations, James Walker's passage from his book 'Race', Rights and the Law in the Supreme Court of Canada is unmatched in depth and detail. Walker points out how the race concept informed and permeated all aspects of Canadian society—including the legal and court systems, which were complicit in upholding race thinking and racist laws. The result is a colour bar every bit as punishing and exclusive as the Jim Crow laws in pre–Civil Rights USA. He also explains how the race concept was manipulated to justify racialized slavery against African Canadians, the dispossession and disempowerment of Canada's Aboriginal peoples, and the blatant exploitation of racialized minorities for the Canada-building project. For those who think of Canada as a largely race-free zone, this introductory article should disabuse them of that notion.

The next article by Robin Winks, 'Negro School Segregation in Ontario and Nova Scotia', is a stark and disturbing reminder that an American-style colour bar existed in Canada. From the earliest black settlers in seventeenth-century Canada to the historical present, Winks describes a Canada that, because of racial stereotypes, consisted of two competing narratives: as a haven of security for various black groups, yet a hell of marginalization as well. The fact that the last racially segregated schools remained on the books in both Ontario and Nova Scotia until the 1960s is a testimony to the tenacity of race thinking even in so-called progressive times. Reading this article should challenge any lingering notion of Canada's so-called moral superiority over the United States in its treatment of blacks.

The passage from James Woodsworth's *Strangers within Our Gates* reveals the inconsistency that characterized race thinking in Canada. With his mixture of compassion and contempt for the racialized others—and often lauded for his progressive ideas—Woodsworth proved a victim of his time. To one side, the so-called Negro race was criticized as climatically unsuitable for Canada—a reminder to readers that race was perceived as a detriment of Canada's development and the purity of the Anglo-Saxon race. To the other side, although Woodsworth believed both immigrant and native-born races (blacks and Aboriginals) to be inferior, he held out hope for them and the future of Canada through their interaction and intermarriage with the superior races.

The extract by John Murray Gibbon on the Canadian mosaic exposes an unmistakable shift in race thinking: that is, racial diversity can make a positive contribution to Canada. The amalgamation of race groups is not only accepted as part of this inclusionary vision, but group characteristics are now seen in terms of history, geography, and social patterns. In other words, innate predispositions are not the only story in defining human differences. Gibbon's indictment of the race concept proved visionary: with Canadians beginning to question race typologies and racial doctrines, the race concept lost its legitimacy, especially following the post-war awareness of Nazi atrocities endured by both Jews and other racialized and undesirable minorities.

The publication of Constance Backhouse's book *Colour-coded* in 1999 proved something of a milestone in deconstructing Canada's race history. The selected excerpt provides an insight into the debates over race for census purposes. A central question revolved around whether 'Eskimos' (Inuit) were racially distinct from Canadian Indians (Aboriginal peoples). Or alternatively, did Canada have a constitutional right to absorb 'Eskimos' into the category of Indians? Backhouse demonstrates the obsessive preoccupation with racial classification as a basis for defining who got what—in this case 'Eskimos' (Inuit)—even as legitimacy for the race concept was eroding.

The enumeration of Canada's racial composition has 'enjoyed' an erratic and checkered history. As the article by Monica Boyd, Gustave Goldmann, and Pamela White points out, three factors prevailed throughout Canada's census history: (1) the presence or absence of a census question relevant to racial classification, (2) variation in the wording so that race is explicit at times and implicit at other times because it is subsumed by an origins question, and (3) shifts in societal ideologies regarding living together with differences. The authors demonstrate how asking a census question on race goes beyond measurement issues; rather, it rests on historically prevailing notions of race relations and models of nation-building. In short, Boyd and her colleagues make it abundantly clear: Census Canada data regarding Canada's racial and ethnic composition is influenced not only by the principles of social survey research but also by societal representations of ethnicity and race.

In an article written for this book, Augie Fleras deconstructs the expression 'playing the race card' by demonstrating how the politics of race clash with the politics of Aboriginal rights in Canada. The inception of a court-mandated Aboriginal fishing industry on the West Coast since 1993 is shown to generate competing reactions. To one side are those who prefer to frame this issue as a race-based preference that is unfair to others. To the other are those who claim that Aboriginal fishing rights are exactly that: Aboriginal rights that Aboriginal peoples are entitled to by virtue of their indigeneity and constitutional guarantees. The article demonstrates the importance of framing issues to not only advance argument but also ensure appropriate solutions.

Cecil Foster's piece from *Where Race Does Not Matter* provides a fitting—if not provocative—conclusion to Part I. According to Foster, for the first time in modern human history references to race no longer matter in terms of who gets what. The emergence of multiculturalism in Canada has created the potential for the dismissal of race in terms of entitlement. Time will tell if this optimism—that we now have an opportunity to create a utopia in which women and men will be judged by the content of their character rather than the colour of their skin—is justified.

Chapter 1

'Race' and the Law

James St. G. Walker

Common Sense

In 1900 a prominent English scholar and humanitarian, Gilbert Murray, expressed a sentiment that was then unchallengeable:

> There is in the world a hierarchy of races. ... [Some] will direct and rule the others, and the lower work of the world will tend in the long run to be done by the lower breeds of men. This much we of the ruling colour will no doubt accept as obvious.[1]

It was indeed 'obvious', for wherever one looked in the world white people were ruling over others. Although themselves colonials, in a world divided by colour Canadians could identify with the ruling 'race' and with the imperial mission. At a 24 May speech in Toronto in 1914, R.B. Bennett explained to his fellow Canadians why 'we' were ruling over places such as India and Egypt:

> We are there because under the Providence of God we are a Christian people that have given the subject races of the world the only kind of decent government they have ever known [applause] . . . and you and I must carry our portion of that responsibility if we are to be the true Imperialists we should be. . . . An Imperialist, to me, means a man who

accepts gladly and bears proudly the responsibilities of his race and breed [applause].[2]

Canadians did not invent 'race': it was the product of a global paradigm emerging from European expansion and conquest. In the vast imperial structures that were created, the world itself became a system in which different peoples were assigned particular economic functions consequent upon their local resources, their power to resist, their geographical location, and ultimately their potential contribution to the enrichment of Europe. Human beings inherit various genetic characteristics from their parents which determine such phenotypes as skin colour, hair texture, and facial structure. Only in certain historical circumstances are these visible features responsible for the assignment of people into groups for social or economic purposes. In ancient Europe, for example, physical differences were noticed and recorded, but they did not govern the roles people played in society.[3] The expansion of Europe into regions with populations bearing dramatically different physical features led to a global stratification of conqueror and conquered, superior and subordinate, by which was created, through military and political means, an observable coincidence between phenotype and social position. The fact that phenotypes are indelible and heritable meant that any individual's position was immediately recognizable and that it would be passed from one generation to the next. Physical features had been rendered significant; persons who were grouped according to phenotype shared with members of the same group not only physical characteristics but functional characteristics as well, particularly social and economic, and a common relationship with members of other groups. Nineteenth-century Europe's attempt to explain these readily observable structural distinctions produced the doctrine that inherited physical attributes were indicative of immutable behavioural traits which suited different people for different roles. Thus was 'race' produced.

By the late nineteenth century a racial typology existed across the world. Positions in the structure had been set and were being accepted as 'natural', and elaborate scientific doctrines were being developed to explain a phenomenon which had evolved circumstantially. Canadians accepted the racial explanation, along with the functional aspects of European supremacy. It was 'common sense'. It did not need to be examined or proved, for it was self-evident. Pierre Bourdieu has commented that 'common sense speaks the clear and simple language of what is plain for all to see'.[4] In an essay entitled 'Common Sense as a Cultural System', Clifford Geertz maintained that common sense is not 'rational', it is 'not a fortunate faculty, like perfect pitch'; rather, 'it is a special frame of mind', 'a cultural system' which reveals 'a loosely connected body of belief and judgment'.[5] The sense of 'race' shared by Canadians in the decades surrounding the *Quong Wing* decision was such a system. It was assumed that 'races' were evolutionary units, fixed in their physical and behavioural characteristics. These units were destined to compete at the group level, for their interests, dictated by biology, were inherently in conflict. Some 'races', it was thought, bore characteristics that were unsuitable as foundation stock for the fledgling Dominion of Canada. Physically, some 'races' could never adjust to the Canadian climate. Fur-

thermore those same 'races' were not equipped to participate in Canada's democratic government and free institutions. If admitted to full participation, they would unwittingly subvert those institutions and ruin them for everyone else. An increasing concern in the early twentieth century was sexual morality. 'Races' less evolved than the Anglo-Saxon were more likely to be driven by base instinct; their presence would not only contaminate the 'moral fibre' of the new nation but would pose a specific threat to white women whose health and safety were essential to the future of the Anglo-Saxon 'race' in Canada, leading to 'race degeneration'.[6] 'Races' who did not possess the appropriate characteristics, or who could not readily gain them through assimilation, would endanger the nation.

The prevailing common sense about 'race' permeated a book written in 1909 by James S. Woodsworth, superintendent of the Methodist All People's Mission in Winnipeg and later to become first leader of the Co-operative Commonwealth Federation. Though it expressed a generous compassion toward new immigrants and revealed its author's experience in Winnipeg's North End immigrant communities, *Strangers within Our Gates, or Coming Canadians* presented and perpetuated the assumption that 'race' determined human behaviour. In Woodsworth's scheme, adopted from leading American commentators of the day, very fine lines divided the different racial categories, making Czechs more intelligent than Slovaks, Magyars less industrious than Slavs, northern Italians more independent-minded than southern. Woodsworth's concern was to ensure the eventual assimilation of these disparate European types into the Anglo-Saxon mainstream of western Canada. The alternative was 'race' conflict and ultimately 'race suicide' for the Anglo-Saxons, who would be degraded to the level of the lowest immigrants. For some 'races', however, the gulf was too wide to make assimilation possible. 'The Mongolians, the Hindus, and the Negroes' would remain forever distinct, creating a 'fatal barrier' to the development of a Canadian nation. The only solution was to exclude this kind of immigrant completely.[7] A more succinct version of the same common sense appeared in a petition organized by the Edmonton Board of Trade in April 1911 to demand the exclusion of African-American migrants: 'It is a matter of common knowledge that it has been proved in the United States that Negroes and whites cannot live in proximity without the occurrence of revolting lawlessness, and the development of bitter race hatred.'[8] In April 1914 the Vancouver City Council passed a resolution calling for the removal of Chinese pupils from the public schools because 'association of the two races must result in a condition detrimental to the future welfare of our children who have nothing to gain, either mentally or morally, by daily association with Orientals'.[9]

Parliamentary debate was equally specific. Prime Minister Sir Wilfrid Laurier confessed that 'racial antagonism' was irreconcilable and 'amalgamation' with Asians was 'neither possible nor desirable'.[10] Nanaimo MP Ralph Smith discovered a 'universal principle' of struggle that was part of the human condition, illustrated 'not only in the conflict of man against man but of race against race'.[11] His colleague R.G. Macpherson from Vancouver told the House of Commons that 'the Oriental and the Caucasian' could never coexist in Canada. 'It is just as impossible to do this as to mix oil and water.'[12] Duncan Ross, from Yale-Cariboo, traced racial antagonism to the biblical Noah, whose sons were assigned different roles on earth by 'an all-wise though inscrutable Providence'; being divinely ordained, 'race prejudice . . . will continue to exist for all time'.[13] Mr Ross quoted the *Edinburgh Review* on the insurmountable differences fixed in the Asian soul:

Should they, conceivably or inconceivably, adopt Christianity, they will produce an entirely different sort of Christian; should they break themselves into the Roman character, they will still read life from right to left. We shall never be able to foretell their mental processes more accurately than those of the cat upon the hearth rug, even had we as favourable opportunities for study.[14]

Unassimilable 'races', such as Asians and Africans, were considered 'dangerous to Canadian interests', a threat to 'the life of this democracy', perpetually and inconvertibly 'alien'. An article by Hilda Glynn-Ward from the *Vancouver World* was read into Hansard:

Between the Orient and the Occident there is more than a mere ocean, there is a great divide, intangible and insurmountable. The leopard cannot change his spots any more than a white man can be Orientalized or an Oriental be brought to live by the customs and laws of the European. The morals of the one are neither worse nor better than the other; but they are different.[15]

In 1922 Prime Minister Mackenzie King drew an analogy to 'Gresham's law of the precious metals': 'the baser metal tended to drive the finer metal out of circulation'. The same thing would happen if lower 'races' were allowed to mingle freely in Canada; Anglo-Saxons would be debased. Opposition Leader Arthur Meighen concurred. For certain 'races', 'their temperaments, their habits, and their very natures are such that assimilation with our people is an impossibility. Assimilation is always an impossibility where marriage itself is forbidden by the very essence of the fact.' It was essential for the future of Canada 'that we maintain here our racial purity'.[16]

These were not intended to be inflammatory remarks, or populist appeals to the fears of Anglo-Canadians; J.S. Woodsworth and the parliamentarians were reflecting, and often quoting, the most advanced scientific opinions of their time. Then in the 1930s scientific orthodoxy began to shift. The definition of 'race' as a biological category lost its precision. American sociologist Robert Park taught that a division of labour imposed by the dominant party created the situation of competition and conflict, resulting in group interests and group consciousness. For the sake of preserving their advantages, the dominant party established fixed structures of privilege and disadvantage according to racial categories.[17] Swedish economist and sociologist Gunnar Myrdal, whose research team produced a massive study of 'race relations' in the United States, proposed that centuries of discrimination, not 'nature', must be held responsible for the distinct characteristics demonstrated by black and white Americans. Far from being insurmountable, according to Myrdal, the observable differences could be eliminated if only American ideals of democracy and equality were applied indiscriminately.[18]

At the very least, this emerging scientific opinion caused confusion about the meaning of 'race' both as a biological term and as a social category. In 1938 John Murray Gibbon published *Canadian Mosaic: The Making of a Northern Nation*, inspired by the 'racial problems' then being manifest in Europe which made it imperative that Canadians 'should examine the progress being made in the amalgamation of their own and other racial groups in the new democracy of the Dominion'.[19] Gibbon took racial differences for granted, but attributed them to cultural habits as well as to biology. His colour illustrations of different ideal 'types'—Scots-Canadian, Dutch-Canadian, Hebrew-Canadian—depended as much on ethnic costume as on physical features. Gibbon's goal was to celebrate those differences and to show how the different types all contributed something positive to Canadian society. The assimilation of the Canadian-born generation, in the most important characteristics, was a well-established trend, while the preservation of Old World folkways, music, and dance merely enriched the Canadian 'mosaic'. Although he considered only immigrants of European ori-

gin, Gibbon's analysis represented a notable movement away from the views offered by Woodsworth only 30 years before.

The biological–cultural ambiguity found in [Gibbon's analysis] was found as well in a study of the 1931 census on 'Racial Origins and Nativity of the Canadian People'. This commissioned study, written by economics professor W. Burton Hurd and published in 1942, was intended 'to measure the progress of assimilation and to discover and evaluate the forces which are working toward that end'.[20] Like Gibbon, Hurd both acknowledged and demonstrated the prevailing lack of confidence in biological 'race'. In his introduction, Hurd wrote that the term 'nativity' presented no problem, but 'unfortunately the same cannot be said of the term "racial origin"'. He elaborated:

> In a strictly biological sense, the term 'race' signifies a subgroup of the human species related by ties of physical kinship. Scientists have attempted to divide and subdivide the human species into groups on the basis of biological traits, such as shape of the head, stature, colour of skin, etc., and to such groups and to such only, would the biologist apply the term 'race'. The use of the term, however, even in this strictly scientific sense is neither definite nor free from confusion, for there is no universally accepted classification. Furthermore, the identification of certain types of culture with definite biological types has led inevitably to the result that, even in the hands of the ethnologist, the term 'race' has acquired a cultural as well as a biological implication.

Hurd went on to explain that most modern nations were composed of different 'races'; even the 'English type, if such exists in the biological sense, is the product of the commingling of perhaps half a dozen primitive stocks'. 'Racial origin' must therefore have both biological and cultural meaning, and the relative importance of each 'is not subject to quantitative measurement'. 'One merely follows popular usage in employing the terms', he admitted. 'Such usage is familiar to the public in general, and only when our "origin" classifications follow such lines can they be collected by a census, be understood by the people or have any significance from the practical standpoint of the development of a Canadian nation.'[21] Data on racial origin were useful as a measurement of immigration and as a means of monitoring the pace of assimilation, but Hurd also offered statistics by 'race' for such things as criminal activity, illiteracy, and insanity, and his 'index of segregation' implicitly attributed segregation to the initiative of the segregated group. 'Immigrants from Scotland show the least tendency to segregate', he observed. 'The Japanese show the greatest tendency to segregate.'[22] In a final demonstration of the ambiguity surrounding racial terminology, Hurd cited the instructions given to enumerators for the 1931 census:

A person whose father is English and whose mother is French will be recorded as of English origin, while a person whose father is French and whose mother is English will be recorded as of French origin, and similarly with other combinations. In the case of the Aboriginal Indian population of Canada, the origin is to be traced through the mother. . . . The children begotten of marriages between white and black or yellow races will be recorded as Negro, Chinese, Japanese, Indian, etc., as the case may be.[23]

Under the Indian Act, Native Indian status was traced through the father. Census and Act were contradictory.

Once again, parliamentary debate offered a confirmation that common sense about 'race' was in a state of flux. About the time that Fred Christie was refused service in the York Tavern and launched his court challenge, Canada's representative to the League of Nations was quoted as saying 'that we did not have any minority problems in Canada'.[24] Not long afterwards Prime Minister King told the House:

The problem is not one of inferior or superior races. It is not a racial problem at all. The problem is one of different civilizations, of different economic structures in the different countries. As long as there are those differences there is bound to be unrest as a consequence of immigration which leads to unfair and undue competition on the part of those who have lower standards of living and who may not assume the same measure of responsibility with regard to their citizenship as do the citizens of the country to which they come. I think it is from that broad point of view, that this question must be faced.[25]

Economic competition had long been regarded as a consequence of racial difference, but the prime minister seemed to be giving it causal significance. Mr King's own certainty about the meaning of biological 'race', as expressed in 1922, had apparently come unstuck.

This direction in thinking about 'race' was being reinforced both by scholarly analyses and by the reverberations from World War II. Psychologists began to theorize that the tendency to discriminate was a characterological defect to be found and explained within the discriminatory individual, rather than a symptom of group competition. John Dollard developed a 'frustration-and-aggression' hypothesis in 1937,[26] in which he proposed that accumulated resentment can turn into aggression against 'acceptable' targets such as racial minorities, compensating for feelings of individual powerlessness. Psychological explanations were made more attractive by the horrors of war, when many people found it impossible to accept that 'normal' individuals could have perpetrated the Holocaust. The most elaborate interpretation was developed by Theodor Adorno and his colleagues at Frankfurt, who discovered what they called 'the authoritarian personality'.[27] They too attributed discrimination to the dysfunctional individual harbouring suppressed anger from childhood, but to suit the image of the Nazi functionary the same individual had to remain respectful and subservient toward authority figures. The Frankfurt scholars identified an 'F-scale', which purported to measure submission to authority above coupled with aggression toward those who are below. Other psychological explanations retained the focus on the prejudiced individual, but enhanced the part played by social context. Since prejudice is so widespread, to the point of orthodoxy in some settings, it must be explicable as a learned behaviour.[28]

Franz Boas, who led the attack on old concepts of the meaning of 'race', wrote in 1936: 'We talk glibly of races and nobody can give us a definite answer to the question what constitutes a race.'[29] This view, considered radical in the 1930s, gained universal endorsement in the UNESCO Statement on Race issued on 18 July 1950, in the midst of the Supreme Court of Canada's deliberations over *Noble and Wolf*. In clause 14 of the statement, the scientists assembled by UNESCO in Paris maintained that

> for all practical purposes 'race' is not so much a biological phenomenon as a social myth. The myth of 'race' has created an enormous amount of human and social damage. In recent years it has taken a heavy toll in human lives and caused untold suffering. It still prevents the normal development of millions of human beings and deprives civilization of the effective co-operation of productive minds.[30]

Canada was not exempt from the impact of the 'war conscience' and the emergence of a new common sense linking racism to inhuman atrocities. Of most significance in attracting Canadian attention to the 'race' issue was the treatment of Japanese Canadians at the hands of their own democratic government. In 1942, when more than 20,000 Japanese Canadians were displaced from their homes in British Columbia, most Canadians were prepared to accept this extreme measure in the face of an alleged threat during wartime. Public opinion was far less tolerant of the government's decision in 1944 to disfranchise the Japanese Canadians who had been moved to other provinces where, until this time, they would have been entitled to vote. Letters and petitions from outraged citizens, church groups, and civil liberties organizations flowed to Ottawa. In the House of Commons, Liberal Arthur Roebuck described racial equality as one of the main principles of Liberalism, yet a Liberal government was disfranchising certain citizens on grounds of 'race'. 'To my untutored mind, to my simple way of thinking, that is race discrimination', Roebuck charged. 'If you keep that up, it will not be long before Canada will be Hitlerized.'[31] North Battleford MP Denise Nielsen insisted that 'Race discrimination is a fascist trend which should have no place in our country.'[32] Acadia's Victor Quelch agreed. 'We are not fighting today merely to defeat Germany and Japan; we are fighting in defence of definite principles. We are fighting for a peace based on justice, and justice must be granted to minorities as well as to majorities. It seems to me that this legislation is a negation of the declaration of principles contained in the Atlantic Charter.'[33] Though the controversial measure was passed, the identification of racial discrimination with the wartime enemy had been established in the prevailing rhetoric.

Discrimination was being viewed as aberrational, and 'new eyes', as the *Vancouver Sun* put it, were seeing Canadian minorities in an entirely different light.[34] 'What is plain for all to see', in Bourdieu's phrase, was undergoing profound change. Not just racial discrimination but 'race' itself came under attack in Parliament. In 1952, not long before Harry Singh walked into the Immigration Office in Toronto, Winnipeg North MP Alistair Stewart denounced the government for using the word 'race' in immigration regulations and the census because 'it is a word which had very little scientific validity'.[35] The discourse of scientists seemed to be en route to the conventional wisdom in Canada, settling the ambiguity about 'race' and consigning racial discrimination to the realm of the unacceptable and the aberrational. By 1956 the popular magazine *Saturday Night* was instructing its readers on 'The Myth of White Supremacy', explaining that 'So far as anyone can tell, all the evidence shows that, within the limits of normality, there is no relation between the character of the mind and either brain weight, brain shape, cranial capacity, or anything physical that we can measure.' Racial prejudices, the article continued, 'are attitudes that have to be cultivated for they do not grow naturally in the young human mind'.[36]

Throughout the period under study, that is the first half of the twentieth century, Canadians also held a 'common sense' view of their judicial system, a 'frame of mind' concerning the nature and meaning of law and the courts and what they were supposed to do in a parliamentary democracy. Its fundamental principle was a belief in 'rule of law'. In a mechanical sense this meant that judges applied the law to particular cases and that everyone in society was subject to the same law. Judges must therefore not only be learned in the law, they must be absolutely impartial in administering it. To ensure judicial impartiality in the application of the law, courts did not themselves initiate proceedings. Cases were brought before them by the contending parties, and the adversary process provided each party with a full opportunity to develop legal arguments on its own behalf for the judges to weigh. Judges served as neutral arbiters in a concrete dispute; their judgment was an adjudication between two

contesting arguments, following their interpretation of the appropriate law relevant to the case at hand. The judges then wrote a legal decision in which they set out not only the result but the reasoning behind it. They clarified the meaning of the disputed law, articulating its underlying principles and, especially in an appellate court, thereby establishing guidelines for future application in comparable cases.

This procedural format emanated from an understanding that an objective judiciary 'discovers' the applicable law. Judges did not insert their personal views or decide what the law ought to be, according to this theory, they simply administered and enforced the law as it was. In 1923 Justice Anglin of the Supreme Court of Canada, soon to become chief justice, defined the judicial process as a search for fixed rules, as in the natural sciences. 'Our common object is to make the administration of justice as nearly certain and scientific as it is possible that any human institution can become.'[37] Although politicians made the law, its explication was entrusted to apolitical judges unaffected by immediate pressures or the balancing of divergent interests. Judges would determine the intent or legislative purpose of any statute, and they would ensure that established principles were incorporated into their interpretation of what the law was saying in any particular set of circumstances. Central to this procedure was the doctrine of *stare decisis*, by which courts followed prior decisions or precedents relevant to the case before them. *Stare decisis* promoted adherence to the rule of law by limiting the individual judges' interpretive scope; they must follow the established authorities, the guidelines produced by their predecessors. Capricious decisions were avoided, and the public could have some reasonable confidence that a sitting judge would not suddenly move in an arbitrary direction. This meant that the law was generally stable and predictable, and as a consequence that change was very gradual.[38]

Also fundamental to the legal context during the period under study was the current understanding of how the British North America Act affected judicial interpretation. According to the preamble of the Act, the new Dominion of Canada was invested with 'a constitution similar in principle to that of the United Kingdom'. On the one hand this meant that the rights of the subject as evolved through legislation and the common law would operate in Canada as in Britain, and the courts would protect those traditional rights against encroachment. On the other hand the British constitution incorporated the principle of parliamentary sovereignty: the elected representatives of the people could 'make or unmake any law whatever', as A.V. Dicey explained in 1885.[39]

In Britain there was only one Parliament, but in Canada, by that same BNA Act, parliamentary authority was divided between federal and provincial legislatures, both of them elected by the people and both of them inheriting the Westminster mantle. What the BNA Act had to do was distribute parliamentary sovereignty between the two legislative levels, primarily through sections 91 and 92 which delineated those powers exclusive to either the central Parliament or the provincial legislatures.[40] In 1912, just as Quong Wing's case was beginning to work its way through the courts, the Privy Council ruled that 'whatever belongs to self-government in Canada belongs either to the Dominion or to the provinces within the limits of the British North America Act'.[41] This 'principle of exhaustive distribution of legislative powers' was the application in Canada of parliamentary sovereignty, as adapted to the requirements of a federal system.[42] Canadian decisions could be appealed to the Privy Council in London where the sovereignty of Parliament was taken for granted and, in addition, where constitutional interpretations tended to favour provincial over federal authority in disputed areas of law.[43] Although it would be argued that there had historically existed 'a convention

against exercise of parliamentary power to abrogate the common law principles which the courts have developed', and in particular a 'received convention of legislative restraint where civil liberties are concerned',[44] the regnant orthodoxy in the early decades of the twentieth century was neatly expressed by Justice W.R. Riddell of the Ontario Supreme Court:

> Parliament can do everything but make a woman a man and a man a woman. . . . An Act of Parliament can do no wrong though it may do several things that look pretty odd.
> . . .
>
> The Legislature within its jurisdiction can do everything which is not naturally impossible, and is restrained by no rule human or divine. . . .
>
> But while we do not allow a court to set aside legislation as unwise or unjust, opposed to natural justice or whatnot, it is sometimes necessary for the Courts to inquire whether the particular legislation of Dominion or Province comes within the ambit of powers conferred by the British North America Act.[45]

When a legislative act was challenged the Canadian judiciary, following the Privy Council example, tended to limit its investigation to the determination of whether the legislature passing the act was operating within its jurisdiction under the BNA Act. In the absence of explicit guarantees, claims to racial equality had to be expressed in terms recognizable to contemporaries, and legal arguments had to be organized under principles which the courts of the time felt themselves equipped to consider.

Such was the 'cultural system' that existed in Canada surrounding the significance of 'race', the propriety of racial discrimination, and the function of the courts. The extent to which this context affected the legal deliberations instigated by Quong Wing, Fred Christie, Bernard Wolf, and

Harry Singh is a major question for the case studies that follow.

Public Policy

In 1938 the German government sought advice on the introduction and implementation of racially discriminatory legislation. One of the places they turned to was Canada. On 14 March the German consul-general in Ottawa, Dr H.U. Granow, wrote to the Department of External Affairs for an account of federal or provincial laws which 'make race (racial origin) of a person a factor of legal consequence'. Herr Granow went on to specify his interest in 'laws governing the exercise of civil and political rights, the marriage, the illegitimate sexual relations, the exercise of a profession, the administration of schools and universities, and the immigration' with any provisions depending on 'race or colour'.[46] It took O.D. Skelton of External Affairs until 27 June to compose a reply. Following a small flurry of letters to different departments, Mr Skelton told the Germans 'that the laws of the Dominion and of the provinces do not make the race of a person a factor of legal consequence'. The only exceptions, the letter continued, were some immigration laws and 'certain provincial laws affecting Asiatics'; otherwise there were 'special provisions' for Native Indians but they were 'protective rather than restrictive' and in any case Indians were free at any time to 'assume the legal status of other Canadians'.[47]

Undersecretary Skelton's reply was not entirely candid. It is true that there was no national policy coordinating 'race' as a 'factor of legal consequence', but there was an inherent logic connecting federal and provincial legislation. By the BNA Act civil rights were a provincial concern, whereas aliens and naturalization were federal matters.[48] The constitutional division of power shaped many of the 'race-related' policies introduced by provincial legislatures and led the provinces to articulate their restrictions in explicitly racial terms to apply to the Canadian-born, for to apply them only to the alien or naturalized subject would be to invade federal jurisdiction and risk disallowance. The Canadian political structure also translated local and provincial concerns to the federal level, so that national policies affecting immigration, military service, and the franchise, to offer some outstanding examples, could be determined by regional interests.

Canada also operated in an imperial context, as part of an empire that justified its existence by its contribution to human equality and progress. Colonial Secretaries insisted that the Empire was free of racial distinctions, at the same time urging Canadian governments to disguise their discriminatory restrictions behind tactical euphemisms such as literacy tests in a European language. Specific British and imperial interests added restraints to Canada's available policy options. Anglo-Japanese treaties guaranteeing personal movement and reciprocal rights forced Canada to modify several policies aimed at Japanese Canadians. Renegotiation of the so-called 'Unequal Treaties' between Britain and China in the 1920s brought imperial pressure to bear upon policies toward Chinese in Canada. India's loyalty to the Empire could not be undermined by thoughtless decisions in Ottawa or the provincial capitals. At the same time Canada was watching other countries design policies to maintain white exclusivity: American, Australian, and South African legislation restricting immigration and limiting civil rights served as an inspiration and a conscious example for the framing of Canadian policies toward minority 'races'.[49]

Within this general environment it is possible to identify policies that trespassed on each of the areas mentioned in Herr Granow's letter. In the 'civil and political' category, regulations were developed to exclude unsuitable persons from the rights, privileges, and duties normally accompanying Canadian birth or naturalization. In one of its first acts after Confederation, the BC legislature in 1872 disfranchised Chinese in the province, adding Japanese and East Indians in 1895 and 1907, respectively, as their numbers began to warrant similar attention. Saskatchewan followed BC's example and disfranchised Chinese residents in 1908. Since the federal franchise derived from provincial qualifications, persons barred by a province were automatically denied the federal vote. Many other rights and privileges depended upon being on the provincial voters' list as well, including the right to public office, jury service, employment in the public service, and the practice of law.[50] Without any direct reference, these regulations greatly extended the distinctions imposed on grounds of 'race'. In the case of Native Indians, explicit legislation at both the federal and provincial levels denied them the vote.[51] Emphasizing their lower-class citizenship, when World War I broke out young men of Native Indian, African, and Asian origin were at first rejected as volunteers by the Canadian Expeditionary Force, on the grounds that their racial qualities made them inadequate soldier material. In late 1915 Native Indians began to be recruited, initially in separate Indian units, and in 1916 a segregated battalion was formed for black volunteers. Although individuals were admitted to regular fighting units on the discretion of their commanders, only Japanese Canadians were widely acceptable as front-line soldiers, and their recruitment began only in 1916 in the midst of a recruitment crisis.[52]

Rules governing 'marriage' and 'sexual relations' were rampant through various versions of the Indian Act,[53] though Mr Skelton would undoubtedly explain that they were 'protective rather than restrictive'. Otherwise the most overt barriers within this category were provincial laws banning the employment of white women by Chinese-Canadian men, as in the case of Quong Wing in 1914, designed to eliminate sexual exploitation. Legally enforced residential and recreational segregation, however, sometimes had the prevention of sexual contact as an admitted motive.[54]

Most elaborate were pieces of legislation restricting economic activity on racial grounds, expressing an underlying principle that certain 'races' were permitted in Canada only to perform certain chores. A racially defined and usually unskilled 'caste' was created and maintained by policies limiting the kinds of employment legally available, or imposing prohibitive conditions to discourage employers from hiring minority group members. British Columbia introduced racially specific laws prohibiting Asian Canadians from employment on public works or in underground mines, from the purchase of Crown lands, and even from cutting timber on Crown property. Liquor licences, in exclusively provincial jurisdiction, were withheld from Asians and Native Indians in British Columbia, and hawkers' licences carried differential fees depending on the 'race' of the applicant.[55] The federal government restricted fishing licences to Japanese Canadians in the 1920s, with the ultimate intention of driving them out of the fisheries.[56] Less directly, an early form of 'contract compliance' was employed to ensure that private contractors working on provincial or federal government projects in BC would not hire Asians. And quite apart from its own enforcement of employment discrimination, the federal government permitted discriminatory practices by private and Crown corporations and by the civil service.[57] During the Depression unemployed Chinese Canadians in Alberta received less than half the relief payment accorded to whites.[58]

In many parts of Canada access to 'schools and universities' was governed by 'race'. In order to enforce their attendance at residential industrial schools, Native Indian children were denied the right to attend provincial schools near their homes.[59] In both Nova Scotia and Ontario the segregation of black schoolchildren was established by law in the nineteenth century and those laws still existed at the time of the Granow inquiry. Nova Scotian legislation further limited the educational benefits of black children by requiring schools with provincial subsidies (including all black schools) to employ teachers with nothing higher than a fourth-class certificate. De facto separate schools existed for black children in New Brunswick, Saskatchewan, and Alberta, supported, but not created, by provincial laws and policies. Several attempts were made to legislate segregated schools for Asian children in British Columbia. The law condoned the widespread use of quotas for the admission of Jewish students to universities, especially in Ontario and Quebec.[60]

Mr Skelton was required to admit that 'some immigration laws' contained provisions making 'the race of a person a factor of legal consequence'. The 1869 Immigration Act, anticipating only British applicants, was silent on the racial issue; by 1910, experience having revealed the error of this expectation, the Act specified 'race' as a ground for admission or exclusion. This was not soon enough for British Columbia, the province chosen by most Asian immigrants. Victoria passed a series of provincial acts banning or limiting Asian immigration, but until the completion of the railroad Ottawa disallowed the exclusion of Chinese labour. Finally in 1885 the federal government passed its own act to discourage the Chinese, imposing a $50 head tax on new arrivals from China. Under continual pressure from BC governments and MPs, Parliament increased the head tax to $100 in 1900 and $500 in 1903, and in 1923 passed the Chinese Immigration Act which virtually ended Chinese admission until after World War II.[61]

Certain other immigrants, though considered just as unsuitable, could not be treated so abruptly as the Chinese. Japan was Britain's Pacific ally, and Japan itself was ready to protest any perceived insult to its dignity as a rising global power. BC's persistent restrictions on Japanese immigrants were as persistently disallowed by Ottawa, usually citing imperial inter-ests. Only when frustrations erupted in a public riot in 1907, directed against Chinese and Japanese districts in Vancouver, was the Laurier government embarrassed into action. A 'Gentleman's Agreement' was negotiated with Japan whereby the number of emigrants permitted to leave for Canada was voluntarily limited.[62] India, as part of the Empire, presented its own complications. The failure of negotiated limitation led to Canada's unique contribution to euphemistic legislation: the 'continuous journey rule'. By Order-in-Council the federal government stipulated that all immigrants must arrive by an unbroken journey from their country of origin.[63] Since no direct travel connections existed with India, Indian migration was eliminated without any specific racial references to disrupt imperial relations. Similarly, restraints operated against an explicit exclusion of African Americans, for despite its domestic treatment of black citizens the United States was not content to see them openly insulted by a neighbouring country. American influence was reinforced by the presence in Nova Scotia and southwestern Ontario of African-Canadian voters who objected to any policy directed against black immigrants. Instead, immigration officials engaged in a campaign to discourage African-American applicants, and rejected them on medical or other grounds rather than 'race'. An Order-in-Council was passed in 1911 to impose a one-year ban upon black immigration, but its implementation proved unnecessary as the informal measures achieved the desired purpose.[64] In these various ways, each one designed to meet specific circumstances, policies excluded immigrants deemed unassimilable. By the 1930s practically no persons of African or Asian origin were entering Canada.

Public policy, whether implemented through openly debated legislation or more surreptitious regulations, can be recognized as the practical application of common sense. It was also a reinforcement, legitimizing common attitudes with the dignity of the law. Legal barriers against Asian immigration, for example, would be a none-too-subtle signal to Canadians that the Asians in their midst were not worthy of equal respect. This cycle of reinforcement was also visible in Native Indian policy. The 'special provisions' for Indians in Canadian law identified by Mr Skelton were not entirely as he represented them in his response to the German consul-general. 'Protection' was undoubtedly a feature of federal policy, though even at its most innocent this suggests a relationship of inequality, but from the very beginning of a formal policy in 1763 'protection' meant 'control'. By Royal Proclamation and by instructions sent to Governor James Murray, Indians were permitted to trade only with government-approved white men, use of alcohol was regulated, credit and debt were allowed only under the strictest supervision, and Indian land could be purchased exclusively by the Crown.[65] In the name of protecting Indians against unscrupulous whites, the law prevented Indians from selling their land or trading their goods or entering a contract with persons of their choice; it kept them dependent on the Crown. By the time of Confederation the assimilation of the Indian population was the avowed purpose of Native policy, while the British North America Act granted responsibility for 'Indians, and lands reserved for Indians' to the federal Parliament.[66] The first consolidated Indian Act in fulfillment of this responsibility was passed in 1876, and it contained at least in embryo the characteristics that would dominate Native policy until World War II.[67]

The 1876 Act outlined the steps to be taken by an Indian who wished to become enfranchised; that is, in Skelton's term, to 'assume the legal status of other Canadians'. First the individual had to be 'sober and industrious' and had to convince his local Indian agent that he was qualified for the franchise. If convinced, the agent gave the applicant a ticket for a parcel of reserve land. After three years of successful cultivation, the Indian would receive personal title to this land. There followed an additional three-year period during which the applicant had to demonstrate 'good behaviour', and if he passed this probationary term satisfactorily he ceased to be an Indian and became an ordinary Canadian.[68]

For those who remained Indians, the federal government assumed control, or at least supervision, of their local affairs, ostensibly to further the project of gradual assimilation. Traditional leaders were replaced by elected chiefs and band councils. This was intended to give Indians experience with democratic processes, but since those elected could be deposed on grounds of intemperance, immorality, dishonesty, or incompetence, the band leadership remained dependent on the goodwill of the Indian agent.[69] An assimilationist motive also lay behind the stipulation that an Indian woman who married a non-Indian man automatically lost her band membership and her Indian status, theoretically becoming an independent Canadian, but it amounted to a direct government imposition in total disregard of individual wishes.[70] Many Native cultural practices, notably the West Coast 'potlatch' and prairie dances, were outlawed because they perpetuated traditional mores and impeded the kind of sobriety and industry considered a prerequisite for full membership in Canadian society.[71] To accelerate assimilation, attendance at residential schools was made compulsory for Indian children.[72] Finally, admitting the failure of contradictory policies, the government actually implemented compulsory enfranchisement in 1920 for those whom the Indian agent considered suitable. This policy was withdrawn in the face of Indian objections in 1922, but it reappeared in somewhat softer terms in 1933 in a mockery of the principle that enfranchisement represented self-reliance.[73]

Other components of the 1876 Act and its many amendments were overtly controlling, with no pretense of preparation for democratic citizenship. The very definition of who was an

Indian, and therefore who was eligible for band membership, treaty considerations, residence on reserves, and so on, was the privilege of the federal government.[74] Intimate details of daily life were subject to government control: who could consume alcohol and under what conditions, sexual morality, responsibility for deserted families, recreation in poolrooms or pubs, the use of band money raised through the sale of goods or services, the dispensation of personal estates, and the appointment of executors; Indians could even be forced to go to the hospital against their will if the agent felt it to be in their best interests. Indian land, as specified in the BNA Act, came under especial scrutiny. Indians could not sell or lease their land, but the government could do so on their behalf, even without their consent. The presence on reserves of non-Indians or Indians from other bands was severely regulated, and even the traffic passing through a reserve was a matter for government regulation. Sanitary provisions on reserves were dictated from Ottawa. In case a band did not like what the federal authorities had done in any instance, the Indian Act was amended in 1927 to prohibit Indians from hiring lawyers to press any claims against the government.[75] None of these conditions could reasonably be expected to promote self-reliance and some regulations, indeed, seemed deliberately designed to *retard* Indian progress toward independence. When prairie Indians became successful agriculturalists in the late nineteenth century, for example, and began selling their surplus produce into local markets, the government introduced a 'permit system' whereby Indians' ability to sell their produce was restricted. At the same time Indians were effectively prevented from utilizing mechanized farm equipment, thus seriously limiting their ability to engage in efficient modern agriculture.[76] Of course not all these regulations were put into effect at the local level,[77] but their existence even in potential is a powerful representation of majority Canadian attitudes toward the Native people and their apparent incapacity to manage their own affairs. The syndrome represented in Canadian Indian policy could not have been established except as part of the evolving common sense about 'race' and imperial responsibility that infused Western culture in the late nineteenth and early twentieth centuries.

But, as was discussed above, the assumptions about 'race' and racial discrimination began to change not long after the exchange of letters between Messrs Granow and Skelton in 1938. When the War began in 1939 the military rejected black volunteers, as had been the case in World War I. A Special Committee on Orientals in BC concluded in October 1940 that both Chinese and Japanese should be excluded from the armed services, and a 1943 federal interdepartmental committee decided that East Indians must not be conscripted and could be accepted as volunteers only if they assimilated to Anglo-Canadian dress and dietary standards.[78] Eventually these barriers would be lowered in the face of overseas military requirements. When called to serve, East Indian and Chinese Canadians took advantage of the opportunity to point out that their citizen's duty to fight in defence of democracy was not matched by a citizen's right to participate in democratic elections in Canada. At the same time African and Jewish Canadians protested racially discriminatory hiring practices in defence industries, and although private employers remained free to discriminate, the government itself eliminated 'race' as an employment criterion in 1942.[79]

Following the unsuccessful campaign over the disfranchisement of Japanese Canadians in 1944, the public conscience was again aroused against the government's attempt to deport certain Japanese Canadians to Japan after the War. A broad coalition of Canadian groups, led by the Co-operative Committee on Japanese Canadians, eventually forced the plan's abandonment by the federal government in 1947.[80] Encouraged, university students demonstrated against Toronto facilities that discriminated against blacks; the Committee for the Repeal of the Chinese Immigration Act united labour and church groups behind the Chinese-Canadian demand for reform; public opinion polls began to show majorities in favour of enfranchising East Indians and Chinese. There was a new concept dawning in international thought, of 'human rights' as a distinct entity with universal applicability. Canadian policy had not recognized this concept early in the War, but through its participation in UN declarations Canada was accepting the international intention to promote fundamental rights. This was reflected in Canada's first Citizenship Act, passed in 1946, which represented the notion that Canadian citizens must share equally in all rights and duties, that there could be no legal distinctions between Canadians on racial or any other grounds. There was, in short, a new Canadian self-image, a new and less restrictive meaning to the very term 'Canadian'.[81]

Racial disadvantage, as it was understood to exist, would have to be addressed. In 1947 Parliament repealed the discriminatory Chinese Immigration Act and enfranchised East Indian and Chinese Canadians; in 1949 the final legal restrictions were removed from Japanese Canadians. A revised Indian Act in 1951 allowed greater autonomy to Indian bands, ended compulsory enfranchisement, and eliminated the increasingly offensive term 'Indian blood' from the requirement for Indian status. In 1960 Native people became eligible to vote in federal elections.[82] But generally there was no sense of urgency to legislate change. The existing 'British freedoms' were understood to protect minorities once the few overt exceptions were removed from public policy, and those ideals also served to restrain legislative interference which could restrict the white majority's freedom of thought, speech, and association. The minorities themselves, however, remained dissatisfied. They

formed pressure groups, produced briefs to provincial cabinets, and conducted educational campaigns through union locals and church groups. By the late 1940s public opinion polls showed a majority of Canadians in favour of legislation protecting individuals against religious or racial discrimination, demonstrating political support to encourage provincial legislatures to act.[83]

As a consequence of these campaigns, prohibitory policies were declared, making racially specific practices illegal. The Fair Employment Practices and Fair Accommodations Practices Acts, passed in Ontario in 1951 and 1954 respectively and soon emulated by the other provinces, contained in their preambles the absolute statement that racial discrimination was contrary to public policy.[84] By the legislation passed in the 1950s, 'race' was eliminated as a legitimate reason to distinguish people's rights and access to public facilities. There was, however, one major exception: access to the country itself. When the Chinese Immigration Act was repealed in 1947 Prime Minister King made his 'classic' statement on Canadian immigration policy, declaring that 'the people of Canada do not wish, as a result of mass immigration, to make a fundamental alteration in the character of our population'. Assimilation, or rather the presumed inability of certain peoples to assimilate, remained the guiding criterion.[85] Continuing international pressures, especially from the 'new Commonwealth', brought forth gestures of equality, such as the decision in 1951 to admit an annual quota of immigrants from India, Pakistan, and Ceylon. Campaigns for further reform achieved one apparently significant change in 1952 when the Immigration Act eliminated the term 'race' as a condition for immigration, substituting the new term 'ethnic group'.[86] It seemed to be a victory for the newly emerging common sense.

Notes

1. Quoted in Michael Banton, *Racial Theories* (Cambridge: Cambridge University Press, 1987), vii.

2. Quoted in Carl Berger, *The Sense of Power: Studies in the Ideas of Canadian Imperialism, 1867–1914* (Toronto: University of Toronto Press, 1970), 230–1.

3. For example, see Frank M. Snowden, Jr, *Before Color Prejudice: The Ancient View of Blacks* (Cambridge, MA: Harvard University Press, 1983).

4. Pierre Bourdieu, *In Other Words: Essays Towards a Reflective Sociology* (Stanford: Stanford University Press, 1990), 52.

5. Clifford Geertz, *Local Knowledge: Further Essays in Interpretive Anthropology* (New York: Basic Books, 1983), 10–11.

6. For example, see Mariana Valverde, *The Age of Light, Soap and Water: Moral Reform in English Canada, 1885–1925* (Toronto: McClelland and Stewart, 1991), esp. Ch. 5, 'Racial Purity, Sexual Purity and Immigration Policy'.

7. James S. Woodsworth, *Strangers within Our Gates, or Coming Canadians*, with an introduction by Marilyn Barber (Toronto: University of Toronto Press, 1909; rpt. ed. 1972), 76, 84, 102, 108–9, 116, 132, 155, 158, 164, 181–2, 230–2.

8. Quoted in R. Bruce Shepard, 'Plain Racism: The Reaction against Oklahoma Black Immigration to the Canadian Plains', *Prairie Forum* 10 (1985): 375. The petition was endorsed by Boards of Trade in Strathcona, Morinville, Fort Saskatchewan and Calgary, Alberta; Yorkton and Saskatoon, Saskatchewan; and Winnipeg, Manitoba.

9. Quoted in Kay J. Anderson, *Vancouver's Chinatown: Racial Discourse in Canada, 1875–1980* (Montreal and Kingston: McGill-Queen's University Press, 1991), 90.

10. Hansard, 27 Mar. 1903, 597–600.

11. Hansard, 16 Dec. 1907, 700.

12. Ibid., 722.

13. Ibid., 732–8.

14. Ibid., 738.

15. Hansard, 18 May 1922, 1510, 1514, 1515, 1516.

16. Ibid., 1555–6, 1562, 1564.

17. For example, Robert E. Park, *Race and Culture* (Glencoe, IL: Free Press, 1950).

18. Gunnar Myrdal, *An American Dilemma: The Negro Problem and Modern Democracy*, 2 vols (New York: Harper & Row, 1944).

19. John Murray Gibbon, *Canadian Mosaic: The Making of a Northern Nation* (Toronto: McClelland and Stewart, 1938), v.

20. W. Burton Hurd, 'Racial Origins and Nativity of the Canadian People', *Census of Canada, 1931*, Vol. 13 (Ottawa: Supply and Services, 1942), vii.

21. Ibid., 567–8.

22. Ibid., 571, 636, 685, 693, 700.

23. Ibid., 827.

24. Hansard, 12 Feb. 1936, 151.

25. Hansard, 17 Feb. 1938, 570.

26. John Dollard, *Caste and Class in a Southern Town* (Garden City, NY: Doubleday, 1937).

27. T. Adorno, E. Frenkel-Brunswick, D. Levinson, and R. Sanforo, *The Authoritarian Personality* (New York: Harper & Row, 1950).

28. For example, see Gordon Allport, *The Nature of Prejudice* (Cambridge, MA: Addison-Wesley, 1954); Thomas F. Pettigrew, 'Personality and Sociocultural Factors in Intergroup Attitudes: A Cross-national Comparison', *Journal of Conflict Resolution* 2 (1958): 29–42.

29. Franz Boas, 'History and Science in Anthropology', *American Anthropology* 38 (1936): 140.

30. For a clause-by-clause discussion of the UNESCO document, see Ashley Montagu, *Statement on Race* (New York: Oxford University Press, 1951).

31. Hansard, 17 July 1944, 4925–6.

32. Ibid., 4929.

33. Ibid., 4935.

34. 'Chinatown! Time was when that foreign quarter . . . had an aura of wickedness for the Vancouver consciousness. . . . How it has changed! Or perhaps, how we, under the impact of World War II have changed. China is now our ally, and visitors look at Chinatown through new eyes' (*Vancouver Sun*, 1 May 1943, quoted in Anderson, *Vancouver's Chinatown*, 177).

35. Hansard, 2 June 1952, 3079.

36. Norman J. Berrill, 'The Myth of White Supremacy', *Saturday Night*, 27 Oct. 1956.

37. Quoted in Ian Bushnell, *The Captive Court: A Study of the Supreme Court of Canada* (Montreal and Kingston: McGill-Queen's University Press, 1992), 56. Justice Anglin's views were reflected as well in the United States Supreme Court in the early years of the twentieth century, where 'the common law was recognized as the distinct subject matter of legal science—as that body of doctrine that emerged when prior judicial decisions were systematically studied with a view to their principled coherence' (Paul W. Kahn, *Legitimacy and History* [New Haven: Yale University Press, 1992], 110).

38. For example, see Donald E. Fouts, 'Policy-making in the Supreme Court of Canada, 1950–1960', in *Comparative Judicial Behavior: Cross-cultural Studies of Political Decision-making in the East and West*, eds Glendon Schubert and David Danelski (New York: Oxford University Press, 1969), 257–91; Mark R. MacGuigan, 'Precedent and Policy in the Supreme Court', *Canadian Bar Review* 45 (1967): 627–65; Patrick J. Monahan, 'Judicial Review and Democracy: A Theory of Judicial Review', *UBC Law Review* 21 (1987): 87–164, and 'Commentary', 165–206; Paul Weiler, *In the Last Resort: A Critical Study of the Supreme Court of Canada* (Toronto: Carswell Methuen, 1974); Bertha Wilson, 'Decision-making in the Supreme Court', *University of Toronto Law Journal* 36 (1986): 227–48.

39. A.V. Dicey, *The Law of the Constitution*, 10th ed. (London: Macmillan, 1965), 39.

40. British Statutes (BS) 1867, c. 3, s. 91 and 92.

41. *AG Ontario* v. *AG Canada (Reference Appeal)*, [1912] AC 571.

42. Peter W. Hogg, *Constitutional Law of Canada*, 2nd ed. (Toronto: Carswell, 1985), 257–9.

43. Ibid., 88–9. In the early years after Confederation, Hogg explains, the federal government dominated the provinces 'akin to a colonial relationship'. But Privy Council decisions, aided by tendencies within Canada toward decentralization, 'elevated the provinces to coordinate status with the Dominion'. This was especially true under the tutelage of Lord Watson (1880–99) and Lord Haldane (1911–28).

44. Bora Laskin, 'An Inquiry into the Diefenbaker Bill of Rights', *Canadian Bar Review* 37 (1959): 77–8. F.R. Scott, *Civil Liberties and Canadian Federalism* (Toronto: University of Toronto Press, 1959), argued that 'if we go back to our constitutional roots in English history we find several notable formulations of rights and liberties, from Magna Carta in 1215 down to the Bill of Rights of 1689. . . . The theoretical sovereignty of the British Parliament has tended to blind us to the reality of the limitations upon that sovereignty residing in the theory of government these documents proclaim. . . . Parliament is restrained in England by certain principles of government almost as effectively as if they were written into a binding constitution' (14–15). Scott further identified 'the established rule that all statutes should be strictly interpreted if they limit or reduce the rights of the citizen. Parliament must always be presumed to have intended the least interference with our freedom, not the most' (26). . . . [T]here were Canadian judges who accepted this tradition of a common law guarantee of equality.

45. W.R. Riddell, *The Constitution of Canada in Its History and Practical Working* (New Haven: Yale University Press, 1920), 98–100. In the first two paragraphs quoted here, Riddell was

repeating verbatim comments from his own judicial decisions in 1909 and 1908, respectively.

46. National Archives (NA), RG 25, G-l, Vol. 1875, file 558, H.U. Granow to O.D. Skelton, 14 Mar. 1938. I am grateful to Myron Momryk of the National Archives for bringing this file to my attention.

47. Ibid., reply, 27 June 1938.

48. Section 91, ss. 25; s. 92, ss. 13.

49. Canada, Parliament, Sessional Papers, Vol. 36, No. 13, 1902, No. 54, *Report of the Royal Commission on Chinese and Japanese Immigration*, including appendices; Robert Huttenback, *Racism and Empire: White Settlers and Colored Immigrants in the British Self-governing Colonies, 1830–1910* (Ithaca: Cornell University Press, 1976).

50. Statutes of British Columbia (SBC) 1872, c. 39; 1895, c. 20; 1907, c. 16; Statutes of Saskatchewan (SS) 1908, c. 2. For a list of the disadvantages deriving from disfranchisement, see Canada, Parliament, Senate, *Proceedings of the Special Committee on Human Rights and Fundamental Freedoms* (Ottawa, 1950), 277–9.

51. For example, Statutes of Canada (SC) 1885, c. 41. Originally 'an Indian normally resident on an Indian reservation' was disqualified from voting. In 1948 the Dominion Elections Act was amended to read 'For the purpose of this provision "Indian" means any person wholly or partly of Indian blood who is entitled to receive any annuity or other benefit under any treaty with the Crown' (SC 1948, c. 46, s. 6, ss. f).

52. For more detail see James W. St. G. Walker, '"Race" and Recruitment in World War I: Enlistment of Visible Minorities in the Canadian Expeditionary Force', *Canadian Historical Review* 70 (1989): 1–26.

53. For example, SC 1879, c. 34, s. 7 and 8; SC 1880, c. 28, s. 95 and 96.

54. For example, Anderson, *Vancouver's Chinatown*, 90.

55. SBC 1884, c. 2; 1899, c. 39; 1900, c. 18; 1908, c. 3; 1910, c. 30.

56. Ken Adachi, *The Enemy That Never Was* (Toronto: McClelland and Stewart, 1976), 142–5; Patricia Roy, 'Educating the "East": British Columbia and the Oriental Question in the Interwar Years', *BC Studies* 18 (1973): 51–2; W. Peter Ward, *White Canada Forever: Popular Attitudes and Public Policy toward Orientals in British Columbia* (Montreal: McGill-Queen's University Press, 1978), 119–23.

57. NA, MG31 E55, Tarnopolsky Papers, Vol. 43, file 4; SBC 1885, c. 30; 1902, c. 39; 1908, c. 50; 1912, c. 34; Hansard, 9, 10, and 23 Mar. 1911, 4930–1, 5038–9, 5941–8; Public Archives of Nova Scotia (PANS), 'Colored Cooks, Stewards and Firemen', file of correspondence concerning Canadian National Steamships.

58. Howard Palmer, *Patterns of Prejudice: A History of Nativism in Alberta* (Toronto: McClelland and Stewart, 1982), 145–8.

59. Chief Joe Mathias and Gary R. Yabsley, 'Conspiracy of Legislation: The Suppression of Indian Rights in Canada', *BC Studies* 89 (1991): 39.

60. Statutes of Nova Scotia (SNS) 1884, c. 29; 1918, c. 9; Revised Statutes of Ontario (RSO) 1960, c. 368; NA, Tarnopolsky Papers, Vol. 44, file 5; V. Carter and W. Akili, *The Window of Our Memories*, Vol. 1 (St Albert, AB: Black Cultural Research Society of Alberta, 1981), 55; Patricia E. Roy, *A White Man's Province: British Columbia Politicians and the Chinese and Japanese Immigrants, 1858–1914* (Vancouver: University of British Columbia Press, 1989), 15, 24–7.

61. SC 1869, c. 10; 1885, c. 71; 1900, c. 32; 1903, c. 8; 1907, c. 50; 1910, c. 27; 1923, c. 38; Hansard, 8 and 14 June 1900, 7052–7, 7406–15, 27 Mar. 1903, 597–612, 23 Mar. 1923, 1443–54; Sessional Papers, 1902, No. 54; Ward, *White Canada Forever*.

62. Howard Sugimoto, 'The Vancouver Riots of 1907: A Canadian Episode', in *East Across the Pacific: Historical and Sociologial Studies of Japanese Immigration and Assimilation*, eds H.

Conroy and T. Miyakawa (Santa Barbara, CA: American Bibliographic Center-Clio Press, 1972), 92–126; NA, MG26 G1(a), Laurier Papers, Vol. 477, correspondence and reports on the riots; Vol. 489, Confidential Report by the Hon. Rodolph Lemieux on his visit to Japan.

63. The final version of this order is found in PC 32, 1914.

64. NA, RG76 Vol. 192, file 72552, 'Immigration of Negros [sic] from the United States to Western Canada'; Hansard, 2, 22, and 23 Mar. and 3 Apr. 1911, 4470, 4471, 5911–13, 5941–8, 6523–8; PC 1324 and 2378, 1911; Shepard, 'Plain Racism', 365–82; Harold Troper, 'The Creek-Negroes of Oklahoma and Canadian Immigration, 1909–11', Canadian Historical Review 53 (1972): 272–88.

65. Treaties and Historical Research Centre, Indian and Northern Affairs, The Historical Development of the Indian Act (Ottawa, 1978), 5–8.

66. Statutes of the Province of Canada 1857, c. 26; BS 1867, c. 3 (British North America Act), s. 91, ss. 24; SC 1869, c. 6.

67. SC 1876, c. 18.

68. Ibid., ss. 86–94.

69. For example, see Vic Satzewich and Linda Mahood, 'Indian Affairs and Band Governance: Deposing Indian Chiefs in Western Canada, 1896–1911', Canadian Ethnic Studies 26 (1994): 40–58; SC 1869, c. 6, s. 10; SC 1880, c. 28, s. 72.

70. For example, Kathleen Jamieson, 'Sex Discrimination and the Indian Act', in Arduous Journey: Canadian Indians and Decolonization, ed. J. Rick Ponting (Toronto: McClelland and Stewart, 1986), 112–36. SC 1869, c. 6, s. 6, said: 'Any Indian woman marrying any other than an Indian shall cease to be an Indian within the meaning of this Act.'

71. For example, Tina Loo, 'Dan Cranmer's Potlatch: Law as Coercion, Symbol, and Rhetoric in British Columbia, 1884–1951', Canadian Historical Review 73 (1992): 125–65; SC 1884, c. 27, s. 3; SC 1895, c. 35, s. 6; SC 1914, c. 35, s. 8.

72. For example, John Tobias, 'Protection, Civilization, Assimilation: An Outline History of Canada's Indian Policy', in As Long as the Sun Shines and Water Flows, eds Ian Getty and Antoine Lussier (Vancouver: University of British Columbia Press, 1983), 39–55; SC 1894, c. 32, s. 11.

73. Historical Development of the Indian Act, 114–15, 124; SC 1920, c. 50; SC 1922, c. 26; SC 1933, c. 42.

74. For example, James S. Frideres, Native Peoples in Canada: Contemporary Conflicts (Scarborough, ON: Prentice Hall, 1988), Ch. 2, 'The Indian Act', 25–38; Historical Development of the Indian Act, 23–5, 61. Section 3, ss. 3 of the 1876 Act defined an Indian as 'Any male person of Indian blood reputed to belong to a particular band; Any child of such person; Any woman who is or was lawfully married to such person.'

75. For example, Mathias and Yabsley, 'Conspiracy of Legislation', 34–45; Howard E. Staats, 'Some Aspects of the Legal Status of Canadian Indians', Osgoode Hall Law Journal 3 (1964): 36–51; Historical Development of the Indian Act.

76. Sarah Carter, Lost Harvests: Prairie Indian Farmers and Government Policy (Montreal and Kingston: McGill-Queen's University Press, 1990).

77. Kenneth Coates, 'Best Left as Indians: The Federal Government and the Indians of the Yukon, 1894–1950', in Out of the Background: Readings on Canadian Native History, eds Robin Fisher and Kenneth Coates (Toronto: Copp Clark Pitman, 1988), 236–55.

78. Department of National Defence (DND), file HQ 61-4-10, 'Sorting Out Coloured Soldiers'; Canada, Parliament, House of Commons, Special Committee on Orientals in British Columbia, Report and Recommendations (Ottawa, 1940); NA, RG24 Vol. 2765, file 6615-4-A, Vol. 5, correspondence and committee minutes on enlistment of 'Asiatics'; RG27 Vol. 130, file 601-3-4, 'Conscription of East Indians for Canadian Army'.

79. NA, RG27 Vol. 1486, file 2-153-1, petitions; DND, file HQ 504-1-7-1, Vol. 1, 'Organization and Administration. Enlistment of Chinese'; Douglas MacLennan, 'Racial Discrimination in Canada', *Canadian Forum* (Oct. 1943): 164–5.

80. Adachi, *Enemy*, 199ff; Peter Ward, 'British Columbia and the Japanese Evacuation', *Canadian Historical Review* 57 (1976): 289–308; Carol Lee, 'The Road to Enfranchisement: Chinese and Japanese in British Columbia', *BC Studies* 30 (1976): 54–60; Hansard, 17 July 1944, 4911–38; SC 1944–45, c. 26.

81. Donna Hill, ed., *A Black Man's Toronto, 1914–1980: The Reminiscences of Harry Gairey* (Toronto: Multicultural History Society of Ontario, 1981), 56–7; F. J. McEvoy, '"A Symbol of Racial Discrimination": The Chinese Immigration Act and Canada's Relations with China, 1942–1947', *Canadian Ethnic Studies* 14 (1982): 34–5; NA, Tarnopolsky Papers, Vol. 32, file 13 and Vol. 36, file 5; RG25 Vol. 1539, file 178, 'immigration to canada of chinese', petitions; SC 1946, c. 15.

82. SC 1951, c. 29; SC 1960, c. 39.

83. NA, MG30 A53, Kaplansky Papers, Vols 20 and 21, 'Reports of Activities for Improved Human Relations, 1946–1956'; Tarnopolsky Papers, especially Vols 36, 40, 41, and 45.

84. Walter Tarnopolsky, 'The Iron Hand in the Velvet Glove: Administration and Enforcement of Human Rights Legislation in Canada', *Canadian Bar Review* 46 (1968): 565–90; 'The Canadian Bill of Rights from Diefenbaker to Drybones', *McGill Law Journal* 17 (1971): 437–75; *Discrimination and the Law in Canada* (Toronto: R. de Boo, 1982); T.C. Hartley, 'Race Relations Law in Ontario', *Public Law* (1970): Pt. 1, 20–35, Pt. 2, 175–95; P.V. MacDonald, 'Race Relations and Canadian Law', *University of Toronto Faculty of Law Review* 18 (1960): 115–27; Mark MacGuigan, 'The Development of Civil Liberties in Canada', *Queen's Quarterly* 72 (1965): 270–88.

85. PC 2115, 1930; Hansard, 11 Feb., 1 May 1947, 307–45, 2644–7.

86. Hansard, 24 Apr. 1952, 4351–3; SC 1952, c. 42; NA, MG28 V75, Jewish Labour Committee of Canada Papers, especially Vols 41 and 42.

Chapter 2

Negro School Segregation in Ontario and Nova Scotia[1]

Robin W. Winks

The Negro has been present in Canada for nearly as long as in the United States, for in 1628, nine years after a Dutch ship unloaded the first cargo of Africans for sale as slaves at Jamestown, David Kirke (or Kertk), the so-called English Conqueror of Quebec, brought a Madagascar slave boy to the French shores. As slaves, Negroes lived in New France and in British North America from that time forward. Although local abolitionist groups moved against slavery in Upper Canada in 1793 and in the Maritime provinces by 1800, slavery continued to be practised in British North America until, in common with all enslaved people within the British Empire, the Canadian slaves were freed by the Imperial Act of 1833.

Canada has been the haven for several disparate groups of Negroes. The United Empire Loyalists who settled in Nova Scotia and the two Canadas often brought their slave property with them, and in the former colony a substantial body of free Black Pioneers took up land grants from the Crown at the end of the American Revolution. In 1796 a large group of exiled Jamaican Maroons were resettled along Nova Scotia's shores, only to be transported to Sierra Leone four years later. During the War of 1812 a number of slaves, largely from the Chesapeake Bay area, sought refuge behind the British lines or on His Majesty's ships standing to in the bay, and they, also, were taken to Nova Scotia, where

they became the perpetual paupers known locally as the Refugees. During the 1840s, and especially after 1850, thousands of new fugitives sought 'freedom under the lion's paw' in order to escape from slave catchers in the United States. While many of these Negroes returned across the border at the end of the Civil War, many others stayed on, principally in Canada West. Less well-known Negro groups came to Canada at a later date. In the 1890s, and again from 1910 until 1914, large contingents of Negroes from the American Plains, predominantly from Oklahoma, made their way into the drylands farming areas of Saskatchewan and Alberta, where they established—at Maidstone, in the former, and near Breton, Wildwood, and Amber Valley in the latter—virtually all-Negro farming communities. They were preceded by Negro settlers on Vancouver Island, to which several hundred had gone in 1859 from California to escape from restrictive legislation there, later to fan out onto the mainland or into Salt Spring Island. These diverse migrant streams were joined in the 1920s by many hundreds of Negroes from the upper South who sought employment on the Canadian railroads, giving such rail centres as Amherst, Montreal, Winnipeg, and Calgary small but quite evident Negro ghettoes, and by elements from Harlem's 'sporting life' who wanted to escape from prohibition. West Indians also began to arrive, until restricted by Canadian immigration laws, to study in French Canada's universities, to work in the steel mills of Cape Breton, or to seek jobs on the vessels of the St Lawrence and in Toronto. Finally, by the 1950s American Negroes from northern cities, tired of ghettoes, broken promises, and second-class status, sought out isolation and equality in Vancouver, Toronto, and Hamilton.

The diversity of sources from which the Negro came into Canada assured that he would have little in common except the colour of his skin. Loyalist Negroes looked upon themselves as among the founders of the new land, as they were, and they wished to have as little as possible to do with the penurious Refugees or the war-like Maroons. West Indians felt themselves to be British or French, having little in common with the Canadians or, as they called the descendants of the fugitive slaves of the 1850s, the Americans. The last, by being the most numerous, tended to assume that they provided the normative values of the twentieth-century Negro community, and they often were intolerant of the groups that had preceded them. The diversity of conditions which confronted the other Negroes, in heritage and in environment, also assured that they would be less militant, less vocal, and therefore less well-known than their American counterparts. One problem which the majority of Negroes shared, however, was that in the two provinces in which they were most numerous, Nova Scotia and Ontario, they were progressively restricted from access to the public schools until, by 1850, both provinces had introduced forms of segregated school systems.

The number of people affected by such schools was small, of course. The total Negro population of Canada at no time numbered more than 4 per cent of the colonial aggregate; after 1900, when those Negroes that remained gradually became more vocal in their protests against the schools and unfair employment and accommodation practices, they were certainly not more than 1 to 1.5 per cent of the total (a figure substantially

larger than the official Canadian census return which, probably erroneously, reported only two-tenths of 1 per cent of the population as black). The Negroes tended to settle, however, in few areas but in substantial numbers: in Halifax County, back of the city, they were 10 per cent of the population, and in Essex and Kent counties, in Canada West, they were as much as a third of the population of pre–Civil War Chatham and Dresden. Observers estimated, with some inflation, that there were 60,000 Negroes in Canada West by the time of the Civil War. Consistently underenumerated, and given many opportunities to pass for white, the Negroes were probably twice as numerous by 1920 as Canada officially recognized; even so, their ranks were thin and —outside certain pockets, or in their own nineteenth-century all-Negro settlements at Wilberforce or Dawn or Elgin—they were not a factor to be reckoned with politically or economically. Hence, white Canada tended to ignore them.

Ignoring Negroes was made easier in the two provinces in which they were relatively numerous because of residential and educational segregation. Although in many respects Canadian culture, even outside Canada East, was substantially different from the developing culture of the United States, on the whole the Canadian response to the question of colour was not unlike that of the nearby northern states of New York, Ohio, or Massachusetts. Most Canadians outside Ontario and Nova Scotia were not even aware of the presence of non-fugitive Negroes, and fewer Canadians yet knew then, or know now, of the resort to segregated schools in those provinces, or of the several anomalies that confronted those who sought their freedom under that lion's paw.

Indeed, most white Canadians would not have learned that there was a Negro problem in Canada at all had they relied upon their own formal schooling. As in the United States, textbooks simply forgot that black men existed after 1865, except in humorous and menial contexts, and only a few Canadian school books gave even passing reference to the influx of fugitive slaves in the 1850s. Most did not mention that Canadians themselves had allowed slavery until 1833, and no Canadian text had occasion to refer to Negroes—or to separate schools—after describing the American Civil War. Until recently most of those few books which purported to analyze social problems for a school-aged audience were imported from the United States, and readers not unnaturally assumed that the racial problems they discussed were unique to the republic.

British North America had much experience with the separate school as an institution, however. Protestant school boards warred within themselves over what a Protestant school was (and in 1874 Newfoundland established a straight denominational system as a result), while separate (or Roman Catholic) schools required constant legislation, and the legislation required constant revision. A legislature could easily establish a provision for yet another form of separation, based on race rather than on religion, with such ready machinery at hand. Canada West did so.

* * *

The twentieth century brought no quick changes in the pattern of segregated schools. In 1918 a new Nova Scotian Education Act provided that the Council of Public Instruction could 'receive the recommendation of any inspector for separate apartments or buildings in any section for the different sexes or different races of pupils, and to make such decisions thereon as it deems proper, subject to the provision that coloured pupils shall not be excluded from instruction in the public school in the section in which they reside . . .'.[2] So the law remained until 1954, when all reference to race was dropped from the statute.

Between 1918 and 1954 the Negro schools continued to fare badly and only the most blind of school inspectors could have pretended that

separate education was also equal education. In the *Annual Reports* of Nova Scotia's superintendent of education there were many references to the uncertainty of the Negro schools: uncertainty whether they would open or not, uncertainty whether a teacher might be found, uncertainty as to the legal status of their property. In 1918 all children near Annapolis and Digby had access to public schools 'except the coloured section of Fundy . . .', where there were 20 children of school age and where there had been no teacher for 10 years. At Joggins, where whites and blacks attended, the latter were permitted to use the school building only one-third of the time until a controversy forced the local inspector to shift all of the whites to Acaciaville. Coloured schools also existed in Inglewood and Weymouth Falls, the latter with a white teacher. In 1927 the Negro ratepayers of Five Mile Plains refused to pay their school taxes, and the Canadian Gypsum Company, a major employer of Negroes, offered them $200 if they would raise an equal sum through taxes, which they ultimately did. In 1912 and in 1919 there was no school for Negroes in Guysborough County because no teacher could be found who would accept the tiny salary. In 1915 two schools for coloured children could not open in Antigonish County for want of teachers, and in 1920 the Negroes of Greenville in Yarmouth County failed to find a teacher; their school remained closed for at least eight years.

During none of this time was Nova Scotia prosperous; after 1929 it was poverty-stricken, and white public schools suffered with separate schools for want of teachers, equipment, and transportation. In 1932, for example, a new school for Negroes was opened on the Guysborough road with 17 pupils; it was the first genuine school for the Negroes of the area to be opened in over 40 years, and they had raised a portion of the funds for it themselves through concerts and benefit suppers, together with a grant from the Department of Education. But in

Greenville there still was no school, and the one in Beechville closed for lack of a teacher; in seven localities Negro schools operated only during the summer. In Annapolis and Digby but one of four instructors was even minimally qualified, and virtually no Negro teacher had gone beyond a permissive licence. Not until 1936 did the Negroes of Birchtown, in Guysborough County, receive any schooling, and then in a mission church. In 1940 the one admittedly uninsurable school in Nova Scotia was a dilapidated building for Negroes near Guysborough.[3]

The same currents of opinion that brought change in other areas of Negro activity between the late 1930s and the 1960s of course influenced education. Environmentalist theories slowly displaced notions of inherent and hereditary racial inequalities. Many liberal-minded Canadians were prepared to explain what they regarded as the manifest inferiority of the Negroes they knew by reference to the institutions which shaped the Negro environment. One such institution was the school, and the separate schools of Nova Scotia and Ontario increasingly came under attack from white and interracial groups as well as from more militant Negro leaders. More and more Negroes, although still relatively few, were successfully completing university degrees, including post-graduate work. No longer was it good Christianity, good politics, good international affairs, good image-building, good human relations, or even good sense to discriminate openly against Negroes, especially in a nation which so prided itself on its moral superiority to the United States. As Canadian newspapers increasingly focused upon the Negro problem across the border, editorials began to sing the praises of non-discriminatory Canadians. This, in turn, produced a reaction, as readers wrote to editors of instances of overt discrimination within the promised land itself. Some newspapers began to overcompensate for their rivals' hortatory praise of the Canadian image and

indulged in unnecessary orgies of self-condemnation, emphasizing each instance of proven or alleged discrimination. By the early 1960s no literate Canadian, regardless of the newspaper he chose to read, could have been unaware of the racial issue in world affairs and that Canada too had its own minorities. More often than not interest in protecting minorities centred upon the Eskimo, numerically no more significant in Canada than the Negro but popularly thought to be uniquely a Canadian problem, or on anti-Semitism. But the Negro, too, became an object of attention.[4]

Given these changing circumstances, separate schools would not survive. Most had closed in Ontario by 1891, in any case, although the permissive legislation had long remained part of the provincial law code. More separate schools existed in Nova Scotia, but most were exclusive to Negroes by virtue of residence rather than separate by force of bylaw. In Alberta a single Negro school continued into the 1960s—at Amber Valley, where the isolated all-Negro settlement maintained a school through the first 10 grades; on occasion, as at Breton in the 1950s, whites protested against a black teacher. Only in Nova Scotia did any substantial number of Negroes continue to have cause for genuine complaint over the school situation.

Public attention once again focused on the reality of de facto segregated schools in 1940 when Negro children were barred openly from public education in Lower Sackville, in Halifax County. Mrs Pleasah Lavinia Caldwell, a Nova Scotian–born Negro who had taught in western Canada for five years, responded by organizing her own school for black children, which she called Maroon Hill in memory of the Jamaican Maroons. For a decade she provided the only instruction available to many Negro children, and when she died in 1950 her 'kitchen school' was a local legend. But her act of personal philanthropy seems not to have moved the provincial authorities, for until 1959 school buses in

Hammonds Plains stopped only in the white section of the community, thus effectively cutting off the more indolent or apathetic Negro students from further formal education.[5]

Mrs Caldwell's school was not without influence outside Nova Scotia, however, for it gave the news media frequent opportunities to remark upon instances of racial discrimination elsewhere in Canada as well. By the mid-1950s church groups, and especially the United Church, were increasingly committed to social reform and temporal equality. As Canadians played ever more intently at the national game of self-identification, attempting to find, define, or invent a coherent Canadianism to pose against the powerful forces of gravity from across the border, they wished to disassociate themselves from the racial crisis so obviously brewing in the United States. We are not basically a prejudiced people, the Canadian press said time and again, although there are pockets of prejudice in Canadian society that must be rooted out. As interest groups pressed more earnestly for provincial legislatures to enact fair employment and fair accommodation acts, or for the national government to enunciate a Canadian Bill of Rights, the outdated and permissive school bills came under close scrutiny.

In truth, the walls came tumbling down in most quarters with little effort, for few Canadians can have wanted to share with the American South the peculiar institution of the segregated school. Custom, inertia, and widespread ignorance of the laws, rather than the active will of white segregationists, had permitted the clauses to remain on the books. Once attention was given to them, in the context of a more generalized and growing Canadian interest in civil rights, the legal foundations for segregation were removed in Ontario and put in course of removal in Nova Scotia. Still, over 10 years were required in each case to achieve such an end.

In 1950 a Royal Commission on Education recommended repeal of the pertinent clauses in Ontario's school law, but they were retained virtually intact in the revised statutes of that year. A minister of the United Church of Canada in Markham, Ontario, thereupon prepared a motion for presentation before the provincial legislature, in 1952, to abolish separate schools for Negroes. Several delegations from Kent County—where, in Dresden, Negroes were informally barred from some restaurants and places of amusement—successfully opposed the motion as superfluous, arguing that such schools no longer existed, although in fact they did, if not in Kent County. Five years later the United Church as a body asked the government to repeal the offending sections of the Common Schools Act, and again a group from Kent County, with support in Essex County, blocked action. In the latter, in North Colchester, it was the Negroes who wished to preserve their separate school for they thought that their children were not prepared to compete with whites. A more militant body of Negroes in nearby Amherstburg, led by Alvin McCurdy, worked to persuade their Colchester brethren that separate education was not equal, but since the Negro school board had a vested interest in maintaining its functions, McCurdy was unsuccessful both then and in 1959 when the United Church, this time through its official organ, *The Observer*, once more protested against the separate school clauses.

The successful drive against the school law, by then 114 years old, began in February 1964, when a newly elected Negro member of the Ontario legislature, Leonard Braithwaite, chose it as the subject of his maiden speech. Braithwaite, a Liberal from Etobicoke, a prosperous suburb of Toronto, was the first Negro to be elected to a provincial legislature in Canada, and while he made it clear that he did not take civil rights as his special province, he felt it fitting that such should be the subject of his first effort. Various human rights groups supported him with petitions. In March the minister of education, William G. Davis, announced that the references to separate schools for Negroes would be removed from the statutes, and on 7 May this was done. By this time the North Colchester school board had begun agitation to improve the physical condition of its school, and a quickly formed Negro organization, the South Essex Citizen's Advancement Association, was protesting retention of the school at all. In November, with the knowledge that the permissive legislation had been struck from the books, the Colchester board held a meeting from which the press was barred. The chairman of the board and the president of the association then issued a joint statement, in which they agreed on a timetable for moving the Negro children, by bus, into other schools and on immediate token integration of the first grade throughout the township. By September 1965, the last segregated school in Ontario closed.[6]

Not surprisingly, change came more slowly to Nova Scotia, and perhaps with cause. The Negroes there were less progressive, less aggressive, and less ambitious than their Ontario counterparts. The majority remained rural, and the most ardent civil rights advocates would have been hard put to argue that immediate integration of the Negro children of New Road Settlement, in particular, was to their advantage. But most recognized that one must begin sometime and somewhere. There were seven formal Negro school districts (and three additional exclusively Negro schools) in the province in 1960,[7] and the Conservative premier, Robert Lorne Stanfield, began with West Hants when in that year he personally and successfully moved the abolition of the three segregated school districts there. By 1964 only four such districts remained, at Beechville, Hammonds Plains, Lucasville, and Cherry Brook,[8] all in Halifax County, and one by one these too were made ready for closing. Two of the exclusively Negro schools also had been breeched, with white children in attendance, and while the permissive legislation remained on the statute books, both it and the separate schools were on a slow road to extinction.[9]

But the present Negro generation in Nova Scotia could not be liberated in any case. The cycle of poverty, ignorance, and unemployment had lasted far too long for anyone but the most idealistic to expect the Nova Scotian Negro to assimilate to Nova Scotian society quickly or easily, or for the Nova Scotian white, however much he might be prepared to concede the Negroes' inherent equality, to think of them as equal in fact as well as in potential. For Negroes were not yet equal in fact and were unlikely to be until the slow curative powers of equal education had made their impact. It was not this generation that had been liberated, but the next.[10]

Notes

1. This article has grown from a general history of Negro activities in Canada. . . . The author would like to thank his university and the Social Science Research Council for providing funds to support his research into Canadian Negro history.

2. *The Revised Statutes of Nova Scotia, 1923* (Halifax), I, 498–500.

3. The school inspectors' reports appear in full from 1879 in the *Journal and Proceedings of the House of Assembly of the Province of Nova Scotia*, and in the *Journal and Proceedings of the Legislative Council of the Province of Nova Scotia*, as well as separately. This and the preceding paragraph is drawn from *Assembly, 1918*, I, 66–9; *Council, 1895–96*, 78; *1910–11*, 74–5; *1912*, 58, 65; *1915*, 66; *1916*, 73; *1919*, 72; *1920*, 63; *1926*, 59, 63, 66–7; *1927*, 65; *1928*,

44, 47; *1931*, 41; *1932*, 34, 37, 68; *1934*, 38–40, 74; *1935*, 34; *1936*, 79; and *1940*, 83.

4. See the proceedings of the 1964 *Human Rights Conference* held at Dalhousie University, Halifax (Institute of Public Affairs, Dalhousie University, publication No. 42 [Halifax, 1965]).

5. Toronto *Globe and Mail*, 28 Nov. 1949; *Time Magazine* (Canadian Edition, Montreal), LV, 2 Jan. 1950, 12; *The Canadian Negro* (Toronto), I (Aug., 1953), 1; Halifax *Chronicle-Herald*, 26 Oct. 1959.

6. Ontario, Sessional Paper No. 43, *Report of the Royal Commission on Education in Ontario, 1950* (Toronto [1951]), 534–6; *Journal of the Legislative Assembly of the Province of Ontario . . . Session, 1951* (Toronto), LXXXV, 15; *. . . Session, 1964*, XCVIII, 97, 105, 136, 149, 160, 168; *Revised Statutes of Ontario, 1950 . . .* (Toronto), IV, 643–80: Separate Schools Act, 356, Pt. 1, s. 2; *Toronto Star*, 17 Apr. 1952; *Canadian Labour Reports* (Montreal), XII (Mar., 1957), 3; *Globe and Mail*, 19 Jan. 1959; Kitchener-Waterloo *Record*, 13 Mar., 19 Nov. 1964; *Canada Week*, I (23 Mar. 1964), 2–3; School Area Board, 16; personal interview with Mr Alvin McCurdy, Amherstburg; Windsor Public Library: scrapbooks on local Negro Activities. For the Act, see *The Ontario Gazette*, XCVII (16 May 1964).

7. A Negro school district formed in 1937 as part of Avonside ceased to exist in 1959 when consolidated with Tracadie. See M.M. MacDonald, *Memorable Years in the History of Antigonish* ([Antigonish], 1964), 192, 195.

8. Nova Scotian place names often underwent minor changes. Both Joggin and Joggins appear in official reports, as do Cherrybrook and Cherry Brook, Hammonds Plains and Hammond Plains, and others. The spellings used here are standardized from Province of Nova Scotia, Department of Mines, *Index of Geographical Names . . .* (Halifax, 1965). Birchtown, as used here, should not be confused with the older community in Shelburne County.

9. *Revised Statutes of Nova Scotia, 1954 . . .* (Halifax); Halifax *Chronicle-Herald*, 25 Feb. 1960; *Canada Week*, I (11 May 1964), 2.

10. Omitted here is any discussion of the educational function of Sunday schools, by nature segregated if their sponsoring churches are, and belonging more properly to a discussion of the Negro church in Canada; of the Nova Scotia Home for Coloured Children; and of recent work by the Adult Education Division of Nova Scotia's Department of Education or the Negro Education and Community Development Council of Halifax County.

Chapter 3

Strangers within Our Gates, or Coming Canadians

James S. Woodsworth

The stranger that sojourneth with you shall be unto you as the homeborn among you, and thou shalt love him as thyself.

—Lev. 19:34

Assemble the people, the men and the women and the little ones, and thy stranger that is within thy gates, that they may hear, and that they may learn, and fear the Lord your God, and observe to do all the words of this law; and that their children, which have not known, may hear, and learn to fear the Lord your God, as long as ye live in the land.

—Deut. 31:12, 13

The Negro and the Indian

Neither the Negro nor the Indian are immigrants, and yet they are so entirely different from the ordinary white population that some mention of them is necessary if we would understand the complexity of our problems. We group them merely because both stand out entirely by themselves.

I. The Negro

Contiguity to the United States is accountable largely for our Negro population. The majority of the 20,000 Negroes now in Canada are the descendants of those who escaped from slavery into British dominions. They are living chiefly in the towns of western Ontario and the Maritime provinces. In the cities they often crowd together and form a 'quarter', where sanitary and moral conditions are most prejudicial to the public welfare. Blood, rather than language or religion, is the chief barrier that separates them from the rest of the community.

John R. Commons, writing in the *Chautauquan* (November 1903), thus describes the Negro:

> In Africa the people are unstable, indifferent to suffering, and 'easily aroused to ferocity by the sight of blood or under great fear'. They exhibit certain qualities which are associated with their descendants in this country, namely, aversion to silence and solitude, love of rhythm, excitability, and lack of reserve. All travellers speak of their impulsiveness, strong sexual passion, and lack of willpower.

He points out what a momentous change it was to this people to be shifted from equatorial Africa to the temperate regions of America; from an environment of savagery to one of civilization. Then he speaks of their present relationship to the free institutions of America.

> The very qualities of intelligence and manliness which are essential for citizenship in a

democracy were systematically expunged from the Negro race through 200 years of slavery. And then, by the cataclysm of a war of emancipation, in which it took no part, this race, after many thousand years of savagery and two centuries of slavery, was suddenly let loose into the liberty of citizenship and the electoral suffrage. The world never before had seen such a triumph of dogmatism and partisanship.

Whether we agree with the conclusion or not, we may be thankful that we have no 'Negro problem' in Canada.

Many Negroes are members of various Protestant churches, and are consistent Christians and highly respected citizens. The African Methodist Episcopal Church, organized in 1816, has about 130 churches, with a membership of 3,000.

II. The Indian

One of the most pathetic sights is that of an Indian stepping off a sidewalk to let a white man pass, or turning out of a prairie trail to give a white man the right of way. Once the Indians were proud autochthones; now they are despised Natives; Aborigines, yet outcasts; belated survivors of an earlier age, strangers in the land of their fathers.

Roughly speaking, the Indians may be divided into three classes—the Indians of eastern Canada, those in the 'North-West', and those in British Columbia. To these might be added the Eskimos of the Far North, who, however, are yet outside our modern civilization. The last census gives 127,932 Indians and half-breeds. The Indians of the East have already taken their place in the new life, and some are as prosperous as their white neighbours. Most of the Indians of the North-West have treaty rights. In general, each man, woman, and child receives annually $5, the councillors $15, and the chiefs $25, with a uniform every three years. In addition there is

an annual allowance of ammunition, tools, etc. Reserves have been set apart allowing about 128 acres per head, and schools are maintained on the reserves. Many of the Indians are becoming successful farmers, but there are serious difficulties. The Rev. Thompson Ferrier writes:

On the reserve the white man's vices have taken a deeper root than his virtues. His firewater has demoralized whole tribes, and the diseases he has introduced have annihilated many. . . . The Indian is growing up with the idea firmly fixed in his head that the Government owes him a living, and his happiness and prosperity depend in no degree upon his individual effort. Rations and treaty are all right for the aged, helpless, and infirm. Strong and able-bodied Indians hang around for rations and treaty, neglecting other duties and the cultivation of their land, in order to secure what in many cases could be earned several times over in the same length of time. The system destroys his energy, push, and independence. . . .

As fast as our Indian, whether of mixed or full blood, is capable of taking care of himself, it is our duty to set him on his feet, and sever forever the ties that bind him either to his tribe or the Government. Both Church and State should have, as a final goal, the destruction and end of treaty and reservation life.

Mr Ferrier thinks that the main hope lies in giving the young generation a good, practical training in specially organized industrial schools.[1]

The Indian population of British Columbia numbers 24,964. The income for 1907 was $1,541,922, or an average of $61.78 for every member of that population. Grouping them in families of four, the income becomes for the family $247.12. Of the British Columbia Indian, Dr Whittington writes:

The sources of this income are catching, curing, and canning fish; fur hunting; logging, boat-building, stevedoring, as sailors, farming, mining, etc. The women, of course, assist materially, and also the children, at inside work in the canneries, also in selling various kinds of handiwork. Apart from this the living of the Indians is easily obtained to a very considerable extent along the lines of fish, venison, and small fruits, as well as farm produce. If it be a question of living, the Indian of today is very much nearer to the civilized white than to his pagan ancestor. Modern homes, modern clothing, modern education are, to a great extent, the order of the day, and are rapidly becoming more so. The Indian is in a transition stage from his old-time to his modern environment. I cannot but say that the journey is more than half done. The white man's vices are the most baneful of all the evil influences at work on the Indian. Another pernicious influence has been the mistaken kindness of the State in helping the Indian instead of simply helping him to help himself.[2]

Much missionary work, evangelistic, educational, industrial, and medical, has been done among the Indians. Many are devout Christians living exemplary lives, but there are still about 10,202 Indians in our Dominion, as grossly pagan as were their ancestors, or still more wretched, half-civilized, only to be debauched. Surely the Indians have a great claim upon Canadian Christians!

* * *

Effects of Immigration

It is extremely undesirable that thousands of foreigners of questionable value from a mental, moral, and physical point of view should be allowed to freely invade well-governed and prosperous communities. They underbid the labour market, raise important and vexatious municipal questions, strain charitable resources to the utmost, increase the cost of government, expose a healthy people to contagious diseases common to the poorer classes of Europe, corrupt the body politic, and in every way complicate a situation none too simple at best.

—Whelpley

So far as mere commercial and material progress is concerned, a heterogeneous people may be as successful as any. But where depth and not breadth is concerned, that freedom from distraction and multiplicity which results from the prevalence of a distinct type and the universality of certain standards and ideals seems almost essential to the development of extraordinary products in any line.

—Hall

Foreign immigration into this country has from the time it first assumed large proportions amounted not to a reinforcement of our population but a replacement of Native by foreign stock. . . . The American shrank from the industrial competition thus thrust upon him. He was unwilling himself to engage in the lowest kind of day labour with these new elements of population; he was even more unwilling to bring sons and daughters into the world to enter into that competition. The more rapidly foreigners came into the United States the smaller was the rate of increase, not merely among the Native population separately, but throughout the population of the country as a whole.

—F.A. Walker

Prescott F. Hall, in his splendid work on *Immigration and Its Effect upon the United States*, classifies the effects under four divisions—racial, economic, social, and political. We cannot do better than adopt his classification, at the same time urging our readers to study carefully this problem, which is essentially the same for the United States and Canada.

I. Racial Effects

America is not American. Canada will not remain Canadian. During the first half of the past century there came to be a fairly well-defined American type—that is, the true American had certain distinctive physical, mental, and social characteristics. But so great has been the alien immigration that it is a question whether the older American type will predominate. New England was English. America is today, in many respects, more nearly German or Irish than it is English. If the Slavic or Latin elements predominate, what will it become?

We in Canada are at the beginning of the process, and can only speculate as to the result. It is conceivable that the various races coming to us might remain absolutely distinct. Canada would then simply be a congeries of races. But such a condition is not possible. Some peoples may not intermarry. The Mongolians, the Hindus, and the Negroes will probably remain largely distinct. Even then the presence of these has a very decided influence on the other races. The Southern States would have had a vastly different history if the slaves had never been imported. The presence of incompatible elements changes the entire social and political life of a country; it is a fatal barrier to the highest national life. But in time most of these peoples will intermarry—Slavs and Celts, Latins and Germans, Hungarian and Semitic peoples, in varying combinations and proportions. From a physical standpoint, what will be the result? Mentally and morally, what type will prevail? Each has something to contribute. What form will each take in combination? All are poured into the crucible. Who can guess the resultant product?

It would be an interesting study to trace some of the modifications that are already taking place in the English people in Canada, some of them

due to the presence of other peoples, some of them to environment. In a score of ways, Canadian English are not the old country type. But we must cross to the United States to see these modifications carried a little further. Physically and socially, what a difference! And these differences in type are bound to react on all our institutions. Grasserie compares the government possible in Latin and Germanic countries:

> The ethnic character has a profound influence on the choice between the two modes of government. With some peoples individual autonomy—independence of character—is strongly traced; for example, among the Germanic nations. Each one engages only his extreme exterior in society. With nations of such temperament family life is strongly developed; the *home* is the sacred ark. With some other peoples—with the Latin nations in general—it is quite different. The autonomy is less refractory, they like to live in society, and prefer to discharge the functions of thinking and wishing upon others. The will not being carefully cultivated, it diminishes, and the State acts for the individual. [quoted in Hyde 1888: 388]

Very decidedly the social life and ideals of the people of the United States have been affected by alien races. Already government—especially the government in the cities where the proportion of foreigners is greatest—is being modified to a large extent.

We can already perceive changes in Canada. The Westerner differs from the Easterner, not merely because east is east and west is west, but because of the mixed character of the population of the West. The character of the Eastern cities, too, is changing. The people on the street differ in physique from those of a decade ago. Social distinctions, hitherto unknown, are being recognized. A hundred years from now who and what shall we be?

There is an unfounded optimism that confidently asserts that all this mingling of the races is in the highest interest of our country. We get the strength of the North, the beauty of the South, and the wisdom of the East; such is the line of thought often presented in after-dinner speeches.

We, too, must confess to a certain optimism, based not altogether on natural law, that ultimately a higher type may be developed. In the older and more permanent races and civilizations there is little variation from type; they are conservative, fixed, stationary. But with the mingling of the races there is a greater tendency to variation. The newer nations are in a state of unstable equilibrium. They are capable of being moved, of developing. There is the opportunity for change. Will the change be for better or worse?

Surely the whole conception of evolution is founded on the implicit faith that the world is moving toward higher things, and that spiritual forces are destined to prevail. Example, training, higher motives, religious impulses are more potent than race characteristics, and will determine the future of our people.

II. Economic Effects

There has been much discussion as to the value of the immigrant. Immigrants from the United States to Canada have often brought thousands of dollars. This seems to be a straight gain to the country. But the amount of money brought from other countries is not great. Hall [1906] has prepared the following table, which shows the amount of money per capita owned by the immigrants at the port of entry in 1900; this will be approximately as true for the same nationalities in Canada as any table that could be compiled from Canadian statistics:

French	37.80	Croatian and	
Greek	28.70	Slavonian	12.51
German	28.53	Slovak	11.69
Bohemian and		Ruthenian	
Moravian	23.12	(Rusniak)	10.51
Italian		Portuguese	10.47
(northern)	22.49	Magyar	10.39
Dutch and		Polish	9.94
Flemish	21.00	Italian	
Cuban	19.34	(southern)	8.84
Scandinavian	16.65	Hebrew	8.67
Russian	14.94	Lithuanian	7.96
Irish	14.50		

In many cases the amount brought in will be more than offset by the money sent out of the country to prepay the immigrant's ticket. It will readily be seen that the immigrant's value lies not in what he has, but in what he is.

How much is he worth? Many have tried to estimate the money cost of 'raising' a man or woman, and have reckoned it at from $500 to $1,000. But such calculations are useless. A man's value to the country consists not in what he costs, but in what he can do—and does. Those who are physically strong can do much of the rough work of a new land. But if they are ignorant or immoral, it is decidedly a question as to whether they are, in the long run, worth much to the country. . . . True prosperity cannot be measured by the volume of trade or bank clearings. It consists in the social and moral welfare of the people.

The competition of races is the competition of standards of living. . . . As rapidly as a race rises in the scale of living and, through organization, begins to demand higher wages and resist the pressure of long hours and overexertion, the employers substitute another race, and the process is repeated. Each race comes from a country lower in the scale than that of the preceding, until finally the ends of the earth have been ransacked in the search for low standards of living, combined with patient industriousness.

Scotch	$41.51	Syrian	$14.31
Japanese	39.59	Chinese	13.98
English	38.90	Finnish	13.06

Europe has been exhausted, Asia has been drawn upon, and there remain but three regions of the temperate zones from which a still lower standard can be expected. These are China, Japan, and India. The Chinese have been excluded by law, the Japanese are coming in increasing numbers, and the Indian coolies remain to be experimented upon.

—John R. Commons,
in March (1904) *Chautauquan*

* * *

Notes

1. See 'Indian Education in the North-West', by Rev. Thompson Ferrier.

2. See 'The British Columbian Indian and His Future', by Rev. R. Whittington, DD.

Chapter 4

Canadian Mosaic: The Making of a Northern Nation

John Murray Gibbon

Preface

'Know Thyself.'
—Plutarch's translation of the Greek motto
inscribed upon the Delphic Oracle

Changes in international boundaries in Europe, due to racial problems, are of vital concern to Canada, since so large a proportion of the Canadian population has originated in disturbed areas, and has crossed the Atlantic to escape from the effects of changes in past years. It seems, therefore, only right that Canadians should make themselves familiar with the countries from which they have come and the reasons why their forebears have taken up Canadian citizenship. They should examine the progress being made in the amalgamation of their own and other racial groups in the new democracy of the Dominion. The old Greek motto of 'Know Thyself' was never so a propos as it is today. 'Make it thy business to know thyself, which is the most difficult business in the world' wrote Cervantes in *Don Quixote*.

While in the first instance many of the settlers in this country have crossed the Atlantic as exiles seeking sanctuary from social or political distress, they have found their sanctuary in Canada not merely a temporary refuge but a home, and in that new home they have acquired a feeling of solidarity which without doubt is moulding a new nation. . . . [T]he Canadians of German descent are turning their eyes not to Berlin but to Ottawa for political guidance and leadership. But each racial group has brought with it some qualities which are worthwhile contributions to Canadian culture—as for instance the national proverb of the Czechs 'Not by might but by the spirit shall ye conquer.'

The War of 1812, the defence of the frontier against Fenian raids in 1866, the Great War of 1914–1918, all served as unifying forces cementing different racial elements of the population, and this supports the belief that in any world conflict Canadians of every racial origin and creed will stand together. . . .

The pact concluded between the four great powers, France, England, Germany, and Italy, to revise the boundaries of Czechoslovakia, will inevitably result in migration of dispossessed citizens of that republic to other countries, and judging by past experience, Canada will receive a quota of such as are considered suitable settlers. . . .

In studying the character of any people, we should consider first the physical background, the kind of country in which that people lives—whether forested or open country, whether mountainous or level, whether any or much of it is lake or river country, whether its climate is temperate or subject to great heat or cold, whether it lends itself to grain or fruit farming, so that it can grow sufficient food, whether it is served by roads, waterways, or railways providing easy communication between its different areas. With a basis of such knowledge, it becomes easier to understand the social qualities of this people, since human beings are so much the creatures of their environment.

As for the social and political conditions, we should ask ourselves—how did the people get there?—are their neighbours friendly?—have they been troubled much by wars with other peoples or by civil wars?—what are their religious beliefs?—are they a home-loving people, or are they restless and inclined to be on the move?—are the women expected to do hard manual labour?—do they have large families?—what sorts of schools do they have?—are they music lovers?—what are their sports?—do they like to work together, or are they inclined to act and get things for themselves?—are they the kind of people who do just what they are told?—or do they like to criticize and think the world should be reformed?

If you can give the answer to these questions, you have at least made a start. But, even then, you have only an outsider's view of your people—a casual or superficial acquaintance.

To know a people, you must know its history and origins, just as to know an individual person requires knowledge of his parents, his upbringing, and his career, as well as the house he lives in and his surroundings.

That is why, if we are to understand the Canadian people, we must know more than just the geography and scenery of Canada, and the customs and habits of the Canadians. We must also study their racial origins.

This we are fortunately able to do, because the Canadian people have not lived long enough together to be set in their ways. They are made up of European racial groups, the members of which are only beginning to get acquainted with each other, and have not yet been blended into one type. Possibly, in another 200 years,

Canadians may be fused together and standardized so that you can recognize them anywhere in a crowd. But, even then, the writers of the future will understand them better if they know what they were like when Canada was younger.

The Canadian race of the future is being superimposed on the original Native Indian races and is being made up of over 30 European racial groups, each of which has its own history, customs, and traditions. Some politicians want to see these merged as quickly as possible into one standard type, just as our neighbours in the United States are hurrying to make every citizen a 100 per cent American. Others believe in trying to preserve for the future Canadian race the most worthwhile qualities and traditions that each racial group has brought with it.

While there is still time, let us make a survey of these racial groups—see where they came from, what relationship, if any, they had with each other in Europe, what culture they enjoyed and how much of that culture they have been able to bring with them.

In the Administrative Report of the Dominion Statistician prefacing the Canadian census of 1931, an outline is given of the plan according to which the racial origins have been decided, and from this the following are extracts:

The term 'origin', as used by the census, has a combined biological, cultural, and geographical significance. It suggests whence our people come and the implied biological strain and cultural background; following popular usage, the terms, 'English stock', 'French stock', 'Italian stock', etc., are employed to describe the sum total of the biological and cultural characteristics which distinguish such groups from others.

In tracing origin in the case of those of European descent, the line is through the father. By applying this rule rigorously, those of mixed family origin are (by the law of large numbers) resolved with a fair degree of accuracy into their constituent elements.

The language spoken by the people of a country has a distinct bearing upon its problems of nationality and assimilation. With the exception of religion, no individual right or heritage is more highly prized or more jealously guarded. In Canada, French as well as English has been an official language from the earliest times. By mother tongue is meant the language commonly spoken in the home; in the case of immigrants it is usually the language spoken before coming to Canada.

Finally, the census requires each person to state what is the religious denomination or community to which he or she adheres or belongs, which he or she favours.

The Canadian people today presents itself as a decorated surface, bright with inlays of separate coloured pieces, not painted in colours blended with brush on palette. The original background in which the inlays are set is still visible, but these inlays cover more space than that background, and so the ensemble may truly be called a mosaic.

The use of the word 'mosaic' in connection with the Canadian people was used for the first time, so far as I know, by an American writer, Victoria Hayward, who used to come every summer to Canada with her friend, Edith Watson, to write about and photograph the country folk, both in the East and in the West. These two collaborated on a book, published in 1922, and this is how Victoria Hayward introduces the word:

The new Canadians, representing many lands and widely separated sections of old Europe, have contributed to the Prairie provinces a variety in the way of church architecture. Cupolas and domes distinctly Eastern, almost Turkish, startle one above the tops of Manitoba maples or the bush of the river banks. These architectural figures of the landscape, apart altogether from their religious significance, are centres where, crossing the threshold on Sundays, one has an opportunity of hearing Swedish music or the rich, deep chanting of the Russian responses; and of viewing at close hand the artistry that goes to make up the interior appointments of these churches transplanted from the East to the West. Here, too, silhouetted against the sky, is the little separate bell-tower and perhaps the three-barred cross of the Eastern Christian Church. Here and there in the corner of a wheat-field, at the cross-section of a Prairie highway, one sees, as in Quebec, the tall, uplifted crucifix set up. It is indeed a mosaic of vast dimensions and great breadth, essayed of the Prairie.

The second writer to use the simile of 'mosaic' was Kate A. Foster (Mrs Percival Foster of Toronto) who made an extensive survey of the foreign-born, or 'new Canadians', as they were coming to be called, for the Dominion Council of the YWCA, and this was published under the title of 'Our Canadian Mosaic' in 1926. It is an excellent survey, running to 150 pages, and must have proved of great value for the purpose for which it was intended, namely, a manual of information for social workers. I did not know of this publication till I had almost completed my own book, and offered to change my title, as she had priority. However, Mrs Foster and the Dominion Council of the YWCA generously agreed to let it stand, considering that the figures in this 1926 survey were in many cases out of date, and there was no immediate intention of reprinting it.

My own book is an elaboration of the talks incidental to a series of 10 musical radio programs which I organized and delivered early in 1938 over the transcontinental network of the Canadian Broadcasting Corporation.

Ever since first I came to Canada 30 years ago, I have been intrigued by the variety of racial types. On the day of my first arrival, I saw a member of the Dominion cabinet, the Hon. Jacques Bureau, on a government tugboat at Quebec, serving ginger ale in his shirt sleeves to a party of newspaper men, and singing the French-Canadian folk song 'En roulant ma boule roulant', and I imagined the kind of letter that some English Colonel would write from his club to the London *Times* if a British cabinet minister were to have done anything of the kind. Ten years after the armistice, Sir Edward Beatty, chairman and president of the Canadian Pacific Railway, authorized me to organize a series of folk-song, folk-dance, and handicraft festivals, starting with Quebec and going west to Winnipeg, Regina, and Calgary, for the new Canadians of the western Prairies; then some Scottish Music Festivals and Highland Games at Banff, as well as a Sea Music Festival at Vancouver, and a Christmas Music Festival at Victoria, BC. These gave me the opportunity of getting to know more about the talent in music and handicraft brought to Canada by the Europeans, and also convinced me that in music these racial groups found contacts which helped greatly in making them understand each other, and in creating goodwill for themselves among Canadians of British stock.

When, therefore, Mr Leonard W. Brockington, the chairman, and Major Gladstone Murray, the general manager, of the Canadian Broadcasting Corporation, both asked me to suggest an idea for their network, it seemed to me that a series of programs which would illustrate the contribution of music brought by the different European Continental groups to Canada could convey a message and an opportunity of mutual understanding to a large audience of listeners scattered from coast to coast over the nine provinces of Canada.

The music identified with these European races is of two kinds: (1) the folk-song and folk-dance tunes of the people; (2) composed instrumental music or art song. As for the songs, the language sung should be the language most widely understood, and the census lists proved that language to be English, most of the Continental immigrants having learned to speak English rather than French. Since English words had to be found, I undertook to write new words on Canadian themes adapted to the spirit of the music and fitting into the general idea of the accompanying talk. This was perhaps a bold innovation, but it worked, judging by the response from a very large number of listeners. Among those listeners were the partners of the publishing firm which asked me to elaborate these talks into a book.

For various reasons, it was decided to confine this survey to the European racial groups in Canada (including those that have come by way of the United States). . . .

Patriotic Canadians have lamented the drain of population into the United States, but such movements are governed by economic laws which Nature has established for the health of mankind. Just as a human body can digest only the amount of food that it needs, so there is a limit to the immigration that a country can absorb. The intervals between meals enable the body to digest what has been eaten, and the intervals between the waves of immigration have enabled Canada to assimilate its new citizens. The health of a country should not be measured by the size of its population. During the depression following the financial crisis of 1932, there were nearly twice as many Americans in receipt of relief as there were inhabitants of Canada. Those who have the ambition to live only in a country with a large population had better go to China.

No province in Canada has shown more stable prosperity than the province of Quebec, and yet we find in the census of the United States for 1930, the foreign white stock includes 1,106,159 from French Canada, or nearly half as many as remained in the province of Quebec (2,290,169).

The turn of the political wheel is shown in the fact that 743,219 of these French Canadians are in New England, the one-time Puritan colony which at the time of the Declaration of Independence considered the French as in league with the Pope and the Devil. In the same census we find listed in the foreign white stock of the United States:

From England	2,522,261
From Scotland	899,591
From Wales	236,667
From Northern Ireland	695,999
From Irish Free State	3,086,522
Total from British Isles	7,441,040

as compared to 5,381,071 of the same racial stocks that are shown in the Canadian census for 1931. All these British and Irish in the United States might have come to Canada, but could we have absorbed them at the time when they entered the United States? Some are coming now, with the proviso that they intend to farm and have sufficient capital to tide them over, and the lists show over 4,000 returning Canadians for the years 1931–36, but they are coming only to occupations where they can be readily absorbed.

The large proportion of British stock in the United States, supplemented by the small though substantial quota of French Canadians, adds to the probability of continued good feeling between the two peoples of North America.

The temporary embargo on immigration resulting from the depression of 1932–37 gave breathing space in which Canada could absorb and assimilate the post-war immigrants. Now there are indications that Canada is ready for more, although this time it will be under some plan of judicious selection.

The revival of the demand for 'self-determination' by racial groups along the Danube Valley, together with the pressure of the great powers adjoining, cannot but result in dislocation of the peoples concerned, to whom the stories of the freedom enjoyed and the success achieved by relatives who have settled in Canada must prove a strong incentive to cross the Atlantic.

Thirty years ago, the name given to the Continental-European immigrant into Canada was 'foreign born'. With the great increase of families born in Canada to parents of European stock, this title is, in many cases, misleading. . . .

The plan I have adopted is to trace the history of each racial group from its original home in Europe, accentuating those incidents that show relationships between such races in Europe previous to their coming to Canada. The history has been documented so far as possible with quotations from contemporary records. These records in recent Canadian history may consist of newspaper items, which the reporter wrote without in the least thinking that he was writing history. In the same way a piece of stone or enamel may eventually provide an interesting note of colour in a mosaic.

Chapter 5

Race Definition Run Amuck: 'Slaying the Dragon of Eskimo Status' in *Re Eskimos*, 1939

Constance Backhouse

At the time, the decision that the Supreme Court of Canada issued on 5 April 1939 was derisively labelled 'an absurd little mouse'. Diamond Jenness, a leading white Canadian anthropologist, coined the phrase, which he borrowed from the Latin poet Horace. In the original Latin, the sentiment was 'Parturiunt montes; nascetur ridiculus mus', meaning: 'The mountains are in labour. From their womb will issue an absurd little mouse.' Such was Jenness's disdain for the ruling that he could find no better way to sum up his scorn for the reasoning of the eminent judges.[1]

The impetus for Jenness's sarcasm was the Supreme Court's *Re Eskimos* decision, in which the judges definitively held that 'Eskimos' were 'Indians' within the Canadian constitutional framework. A landmark judicial opinion on racial definition, the most noteworthy feature of the case is the breathtaking sense of certitude that accompanied the court's pronouncement.[2]

The legal definition of 'Indian' had long occupied Canadian legislators and judges, who tinkered and fretted over the language in the successive enactments of the Indian Act. Now the perplexing question of whether the word 'Eskimo' was subsumed within the word 'Indian' was at last resolved. And Jenness was properly irked. As well he might have been, since he had testified as an expert witness that 'Eskimos' and 'Indians' were 'racially' distinct.

Diamond Jenness was, by all accounts, a fascinating and irrepressible scholar, possessed of a bitingly funny wit and apt to dispense disarmingly frank, droll comments on any range of intellectual issues. Born in Wellington, New Zealand, he obtained his academic degrees at the University of New Zealand and Oxford, where he trained in classics. Toward the end of his studies, he embraced the subject of anthropology and picked up a 'diploma' in the newly emerging discipline. In 1911, he began his fieldwork in the steamy jungles of Papua New Guinea, and then in 1913, looking for a change of pace, he hired on with Vilhaljmur Stefansson's Arctic expedition. Jenness spent an extraordinary period of three years travelling and living among the Arctic peoples, examining their culture, and recording his observations for posterity. In 1926, he was appointed chief anthropologist for the National Museum of Canada, where his steady stream of papers, articles, and books inspired others to christen him 'Canada's most distinguished anthropologist' and 'one of the world's most respected Eskimologists'.[3]

Testifying before the Supreme Court, Diamond Jenness had offered his opinion that both 'Eskimos' and Indians had 'a very strong infusion or percentage of Mongoloid blood', and that there was a 'strong racial resemblance, a strong community of race between all the inhabitants' of North and South America. There were, however, sharp distinctions. In addition to different language, customs, and religion, the 'Eskimo' 'diverge[d] considerably from the other Aborigines' in physical appearance. 'The Eskimo may well have inherited some of the same racial elements as the Indians,' noted Jenness, 'but may have deviated so greatly, owing to his peculiar environment, that he now forms a distinct subtype.'[4]

Trying to clarify matters, one of the lawyers had asked Jenness whether the difference between the 'Eskimo' and the Pacific Coast Indians, for example, could be compared 'with the difference between the Englishman and the Hindu'. Although he was careful to qualify his answer, noting that it was 'hard to define the uniform Englishman or the uniform Hindu', Jenness had no difficulty formulating a reply. A man with a genius for calculating his words, Jenness may have gazed steadily out at the bench of six white Supreme Court judges when he offered up this astute assessment: 'I should think the difference between the Eskimo and your Siwash [Indians] on the Pacific coast would be about as great as between, say, an Englishman and an Italian or Greek; possibly between an Englishman and certain Hindus.'[5]

This evidence must have given some pause. The judicial panel was composed of Sir Lyman Poore Duff, Patrick Kerwin, Oswald Smith Crocket, Henry Hague Davis, Albert Blellock Hudson, and Lawrence Cannon. They were a bit out of their league in trying to assess the racial affinity between the 'Eskimo' and the 'Indian', lacking any personal reference base from their own sense of the world. Now the litigants were attempting to lob the problem back onto more familiar territory. All of the judges knew instinctively what an 'Englishman' was. Some of them were such. Had they glanced down the bench, they would have found no one of Italian or Greek heritage. Nor was there anyone who professed the Hindu religion. With the exception of Lawrence Cannon, whose mother, Aurelie Dumoulin, was francophone, all of them came from a homogeneous English, Scottish, and Irish background.[6] What ran through their minds as they pondered the difference between their own ethnic heritage and that of a Hindu? Did they surreptitiously scan the faces of their colleagues, searching for skin pigmentation, skull shapes, nostril alignment, and eye characteristics? Just how distinct did they feel themselves, linguistically, socially, economically, culturally, and physically, from Hindus, Italians, and Greeks?

Diamond Jenness meant the judges to recognize intuitively the vast chasm between themselves and the specific groups he chose for comparison. He wanted the judges to draw a legal distinction between the 'Eskimo' and the 'Indian' on a racial basis:

> The Eskimo of the Arctic and subarctic coastline diverges considerably from the other Aborigines. His skin is lighter in colour, verging toward a yellowish white, his head longer and often keel-shaped, the face wider and flatter, the eyes more often and more markedly oblique, and the nasal aperture unusually small. The cranial capacity slightly exceeds that of the average European, whereas the capacity of Indian skulls is slightly less.[7]

The reference to skin colour alone ought to have scored a few points. The official Canadian census divided the 'races' into four: white, red, black, and yellow. The 'red' were the 'American Indian', and the 'yellow' the 'Mongolian (Japanese and Chinese)'. When Jenness characterized the skin colour of Arctic peoples as 'yellowish white', it was a pigmentation resistant to any simple amalgamation within the four tidy boxes. Jenness summed up the anthropological data with confidence and certitude. The 'Eskimos' were 'a people distinct in physical appearance, in language, and in customs from all the Indian tribes of America'.[8] What possessed the Supreme Court justices in unanimous agreement to sweep aside the conclusions of Canada's pre-eminent 'Eskimologist', and collapse the two 'racial' groups into one under the law?

The Legal Definition of 'Indian'

The preliminary issue of how to define 'Indian' had posed a conundrum for years. The earliest statute on record, passed for Lower Canada in 1850, included four categories of individuals: (1) persons of Indian blood, reputed to belong to the particular body or tribe, and their descendants; (2) persons intermarried with any such Indians and residing among them, and their descendants; (3) persons residing among such Indians, whose parents on either side were or are Indians, or entitled to be considered as such; and (4) persons adopted in infancy by any such Indians, and residing in the village or upon the lands of such tribe or body of Indians, and their descendants.[9] This is a fulsome description by any reckoning, and it provides some glimpse into the racial understanding of the time. The concept of 'Indian blood' suggests that the legislators believed there was a biological difference between 'Indians' and other races. Yet the definition is not restricted to the 'bloodline' alone. Reputation is sufficient to garner Indian status. And for those who choose to reside among 'Indians', intermarriage and adoption are also passable.

The history of race definition shows a remarkable mutability, with terms no sooner articulated than they come under pressure for displacement. One year after the first legislative formulation, the sweeping definition was pinched and squeezed a bit. Adoptees were stricken from the record, and status through intermarriage was reduced to women only, defying centuries of Aboriginal tradition.[10] The first federal statute passed in 1868 temporarily embraced this version of racial designation.[11] One year later, the central government began to whittle deeper into the constricting definition. In 1869, federal legislation stipulated that no person 'of less than one-fourth Indian blood' could share in any annuity monies, interest, or rent owing to a band.[12]

By 1876, the Indian Act defined an 'Indian' as 'any male person of Indian blood reputed to belong to a particular band, any child of such person, and any woman who is or was lawfully married to such person'.[13] The unabashed male chauvinism clearly in the ascendancy here makes Indian status pivotal to one's relationship with an Indian man.[14] Other provisos began to erode the status of children born out of wedlock and individuals who had resided for more than five years in a foreign country.[15] For the first time, the concept of a 'half-breed' was given reification in a statute, but only to indicate that 'no half-breed in Manitoba who has shared in the distribution of half-breed lands shall be accounted an Indian'. Curiously, the Act contained no definition for 'half-breed'.[16]

The 1876 Indian Act also contained the rather startling statement that the word 'person' did not include an 'Indian'.[17] The arrogance of the federal government knew no bounds in taking upon itself the unilateral authority to draw such definitions. In 1887, Parliament purported to make the superintendent general of Indian Affairs the complete arbiter of 'membership in an Indian band'.[18] There was no consultation with First Nations communities on definitional matters. Aboriginal spokespersons might have advised on the multiplicity of Indigenous ways of defining identity, devised across centuries of political, economic, and spiritual experience. Aboriginal history and culture went dismissively unheeded in the development of the legal definitions.[19]

The provincial governments were inclined to use slightly different race formulations. None seemed prepared to embrace the decision taken by the federal government to exclude Aboriginal people from the definition of 'person'. Yet the phrasing of provincial legislators proved little more edifying than that of their federal counterparts. British Columbia, concerned to ensure that First Nations peoples were prohibited from voting in provincial elections, defined an 'Indian' in 1903 as 'any person of pure Indian blood, and any person of Indian extraction having his home upon or within the confines of an Indian reserve'.[20] In the 1922 statute that barred Indians from voting at public school meetings, the British Columbia legislature described an 'Indian' as 'any person who is either a full-blooded Indian, or any person with Indian blood in him who is living the Indian life on an Indian reserve'.[21] To clarify what was meant by the phrase 'Indian woman or girl' in another statute, the same legislators proclaimed it to encompass 'any woman or girl of pure Indian blood or Indian extraction'.[22]

The fascination with blood is no significant departure from the federal perspective, but the British Columbian legislators seem to have been particularly interested in the purity of that blood. The notion that race definition has something to do with residence on a reserve is also familiar, but the phrase 'living the Indian life' signifies a whole new point of definitional departure. Exactly what could the legislators have had in mind here? What thinking went through their collective mind as to the peculiarities and racially distinctive features of the Aboriginal 'lifestyle'? A 1950 statute authorizing an inquiry into 'Indian rights' defined 'Indian' somewhat more sweepingly as 'a person resident in this province of the North American Indian race'.[23] Here the dozens of Aboriginal nations, from the interior Salish to the plateau Athapaskans to the coastal Haida, were simply conflated into one amorphous mix.[24]

Saskatchewan and Alberta were more content to follow the lead of the federal government, albeit in a relatively simplified formula. In their early twentieth-century statutes prohibiting First Nations peoples from voting, the two Prairie provinces defined 'Indians' as 'all persons of Indian blood' who 'belong or are reputed to belong' to a band.[25] Blood and reputation seem to mix in an uneasy blend of disparate clues and characteristics. Alberta took greater care with its designations of racial intermixture than the federal government. 'Métis' was defined in a 1938 statute as 'a person of mixed white and Indian blood' who was not 'an Indian or a non-treaty Indian as defined in the Indian Act'.[26] Obviously worried that this might be too encompassing, the Alberta legislature amended the definition in 1940 to stipulate that only individuals who had 'not less than one-quarter Indian blood' were meant.[27] The province of Ontario refrained from making any legislative pronouncements about the definition of 'Indian', but was anxious to indicate that the word 'person' in the context of its game and fisheries legislation definitely encompassed an 'Indian', whatever that might be construed to mean.[28]

The tangled legal definitions were surpassed only by the tangled evidence that often emerged before the courts. Despite the complexity of people's lives, the courts typically took a no-nonsense approach to sorting out the confusing welter of data. *Rex* v. *Tronson*, a 1931 British Columbia case, involved a man named George Tronson who had been born on the 'Okanagan Indian Reserve'.[29] The evidence on Tronson's parentage is fragmentary, but he apparently had an 'Indian' grandmother, an 'Indian' uncle, and an 'Indian' wife. The court described his father as 'a white man' who was 'one of the old-time large cattle ranchers of the Okanagan District'. The evidence also indicated that Tronson had exercised certain racial privileges available only to whites—voting in provincial elections and filing for land grants not open to 'Indians'. Although Tronson was reputed to belong to the 'Head of the Lake Indian Reserve', and had lived on and off the 'Okanagan Reserve' throughout his life, the superintendent general had not seen fit to list his name on the membership rolls, and the government challenged his right to reside there. First Nations witnesses expressed their agreement to having Tronson reside with his First Nations wife in their community. The court would have none of it. Tronson 'cannot in one breath say in effect that he is a white man, and in the next say that he is an Indian', railed the judge. He 'cannot blow hot and blow cold'. Without further explanation of why, the judge concluded it was 'abundantly clear' that Tronson was not an 'Indian', and ordered him off the 'reserve'.[30]

Some of the legal debates regarding racial definitions were provoked by alcohol prosecutions. Liquor had long functioned as a staple of the fur trade, a bartering tool used by unscrupulous white traders to inflate profits and crush Aboriginal resistance to European control.[31] The overwhelming problems of violence and social dislocation wrought by alcoholism caused successive provincial and federal governments to enact a series of statutes prohibiting the sale of liquor to First Nations peoples.[32] Court after court encountered defendants accused of selling alcohol to Indians who tried to avoid conviction by tangling up the authorities with questions of racial definition. Who could be certain that the individual to whom the accused had sold liquor was in fact an 'Indian'?

One of the most famous cases to rule on this was *Regina* v. *Howson*, an 1894 decision of the Northwest Territories Supreme Court.[33] The accused had sold liquor to Henry Bear, described in the case as a 'half-breed' residing on the 'Muscow-equan Reserve'. Bear's father was described as a 'Frenchman' and his mother 'an Indian'. Defending himself against conviction, the accused argued that Henry Bear was not 'an Indian of pure blood', and as such did not count. That Bear's father was 'white' was another plank in the accused's argument, and his lawyer insisted that paternal racial inheritance ought to be definitive.

Turning to the Indian Act definition, 'any male person of Indian blood', the court held that this must mean 'any person with Indian blood in his veins, whether such blood is obtained from the father or mother'. Forcing the prosecution to prove purity of the bloodline, or patriarchal Aboriginal lineage, would be a stark impossibil-

ity in vast numbers of cases. Skin colour ought to play a distant second to the characteristics of language and 'lifestyle', according to the court: '[T]he alleged Indian might so far as his skin was concerned be as white as a Spaniard or an Italian or as many Englishmen or Frenchmen for that matter, and yet not understand a word of any European language, and be in thought, association, and surrounding altogether Indian.' Throwing up its hands in despair over this problematic lineup of pigmentation, the court eschewed skin colour, insisting that 'reputation' ought to prevail instead:

> It is notorious that there are persons in those bands who are not full-blooded Indians, who are possessed of Caucasian blood, in many of them the Caucasian blood very large predominates, but whose associations, habits, modes of life, and surroundings generally are essentially Indian, and the intention of the legislature is to bring such persons within the provisions and object of the Act . . .[34]

Directly on the heels of this decision, Parliament amended the definition of 'Indian' in the Indian Act as it related specifically to the liquor prohibition. 'In addition to its ordinary signification', the meaning was extended to include 'any person, male or female, who is reputed to belong to a particular band, or who follows the Indian mode of life, or any child of such person'. The 'mode of life' phrase was lifted straight out of the *Howson* decision.[35]

The concept of an 'Indian mode of life' being rather nebulous, clarification awaited further judicial pronouncements. Affirmed in its definitional prowess, the Northwest Territories Supreme Court branched out even further in *The Queen* v. *Mellon* in 1900.[36] The man to whom the liquor had been sold, Charles Pepin, conceded that he was a 'half-breed'. But he spoke English 'fluently', 'never dressed like an Indian', 'never wore moccasins', and had been employed to move freight between Calgary and Edmonton for several summers. The judge took one look at the man and pronounced that he 'dress[ed] better than many ordinary white men'. In fact, he said, 'there is no indication whatsoever in his appearance, in his language, or in his general demeanour, that he does not belong to the better class of half-breeds'. With some despatch, the judge dismissed all charges, ruling that it was nonsense to convict a liquor seller who could not have known his customer was an 'Indian'. The Indian mode of life seems to be deftly fashioned from attire, linguistic facility, demeanour, and employment history.[37]

The Edmonton District Court had an opportunity to pursue this further in *The King* v. *Pickard* in 1908.[38] In that case a shop-owner sold a bottle of liquor to an individual named Ward. The legal question was whether the shop-owner ought to have known or suspected that Ward, who resided at Stony Plain, was 'Indian'. In contrast with the absence of 'Indian' characteristics in *Mellon*, here there was a surfeit of pointers. There was the now familiar reference to moccasins, which Ward wore. The linguistic signs were definitive, for Ward 'could speak little or no English'. In fact, he purchased a calendar from the shop-owner by 'pointing' and 'asking in Cree'. Skin colour seems to have been equally determinative, with the judge noting that Ward was 'fairly dark'. Without further elaboration, he concluded that the man looked 'a good deal like an Indian'. The judge's certainty is belied in part by a shrewd tactic employed by the defence lawyer, who brought into court that day a number of individuals whose race was difficult to discern from appearance. 'It is true that there are many half-breeds that look like Indians', the judge admitted,

and the counsel for the accused brought into court many for that purpose, but to my mind, this makes my contention all the

stronger that Pickard, knowing how difficult it was to distinguish the Indian from the half-breed, should have been on his guard and refused the liquor till he found out whether they were Indians or half-breeds.[39]

In what seems the most far-fetched variable to date, racial status seems also to have been ascertained by the company Ward kept. The judge reconstructed in depth the racial designation of Ward's companion, a man named Bonenose, who had accompanied him into the store: he also wore moccasins; he, too, bought a calendar by asking for it in Cree; he 'was rather darker than Ward' and was 'very much like an Indian, in appearance, even more so than Ward'. Since the shop-owner was not charged with selling liquor to Bonenose, there was no need to delve into his racial attributes. It was solely his value as companion to Ward that was under appraisal. One's racial status seems to turn here in part on the racial designation of one's friends and acquaintances. In the end, the court concluded Ward was indeed 'Indian', and that the shop-owner had unlawfully sold him alcohol.[40]

Once having determined the meaning of an 'Indian mode of life', it behooved the court to consider when someone could be held to have 'abandoned the Indian mode of life'. *Rex* v. *Verdi* offered the Halifax County Court the opportunity to dwell on this fine point at length in 1914.[41] Mr Lambkin was born of mixed heritage, and the court pronounced his father 'French', and using the most racist appellation available, his mother a 'squaw'.[42] Raised in a Mi'kmaq community in New Brunswick, Lambkin left his reserve and moved to Nova Scotia. Although he conceded that he 'lived amongst Indians in Nova Scotia', and had spent short periods on a Nova Scotia 'Indian reserve', for the previous 10 years he had been living away. He was employed in farming and 'travelling for a living', and testified that he lived 'like a white man' and paid municipal taxes. The court was poised to classify him as non-Indian until it determined that Lambkin had voted at the last election of a Mi'kmaq chief. This tipped the balance the other way, and the liquor seller was convicted.[43]

The complexity of defining what is meant by 'Indian' is baldly obvious. The intricate ways in which people group themselves and live their lives presents a host of enigmatic possibilities. To try to capture such a dizzying array of human combination with a watertight definitional framework is destined for disaster, no matter how earnest or multi-textured the effort. The multiplicity of legislative formulae, inconsistent between governments and over time, is reflective of the insoluble difficulties. What is most remarkable is the apparent readiness of Canadian authorities to use the law to draw racial boundaries, cutting through the morass, in case after case, to concretize distinction and to create a hierarchy of racial designation.

Separate Recognition of 'Eskimo' Status

The origin of the word 'Eskimo' is often attributed to an Algonquian term (from Plains Cree), 'a´yaskime´w', meaning 'eater of raw meat'. Others claim that the term was derived from a completely different Montagnais word, 'ayassime´w', meaning 'those who speak a strange language', which was disseminated through Spanish-speaking Basque whalers as 'esquimaos'. Europeans who tried to capture the word in writing fashioned a multiplicity of possible spellings, ranging from 'Eskeimoes' through 'Iskemay', to 'Usquemaw' and 'Huskemaw'.[44] None of these terms bore the slightest resemblance to the name the Aboriginal people of the Arctic had given themselves: 'Inuit' (meaning 'the people') and 'Inuk' (for the singular 'person') in their Inuktitut language.[45]

Various European spellings of 'Eskimo', 'Esquimau', and 'Eskimaux' made their way into Canadian statutes during the first half of the twentieth century. In 1919, the Quebec legisla-

ture enacted an exemption for 'Eskimos' under the fish and game laws.[46] The Northwest Territories passed an ordinance in 1930 to protect 'Eskimo ruins' from unauthorized excavation.[47] The federal government used the term 'Esquimau' when it disqualified the group from voting in 1934.[48] The Northwest Territories barred sales of liquor and prohibited drinking for 'Eskimos', or 'any person, male or female, who follows the Eskimo mode of life', as well as 'any child of such person'.[49] An 1882 Newfoundland statute baldly conflated two terms when it prohibited the sale and delivery of intoxicating liquors 'to any Esquimaux Indian'.[50]

The federal government never enacted an Eskimo Act to be the counterpart of the Indian Act, and seemed to be of two minds whether to include 'Eskimos' under the latter. In 1924, Parliament debated whether it should bring 'Eskimos' into the Indian Act, and resolved not to do so.[51] Instead, the legislators specified that the superintendent general of Indian Affairs was to have 'charge of Eskimo affairs'. Speaking for the federal government at the time, the Liberal Minister of the Interior, Charles Stewart, pronounced definitively on the racial status of 'Eskimos'. 'No', he posited, 'Eskimos are not Indians. While they may be of a somewhat similar character, they are not looked upon as Indians in the real sense of the word.'[52]

Six years later, 'Eskimo affairs' was brusquely separated from 'Indian affairs' once more, with Stewart advising that it was administratively more efficient to transfer the responsibility back to the Department of the Interior. The move occasioned further debate in the House of Commons over racial designation. All seemed to agree that 'Eskimos' were not 'Indians', but opinions divided on the variables of distinction. Challenged to delineate the differences, Charles Stewart itemized three: 'appearance', 'language', and 'habits'. Sir George Halsey Perley, Conservative Opposition MP for the Quebec riding of Argenteuil, remained sceptical. 'The minister says that a person could tell the difference between them by their appearance, but the minister himself is not going to decide which of these thousands of people are Eskimos and which are Indians', he fussed. 'I do not see how the minister can draft a definition which will hold water in all cases.' The response from Charles Stewart was dismissive and peremptory: 'There is no doubt that the racial distinction between even the most northern Indian and the Eskimo is very marked. I do not think anyone would have a great deal of difficulty in distinguishing one from the other.'[53]

Endeavouring to get to the root of the matter, Hugh Guthrie, Conservative MP from an Ontario riding near Guelph, asked his parliamentary colleagues a simple question. If 'Eskimos' are not Indians, 'what race are they?' This provoked some hesitation. Some of the legislators ventured that 'Eskimos' were originally 'Mongolian'. Others jocularly adverted to substantial sexual intermingling in the North by speculating that 'some people say they are Scotch'.[54]

The issue of racial purity seems to flutter at the margins of debates over racial designation. Most anthropologists conceded that racial intermixture flourished virtually everywhere. The Arctic was perhaps something of an exception, as Diamond Jenness pointed out, in that 'two grim sentinels, Cold and Silence, guarded the retreats of the Eskimos', repelling most European adventurers who tried to 'storm their gates'. Relying on the male lexicon of his generation, Jenness pronounced it 'a land where the climate demanded that men be men'. By the late nineteenth century, however, intrepid whalers from Britain, Holland, Spain, France, Russia, and the United States showed they had the stamina to 'breach the walls'.[55] Tracking the changes the whalers wrought to 'Eskimo' culture, Jenness discovered that the commanders, officers, and crews of the whaling ships routinely 'frequented with local Eskimo women'. The racial blending was dramatic: 'In the veins of increasing numbers [of Eskimos] coursed European blood that modified their forms and their features'. On the heels of the whalers came fur traders, police, missionaries, and anthropologists, many of whom continued to contribute to the cross-fertilization.[56]

In the eastern Arctic, for centuries the Inuit had 'jostled and intermarried' with neighbour Algonkian peoples. On the West Coast, there was also interbreeding between Inuit and some Africans, Asians, and Polynesians.[57] What is more, anthropologists had discovered in France an ancient skull that they believed came from 'Eskimo' stock. Another find of an alleged 'Eskimo skull' at Obercassel, near Bonn in Germany, created more consternation. 'Theoretically, it would seem not impossible that the generalized Eskimo type established itself somewhere in the Old World toward the close of the glacial period, and that some of its representatives penetrated to western Europe', explained Jenness.[58] But if 'Eskimos' had migrated to France and Germany, what were the implications for the purity of racial theory? Racial blending made mincemeat of the already imponderable task of quantifying and delineating racial characteristics. The most bizarre thing was how few seemed to recognize that, before one could articulate racial definitions, one had to be certain exactly whom one was measuring.

None of this seemed to bother Canadian legislators, who tossed about racial terminology, without even a semblance of reflection. Statutes drew multiple distinctions between 'Indians' and 'Eskimos' without clarifying what the difference encompassed.[59] In fact, few of the enactments attempted to define their terms at all. When the legislators tried their hand at the task, they came up with circular depictions. The Newfoundland legislature defined 'Esquimaux' in 1911 to mean 'Native residents of the coast of Labrador who are commonly known as Esquimaux'.[60] The Northwest Territories defined 'Eskimo' under the game law as including 'a half-breed of Eskimo blood leading the life of an Eskimo'.[61] The notions of 'blood' and 'lifestyle' are reminiscent of earlier pronouncements relating to 'Indians'. The Indian Act of 1951 made reference to 'the race of Aborigines commonly referred to as Eskimos'. Here the federal Parliament seemingly contemplated the group as a distinct 'race' but remained helpless to delineate the individuals within it, except by using the term others customarily applied to them.[62]

* * *

Notes

1. Richard J. Diubaldo, 'The Absurd Little Mouse: When Eskimos Became Indians,' *Journal of Canadian Studies* 16, 2 (Summer 1981): 34, at 34.

2. *Re Eskimos* [1939] 80 SCR 104; [1939] 2 DLR 417.

3. Jenness held an MA degree in honours classics from the University of New Zealand, and an honours MA in classics from Oxford. In 1910, he was awarded a diploma in the 'relatively new field' of anthropology under Dr R.R. Marett. At the time of testifying, he held an honorary doctorate of literature from New Zealand University, and served as a Fellow of the Royal Society of Canada, an honorary corresponding member of the Danish Geographical Society, and President of the Society for American Archaeology. See 'Foreword' by William E. Taylor, Jr, Director, National Museum of Man, Ottawa, Canada, July 1977, in Diamond Jenness, *Indians of Canada* (Ottawa: National Museum of Canada, 1932; repub. Ministry of Supply & Services Canada, 1977), at p.v; 'Case on Behalf of the Attorney General of Canada, in the Supreme Court of Canada, in the Matter of a Reference as to Whether the Term "Indians" in Head 24 of Section 91 of the British North America Act, 1867, Includes Eskimo Inhabitants of the Province of Quebec' (Ottawa: King's Printer, 1938) [hereafter 'Canada Case'], at 16; B.L. Clark, 'Diamond Jenness 1886–1969' in *Development of Caribou Eskimo Culture—A Diamond Jenness Memorial Volume* (Ottawa: National Museum of Canada, 1977); W. Stewart Wallace, ed., 'Jenness, Diamond', *The Macmillan Dictionary of Canadian Biography* 4th ed. (Toronto: Macmillan of Canada, 1978), at 390.

4. 'Factum on Behalf of the Attorney General of Canada, In the Supreme Court of Canada, In the Matter of a Reference as to whether the term "Indians" in Head 24 of section 91 of the British North America Act, 1867, Includes Eskimo Inhabitants of the Province of Quebec', at 26–7 [hereinafter cited as Canada Factum]; 'Exhibit C-47, Canada Case', at 303; Diamond Jenness, *Indians of Canada*, at 6.

5. Canada Factum, at 19–20. Jenness was not the first to draw a comparison between the English and the Italians, on one hand, and the Indians and Eskimos, on the other. In 1927, W.H.B. Hoare, a Department of the Interior field man living in the Barren Lands, had written to his superior, O.S. Finnie, the first director of the Northwest Territories Branch of the Department of the Interior, arguing that 'the Inuit could not [be] treated or dealt with like the Indians, as they were as widely different from one another as is the Englishman from the Italian. [. . .] The Indian is of low mentality, and seems a dour, discontented fellow with no ambition to better his conditions either materially or intellectually. [. . .] The Eskimo looks upon himself as the equal of any white man.' See Public Archives of Canada, RG22/253/40-8-1/1.

6. On the group cohesiveness of Englishmen, Scotsmen, Welshmen, and Ulstermen who emigrated to Canada, and the development of the pan-British identity in North America, see Ross

McCormack, 'Cloth Caps and Jobs: The Ethnicity of English Immigrants in Canada 1900–1914', in *Interpreting Canada's Past: Vol. II, After Confederation*, ed. J.M. Bumsted (Toronto: Oxford University Press, 1986), at 175–91. Duff's father, Reverend Charles Duff, born in England, was of Scottish and English descent; his mother, Isabella Johnson, was born in Iowa of parents who had immigrated from Scotland but were of Irish descent. Cannon's father, Lawrence John Cannon, was Irish and his mother, Aurelie Dumoulin, was French; he was Roman Catholic by religion. Kerwin's parents, Patrick Kerwin and Ellen Gavin, were of Irish Catholic background. Crocket's parents, William and Marion Crocket, were of Scottish descent. Davis was born in Brockville, to Anglican parents named William Henry Davis and Eliza Dowsley, whose ethnic origins were British. Hudson, whose parents were Albert and Elizabeth Hudson, was a Presbyterian of British origin. The ethnic and religious diversification of the Supreme Court of Canada would not begin until more than thirty years later. Bora Laskin became the first Jewish Supreme Court justice, when he was appointed in 1970. John Sopinka, whose parents emigrated from the Ukraine, appears to have been the first appointee to the Supreme Court of Canada to identify himself as a member of an 'ethnic minority'. His appointment in 1988 followed a promise from the Prime Minister to the Ethno-Cultural Council to appoint more minority members of the court. Frank Iaccobucci, whose parents were Italian-Canadian, was appointed in 1991. See Gerald A. Beaudoin, *The Supreme Court of Canada: Proceedings of the October 1985 Conference* (Cowansville, Que.: Editions Y. Blais, 1986) at 398–400; Ian Bushnell, *The Captive Court: A Study of the Supreme Court of Canada* (Montreal: McGill-Queen's University Press, 1992), at 246, 343–4, 488, 491; correspondence from Ian Bushnell to the author, 5 February 1998; David R. Williams, *Duff: A Life*

in the Law (Vancouver: University of British Columbia Press, 1984), at 2 and 4.

7. 'Exhibit C-47', Canada Case, at 303, citing Jenness, *Indians of Canada*, at 6.

8. Jenness, *Indians of Canada*, at 405.

9. 'An Act for the Better Protection of the Lands and Property of the Indians in Lower Canada' S. Prov. C. 1850, c. 42, s. 5. The statute appointed a Commissioner of Indian Lands who was authorized to concede, lease, or charge lands held by the Crown in trust for Indians.

10. 'An Act to Repeal in Part and to Amend an Act, Intituled, "An Act for the Better Protection of the Lands and Property of the Indians in Lower Canada"' S. Prov. C. 1851, c. 59, s. 2. This definition is also utilized in 'An Act Respecting Indians and Indian Lands' CSLC 1861, c. 14, s. 11.

11. 'An Act Providing for the Organisation of the Department of the Secretary of State of Canada, and for the Management of Indian and Ordnance Lands' SC 1868, c. 42, s. 15.

12. 'An Act for the Gradual Enfranchisement of Indians, the Better Management of Indian Affairs, and to Extend the Provisions of the Act 31st Victoria, Chapter 42' SC 1869, c. 6, s. 4. Section 6 also spells out the gender-based marital provision more explicitly: 'Provided always that any Indian woman marrying any other than an Indian, shall cease to be an Indian within the meaning of this Act, nor shall the children issue of such marriage be considered as Indians within the meaning of this Act; Provided also, that any Indian woman marrying an Indian of any other tribe, band or body shall cease to be a member of the tribe, band or body to which she formerly belonged, and become a member of the tribe, band or body of which her husband is a member, and the children, issue of this marriage, shall belong to their father's tribe only.' See also 'An Act to Amend Certain Laws Respecting Indians, and to Extend Certain Laws Relating to Matters Connected with Indians to the Provinces of Manitoba and British

Columbia' SC 1874, c. 21, s. 8.

'An Act for the Gradual Enfranchisement of Indians, the Better Management of Indian Affairs, and to Extend the Provisions of the Act 31st Victoria, Chapter 42' SC 1869, c. 6, s. 13 also establishes a process for 'enfranchisement' whereby an 'Indian' could obtain the right to own land in fee simple. See also 'The Indian Act, 1876' SC 1876, c. 18, s. 3(5), 86–88, 93; 'An Act Further to Amend "The Indian Act, 1880"' SC 1884, c. 27, s. 16; 'The Indian Act' RSC 1886, c. 43, s. 2(j). The 'Indian Act' RSC 1906, c. 81, s. 107–23 stipulates that an 'enfranchised Indian', his wife, and his minor unmarried children would 'no longer be deemed Indians'. See also 'Indian Act' RSC 1927, c. 98, s. 114(2); 'The Indian Act' SC 1951, c. 29, s. 12, 109.

13. 'The Indian Act, 1876' SC 1876, c. 18, s. 3. See also 'The Indian Act' RSC 1886, c. 43, s. 2(h); 'Indian Act' RSC 1906, c. 81, s. 2(f); 'An Act Respecting Indians' RSC 1927, c. 98, s. 2(d). The first major change to this definition came in 'An Act Respecting Indians' SC 1951, c. 29, s. 2(g) which defines 'Indian' as 'a person who persuant [sic] to this Act is registered as an Indian or is entitled to be registered as an Indian.' Section 5 establishes an 'Indian Register', to record 'the name of every person who is entitled to be registered as an Indian'. Section 11 provides: 'Subject to section twelve, a person is entitled to be registered if that person

(a) on the twenty-sixth of May, eighteen hundred and seventy-four, was, for the purposes of An Act Providing for the Organization of the Department of the Secretary of State of Canada, and for the management of Indian and Ordnance Lands, chapter forty-two of the statutes of 1868, as amended by section six of chapter six of the statutes of 1869, and section eight of chapter twenty-one of the statutes of 1874, considered to be entitled to hold, use or enjoy the lands and other immovable property belonging to or appropriated to the use of the various tribes, bands or bodies of Indians in Canada,

(b) is a member of a band

(i) for whose use and benefit, in common, lands have been set apart or since the twenty-sixth day of May, 1874 have been agreed by treaty to be set apart, or

(ii) that has been declared by the Governor in Council to be a band for the purposes of this Act,

(c) is a male person who is a direct descendant in the male line of a male person described in paragraph (a) or (b),

(d) is the legitimate child of

(i) a male person described in paragraph (a) or (b), or

(ii) a person described in paragraph (c).

(e) is the illegitimate child of a female person described in paragraph (a), (b) or (d), unless the Registrar is satisfied that the father of the child was not an Indian and the Registrar has declared that the child is not entitled to be registered, or

(f) is the wife or widow of a person who is entitled to be registered by virtue of paragraph (a), (b), (c), (d) or (e).'

14. Section 3(c) states: 'Provided that any Indian woman marrying any other than an Indian or a non-treaty Indian shall cease to be an Indian in any respect within the meaning of this Act, except that she shall be entitled to share equally with the members of the band to which she formerly belonged, in the annual or semi-annual distribution of their annuities, interest moneys and rents; but this income may be commuted to her at any time at ten years' purchase with the consent of the band.' Section 3(d) states: 'Provided that any Indian woman marrying an Indian of any other band, or a non-treaty Indian shall cease to be a member of the band to which she formerly belonged, and become a member of the band or irregular band of which her husband is a member.' An earlier version of this is

found in 'An Act for the Gradual Enfranchisement of Indians, the Better Management of Indian Affairs, and to Extend the Provisions of the Act 31st Victoria, Chapter 42' SC 1869, s. 6. See also 'The Indian Act, 1880' SC 1880, c. 28, s. 12–13; 'The Indian Act' RSC 1886, c. 43, s. 11–12; 'Indian Act' RSC 1906, c. 81, s. 14–15. 'An Act to Amend the Indian Act' SC 1919–20, c. 50, s. 2 takes away from the band the power to consent to buying out a woman's rights with a ten year payment, and places it exclusively with the Superintendent-General. See also 'An Act Respecting Indians' RSC 1927, c. 98, s. 14–15; 'An Act Respecting Indians' SC 1951, c. 29, s. 12(1)(b), 14.

15. Section 3(a) states: 'Provided that any illegitimate child, unless having shared with the consent of the band in the distribution moneys of such band for a period exceeding two years, may, at any time, be excluded from the membership thereof by the band, if such proceeding be sanctioned by the Superintendent-General.' 'The Indian Act, 1880' SC 1880, c. 28, s. 10 revises this so that the exclusion is completely under the control of the Superintendent-General. See also 'The Indian Act' RSC 1886, c. 43, s. 9; 'Indian Act' RSC 1906, c. 81, s. 12; 'An Act Respecting Indians' RSC 1927, c. 98, s. 12; 'An Act Respecting Indians' SC 1951, c. 29, s. 11(d) and (e). Section 3(b) states: 'Provided that any Indian having for five years continuously resided in a foreign country shall with the sanction of the Superintendent-General, cease to be a member thereof and shall not be permitted to become again a member thereof, or of any other band, unless the consent of the band with the approval of the Superintendent-General or his agent, be first had and obtained; but this provision shall not apply to any professional man, mechanic, missionary, teacher or interpreter, while discharging his or her duty as such.' See also 'The Indian Act, 1880' SC 1880, c. 28, s. 11; 'The Indian Act' RSC 1886, c. 43, s. 10; 'Indian Act' RSC 1906, c. 81, s. 13; 'An Act

Respecting Indians' RSC 1927, c. 98, s. 13.

16. Section 3(e) states: 'Provided also that no half-breed in Manitoba who has shared in the distribution of half-breed lands shall be accounted an Indian; and that no half-breed head of a family (except the widow of an Indian, or a half-breed who has already been admitted into a treaty), shall, unless under very special circumstances, to be determined by the Superintendent-General or his agent, be accounted an Indian, or entitled to be admitted into any Indian treaty.' Additional provisions are added in 'The Indian Act, 1880' SC 1880, c. 28, s. 14: 'any half-breed who may have been admitted into a treaty shall be allowed to withdraw therefrom on refunding all annuity money received by him or her under the said treaty, or suffering a corresponding reduction in the quantity of any land, or scrip, which such half-breed, as such, may be entitled to receive from the Government.' See also s. 14(2): 'The Half-breeds who are by the father's side either wholly or partly of Indian blood now settled in the Seigniory of Caughnawaga, and who have inhabited the said Seigniory for the last twenty years, are hereby confirmed in their possession and right of residence and property, but not beyond the tribal rights and usages which others of the band enjoy.' See also 'The Indian Act' RSC 1886, c. 43, s. 13; 'Indian Act' RSC 1906, c. 81, s. 16; 'An Act to Amend the Indian Act' SC 1914, c. 35, s. 3–4; 'An Act Respecting Indians' RSC 1927, c. 98, s. 16; 'An Act Respecting Indians' SC 1951, c. 29, s. 12(1).

17. 'The Indian Act, 1876' SC 1876, c. 18, s. 3(12) states: 'The term "person" means an individual other than an Indian, unless the context clearly requires another construction.' 'The Indian Act' RSC 1886, c. 43, s. 2(c) states: 'The expression "person" means any individual other than an Indian.' See also 'Indian Act' RSC 1906, c. 81, s. 2(c); 'An Act Respecting Indians' RSC 1927, c. 98, s. 2(i). This offensive provision was not removed until 1951: see 'An Act Respecting Indians' SC 1951, c. 29. In *The Queen* v. *Murdock*

(1900), 4 CCC 82, at 86 the Ontario Court of Appeal indicated that 'person' must encompass 'a white man, woman, or child, a non-treaty Indian, and perhaps an enfranchised Indian'.

18. 'An Act to Amend "The Indian Act"' SC 1887, c. 33, s. 1 states: 'The Superintendent General may, from time to time, upon the report of an officer, or other person specially appointed by him to make an inquiry, determine who is or who is not a member of any band of Indians entitled to share in the property and annuities of the band; and the decision of the Superintendent General in any such matter shall be final and conclusive, subject to an appeal to the Governor in Council.' Given the proviso that 'person' did not include 'Indian', it appears that only non-Indians are authorized to investigate or decide such matters. See also 'An Act Respecting Indians' RSC 1927, c. 98, s. 18. Bradford W. Morse, ed., *Aboriginal Peoples and the Law* (Ottawa: Carleton University Press, 1985) notes at 1 that 'The registration system was implemented by sending an Indian agent, appointed by the government, to the Indian nations to enumerate persons in order to develop treaty payment lists or band lists. If people were away on hunting parties, out on their traplines, or off fishing, or if bands were in remote areas, then they simply were not registered under the Indian Act.'

19. George Manuel and Michael Posluns, *The Fourth World: An Indian Reality* (Don Mills, ON: Collier-Macmillan Canada, 1974), note at 21 that 'the Indian Act . . . was passed into law by Parliament without any reference to the realities of Indian life as Indian spokesmen might have explained them'. Critiquing the narrowing of definition, they state at 22: 'It was no longer a question of a person being "reputed to be an Indian", a phrase that could be taken to mean accepted by the band as a member, rather than a strict tracing of male bloodline, an English way of tracing lineage not accepted by very many Indian societies.' Manuel and Posluns add

at 241: 'Indian customs of inheritance and for defining identity have varied from nation to nation according to political and economic structure and religious beliefs. Many trace through the mother's line, some through the father's. My own [i.e., Manuel's] people [Shushwap Nation] work through a mixture of both, as do many of our neighbours.'

20. 'An Act to Consolidate and Amend the Law Respecting the Qualification and Registration of Electors, the Regulation of Elections of Members of the Provincial Legislative Assembly, and the Trial of Controverted Elections' SBC 1903–04, c. 17, s. 3. See also 'An Act Respecting Elections of Members of the Legislative Assembly' SBC 1920, c. 27, s. 2(1).

21. 'An Act to Amend and Consolidate the "Public Schools Act"' SBC 1922, c. 64, s. 2.

22. 'An Act for the Protection of Women and Girls in Certain Cases' SBC 1923, c. 76, s. 2.

23. 'An Act Authorizing an Inquiry into the Status and Rights of Indians in the Province' SBC 1950, c. 32, s. 2, also noting 'unless the context otherwise requires...'.

24. Robert Berkhofer, *The White Man's Indian: Images of the American Indian from Columbus to the Present* (New York: Knopf, 1978), suggests that, as Europeans developed the idea of 'Indian', they collapsed into a single group all of the diverse cultures, societies, language groups, and identities of Indigenous peoples of the Americas—people who did not think of themselves as one group or one continental people when they were first encountered.

25. 'An Act Respecting Elections of Members of the Legislative Assembly' SS 1908, c. 2, s. 2(12) states: '"Indian" means and includes all persons of Indian blood who belong or are reputed to belong to any band or irregular band of Indians; and the words "band" and "irregular band" as used in this clause shall have the meaning given to them respectively by *The Indian Act*, being chapter 81 of *The Revised Statues of Canada 1906*'. See also 'An Act Respecting Elections of

Members of the Legislative Assembly' RSS 1930, c. 4, s. 2(12). The Alberta statute, exactly the same, is 'An Act Respecting Elections of Members of the Legislative Assembly' SA 1909, c. 3, s. 2(12). 'An Act for the Protection of Game' SA 1946, c. 4, s. 2(y) is somewhat more fulsome, but also follows the federal format, defining 'Indian' as: (i) any male person of Indian blood reputed to belong to a particular band or an irregular band; (ii) any child of such person; (iii) any person who is or was lawfully married to such person.

26. 'An Act Respecting the Métis Population of the Province' SA 1938 (2nd Sess.), c. 6, s. 2(a), with the proviso 'unless the context otherwise requires'. Some individuals of mixed white and Aboriginal ancestry appear to have identified primarily with either their First Nations' or their European inheritance. Others established a unique racial identity described as 'Métis', especially in the fur trade areas of Rupert's Land and the Great Lakes region. On the creation of the separate Métis identity in Canada, see Jennifer S.H. Brown, *Strangers in Blood: Fur Trade Company Families in Indian Country* (Vancouver: University of British Columbia Press, 1980); Sylvia Van Kirk, *'Many Tender Ties': Women in Fur-Trade Society, 1670–1870* (Winnipeg: Watson & Dwyer, 1980); Jacqueline Peterson and Jennifer S.H. Brown, *The New Peoples: Being and Becoming Métis in North America* (Winnipeg: University of Manitoba Press, 1985); John E. Foster, 'The Origins of the Mixed Bloods in the Canadian West', in Lewis H. Thomas, ed., *Essays on Western History, in Honour of Lewis Gwynne Thomas* (Edmonton: University of Alberta Press, 1976): 71–80; John E. Foster 'The Métis: The People and the Term', *Prairie Forum* 3 (1978) 79–90; Olive P. Dickason 'From "One Nation" in the Northeast to "New Nation" in the Northwest: A Look at the Emergence of the Métis', in Peterson & Brown, eds, *New Peoples*: 19–36; Jacqueline Peterson 'Prelude to Red River: A Social Portrait of the Great Lakes

Métis', *Ethnohistory* 25 (1978): 41–67; Jacqueline Peterson 'The People in Between: Indian-White Marriage and the Genesis of a Métis Society and Culture in the Great Lakes Region, 1680–1830', Ph.D. Thesis (University of Chicago: 1981); Jacqueline Peterson 'Many Roads to Red River: Métis Genesis in the Great Lakes Region, 1680–1815', in Peterson and Brown, eds, *The New Peoples*: 31–71; R. David Edmunds, '"Unacquainted with the Laws of the Civilized World": American Attitudes Toward the Métis Communities in the Old Northwest', in Peterson & Brown, eds, *The New Peoples*: 185–93; Robert E. Bieder, 'Scientific Attitudes Toward Indian Mixed-Bloods in Early Nineteenth Century America', *Journal of Ethnic Studies* 8 (1980): 17–30; John E. Foster, 'The Plains Métis', in Bruce Morrison and R.C. Wilson, eds, *Native Peoples: The Canadian Experience* (Toronto: McClelland & Stewart, 1986): 375–403; Sylvia Van Kirk '"What if Mama Is an Indian?": The Cultural Ambivalence of the Alexander Ross Family', in Peterson & Brown, eds, *The New Peoples*: 207–17; John E. Foster, 'Some Questions and Perspectives on the Problem of Métis Roots', in Peterson & Brown, eds, *The New Peoples*: 73–91; Irene M. Spry, 'The Métis and Mixed-Bloods of Rupert's Land Before 1870', in Peterson & Brown, eds, *The New Peoples*: 95–118; Jennifer S.H. Brown, 'Women as Centre and Symbol in the Emergence of Métis Communities', *Canadian Journal of Native Studies* 3 (1983): 39–46; Carol M. Judd, 'Moose Factory Was Not Red River: A Comparison of Mixed-Blood Experiences', in Duncan Cameron, ed., *Exploration in Canadian Economic History: Essays in Honour of Irene M. Spry* (Ottawa: University of Ottawa Press, 1985): 251–68; K.S. Coates and W.R. Morrison, 'More Than a Matter of Blood: The Federal Government, the Churches and the Mixed Blood Populations of the Yukon and the Mackenzie River Valley, 1890–1950', in F. L. Barron and James B. Waldram, eds *1885 and*

After: Native Society in Transition (Regina: Canadian Plains Research Center, 1986): 253–77; Dennis F.K. Madill, 'Riel, Red River, and Beyond: New Developments in Métis History', in Colin G. Calloway, ed., *New Directions in American Indian History* (Norman, Oklahoma: University of Oklahoma Press, 1988): 49–78.

27. 'An Act to Amend and Consolidate the Métis Population Betterment Act' SA 1940, c. 6, s. 2.

28. 'An Act Respecting the Game, Fur-Bearing Animals and Fisheries of Ontario' SO 1927, c. 86, s. 3. See also 'The Game and Fisheries Act, 1946' SO 1946, c. 33, s. 1(s).

29. *Rex v. Tronson* (1931), 57 CCC 383 (BC County Ct.).

30. *Rex v. Tronson*, at 518–21.

31. See Jan Noel, *Canada Dry: Temperance Crusades before Confederation* (Toronto: University of Toronto Press, 1995), at 183, 187–90; Robert A. Campbell, *Demon Rum or Easy Money: Government Control of Liquor in British Columbia from Prohibition to Privatization* (Ottawa: Carleton University Press, 1991), at 9; Andre Vachon, 'L'eau-de-vie dans la societe indienne', *Canadian Historical Association Annual Report*: 23–32; Peter C. Mancall, *Deadly Medicine: Indians and Alcohol in Early America* (Ithaca, NY: Cornell University Press, 1995); Edwin M. Lemert, *Alcohol and the Northwest Coast Indians* (Berkeley: University of California Press, 1954); J.F. Mosher, 'Liquor Legislation and Native Americans: History and Perspective' (Berkeley: University of California, Boalt Hall School of Law, 1975); Anastasia Shkilnyk, *A Poison Stronger than Love: The Destruction of an Ojibwa Community* (New Haven: Yale University Press, 1985); Arthur Ray, *Indians in the Fur Trade* (Toronto: University of Toronto Press, 1974); Sidney L. Harring, *Crow Dog's Case: American Indian Sovereignty, Tribal Law, and United States Law in the Nineteenth Century* (New York: Cambridge University Press, 1994), at 163, 278.

32. For a more detailed account of the legislation regarding alcohol and First Nations peoples, which was punitive in its effect and failed miserably in its capacity to offer support to First Nations communities, see Constance Backhouse, '"Your Conscience Will Be Your Own Punishment": The Racially-motivated Murder of Gus Ninham, Ontario, 1902', in *Essays in the History of Canadian Law*, eds Blaine Baker and Jim Phillips (Toronto: The Osgoode Society, 1999). Provincial governments enacted a series of statutes to outlaw the sale of alcohol to Aboriginal peoples. The first legislative prohibition appeared in Quebec in 1777: 'An Ordinance to Prevent the Selling of Strong Liquors to the Indians in the Province of Quebec' 17 Geo. III, c. 7 (reprinted in RSLC 1845 at 572); see also 'Ordinances of the Late Province of Quebec' RSUC 1792–1840; 'An Act Respecting Indians and Indian Lands' CSLC 1861, c. 14, s. 1–3. Other jurisdictions began by prohibiting liquor sales to specific Aboriginal groups [see the 1801 statute 'An Act to Prevent the Sale of Spirituous Liquors and Strong Waters in the Tract Occupied by the Moravian Indians on the River Thames, in the Western District' RSUC 1792–1840, c. 8] and then legislating more broadly [see the 1840 statute 'An Act to Amend and Make Permanent an Act Passed in the 5th Year of His Late Majesty's Reign, Intituled, "An Act to Prevent the Sale of Spirituous Liquors to Indians"' RSUC 1792–1840, c. 13]. Additional statutes passed in the geographic area that came to be known as Ontario include: 'An Act for the Protection of the Indians in Upper Canada from Imposition, and the Property Occupied or Enjoyed by them from Trespass and Injury' S. Prov. C. 1850, c. 74, s. 6–7; 'An Act Respecting Civilization and Enfranchisement of Certain Indians' CSC 1859, c. 9, s. 3–4; 'An Act to Amend the Ninth Chapter of the Consolidated Statutes of Canada, Intituled: "An Act Respecting Civilization and Enfranchisement of Certain Indians"' S. Prov. C. 1860, c. 38, s. 2. Nova Scotia first legislated in

1829: 'An Act to Prevent the Sale of Spirituous Liquors to Indians, and to Provide for their Instruction' SNS 1829, c. 29, s. 1–3. See also 'Of Licenses for the Sale of Intoxicating Liquors' RSNS 1864, c. 19, s. 30; 'Of Licenses for the Sale of Intoxicating Liquors' RSNS 1884, c. 75, s. 46. British Columbia prohibitions are contained in: 'An Act Prohibiting the Gift or Sale of Intoxicating Liquours to Indians' Colony of Vancouver Island, Passed by Council 3 Aug. 1854; 'Proclamation Respecting Sale or Gift of Intoxicating Liquors to Indians' Colony of British Columbia, 6 Sept. 1858; 'Indian Liquor Act, 1860' Colony of Vancouver Island, 1860, No. 16, s. 2–3; 'The Indian Liquor Ordinance, 1865' Colony of British Columbia, 1865, No. 16; 'The Indian Liquor Ordinance, 1867' Colony of British Columbia, 1867, No. 28 [reprinted in Laws of British Columbia 1871, No. 85]; 'Indian Liquor Ordinance, 1867' CSBC 1877, c. 87; 'An Act Respecting Liquor Licences' SBC 1900, c. 18, s. 2(g) and (h), 37; 'An Act to Amend the "Liquor Licence Act, 1900"' SBC 1902, c. 40, s. 2; 'An Act Respecting Liquor Licences and the Traffic in Intoxicating Liquors' SBC 1910, c. 30, s. 65(c), 75(i); 'An Act Respecting Municipalities' RSBC 1911, c. 170. s. 349(f); 'An Act Respecting Liquor Licences and the Traffic in Intoxicating Liquors' RSBC 1911, c. 142; 'An Act to Amend the "Liquor Licence Act"' SBC 1912, c. 20, s. 5; 'An Act to Amend the "Liquor Licence Act"' SBC 1913, c. 40, s. 8; 'An Act to Provide for Government Control and Sale of Alcoholic Liquors' SBC 1921 (First Session), c. 30, s. 36; 'An Act to Provide for Government Control and Sale of Alcoholic Liquors' RSBC 1924, c. 146, s. 41; 'An Act to Amend the "Government Liquor Act"' SBC 1926–27, c. 38, s. 11; 'An Act to Provide for Government Control and Sale of Alcoholic Liquors' RSBC 1936, c. 160, s. 43; 'An Act to Amend the "Government Liquor Act"' SBC 1947, c. 53, s. 16; 'An Act to Provide for Government Control and Sale of Alcoholic Liquors' RSBC 1948, c.

192. Newfoundland's prohibition is found in 'An Act Regulating Sale of Intoxicating Liquors on the Coast of Labrador' S.Nfld. 1882, c. 8, s. 6. After the turn of the century, other jurisdictions followed suit. Prairie province enactments include: 'An Act to Provide for Government Control and Sale of Liquor' SM 1928, c. 31, s. 38(1)(e); 'An Act to Amend the Liquor License Act' SS 1909, c. 38, s. 12; 'An Act to Amend the Government Liquor Control Act of Alberta' SA 1927, c. 35, s. 5. The Northwest Territories prohibited liquor sales to Indians and Eskimos: 'An Ordinance to Provide for the Control, Regulation and Sale of Liquor in the Northwest Territories' Ord. NWT 1948, c. 23, s. 15(1)(e), 26–28. Prince Edward Island prohibited 'Indians' from voting on prohibition: 'An Act to Provide for a Plebiscite on Questions Relating to the Control and Suppression of Traffic in Alcoholic Liquors' SPEI 1929, c. 15, s. 6. When the federal government obtained constitutional jurisdiction over 'Indians' after confederation, it enacted a host of prohibitions as well: 'An Act Providing for the Organisation of the Department of the Secretary of State of Canada, and for the Management of Indian and Ordnance Lands' SC 1868, c. 42, s. 9, 12–13; 'An Act for the Gradual Enfranchisement of Indians, the Better Management of Indian Affairs, and to Extend the Provisions of the Act 31st Victoria, Chapter 42' SC 1869, c. 6, s. 3; 'An Act to Amend Certain Laws Respecting Indians, and to Extend Certain Laws Relating to Matters Connected with Indians to the Provinces of Manitoba and British Columbia' SC 1874, c. 21, s. 1; 'The Indian Act, 1876' SC 1876, c. 18, s. 27, 68, 79–85; 'The Indian Act, 1880' SC 1880, c. 28, s. 90; 'An Act to Further Amend "The Indian Act, 1880"' SC 1882, c. 30, s. 5; 'The Indian Act' RSC 1886, c. 43, s. 94–105; 'An Act to Amend "The Indian Act"' SC 1887, c. 33, s. 10; 'An Act to Further Amend "The Indian Act", Chapter Forty-three of the Revised Statutes' SC 1888, c. 22, s. 4; 'An Act Further to Amend

"The Indian Act", Chapter Forty-three of the Revised Statutes' SC 1890, c. 29, s. 8; 'An Act Further to Amend "The Indian Act"' SC 1894, c. 32, s. 6–7; 'The Indian Act' RSC 1906, c. 81, s. 135–46; 'An Act to Amend the Indian Act' SC 1919–20, c. 50, s. 4; 'Indian Act' RSC 1927, c. 98; 'An Act to Amend the Indian Act' SC 1930, c. 25, s. 13–14; 'An Act to Amend the Indian Act' SC 1936, c. 20, s. 6–12; 'The Indian Act' SC 1951, c. 29, s. 93–102.

33. *Regina* v. *Howson* (1894), 1 Terr. LR 492.

34. *Regina* v. *Howson*, at 493–6.

35. 'An Act Further to Amend "The Indian Act"' SC 1894, c. 32, s. 6. See also 'Indian Act' RSC 1906, c. 81, s. 135. The federal provisions were not altered until 'The Indian Act' SC 1951, c. 29, s. 93 reconstructed the offence to prohibit the sale or supply of liquor to 'any person on a reserve' or 'an Indian outside a reserve'. Strangely enough, some of the earlier provincial statutes prohibiting the sale of alcohol to Indians had failed to define the term 'Indian' at all. Most striking is 'The Indian Liquor Ordinance, 1867' Colony of British Columbia, 1867, No. 28 [reprinted in Laws of British Columbia 1871, No. 85], which contains an intricate 'interpretation clause' as follows: 'In the construction of this Ordinance, the word "Governor" shall be held to mean the Governor of this Colony, or other Officer administering the Government of this Colony for the time being, and whenever in this Ordinance in describing or referring to any person or party, matter or thing, any word importing the masculine gender or singular number is used, the same shall be understood to include and be applicable to several persons and parties as well as one person or party, and females as well as males, and bodies corporate as well as individuals, and several matters and things as well as one matter or thing, unless it be otherwise provided or there be something in the subject or context repugnant to such construction.' Clearly the legislators turned their minds to questions of definition, and yet there is no attempt to define 'Indian' whatsoever.

36. *The Queen* v. *Mellon* (1900), 7 CCC 179.

37. *The Queen* v. *Mellon*, at 180–1. On the *mens rea* requirements for the offence, see *Rex* v. *Brown* (1930), 55 CCC 29 (Toronto Police Ct.), where it is stated at 32–3: 'Under the decisions, *mens rea* must be proved . . . The evidence must amount to positive knowledge on the part of the accused as to the nationality of the purchaser, no matter how stupid he may have been'. See also *Rex* v. *Hughes* (1906), 12 BCR 290 (New Westminster County Court); *Rex* v. *Webb* (1943), 80 CCC 151 (Sask. KB).

38. *The King* v. *Pickard* (1908), 14 CCC 33.

39. *The King* v. *Pickard*, at 33–5. *Rex* v. *Bennett* (1930), 55 CCC 27 (Ont. County Ct.), would tangle with the issue of deceptive appearances as well. The accused had been convicted of selling wine to Jack Post, an 'Indian'. On appeal, the defence argued that the accused 'did not know or believe or suspect him to be an Indian', but thought he 'was a Japanese'. The appeal court adjourned the hearing so that the judge might take a look at the individual concerned. 'He is typically Indian in appearance', pronounced the presiding judge, 'and I do not see how the accused could have very well taken him for other than an Indian. Certainly his appearance would at least cause the accused to suspect him to be an Indian.'

40. *The King* v. *Pickard*, at 33–5.

41. *Rex* v. *Verdi* (1914), 23 CCC 47.

42. Emma LaRoque states that 'there are some words that are not reclaimable and "squaw" is one of them', representing 'rapist imagery, where rape and murder merge [and] the grossest acts of the objectification of human beings'. Harmut Lutz notes that one of the definitions of 'squaw' from the *Oxford English Dictionary* is 'a kneeling figure used for target practice', and also 'a certain position in which a barrel is held when it is tapped', so that it is 'a term denoting sexual penetration and violence'. See the text of

this conversation in Harmut Lutz, *Contemporary Challenges: Conversations with Canadian Native Authors* (Saskatoon: Fifth House, 1991), at 191–2, 201–2.

43. *Rex v. Verdi*, at 48–9. The court held: 'The fact that this man voted last summer and did not since resign from the tribe, together with the other facts in evidence, satisfy me that he is an "Indian".'

44. Pauktuutit, *The Inuit Way: A Guide to Inuit Culture* (Ottawa: Pauktuutit, Inuit Women's Association, 1989), at 4; David Damas, 'Arctic', in *Handbook of North American Indians*, Vol. 5, ed. William C. Sturtevant (Washington: Smithsonian Institution, 1984), at 6–7. Marie Wadc , *Nitassinan: The Innu Struggle to Reclaim Tı Homeland* (Vancouver: Douglas & McInty 1991), notes at 26: 'According to [ethnoli guist] José Mailhot, it was the Innu, in conve sation with the Basques, who coined the terr *aiskimeu* to refer to their Inuit neighbours. She believes the word meant "those who speak a strange language", not "eaters of raw meat" as is popularly believed. The Innu word was eventually spelled "esquimaux" by the French and "eskimo" by the English.' Damas also suggests another possible First Nations source: the Ojibwa 'e-skipot'. Damas mentions additional alternative spellings: Esquimawes, Esquimaud, Esquimos, Eskemoes, Eskima, Eskimeaux, Esquimeaux, Excomminquois, Exquimaux, Ehuskemay, Uskemau, Uskimay, Eusquemay, and Usquemow.

45. Pauktuutit, *The Inuit Way*, at 4. Damas, 'Arctic', notes at 7 that the commonest self-designation within the Canadian Arctic is 'Inuit', with several other terms also in use: 'Inupiat (for those of north Alaska), Yupik (southwestern Alaska), and Yuit (Siberia and Saint Lawrence Island).' The 1977 Inuit Circumpolar Conference in Barrow, Alaska, officially adopted 'Inuit' as a designation for all, regardless of local usages.

46. 'An Act to Amend the Quebec Fish and Game Laws' SQ 1919, c. 31, s. 5, amending Article 2313 of the Revised Statutes, 1909, as enacted by the act 7 George V, chapter 26, section 1, and amended by the act 8 George V, chapter 36, section 2, provides: 'It is forbidden . . . to hunt, kill or take [...] (c) At any time of the year, any wild swan, wood duck, eider duck, curlew, sandpiper or other shore bird or wader (except woodcock, snipe, black-breasted or golden plover and the greater and lesser yellow-legs), or any of the following species of migratory non-game birds: auks, auklets, bitterns, fulmars, gannets, grebes, guillemots, gulls, herons, jeagers, loons, murres, petrels, puffins, shearwaters, and terns. Nevertheless, Eskimos and Indians may take at any time auks, auklets, guillemots, murres and puffin and their eggs for food and their skins for clothing; but any birds or eggs so taken shall not be sold or offered for sale.'

47. 'An Ordinance Respecting the Protection and Care of Eskimo Ruins' Ord. NWT, 5 February 1930, s. 1 provides: 'No Eskimo ruins shall be excavated or investigated nor shall any objects of archaeological or ethnological importance or interest be exported or taken from the Territories save by permission of and in accordance with regulations made by the Commissioner of the Northwest Territories.'

      'An Act Respecting the Franchise of Electors at Elections of Members of the House of Commons' SC 1934, c. 51, s. 4 states: 'Provided that the following persons are disqualified from voting at an election and incapable of being registered as electors and shall not be so registered, that is to say—(vi) every Esquimau person, whether born in Canada or elsewhere.' See also An Act Respecting the Franchise of Electors and the Election of Members of the House of Commons' SC 1938, c. 46, s. 14(2)(e).

49. 'An Ordinance to Provide for the Control, Regulation and Sale of Liquor in the Northwest Territories' Ord. NWT 1948, c. 23, s. 15(1)(e), 26–28.

50. 'An Act Regulating Sale of Intoxicating Liquors

on the Coast of Labrador' S.Nfld. 1882, c. 8, s. 6 states: 'No Intoxicating Liquors shall be sold, given or delivered to any Esquimaux Indian, under a penalty of Two Hundred Dollars.' Later versions of this legislation would alter the wording to prohibit sales of alcoholic liquor 'to any Esquimaux or Indian'; see 'Alcoholic Liquors Act' S.Nfld. 1924, c. 9, s. 23(e); S.Nfld. 1933, c. 19, s. 27(1)(e); R.S.Nfld. 1952, c. 93, s. 69(1)(i). Surprisingly, the 1882 statute would be the only one cited by the Supreme Court of Canada in its ultimate decision: *Re Eskimos* at 114. The judges ignored the 1924 amendment to the Newfoundland statute separating 'Esquimaux' from 'Indian'.

51. The Minister of the Interior, Hon. Charles A. Stewart, initially proposed to add the following section to the Indian Act: 'The Superintendent General of Indian Affairs shall have the control and management of the lands and property of the Eskimos in Canada and the provisions of Part I of the Indian Act shall apply to the said Eskimo insofar as they are applicable to their condition and mode of life, and the Department of Indian Affairs shall have the management, charge and direction of Eskimo affairs.' Stewart's explanation was that, with the expansion of the fur trade, there was increasing connection between whites and Eskimos, police posts were being set up in the North, and there was need to establish greater governmental coordination in dealing with the Eskimo. Several legislators objected to the draft provision. One questioned whether 'any request had been made to the government by the Eskimos through their chiefs that they be brought within the provisions of the Indian Act'. No answer was forthcoming. The Leader of the Opposition, Arthur Meighen, objected strenuously to equating Eskimos with Indians, arguing that decades of governmental wardship had not improved the status of Indians, and that there was no need to 'put our wings all around [the Eskimo's] property and tell him he is our ward and that we will look

after him. [. . .] My own opinion would be to leave them alone—make them comply with our criminal law and give them all the benefit of our civil law; in other words, treat them as everybody else is treated. I should not like to see the same policy precisely applied to the Eskimos as we have applied to the Indians.' Meighen's position carried the day, and the provision was shortened to state only that the superintendent general should have charge of Eskimo affairs. See Canada, House of Commons, *Parliamentary Debates* [Hansard; hereinafter cited as *Debates*], 10 June 1924, at 2992–3; 30 June 1924, at 3823–7; 14 July 1924, at 4409–13.

52. 'An Act to Amend the Indian Act', SC 1924, c. 47, s. 1; *Debates* 14 July 1924, at 4409.

53. 'An Act to Amend the Indian Act', SC 1930, c. 25, s. 1. The Indian Act, SC 1951, c. 29, s. 4(1), provides: 'This Act does not apply to the race of Aborigines commonly referred to as Eskimos.' *Debates*, 31 Mar. 1930, at 1091–101.

54. *Debates*, 31 Mar. 1930, at 1092. The 'Scotch' reference was supplied by the Hon. Charles A. Dunning, Minister of Finance.

55. Diamond Jenness, *Eskimo Administration: II. Canada* (Montreal: Arctic Institute of North America, 1964), at 10, 22; Bobbie Kalman and Ken Faris, *Arctic Whales and Whaling* (New York: Crabtree, 1988).

56. Jenness, *Eskimo Administration*, adds at 10–13, 26 that the sexual intermixture was accentuated by the 'moral code' of Inuit culture, which 'permitted [Eskimo women] the same freedom as prevailed among the Polynesian islanders in the days of Captain James Cook'. K.S. Coates, 'Furs along the Yukon: Hudson's Bay Company–Native Trade in the Yukon River Basin, 1830–1893', MA Thesis (University of Manitoba: 1979) notes at 153–4 that within Inuit culture, sexual relationships between Inuit women and European whalers and traders were frequently encouraged as a systemic mechanism to solidify trading ties. See also William R. Morrison, *Under the Flag: Canadian Sovereignty and the*

Native People in Northern Canada (Ottawa: Indian and Northern Affairs Canada, 1984) at 71–4.

57. On the eastern Arctic, see 'Factum on Behalf of the Attorney General of the Province of Quebec, in the Supreme Court of Canada, in the Matter of a Reference as to Whether the Term "Indians" in Head 24 of Section 91 of the British North America Act, 1867, Includes Eskimo Inhabitants of the Province of Quebec' [hereinafter cited as Quebec Factum], at 24, citing Jenness. On the western Arctic, see Emoke J.E. Szathmary, 'Human Biology of the Arctic', in *Handbook of North American Indians*, ed. Sturtevant, at 64. Dorothy Harley Eber, *Images of Justice* (Montreal and Kingston: McGill-Queen's University Press, 1997), describes at 51 the travels of Morris Pokiak, 'half Inuk, half black', who used to trade by boat along the Arctic coast in the 1920s and 1930s.

58. Quebec Factum, at 7. The original reference comes from Jenness, *Indians of Canada*, at 247.

59. For example, 'An Act Respecting the Franchise of Electors at Elections of Members of the House of Commons' SC 1934, c. 51, s. 4 distinguishes between 'Esquimau persons' and 'Indian persons', when disqualifying both from voting. Other statutes drawing a distinction without further explanation include: 'An Act Respecting the Franchise of Electors and the Election of Members of the House of Commons' SC 1938, c. 46, s. 14(2); 'An Ordinance to Provide for the Control, Regulation and Sale of Liquor in the Northwest Territories' Ord. NWT 1948, c. 23, s. 15(1)(e); 'An Act Respecting the Esquimaux and Indians Resident in Labrador' S.Nfld. 1911, c. 4, s. 1; 'Of the Protection of Esquimaux and Indians' C.S.Nfld. 1916, c. 80; 'An Ordinance Respecting the Preservation of Game in the Northwest Territories' Ord. NWT 1949, c. 12, s. 2(1)(d), 12, 24(2), 33(1), 44(1), 66(5); 'An Ordinance to Amend an Ordinance Respecting the Preservation of Game in the Northwest Territories' Ord. NWT 1949, c. 27, s.

1; 'An Act to Amend the Quebec Fish and Game Laws' SQ 1919, c. 31, s. 5.

60. 'An Act Respecting the Esquimaux and Indians Resident in Labrador' S.Nfld. 1911, c. 4 provides:

> s. 1. Without the permission of the Governor in Council first obtained, it shall be unlawful for any person to enter into any agreement with an Esquimaux, Nascopee, or Mountaineer Indian to leave this Colony or its dependencies for the purpose of performing any services in any place outside this Colony or its dependencies, or to pay or promise to pay any money, or give or promise to give any article to any Esquimaux, Nascopee, or Mountaineer Indian as a reward or inducement for leaving this Colony, or to transport or furnish the means of transporting any Esquimaux, Nascopee, or Mountaineer Indian from this Colony to any place outside this Colony; provided that nothing in this section shall prevent the employment of Esquimaux, Nascopee, or Mountaineer Indians by any person for the purpose of fishing, hunting, or exploring upon any part of the coast or territories of the Canadian Labrador.
>
> s. 2. Any person violating any one of the provisions of the first section of this Act shall be liable to a penalty not exceeding five hundred dollars, or in default of payment, to imprisonment not exceeding six months, to be removed or imposed upon the complaint of any person in a summary manner before a stipendiary Magistrate.
>
> s. 3. In this Act, 'Esquimaux' shall mean native residents of the Coast of Labrador who are commonly known as Esquimaux.

The impetus for the statute was a desire to prevent the exploitation of Eskimo in travelling exhibitions in Europe and the United States. Certain Eskimo had contracted with wild animal exhibitors to participate in such displays, and been left destitute without funds to return home. On one occasion, the Newfoundland government had to pay return travel costs to Labrador. On another, an Eskimo contracted a most loathsome disease during the time away. The motivation to include the 'Indian' groups came from the Right Honourable Sir Robert Bond, who suggested that if deportation of Eskimo was prohibited, exhibitors would turn to groups such as the Mountaineer Indians. See House of Assembly Proceedings 24 February 1911, at 204-6; St. John's Daily News 21 March 1911.

61. 'An Ordinance Respecting the Preservation of Game in the Northwest Territories' Ord. NWT 1949, c. 12, s. 2(1)(d) provides:

s. 12. No person shall employ or enter into a contract or agreement with an Indian, Eskimo, or other person to hunt, kill, or take game or to take any egg or nest or part thereof contrary to the provisions of this Ordinance.

s. 24(1). Except as authorized by this Ordinance, no person shall hunt in a game preserve.

(2). An Indian or Eskimo who was born in the Territories and who holds a general hunting licence may hunt in a game preserve.

s. 33(1). An Indian or Eskimo who holds a general hunting licence may take or kill male barren-ground caribou during the month of March in the year for which the licence was issued to provide meat for food for himself and his immediate family, but not for sale or barter.

s. 44(1). A general hunting licence may be issued to a person over the age of sixteen years who is,

(a) an Indian or Eskimo and who

(i) has resided continuously in the Territories since his birth, or

(ii) is a member of a family or group of Indians or Eskimos that, prior to the commencement of this Ordinance, hunted in the Territories as a means of livelihood;

s. 66(5) The widow of an Indian or Eskimo in needy circumstances, or the head of a family who is the holder of a general hunting licence may be issued a licence to take not more than ten beaver.

See also 'An Ordinance to Amend an Ordinance Respecting the Preservation of Game in the Northwest Territories' Ord. NWT 1949, c. 27, s. 1, which provides: 'An Indian or Eskimo who holds a general hunting licence may take or kill male barren-ground caribou in any part of the Territories except Baffin Island and Bylot Island during the month of March in the year for which the licence was issued to provide meat for food for himself and his immediate family, but not for sale or barter.'

62 'The Indian Act' SC 1951, c. 29, s. 4(1).

Chapter 6

Race in the Canadian Census

Monica Boyd, Gustave Goldmann, and Pamela White

Unlike her neighbour to the south, Canada has an erratic history of enumerating the racial composition of her population. This enumeration history is characterized by three components: (1) temporal variation in the presence, or absence, of a census question relevant to the collection of racial data; (2) variation in question wording such that at times 'race' is explicit and at other [times] subsumed by the 'origin' concept; and (3) variation in the larger societal ideologies of race relations that motivate data collection.

At the moment, Canada is at a crossroad. Considerable demand for data on 'visible minorities' currently exists as a result of changing models of social inequality and related public policies of multiculturalism and employment equity. Public discourse on 'racism' and racial discrimination has also fuelled such data demands. However, the 1991 census failed to include a question that explicitly asks for 'race', despite formal consultation by Statistics Canada and considerable public attention to the issue. The 1996 census asked a question on the country's visible minority population for the first time. Yet, during the 1996 census collection, diverse blocks of public opinion threatened to perpetuate societal and statistical ambivalence about asking the question at all.

The purpose of this paper is twofold: (1) to document the variations in the Canadian census with regard to enumerating race; and (2) to show

that such variations co-vary with changing conceptualizations of race and race relations. Pursuit of these objectives serves to confirm both common sense and expert assessments of ethnic and racial origin questions. How and when ancestry and/or phenotypical or somatic characteristics are collected by the census is determined not only by the principles of social survey research but also by laws, politics, and broader societal representations of ethnicity and race (Goldmann and McKenney 1993).

In order to provide background information on the census as a measuring instrument, we present a brief overview of census-taking in Canada. We then discuss the changing history of enumerating race in Canadian censuses. Temporal variations exist in approaches to the enumeration of race. These variations reflect prevailing models of racial discourse and nation-building. In a subsequent section, we examine the specific issues that [are] associated with attempts to devise a question on race for the 1991 census. We conclude with a brief assessment of the issues which must be confronted in renewing attempts to field a race question in the 1996 census.

Taking Stock

As Priest (1990: 1) observes, '[i]t is difficult to discuss the collection and use of ethnicity [and, we add, race] in the Canadian census without recounting . . . the struggle of the French and the British for control of the North American continent and to consider the history of census-taking itself'. Priest's review enriches the context of early census-taking, beginning in 1665 with Jean Talon's enumeration of the population in the French territory which is now part of Quebec. Motivated by questions of political and economic domination through the mechanism of European settlement, these early censuses focused on age, sex, marital status, professions, and trades. Race, religion, and origins were new dimensions added to the 1767 British-instigated censuses in Nova Scotia, and race and origins reappeared in the 1824 census in New Brunswick (Priest 1990).

To the extent that race, religion, and origins were found in other earlier censuses, much of the emphasis was on collecting data by religion and/or birthplace. Such information was central to broader issues of nation-building and sovereignty in a land whose colonization had been so much contested in the preceding two centuries. However, the demographic and economic expansion of Canada's western regions during the late 1800s brought with it increasing awareness of, and conflict with, the Aboriginal populations resident there. Following the uprising of Louis Riel and his Métis force, an 1885 census of Assiniboia, Saskatchewan, and Alberta included a count of wigwams and introduced the concept of 'half-breeds' through a modification of the origin question.

The British North America Act, 1867, formalized nation-building endeavours. To meet the administrative needs of the Canadian government it provided the legal mechanism for the continuation of decennial censuses undertaken in 1851 and 1861. Since then the government of Canada has been required to conduct a census of population in the first full year of every decade. More recently the decennial census has been conducted under the authority of the Constitution Act, 1982. National quinquennial censuses

began in 1956 and since this time Canada has held a census every five years (Statistics Act 1985).

Immigration was a major component of Canada's growth and national development in the centuries following the travels of the early European explorers. As Miles (1992) notes, how racially and ethnically diverse newcomers are to be incorporated is a major question facing such countries both then and now. Similar concerns and administrative needs appear to underlie the continued interest in enumerating the origins of Canada's population during the 1800s. Nevertheless, race as an explicit term did not then enter into the census-taking. Table 6.1 shows the temporal variations in the focus on origins, race, and visible minority group.

Between 1851 and 1881, the primary focus was on the origins of the Canadian population. However, a discernible shift occurred following the 1891 census, in which no question on origins or race was present, though information on persons of French-Canadian background was collected. Between 1901 and 1941, racial origins were an explicit part of the wording of census questions. Enumerators were provided with rules of enumeration that emphasized categorization according to lineage or descent. In 1951, however, explicit references to 'race' were abruptly dropped. Between 1951 and 1991, data collection efforts relied on an ethnic origin question. In 1996, questions on ethnic origin, Aboriginal identity, and visible minority group were asked.

If the explicit formulations of race questions vary, so too do the underlying conceptualizations of race. Given Canada's European settlement and attachments it is not surprising to find that images of, and discussion about, race parallel northern European changes in conceptualizing it. Miles (1989: 31) argues that the idea of 'race' emerged in the English language in the early sixteenth century, as part of nation-building and it largely referred to populations of emergent nation-states. In its early usage in Europe the

Table 6.1: Historical Overview of Canada's Collection of Ethnic and Racial Origin Data by Census Year, 1767 to 1996

Census Year	Origins	Racial Origins	Ethnic Origins	Visible Minority Group
1767	X	X		
1824		X		
1851	X			
1861	X			
1871	X			
1881	X			
1891	NA	NA	NA	NA
1901		X		
1911		X		
1921		X		
1931		X		
1941		X		
1951			X	
1961			X	
1971			X	
1981			X	
1986			X	X*
1991			X	X*
1996			X	X*

X* Derived counts of visible minority population based on employment equity definitions.
NA = Not asked.
Source: White, Badets, and Renaud (1993). Modified to reflect 1996 census.

term 'race' meant lineage or common descent and identified a population with a common origin and history, but not a population with a fixed biological character. However, the idea of race took on a new meaning with the development of science, its application to the natural world, and its extension to a social world (Miles 1989). By the late 1800s, social Darwinism had permeated public and academic discourse.

Between 1901 and 1941, Canadian censuses not only explicitly used the terms 'race' and 'racial origin' but also they contained elaborate instructions to enumerators on how to properly categorize respondents on the basis of race. The categories changed somewhat over time, but the emphasis was on demarcating a 'white' population from groups which today are considered African, Asian, or Aboriginal. . . . [P]aternal ancestry was used to classify the European 'white' groups. Indians [sic] were to be classified by the origin of the mother and all offspring of children of mixed marriages between white and other 'races' were classified as belonging to the non-white 'race'.

In the Canadian census questions on 'race', the descent rules which were *de rigueur* up to 1941 are highly consistent with evolutionary theory. According to the nineteenth-century evolutionary schemes, societies were classified on a scale that, based on Lewis Henry Morgan's interpretation, spanned a continuum from 'savagery' to 'barbarism' to 'civilization' (Zeitlin 1990). Evolutionists commonly believed that in 'civilized' societies descent was determined along patrilineal lines. They also believed that among 'barbaric' societies descent was matrilineally based and that among 'savages' it was based on 'tribal' affiliation. With regard to Canada's census, it is interesting to note that according to this logic the Aboriginal population 'evolved' from savagery to barbarism during the period 1901 to 1911. This contrasted with the specification of rights in the Indian Act which designated lineage according to patrilineal descent until changes were made by Bill C-31 (1985).

However, if one focuses on the descent rules in the 1901–1941 Canadian censuses as reflecting the then-existing conceptualizations of race one risks missing the broader motivating forces behind the adoption of such conceptualization and measurement. Migration involves contact with new societies, and in Canada's history it certainly concerned the twofold activities of dominating the Indigenous populations and creating a nation out of diverse peoples. Miles (1989: 11) argues that such migration generates and reshapes imagery, beliefs, and evaluations about the 'other' in order to formulate a strategy for interaction. In Canada, prior to the mid-1900s, the representations of the 'other' in 'racial' terms emphasized biological properties associated with blood lineage. These representations, as embodied in descent rules, took different forms depending on the twin projects of colonialism and nationhood.

Colonialism is often defined as the military, political, and/or economic dominance of one nation over a subordinate country. Internal colonialism exists where Europeans have settled in new lands, established European institutions, and subjugated both Indigenous and non-Indigenous peoples (Satzewich and Wotherspoon 1992). There are a number of dimensions to this internal colonialism, but one aspect of the colonization process is the creation of racism and a colour line to regulate social interaction between groups.

The settlement of the Prairies carried with it an agenda for the agricultural development of the region and the wresting away of control from the Indigenous peoples. The establishment of a permanent Canadian presence in the West also diminished American influences. Evolutionary theory made it possible to develop a discourse of race that represented Aboriginals as the 'other', with capacities and achievements fixed by biological, natural, and unalterable conditions (Miles 1989). As observed by Satzewich and Wotherspoon (1992: 8), 'ideologies of biological superiority and inferiority emerge[d] to justify the exploitation of Aboriginal people and their resources, to break down their resistance and to deter them from becoming full members of Canadian society'. The Indian Act was a significant legislative instrument of policy, used by the Canadian government to maintain control over Indigenous groups and to instill the notion of 'other'.

However, non-European groups from abroad were not immune to social characterization. Late nineteenth-century reactions against the immigration of Chinese existed, with a head tax being imposed in 1886 and increased in 1900 and 1903. Indeed, the rules of descent as operationalized in the census for the years 1901 to 1941 approximated the notion of the 'one drop rule'. This form of categorization had been in existence in the United States and prevented successive generations of mixed marriage offspring from ever being classified 'white' (Davis 1991).

As well, reputed biological properties were the basis of many admonitions against admitting European groups of dubious 'suitability'. As Porter (1965: 64–5) notes British immigrants were never considered foreigners, but changing immigration patterns, reducing the proportion of northern European and British settlers in favour of eastern and southern Europeans provoked debate about the desirability of other groups. Central to this debate was a focus on certain traits as biological, although there was much variation in opinion as to whether these traits were to be considered as cultural in origin, or as genetic, inherited and thus unalterable.

The 1908 book *Strangers within Our Gates*, written by J.S. Woodsworth, epitomized many of the beliefs and tensions regarding the relative desirability of various white 'races'. However, Woodsworth was not alone in his views. Such attitudes lasted well into the 1940s and served to exclude many groups from entry into Canada. For example, Abella and Tropper (1982) document the tragic consequences of Canadian immigration policies which prevented admission of Jews to Canada both before and after the Second World War.

The resulting schema of ranking clearly acknowledged the dominance of the British-origin group in Canada's economic, political, and social life. For almost two centuries following the battle between British and French forces on the Plains of Abraham, international migration reinforced British domination. The Immigration Acts of 1910, 1927, and 1952 continued the exclusion of groups deemed undesirable according to ethnic/racial criteria and continued to favour the migration of people from the British Isles, northern Europe, and—if all else failed—other European areas (Harney 1988). In actual fact, during the late 1800s and through the 1900s, migration from Europe ensured substantial ethnic diversification, yet the prevailing model remained that of assimilation to a British ethnic prototype (Breton 1988; Harney 1988). The cre-

ation of a common 'Anglo' ideology and set of institutions and the pressing agenda of developing the western Interior of Canada provided important contexts for debates on the characteristics of south and east European migrants. These debates accorded much attention to the ability of such groups to be assimilated and to strengthen Canada's nation-building endeavours.

To summarize: between 1901 and 1941 the context surrounding the 'race' questions generated two models of incorporation into the Canadian mainstream. Both emphasized lineage and invoked distinctions between 'we' and 'they'. In one model, firm unalterable boundaries existed around non-white groups. In the context of the Canadian census, the instructions to census enumerators specified that the offspring of mixed marriages (white/non-white) were to be assigned the non-white 'race'. These boundaries both derived from and reaffirmed prevailing ideologies in which white was superior and dominant in relation to other non-white groups.

The second model permitted boundary crossing for the white population. Although various 'white' immigrant groups were considered races, categorization in the census was traced through the father's side. As a result, intermarriage for the white population could, and did, change the categorization of offspring. Such fluidity is consistent with the early twentieth-century model of Anglo assimilation and with the transformation of the white 'other' into the 'self'.

Post–Second World War View: Out with Race, In with Culture

The period between 1941 and 1951 was in many respects a watershed. World War II sensitized the Western world to the genocidal policies that could—and did—accompany the conceptualization of race as biological and unalterable. This most certainly had an impact on the way in which the population was counted and classified in Canadian censuses from that point on. The 1951 census origins question contained no mention of 'race' either in the instructions to enumerators or in the question description and wording. Instead, the emphasis was on ancestry or cultural origins on the father's side. Aboriginal peoples, Africans, and persons of colour or with distinctive features continued to be enumerated as such, but the vocabulary of labelling and categorization officially changed to that of origin instead of race. With minor alterations, the approach adopted in the 1951 census was repeated in 1961 and 1971. From 1981 onward, instructions to link origins to the paternal side were dropped and multiple responses were permitted.

While an important factor in the move away from an explicit 'race' question, horror at Nazi termination policies does not adequately account for the protracted post-war history of census questions on ethnic origins as opposed to race. Nation-building was again an important factor although the earlier ideologies of Anglo-conformity and colonialism were to be replaced by issues of multiculturalism and sovereignty.

In addition to Anglo–French relations (Breton 1988), demographic change in the form of large post-war immigration provided an important impetus to development of the concept of nationhood and its legislative and institutional representations. During and after World War I the large numbers of migrants to Canada slowed considerably and became a trickle during the Depression years of the 1930s. After World War II, however, not only was Europe on the move, with the migration of displaced persons, but also there was an awareness in the Canadian government, due to the war, of the dangers of a sparsely settled country. In his 1947 statement to Parliament on immigration Prime Minister Mackenzie King explicitly noted that immigration would shore up Canada's small population. Europe was clearly the source for such reinforcements, given King's announcement that Canada

did not wish there to be, as a result of mass immigration, any fundamental alteration in the character of the Canadian population. However, in 1962 and in 1967 changes in Canadian immigration regulations opened the doors to non-European groups. These changes, later embodied in the Immigration Act, 1976, replaced the national origins criteria for admission with those emphasizing family reunification and labour-market contribution. Groups which previously could not immigrate to Canada because they were not from designated European countries were now admitted if they met family reunification, labour-market, or humanitarian criteria.

These policy changes altered the composition of Canada's migration flows and diversified the Canadian population. Of immigrants arriving before 1961 over 90 per cent were born in the United States and Europe, while between 1 to 2 per cent were Asian-born. In contrast, of those immigrating in the late 1980s, a little over 30 per cent were from the United States and Europe, compared with over 40 per cent from Asia. Today, close to three-quarters of immigrants come from regions other than Europe and the United States.

Harney (1988) argues that the resultant ethnic diversity belied the old images of Canadian society and thus fuelled the search for a principle of collective national identity in the 1980s. However, the need to unify a country with major regional and linguistic/ethnic cleavages had been recognized by politicians much earlier. Starting in the late 1950s under Diefenbaker, and continuing under the Liberal governments of the 1960s and 1970s, a series of policies and actions were initiated which deliberately and directly appealed to Canada's inhabitants as Canadian regardless of where they lived or what language they spoke (Smith 1989).

The development of Canada's multiculturalism policy can be interpreted as part of the efforts of the Canadian state to given recognition to the role that ethnic diversity plays in the forging of a

Canadian identity. The original impetus for such a policy came from the Royal Commission on Bilingualism and Biculturalism, which was intended to review the status of the British and the French 'founding peoples'. However, non-British and French groups stressed in public hearings that their status too must be recognized (Sheridan and Saouab 1992). As Stasiulis (1991) observes, various groups sought a policy of multiculturalism as a strategy for affirming their place in the nation's ethnocultural symbolic order.

Established in 1971, Canada's multiculturalism policy has gone through several evolutions (Sheridan and Saouab 1992). In respect of data demands, the most significant events have been legislative. During the 1980s and early 1990s additional significant legislative developments included the creation of the Department of Multiculturalism and Citizenship. Major programs managed by this federal department, currently known as Heritage Canada, include: Race Relations and Cross-cultural Understanding; Heritage Cultures and Languages; and Community Support and Participation. The data requirements of these programs were reinforced by two additional documents. The first was the Canadian Charter of Rights and Freedoms, 1982, which guaranteed rights regardless of origin, race, gender, age, or disability. The second was the Employment Equity Act, 1986, which established a monitoring of hiring and promotion practices affecting visible minorities, women, Aboriginal peoples, and persons with disabilities in federally regulated businesses.

Together, the creation of a federal department, the Charter, and the Employment Equity Act created the policy rationales for collecting and disseminating information on various ethnocultural groups in Canada. Such matters as how the ethnic origin question is worded, whether ancestral origins, identity, or visible minority status is captured or derived, and whether or not multiple responses are permitted have become contested

terrain for a large body of potential users including researchers, government agencies, and ethnocultural groups. The debate in the public arena, discussed elsewhere (Boyd 1993a; 1993b), derives as much from the politics of numbers as from the application of principles of sound survey design.

The Challenge of the 1990s

From 1971 onward, the collection of census data through enumerators has been replaced by a methodology that primarily relies on self-reporting by respondents. As a result, Canadian census planning now includes extensive pretesting of census questions and nationwide public consultation. Ethnocultural questions are an integral subset of such pretests and consultations. After a hiatus of nearly 50 years, the need to collect data on race was actively discussed and explicitly tested as part of the 1991 and the 1996 census consultation and testing.

In a contrast to earlier practices the question on race was now motivated by reformulated concepts of equality and a growing concern with discrimination and racism in Canadian society. As in the United States (Blauner 1991) structural models of inequality emphasizing institutionalized barriers and discrimination had come, by the 1980s, to replace earlier individualist models of inequality, in which the central concern was lack of opportunity for individual achievement (Agocs and Boyd 1993). In addition to academic research and public discourse, this paradigmatic shift also characterized legislation and policy. For example, section 15(2) of the Canadian Charter of Rights and Freedoms, 1982, removed obstacles to the subsequent passage of the Employment Equity Act, 1986. This Act and accompanying regulations were reviewed and strengthened in 1996.

The foundation document of Canadian employment equity policy was the 1984 Report of the Royal Commission on Equality in Employment (Abella 1984). This report corroborated the changed approaches to stratification, in which issues of difference were replaced in the 1960s by preoccupations with equality of opportunity. More recently, analysts have begun to emphasize the covert sources of disadvantage, produced as a result of traditional hiring and promotional practices (Agocs and Boyd 1993).

Seeking to redress the effects of systemic discrimination, the Report of the Royal Commission on Equality in Employment recommended that the government of Canada pass legislation making employment equity mandatory for employers in the public and private sectors, and that there be effective arrangements to monitor compliance and impose sanctions for failure to demonstrate good faith efforts to attain employment equity goals. In response, the Conservative government of the day introduced two initiatives in 1986: the Employment Equity Act and the Federal Contractors Program.

Within the context of the Act, visible minorities are defined as 'persons other than Aboriginal persons, who are non-Caucasian in race or non-white in colour and who so identify themselves to an employer or agree to be so identified by an employer for the purpose of the Employment Equality Act' (Employment and Immigration Canada 1989: 25). The underlying concept of this definition is race. In the terminology the choice of 'visible minority' is itself noteworthy. The term came into usage in the early 1980s. Given alternatives such as race (United States) and 'ethnic minorities' (United Kingdom, Germany, Netherlands) an interesting question is what was the reason for constructing of a new nuance. While the answer may be partly found in the identity politics already practised by Aboriginal people, another part of it may lie in the studied avoidance of the term 'race' since the 1950s. Critics charge that this avoidance, and the accompanied nuances of 'visible minorities', is also avoidance of the issue of racism (Stasiulis 1991).

Under the Employment Equity Act, 1986 (and as reaffirmed in the 1996 legislation), federally regulated businesses are required to submit annual reports indicating their employment profiles in regard to the four target groups. These target populations are visible minorities, Aboriginal peoples, women, and persons with disabilities. Self-identification categories for visible minority groups are black, Chinese, Japanese, Korean, Filipino, Indo-Pakistani, West Asian and Arab, Southeast Asian, Latin American, Indonesian, and Pacific Islander (Employment and Immigration Canada 1986). Compliance with the Act involves comparisons with a reference [to] population, usually that of the local labour market. Given this methodology and the implied requirements for geographically defined information, census data represent a potentially important source.

These legislative demands have obliged Statistics Canada to provide data on a new construct. The methodology developed for the 1981, 1986, and 1991 census data derives visible minority status from responses to census questions on birthplace, ethnic origins, mother tongue, and religion (the latter was not collected in the 1986 census). These procedures were developed in collaboration with the federal departments responsible for the Employment Equity Act. The reliance on existing census questions means that self-identification plays no role in defining 'visible minority', unlike the methodology used to collect data at the business firm level.

It is important to note that Statistics Canada has experienced considerable difficulty in measuring ethnic and cultural self-identification. In 1986, for example, a question asking persons of Aboriginal background whether they 'considered themselves to be an Aboriginal or Native person of Canada' produced a high level of 'false positive response' on the part of respondents who did not understand such terms as Aboriginal and Inuit. At this time, Statistics Canada concluded that an identity question should not be edited for consistency with other responses, since the response provided was one based on respondent opinion and self-identity rather than fact. Data from this 1986 census question were not published.

Similarly, testing after the 1986 census revealed that the Federal Public Service question, which asked respondents to identify the visible minority group to which they considered themselves to belong, produced poor-quality data when used in the 1986 census Overcoverage Survey (White 1988). In this instance, respondents reported 'immigrant', 'Quebecois', and 'senior' as being the visible minority groups to which they belonged.

For the 1991 census, questions were developed which asked respondents to report their ethnic origin while a certain subset of the population who completed the Aboriginal Peoples Survey responded to a question on Aboriginal identity. In 1996, however, the range of questions was expanded to include visible minority status, ethnic origin, and Aboriginal identity.

Conscious of the need for data on the new concept of visible minority, Statistics Canada sought to determine if a direct question on race or visible minority status should be asked in the 1991 and the 1996 censuses. During the census content consultations, data users, ethnocultural groups, and advisory bodies to Statistics Canada were asked to ponder the inclusion of a question on race, and its wording. In preparation for the 1991 and the 1996 censuses, respondents to various surveys and pretests were asked a question on race, and qualitative assessments by focus groups on these questions were also undertaken (Breedon 1988; White 1988; Statistics Canada 1994a).

The inquiry into racial differentiation of the Canadian population marked a fundamental turning point for the agency. Statistics Canada has been criticized in the past for being slow to measure social phenomena. To discuss the concepts of race, and to consider the measurement of race in a country which has frequently over-

looked its racialized history (Abele and Stasiulis 1989; Walker 1985) is remarkable. The shift occurred in the aftermath of the 1980s, which was a turbulent period in the history of Canadian nation-building. Issues of Canadian identity, multiculturalism, and the place of Quebec in a renewed federalism (Spicer 1991) captured public attention, influenced census consultations, and generated discussions of the collection of visible minority and 'Canadian' ethnic origin data (Boyd 1993a; 1996; Pryor et al. 1992). . . .

1996 Census: Direct Question on Visible Minorities

Given legislative requirements and a public that is increasingly aware of employment equity issues, race relations, and racism, the issue of including a question on race in Canada's census did not fade away. Instead, it resurfaced with the 1996 census-taking efforts. In these the past activities with respect to the 1991 census have informed the ongoing debate.

The 1991 census ethnic origin question, as previously discussed, was designed to collect information required for employment equity and multiculturalism programs. Negative public reactions to the mark-in entry 'black' by Afro-Canadian groups, who viewed it as a 'racial' term, rather than an ethnic category (White 1992), as well as increasing support for the specification of the ethnic origin 'Canadian', resulted in continued consultation and testing prior to the 1996 census.

The issue of 'Canadian' further complicated the issue of meeting visible minority data needs. 'Canadian' was the fifth-largest single-response ethnic group in the 1991 census. The practice in past censuses has been to list the ethnic groups in numerical order. If this practice were continued, the category 'Canadian' would have to be included among the list of examples of ethnic groups shown for the ethnic origin question in

1996. For example, if a mark-in question were to be developed, 'Canadian' would have been shown as the fifth mark-in entry. Or, if only write-in entries were permitted, then 'Canadian' would be the fifth group shown in the list of examples of ethnic entries.

In addition to public reaction and the potential consequences of 'Canadian' responses, another ground for change was the derivation of visible minority groups from ethnocultural questions. The decision to continue with the derivation of visible minority counts from the ethnic origin, place of birth, religion, and language questions was not without its critics. During the 1996 census consultation, the majority of data users voiced support for the testing and inclusion in the 1996 census of a direct question designed to count the country's visible minority population (Statistics Canada 1994b). The ethnic origin question, in particular, came under criticism from Canadian black groups, who expressed a strong preference for reporting their ethnic background as, for example, Haitian, Jamaican, or African Canadian. Aboriginal peoples indicated that they too wished to report a tribal or First Nation origin rather than mark the entry 'North American Indian' which had appeared in earlier censuses.

In sum, three forces underlay the decision to test a different set of ethnocultural questions in the 1996 National Census Test, fielded in November 1993: (1) the renewed interest and support for a direct question on visible minorities; (2) the need to change pre-specified categories; and (3) the requirement to include 'Canadian' in the listing of examples of ethnic groups shown on the questionnaire. The November 1993 NCT asked a series of questions on ethnic origin, Aboriginal identity, visible minority group, Status/Treaty Indian, and band/First Nation. Various language questions were also asked (first language learned, home language, official and non-official language knowledge, language used at work, and language

of schooling). Prior to the inclusion of these questions in the National Census Test extensive qualitative testing was undertaken on such topics as respondent reactions to terms, response to direct questions, and the understanding of why questions were asked.

The results of the 1993 National Census Test indicated that about 30 per cent of respondents would report 'Canadian' to the ethnic origin question (Statistics Canada 1994a). Discrepancies also existed between responses to the ethnic origin question and responses to direct questions on Aboriginal identity and visible minority group. Inspection of responses to the latter direct questions revealed that some Aboriginal and visible minority respondents provided responses that appeared to be inconsistent. That is, they reported their ethnic origin as being Canadian, English, French, or Spanish. As well, there was some reporting of 'white' by members of some designated visible minority groups.

The results of the testing undertaken prior to the 1996 census led Statistics Canada to conclude that a direct visible minority question would yield estimates of improved data quality, as compared with those [of] the ethnic origin approach (Statistics Canada 1994b). The primary rationales for including a direct visible minority question in the 1996 census were threefold: (1) the overall high quality of responses to the visible minority question; (2) a low level of non-response and few nonsense or backlash responses (Renaud 1994b; 1994b); and (3) the legislated requirement to provide data on visible minorities.

During the interval between the testing of the 1996 census question in 1993 and the date of the census (14 May 1996), several factors intervened which brought the issue of employment equity and the 1996 census question under close scrutiny. One was the election in Ontario of a government which adopted as one of its major election issues the elimination of *provincial* employment equity legislation. Another was a concern regarding the continuation of high immigration levels during a time of poor economic performance and the concentration of certain groups in major urban centres.

The public media reaction was swift once the 1996 census questions were published in [the] *Canada Gazette* on 22 August 1995 (Mitchell 1995). Criticism of the question focused on the usefulness of the federal employment equity legislation. Certain commentators felt such a census question was based on outmoded ideas of race and had the potential to be socially divisive (Gardner 1995; Loney 1995). It should also be noted that during this period social tensions were heightened by such issues as a need for social cohesion and the apparent lack of common vision for the country as it faced the outcome of the 30 October 1995 referendum in Quebec.

Media reaction therefore focused on three topics: (1) the need for data showing various ethnic and visible minority groups; (2) the aims of employment equity and multiculturalism legislation; and (3) the perception of some Canadians that identification of groups as being other than 'Canadian' contributed to a lack of social cohesion and national identity. In addition, certain commentators questioned the premise of economically based racial discrimination (Greenfield 1996), though this point of view was questioned by Pendakur and Pendakur (1996). In addition to these themes, reaction also focused on question content. Some commentators disagreed with the categories and examples shown on the questionnaire. The inclusion of some groups and not others was criticized (Gwyn 1996). The category 'white' was also seen by some as being unacceptable (Gunter 1996).

In response, members of the visible minority community (Cardozo 1996), the ethnic media (Editorial, *Share* 1996), as well as journalists writing for the major daily papers (Editorial, *Edmonton Journal* 1995) provided support for the questions, for employment equity legislation,

and subsequent collection of data by the 1996 census. Thus the debate on the appropriateness of the census question, the usefulness of the legislation and the deeper question of the divisions—real or apparent—in Canadian society, had become intense well before the 14 May 1996 Census Day.

In the year following the 1996 census, media and public concern and confusion regarding the potential impacts of a direct question on race had not abated. A private member's motion (M-277) introduced by the Reform Party member for Beaver River, Debra Grey, was discussed in Parliament on 26 November 1996. This motion proposed that the government return to the word 'Canadian' in questions of ethnic origin in the Canadian census (Hansard, 26 November 1996). In fact, the 'Canadian' category was included in the list of examples of ethnic groups shown on the 1996 census form. Comments accompanying the motion indicate that it was the omission of 'Canadian' from the visible minority question that was of concern. Grey's comments, as well as those made by other Members of Parliament in subsequent discussions on Motion M-277, indicate considerable confusion between the two questions (ethnic origin and visible minority). Legislative rationales for asking a question on the visible minority population appear either to have been poorly understood or judged to be offensive. Moreover, the topic of Canadian unity and the importance of being able to classify oneself as Canadian were themes addressed both by Grey and by others speaking to the motion.

Summary: Racial Discourse

Motion M-277 continues the themes found throughout the late 1980s and early 1990s in the larger public arena. What is clear is the considerable lack of consensus regarding the Canadian racialized identities in a public increasingly concerned about what Canada is and what it, as a nation, will become. In fact, general dismay regarding the future of the Canadian state, following the 1995 Quebec referendum, the pressures of social adaptation required by high levels of immigration, and a troubling economic situation in the early 1990s, combined to focus attention on the means of achieving a sense of pan-Canadian identity in a context of policies, viewed as competing, with multiculturalism, employment equity, and Aboriginal rights. To see Canadian society as being racially constructed was antithetical to the attributes of many people. To have the racialized and ethnic character of the country measured in a national census reinforces stereotypes for some while for others this procedure confirms the structure of the Canadian social fabric.

Thus, in the 130 years since Confederation (1867) the use of the term 'race' and the collection of 'race' data have been erratic and changing. Asking a question on race in the Canadian census is an exercise that goes beyond measurement issues. The questions asked between 1901 and 1941 rested on prevailing race relations and models of nation-building and incorporation. Recent initiatives to return to a question on 'race' also incorporate models of nation-building, integration, and race relations although all the parameters of all three have greatly changed since the first half of the century.

Chapter 7

'Playing the Aboriginal Card': Race or Rights?

Augie Fleras

Introduction: Framing Race

The media work in mystifying ways. Instead of telling us what to think, media messages are more inclined to tell us what to think about. The framing of issues is critical to this information processing dynamic. By making issues both less complex yet more compelling, frames encourage a preferred reading, mainly by drawing attention to some aspects of reality as necessary, normal, or superior, while other aspects are dismissed or demonized. The consequences are not inconsequential. How issues are framed will influence their debate in public discourse, patterns of public response, and proposed solutions. For example, if racism is framed as a personal problem reflecting prejudicial attitudes, solutions will emphasize changing individual mindsets through education or exposure; if racism is framed as a structural or systemic problem, endorsed instead are institutional changes through the removal of discriminatory barriers.

Clearly, then, media frames are critical to our understanding of reality. In the absence of personal experiences about the world out there, Canadians increasingly rely on news media as a preliminary and primary source of information (Fleras 2003). Nowhere is this more evident than in the framing of Aboriginal politics around either 'race' or 'rights'. For some, Aboriginal politics are about advancing Aboriginal rights; for others, references to Aboriginal rights are little more than a smokescreen for race-based privileges. A conflict of interest is evident: to one side are those who endorse Aboriginal peoples' rights as inherent and inalienable; to the other side are those who oppose the principle and assertion of Aboriginal rights as race-based and racist. Not surprisingly, critics of the critics accuse the latter of race card politics by framing Aboriginal rights as reverse racism. To put this argument to the test, this paper deconstructs the concept of playing the race card, provides an example of how the race card is played out in allocating fishing quotas, and explores the implications of framing Aboriginal politics as race rather than rights.

Invoking the Race Card: A Conceptualization

We've heard the expression countless times, yet few can clearly articulate the meaning of 'playing the race card'. Analogies with select card games might be useful, including bridge in which playing a trump card is critical to the outcome. Trumps are all about securing an advantage over your opponent; playing a trump card renders a non-trump hand virtually useless for trick-taking purposes. Of course, the analogy between cards and reality can only be taken so far. In contract or duplicate bridge, for example, there is a bidding war to determine whose trumps prevail; opponents' trump cards are usually drawn as quickly as possible to weaken the hand; higher trump cards can trump those of lower values, and trump cards can only be played when conventional sequences have exhausted the suit cards. Still, the analogy provides a useful metaphor for navigating our way through the tricky thickets of social reality. Consider some examples of playing (up) the race card:

- A *Survivor* series that divided the cast into race-based teams was accused of playing the race card in hopes of bolstering ratings (Eracism 2006).
- The accusation of playing the race card is levelled at black separatists whose Afrocentrism exploits racial pride to create a bitterly divided society (Collier and Horowitz 2004).
- Democrats are accused of playing the race card as a wedge issue by accusing Republicans of ignoring race and race relations in rehabilitating post-Katrina New Orleans. A racial divide between the haves and the have-nots is reflected in who is getting what in relief (Hinton 2007).
- New Zealand opposition leaders have demanded an end to special funding for Indigenous Maori. Proposed instead is funding on the basis of merit rather than race or political correctness. For critics, any concession to Indigenous peoples is race-based and racist; for counter critics, the critics themselves are criticized for playing the race card from the bottom of the deck.
- Criminal Code changes in 1996 directed judges to incorporate the special circumstances of Aboriginal peoples. In 1999, the Supreme Court ruled that judges must consider alternatives to prison when sentencing Aboriginal offenders (80 per cent of Saskatchewan prison space is occupied by Aboriginal peoples who constitute 10 per cent of the province's population). Those opposed

to the concept of Aboriginal sentencing criticize the concession as a kind of 'get out of jail race card'.

Is there a common denominator that connects and reinforces? Generally speaking, it would appear playing the race card refers to a manipulative process whereby the issue of race or racism is deliberately—but unnecessarily or even falsely—inserted into debate in order to inflame, accuse, confuse, deflect, or silence. By focusing almost exclusively on the racial dimension instead of other factors, or as part of the larger context, the race card is invoked as a smokescreen—an observation espoused by Booker T. Washington who said:

> There is a class of coloured people who make a business of keeping the troubles, the wrongs, and the hardships of the Negro race before the public. Having learned that they are able to make a living out of their troubles, they have grown into the settled habit of advertising their wrongs—partly because they want sympathy, and partly because it pays. Some of these people do not want the Negro to lose his grievances, because they do not want to lose their jobs. (in Buchanan 2001)

Playing up the race card promotes personal agendas or political advantages. A person may accuse another of being a racist to shut down debate or deflect from related issues. Playing the race card can also entail the use of racial prejudices for political gain, in part by playing upon racist fears to frighten the public (Williams 2002). For example, according to the BBC News (2001), the expression was first coined in the UK during the 1960s when a Conservative candidate in a by-election used the slogan 'If you want a nigger neighbour—vote Labour.' He won the seat. Not surprisingly, the effectiveness of playing up the race card reflects its ability to elicit powerful emotional responses, from hatred to fear.

Consider how references to race conjure up widely detested images associated with the Ku Klux Klan or South Africa's apartheid. In short, reference to race resonates with this negativity, including images of actions or inactions that capitalize on white guilt to drive the dynamics (Collier and Horowitz 2004).

Playing a race card is highly political (Doane 2006). Many whites believe that racialized minorities inflate charges of racism in situations where the charge is inappropriate—thus playing up the race card to gain sympathy, extract concessions, or detract from their own shortcomings (see Wise 2006). According to this perception, minorities manipulate race as a crutch to camouflage their inadequacies, while heaping guilt on whites for their lack of action. Yet two can play with the same deck of cards. Minorities believe that whites are no less guilty of playing the race card by denying realities of race and racism. Insofar as racism is a real and persistent presence in their lives, yet dismissed by whites, its denial card constitutes the trump card that ensures a 'white-o-centric' status quo, according to anti-racist educator Tim Wise:

> Precisely because white denial has long trumped claims of racism, people of colour tend to under-report their experiences with racial bias, rather than exaggerate them. Again, when it comes to playing the race card, it is more accurate to say that whites are the dealers with the loaded decks, shooting down any evidence of racism as little more than the fantasies of unhinged blacks, unwilling to take personal responsibility for their own problems in life. (Wise 2006: 4)

In short, both the powerful and powerless can play the race card. The privileged play up the race card by accusing minorities of deliberate overaction to racism. Conversely, the raced may accuse whites of playing down the race card by deliberately underplaying the realities of racism.

For one, playing up the race card secures an existing advantage; for the other, it's to challenge an unequal status quo.

Aboriginal Peoples' Politics: Race or Rights?

Aboriginal peoples' politics have leapt to the forefront of Canada's constitutional debate. Two mutually opposed sides can be isolated—at least for purposes of analysis (Maaka and Fleras 2005): to one side are the assimilationists who believe Aboriginal peoples must modernize (i.e., become more like us) if they hope to prosper (Flanagan 2000; Fiss 2004); to the other side are the autonomists who argue that Aboriginal peoples must embrace self-determining autonomy (i.e., become less like us) to secure survival and prosperity (Alfred 2005; Turner 2006). The assimilationists take a dim view of Aboriginal rights, preferring to see them as irrelevant, illiberal (anti-meritocratic), repressive, or racist. By contrast, autonomists uphold the legitimacy of Aboriginal rights as constitutionally grounded or treaty-based rather than a race privilege. A conflict of interest is discernible: there are those who believe that any preferential treatment because of race is racist versus those who frame the primacy of Aboriginal claims as rooted in rights, arguing that individuals who claim race-based rights are themselves racist by stacking the deck to frighten, confuse, or intimidate.

Canada introduced an Aboriginal Fishing Strategy in 1992 in response to the 1990 Supreme Court's *Sparrow* decision which established an Aboriginal's right to fish for food and for ceremonial purposes (Dolha 2006). Although *Sparrow* did not deal specifically with Aboriginal commercial fishing rights, the federal government expanded Aboriginal peoples' role in the fisheries without depleting stocks in the process or disrupting a stable environment for resource sharing. Under the AFS, the Department of Fisheries and Oceans began a buyback of commercial fishing licences; 75 were repatriated, then mothballed to offset the Aboriginal annual allocation of 800,000 fish. But critics are vehemently opposed to what they call a race-based commercial fishery. In establishing an Aboriginal-only commercial fishery, the AFS is criticized for creating two classes of BC fishers based primarily on bloodlines (*National Post* 2004; Carpay 2007). Fishery was opened to three Aboriginal bands during special periods when only they could fish, prompting non-Natives to argue that stocks were prematurely depleted. Although the program was shut down in 2004 by provincial courts on the grounds that it constituted a government-sponsored racism that privileged race, the BC Supreme Court overturned the ruling, arguing that the good intentions of the AFS do not contravene the Charter of Rights and Freedoms. To further sow confusion, while Prime Minister Stephen Harper has reiterated his intent to abolish so-called race-based and racially divided fisheries on the West Coast, the Supreme Court of Canada recently upheld the constitutional validity of the 1992 pilot program (Carpay 2008).

Conclusion: Revoking the Race Card

Race remains a paradox. Race once mattered in that people were routinely pigeonholed into fixed and bounded categories that justified their exclusion or exploitation. That race continues to matter as explanation, justification, or vilification is an issue of grave concern. Yet another paradox: many claim to be victims of racism, yet no one openly expresses or defends racist bigotry. How do we account for this world of racism without racists? Are people lying? Is racism so broadly defined that everything is racism? Are people playing the race card to distract, shift blame, or as a ploy for advantage? Is playing the race card inevitable in a world of subtle and polite bias so that it's a virtue to assume the worst when confronting ambiguous situations (Ford 2008)?

To associate Canada's Aboriginal peoples with playing up the race card is not without consequences. First, a race-card discourse reduces the status of Aboriginal/Indigenous peoples to the level of racial minorities, with entitlements consistent with normal citizenship. But Aboriginal peoples do not see themselves as racialized citizens whose concerns revolve around 'fitting in' by way of institutional integration. Rather, they define themselves as peoples or nations who have been forcibly incorporated into someone else's system. Aboriginal peoples claim they are political communities who are sovereign in their own right, while sharing the sovereignty of Canada through multiple and overlapping jurisdictions. By virtue of their original occupation and political rights, Aboriginal peoples possess a special (nation-to-nation) relationship with the Crown, together with a corresponding set of entitlements (rights) that flow from this relationship.

Second, equating Aboriginality with race also compromises their rights as nations within Canada (Fleras and Elliott 1992). In playing up the race card to criticize Aboriginal politics, its effectiveness resides in driving hidden agendas while framing issues in ways that reflect and reinforce vested interests. Governments would prefer to frame Aboriginal peoples as a problem people with needs that can be solved by working within the system. But Aboriginal peoples do not see themselves as a problem for solution, but as people with rights that are both collective and inherent, including the right to Aboriginal models of self-determining autonomy over land, identity, and political voice that has never been extinguished. Clearly, then, the discourse of rights must supersede that of race in any debate over constitutional change (Maaka and Fleras 2005). And only by trumping race by playing the *rights* card is there much likelihood of a post-colonial social contract between Aboriginal peoples and Canada based on the principles of power sharing, partnership, and participation.

Chapter 8

Where Race Does Not Matter: The New Spirit of Modernity

Cecil Foster

. . . Indeed, at a cursory glance, Canadians are doing all the things that the men and women of old had made taboo in the quest for a patriotism and a nationalism that were strong, healthy, and durable. Most taboo of all is that old proscription that there should be a primacy of civilization, especially one that claims to be both European and Christian, or even African and Christian. Good Christians like [Jan] Smuts and [Marcus] Garvey would have been mortified by what civilization has come to—and in Canada, of all places. Just a generation ago, multi-ethnicity and multiculturalism were only dreams. But one man's dream is often another's nightmare. Where one person sees a coming delight and a new life, another imagines only fear and death.

Such was the fear of the longest-serving prime minister of Canada, a man who said that his service to his people would have been in vain if he had overseen anything other than the preservation of a white man's country. Prime Minister William Lyon Mackenzie King was a good friend and associate of Smuts's, and the two men, intent on achieving the same goals, bound their countries in a special relationship. Their dream was shared by the president of the United States, Woodrow Wilson, a man who also aimed to save humanity from its own imagining and warlike tendencies.

With Smuts at his side at the International Peace Conference in 1919, Wilson promoted the League of Nations as the pinnacle of human achievement. With Smuts at his side at the various imperial conferences of the British Empire, King fashioned a special relationship between the Confederation of Canada and the Union of South Africa. Together, the three men hoped to maintain an international order based on dividing the world into superior and inferior groups. Wilson, we must recall, was the president who effectively reintroduced race officially into the American nation-state by instituting segregationist policies, taking people with black skin out of the modern nation-state. This was particularly the case when he allowed segregation to occur in federal institutions, especially the post office. In that one act, he reversed efforts by the federal government that had been ongoing since the creation of the United States, through the expansion of the Louisiana Purchase and the turmoil of the American Civil War, to champion the rights of African Americans. In the world of Smuts, King, and Wilson, blacks were relegated to second-class status.

These men were products of their times and their history. Fortunately, time has moved on. We can pass judgment on them, but we must do so in the knowledge that soon others will pass judgment on us. History does not end, even if, in moving on, it is always passing judgment on the past.

Today, the nightmares so feared by these three international statesmen are part of the reality of living in the modern world. Black skin is fast losing its relevance as a means of setting limits on ambitions and citizenship. Are we approaching the day Martin Luther King, Jr, spoke of almost a half-century ago when he predicted that 'the sons of former slaves and the sons of former slave owners will be able to sit down together at the table of brotherhood'? Are we at last nearing a time when boys and girls will be 'judged not by the colour of their skin but by the content of their character'? Is this the reality we can now offer to young black boys and girls not only in Montgomery, Atlanta, Buxton, and Johannesburg but also in Toronto, Montreal, Calgary, Halifax, and Sudbury?

. . . [W]e now have the opportunity to produce such times. This would allow what is euphemistically still called Western civilization to enter into a new millennium, or a new spirit of modenity, *an era in which, for the first time in the modern human experience, race does not matter*. In this new era, the intentions that precede the actions in any social relationship will be for a good that is raceless. If our actions follow our thoughts, this new good will be upon us, or at least we will have made our best efforts to bring it about.

The beginnings of this new era can be seen in the multicultural composition of Canada, and in the ease with which young Canadians accept the multicultural nature of their state and their citizenship. It can be seen in England, where, according to the census, more communities are becoming predominantly black. It can be seen in South Africa, where power has shifted, with seemingly few hiccups, from white hands to black. It can be seen in the southern United States, where a growing number of police chiefs, governors, and other elected officials are black. And it can be seen in popular culture the world over, where it is now acceptable for a black man to appear as God in the movies, for black actors to carry off top awards, and for much of modern music to be drawn from black culture.

Most of all, it can be seen in what Western civilization is coming to mean: a way of life that draws on the strengths of people from all parts of the world. Indeed, having dispensed with using race as a method for national development, we have also dropped from favour the idea of dividing humanity into separate civilizations, into worlds that are ranked from first through third. Now we know that countries once considered to be of one world can have regions within them from different and contradictory worlds. There is unity in diversity. The boundaries between our thoughts and our actions have been fused. Now we must make sure that the potential in this moment comes forth.

But for many, this lived experience was not supposed to be. (So much for purposefulness when devised by human minds!) Thankfully, the world marched to its own beat and, over time, followed its own designs. Indeed, in the long-run everything turned out for the good. But at the beginning of modernity, blacks were intentionally excluded from the affairs of state. Their skin declared to others first their biological and then their cultural inferiority. They had no official place, no standing, no privileges in the modern state or in international affairs. Modernity worked out of European and Christian civilizations. Its goal was to create an environment to allow the greatest in human achievements. Society, it was believed, would provide individuals with a culture that would, in due course, civilize them, turning them almost into gods, but for the fact that unlike gods they would die. The attainment of citizenship in these cultures marked the achievement of the highest levels of human perfection. Hence, citizens became the most endowed and privileged individuals. This we see in the rise of jingoism, patriotism, and nationalism. Citizenship was predicated predominantly on separation. Exclusion was based, in the main, on the colour of the skin, ethnicity, or culture. The nation-state was the finishing school for the elites of humanity, those who would become citizens of a white and European-style nation-state. Looking back, we can now claim with a morality borne out by history that such attempts to exclude specific groups from the nation-state were evil and should not be continued in the present or carried forward into the future.

Black-skinned people were considered to be less than human, or at least less fully realized than those perfected beings of the higher-achieving civilizations, cultures, and nation-states. They were held as chattel slaves and then in apprenticeship and tutelage until the white elites of the world deemed them civilized enough to govern themselves. Theirs was a culture marked by permanent alienation, a culture where the lived experience was always lagging behind the perfection attained when humans reach their full potential. And those who argued against modernity's dominant model were often themselves ostracized and excluded from society.

Other non-European groups, according to the dominant Western view, would naturally make their own attempts at state formation. But because they were perceived as inferior in thoughts and actions to Europeans, they would, naturally, apply inferior structures and methods, have inferior goals, and experience poor-quality results. Europeans would produce the gem of a superior Western civilization. This was the natural order of the world, the foundation on which long-lasting social and ethical relations would be based. At the heart of this thinking was always *race*, which was so much more than the colour of the skin, the shape of nose, the curl of the hair, or the fullness of the lips. Even when physically free, blacks and other visible and racialized minorities were to be excluded from the prototypical state and from involvement in all the modern institutions and agencies. This was the thinking behind segregation in the United States, apartheid in South Africa, reservations and ethnic homelands in Canada, and the expulsions of criminals and the mentally and physically disabled from states around the world.

But today, those who were once excluded are taking up leading roles in institutions, agencies, and states that were once intended exclusively for a different people. This is not to suggest that there is no longer any racism, or that there is an equitable distribution of blacks and other minorities within national institutions or in business. But the attitude toward blacks and other minorities and their place in society has changed. As long as the intentions remain good, positive actions will follow, even if slowly. The journey is incremental: a slow forward pass rather than a quick dash to the finish line. What's important is that there is no official turning back to reclaim and reconstitute ideals that are now discredited. New social relationships are becoming set and, in many cases, have been fully accepted by the elites of society. The ideological turn has already happened, and that is the hardest part to achieve. We must feed the spirit of a new time and seize its goodness.

In the current social climate, there are a few cases where racial discrimination and profiling are still viewed as ethically acceptable, although it is usually for those who are not considered part of the nation-state. We see this, for example, with the racial profiling the United States has engaged in to combat terrorism, when individuals who show up at airports are required to prove their citizenship and automatic right of (re)entry. Why is racism practised in the breach rather than as the norm? And does this mean that the modern state has been built on a shifting foundation?

It has not been easy to overcome racism in Canada or internationally. And the debates over racial profiling, black youth gangs, and the place in the social hierarchy of immigrants from predominantly black countries prove that in some areas the struggle still continues. There is an ocular deficit that is emblematic of the alienation that still exists in Canada. In other words, what we see—in terms of the numbers of visible minorities in various government institutions and agencies and in business in general—is very different from what the ideal would suggest. It is the difference between the dream of full citizenship and the current realities of the difficulty attaining it. The deficit can be a measurement of hope or of despair, of what is achievable but is viewed as very unlikely. It is a deficit that, we hope, gets smaller every day.

The unreconciled visions of Canada, where the theory promises one thing and the lived reality is very different, are generational. One look at the top echelons of government and business reveals them still to be disproportionately white. But it also reveals that our leaders are aging. Soon, they will need to be replaced, and then Canada will have a chance to reconcile theory and practice by filling the vacated positions according to new rules and regulations. The future seems to point toward a world in which black skin colour will have no bearing on how we see ourselves constitutively, as nations or citizens. In the absence of full sight and knowledge, we operate in the spirit of hope.

But do these developments mean that blackness now has no real social or ethical purpose? Do they mean that we are marching inevitably toward a new modernity? . . . [A]s a point of pride, there should always be meaning to having black skin. This meaning has always been a hidden element of modernity, and it is caught in much of the mythology of Western civilization—including the mythology captured in the dreams of Martin Luther King, Jr, and others like him. Black skin is a mark from the gods, a reminder that we are all human and that none of us, black or white, should ever forget our humanity. We must not forget how easy it is for some groups of people to declare themselves morally and ethically superior. We must not forget how easy it is to find reasons to enslave others, whether physically or mentally.

People with black skin must stand as a reminder that we are all the sons and daughters of slaves, and that none of us is a descendant of gods. They will continue to carry this responsibility—which some may call a burden, but I view as an issue of pride and self-consciousness—into the future. We are all human. On this score, the body never lies. Like the state, it always dies. And we see the face of humanity in all the places and positions of the world, even in locations where some were not supposed to be but have claimed triumphantly. They have defeated race by lifting up hope and faith.

* * *

Questions

1. What is meant by the expression 'race is a social construction and not a biological reality'?
2. What is meant by the expression 'the concept of race represents an explanatory framework, a key variable in influencing behaviour, a discourse in defence of ideology, and a rationalization for justifying actions'? Provide an example of each.
3. Demonstrate how the legal system in Canada was actively complicit in reinforcing racism and racial discrimination in Canada.
4. Demonstrate how the articles by both Woodsworth and Gibbon reflected a shift in race thinking, that is, from race as an exclusive explanatory framework to more complex notions for explaining patterns of human difference and behaviour.
5. Explain how asking race questions on Canada's national census went beyond a simple enumeration process, but said a lot about people's perceptions of race and race relations and their relationship to Canada's national identity and nation-building.
6. What is meant by the concept of 'playing the race card'? Demonstrate your knowledge of the concept by reference to the politics of Aboriginal fishing allocation in British Columbia.
7. Why does Cecil Foster believe that race is losing its relevance in Canada? Do you agree or disagree with his assessment?

Websites

African Canadian Legal Clinic: http://www.aclc.net
Canadian Heritage: http://www.pch.gc.ca
National Anti-racism Council of Canada: http://www.narcc.ca

Suggested Readings

Backhouse, Constance. 1999. *Colour-coded: A Legal History of Racism in Canada 1900–1950* (Toronto: University of Toronto Press for The Osgoode Society for Canadian Legal History).
Brace, C. Loring. 2005. *'Race' Is a Four-letter Word* (New York: Oxford University Press).
Mills, Charles W. 1997. *The Racial Contract* (Ithaca, NY: Cornell University Press).
Omi, M., and H. Winant. 1994. *Racial Formation in the United States: From the 1960s to the 1990s*, 2nd edn (New York: Routledge).
Tator, Carol, and Frances Henry. 2006. *Racial Profiling in Canada* (Toronto: University of Toronto Press).
Thobani, Sunera. 2007. *Exalted Subjects* (Toronto: University of Toronto Press).
Walker, James St. G. 1997. *'Race', Rights and the Law in the Supreme Court of Canada* (Waterloo, ON: Wilfrid Laurier University Press for The Osgoode Society for Canadian Legal History).

Systemic Racism: Theorizing Racism as Structural Exclusion

Explicit references to race or race-based thinking in Canada shift and begin to focus on human rights, and eventually to a structural analysis of social exclusion. This shift is officially marked in 1984 with the publication of the Abella Report on employment equity. While Canadian human rights legislation focused exclusively on the individual's intent to discriminate, Canada's Multiculturalism Policy officially encouraged tolerance by respecting differences. Canada's implicit approach to race embedded in the Multiculturalism Act is seen as a strategy that focuses more on public relations than addressing social inequality (Bannerji 2000; Dua and Robertson 1999). The federal employment equity legislation was established in response to community pressure to address systemic patterns of exclusion.

In modern liberal societies, when the rhetoric calls for a universal claim to 'human rights', what is denied are systemic, structural ways groups of people are excluded from society's rights and resources. Canadian society continues to socially construct groups of people as the 'other' and subsequently deserving of a particular social location in this nation. Systemic racism has been defined as the result of supposedly neutral organizational policies and procedures that have a differential impact on groups of people (Henry 1995; Das Gupta 1996). It can also be defined as racial biases so deeply embedded within institutional structures, principles, and processes that their controlling power often goes undetected except as consequences or effects. To gain an understanding of how systemic racism is articulated in institutions and society in general, one must examine the patterns and/or 'common sense' understanding of lived experiences, and must also interrogate certain silences in society.

Part II begins with the Introduction to *The Politics of Community Services*, the pioneering research by Roxana Ng on the systemic ways 'immigrant women' are produced in the Canadian labour market. Through macro social processes such as immigration policies, which are in turn reinforced by policies of labour-market recruitment, immigrant women are socially constructed to occupy the lower end of the occupational hierarchy. Using the method of an institutional ethnography, Roxana Ng examines the production and reproduction of immigrant women in the Canadian class system. This capitalist economy further stratifies women by ethnicity and race. Ng illustrates how legal categories such as the 'sponsored' category in Canadian immigration policies, employer–client relations in a non-profit community agency, and class, gender, and ethnic fragmentation in the Canadian labour market organize social processes that exert the hegemony of the dominant classes. In this way Ng's analysis illuminates the connection between immigration policies and documentary demands in institutions. This detailed examination illustrates how 'class rule is accomplished as an ongoing practice in people's activities in the everyday world . . .' (Ng 1988: 14).

The systemic nature of racism is explored further by Daiva Stasiulis's important article, 'Theorizing Connections: Gender, Race, Ethnicity, and Class'. Stasiulis analyzes debates that give a priori privilege to class divisions and/or gender divisions over race divisions and racism. She reviews black feminist analyses that reveal the relationship of the family, state, production, and reproduction to class interests, gender divisions, and white supremacist logic. Rather than being treated as 'add-ons' or as simple references to axes of domination, gender, race, and class need to be seen as different sites of power, exploitation, and oppression within the larger context of global and national economic and political realities. Only such an integrated analysis, Stasiulis concludes, can help us 'develop a politics of social transformation that truly moves beyond the fragments' (1990: 295).

The third article in Part II is taken from the seminal work by Frances Henry et al., *The Colour of Democracy: Racism in Canadian Society*. The authors provide an explanation for what they describe as 'the racist attitudes and behaviours of individuals, the maintenance of racist policies and practices in Canadian institutions, and the promulgation of racist doctrines and laws by the state' (2000: 15). Systemic racism in Canada is legitimized by the existence of 'democratic racism', the coexistence of liberal beliefs in freedom and equality, and the continued 'marginalization, exclusion, and domination of people of colour in Canadian society' (2000: 16). Democratic racism also explains the hostility in Canadian society that greets policies and practices that could ameliorate this social inequality. As a result, the authors conclude, there is a moral tension between universal principles and values of social justice, and the continued marginalization and exploitation of racialized Canadian citizens.

Finally, in 'Geopolitics, Culture Clash, and Gender after September 11', Sherene Razack tackles how racism is articulated and legitimized after the attacks on the World Trade Center and Pentagon on September 11, 2001. She analyzes how the discourse of racism is gendered when the grounds of gender equality are used to defend and legitimize the US bid for empire. An analysis of how 'culture' is taken up, then combined with 'a disturbing spatializing of morality' (2005: 15), reveals assumptions of Western superiority and the motivation of empire disguised as a 'clash of civilizations'. Razack calls for an understanding of historical contexts, and concludes by calling on women in the West to 'refuse to come into being as subjects against women constituted as culturally different' (2005: 28).

In summary, all four articles in Part II examine the systemic, structural articulations of the Canadian state, popular culture, various processes of knowledge production, and power dynamics that work to signify race. They also analyze the material and symbolic consequences of such signification, and suggest ways to establish anti-racist theorizations and practice to resist these 'taken-for-granted-as-natural' social practices.

Chapter 9

Immigrant Women, Community Work, and Class Relations

Roxana Ng

Introduction

When I began this study in 1980, it was to be an investigation of immigrant women in the paid labour force. Specifically, I wanted to investigate *how* immigrant women were organized into the positions they occupied in the labour market hierarchy (cf. Boyd 1975; 1986; Arnopoulos 1979; Jenke and Yaron 1979). It ended as an analysis of the internal transformation of a community employment agency for immigrant women. As well, through observing the counsellors' daily work of job counselling and placement, I came to see how 'immigrant women' were *produced* as a labour market category. In other words, I saw how class relations were reproduced in the ordinary activities of daily life. Thus, it can be said that this [study] captures a moment in the production and reproduction of class in Canadian society.

After finishing a study on immigrant housewives in 1980 (Ng and Ramirez 1981), I decided to conduct a parallel study on women's situations in the labour force. The employment agency recommended to me, by a number of activists in the immigrant community, was a group which was successful in helping women to find employment and in securing government funding at a time when overall government spending on community groups had been reduced.

The employment agency was a voluntary nonprofit organization, registered under the Incorporation Act, which provided job counselling and placement services for non-English-speaking and black women. It was established by activists in the immigrant community of a metropolitan city in Ontario, who were dissatisfied with existing services by other organizations. They rallied community support, and lobbied the state to provide funding to set up the agency, which had a clear advocacy role. That is, the agency claimed to work in the interest of immigrant women and help them overcome barriers in the labour market. In so doing, members of the agency also intended to improve the overall status of immigrant women in the labour force.

At the time of my research, the employment agency was funded through the Outreach Program of the federal Department of Employment and Immigration (EIC). By examining the work process of the agency in terms of state and labour market relations, I discovered that the agency's operation underwent certain transformations from its inception, so that it came to function on behalf of the state apparatus in organizing and producing immigrant women as a distinctive kind of labour, as 'commodities', in the Canadian labour market.

As a result of its funding arrangement, the employment agency now entered into a subcontractual relationship with the state. The funding protocol was such that the agency had to produce a 'product' for the state in return for funding. The nature and parameter of this 'product' was defined by a legal contract, signed by the board of directors, who were legally accountable to the state and 'the public' for the agency's financial welfare. As such, they became the internal representatives of the state within the agency.

This 'product' was given visibility and definition through an elaborate accounting system which was to be executed by the agency staff. The requirements of the funding program, as well as the expanded capacity of the agency, led to an internal fragmentation of the work process within the agency itself. This in turn led to certain tensions and contradictions inside the agency: tension between the board and the staff; tension between the 'paperwork' and services to clients (immigrant women).

The 'product' for which state funding was remunerated was defined not so much in terms of advocacy as in terms of services to *both* clients and employers, the buyers of the labour of immigrant women. The placement of women in job openings, therefore, progressively became a major consideration. In order for the agency to place women in jobs (i.e., as the agency entered into labour market relations with employers), good relations with employers became paramount for the agency to secure a continual supply of job orders. This, to a certain extent, undermined the advocacy capacity of the agency, so that the work of the agency came to take on a contradictory character vis-à-vis immigrant women. In effect, the successful placement of clients depended upon conformity to employers' requirements for labour. In this way, the requirements for certain kinds of experiences and skills, the 'quality' and 'personality' of the clients, came to dominate the selection and matching process of immigrant women in relation to job openings. In the job counselling and placement process, then, what we will see is the production of immigrant women as 'commodities' for employers, the buyers of these commodities. This process was partially accomplished through documents, which served to delineate and define the characteristics of these 'commodities' specified by the 'buyers'.

In this way, the counselling and placement process was a moment in organizing the class locations of immigrant women in the Canadian social structure. The work of employment counsellors in 'matching' immigrant women to available job openings, based on their marketable skills, work experiences, and the requirements of employers, was part of the process whereby a labour market stratified by gender and ethnicity was maintained and reproduced in a capitalist economy. Thus, the agency did not only organize, but actually helped rationalize, labour market processes on behalf of the state.

As I conducted fieldwork there, the tensions and contradictions which underlay the work processes of the agency became visible. After I had spent a certain period of time at the agency, it was difficult not to notice the frustration and exhaustion experienced by employment counsellors in their work. For example, while the agency's goal was to place immigrant women in the best possible job openings with some degree of upward mobility, a consistent feature was that clients of the agency ended up in minimum wage, assembly-line jobs or as restaurant and domestic help. Unless a client had a high level of command of English and officially recognized educational credentials, it was almost impossible to enrol her in a skill-upgrading or job-training program. In this regard, attempting to obtain government subsidies for clients, who were mostly 'sponsored immigrants'. . . , to take basic English language training was a constant struggle between the counsellors and Employment and Immigration personnel.

Although funding from the Outreach program had enabled the agency to expand its services, the agency also experienced a concomitant increase in client intake because of increasing demand. On the day-to-day level, there was a persistent tension between the provision of services to clients, and the rising demand for producing documentary materials, from time sheets recording the counsellors' working hours to statistical and case records on clients, not to mention bookkeeping and other financial records.

When the workload became impossible to manage, one way of coping, for the counsellors, was to close the agency's door for a day or an afternoon and refuse to admit clients. Occasionally, instead of giving clients extended counselling sessions, the counsellor would make a placement as quickly as possible. When, initially, the counsellor had attempted to act as an advocate for her clients, as time went on, she began to adopt an 'objective' and non-committal stance in client–employer disputes so as not to offend employers. In her daily work, the counsellor constantly had to strike a balance between her role as an advocate and her relationship with government officials and employers on whom the agency depended for funding and for a continual supply of job orders.

In terms of its structure, there was increasing animosity between board and staff members over decision-making affecting the operation of the agency. The agency was caught in the dilemma of striving toward a more or less egalitarian mode of operation and an emerging hierarchy resulting from the incorporation and funding procedures. The various funding crises had created and deepened the division between paid staff and volunteers in their role as board members, who had previously worked co-operatively to further the well-being of the agency. The tensions underpinning these changes were experienced by the agency as a series of never-ending crises, which the staff, as well as the board, had to deal with on a continual basis.

＋ This [study] is an investigation into the way in which the employment agency was organized by state and labour market processes so that its services came to have this contradictory character vis-à-vis the interest of immigrant women. In so doing, it illuminates how class rule is accomplished as an ongoing practice in people's activities in the everyday world: as people go about looking for work and as they go about doing their jobs. Through this analysis, we see that class is not merely a theoretical category; nor can it be reduced to a set of occupational and economic indicators. It is a *process* which is enacted and re-enacted by people's daily activities in securing their livelihood.

The remainder of this chapter will discuss the usage of the term 'immigrant women' and the theoretical and methodological procedures employed for the study. . . .

The Social Construction of Immigrant Women

Technically, the term 'immigrant women' refers to women who are landed immigrants in Canada. Using this definition, many researchers found that these women tended to concentrate at the top and bottom of the occupational hierarchy, either in skilled professional jobs or in non-skilled and dead-end positions (e.g., Boyd 1975; 1986; Arnopoulos 1979). In everyday life, however, women who are white, educated, and English-speaking are rarely considered to be immigrant women.

The term conjures up the image of a woman who does not speak English or who speaks English with an accent; who is from the Third World or a member of a visible minority group; and who has a certain type of job (e.g., a sewing machine operator or a cleaning lady). Thus, 'immigrant women' is a socially constructed category presupposing, among other things, a labour market relation.

Women who are considered to be immigrants in Canada have not always been so considered. They *become* immigrant women when they immigrate to Canada and enter certain positions in the labour market. Thus, when we call some-

...c an 'immigrant woman' we are in fact naming a process whereby this individual comes to be identified as an immigrant woman.

In this [study], I will adopt the common sense usage of the term 'immigrant women'. My purpose is to discover *how* some women *become* immigrant women in Canadian society. What we will see is that the work of employment counsellors is one 'moment' in the social construction of immigrant women as the employment agency entered into relations with the state and with employers.

Historically, immigrant women are the product of capitalist development, which displaces segments of the population from their Indigenous livelihood and draws them to centres of new industrial development. There, they are more and more tied to an economy based on profit-making: a monetary economy. Immigrant women become a social entity after the rise of the phenomenon of immigration, which in turn indicates a process whereby different labour supply systems are integrated into the world capitalist economy (see Sassen-Koob 1981).

In Canada, immigrant women become a visible social category when female labour is employed in large numbers, such as in the latter half of the nineteenth century when England experienced a surplus of single, unemployed women, whereas the colonies, including Canada and Australia, were in need of domestic labour and wives (see Lay 1980), and more recently when male immigrants were allowed to bring their families into Canada as permanent residents. In the 1970s, this pattern of female immigration coincided with the downturn of the Canadian economy when the quota for 'independent immigrants' was cut down and the policy of 'family reunification' was stressed.

The Canadian state plays a crucial role in determining the position of immigrant women through the Immigration Act. Immigration policies have always been designed to meet and regulate the needs of the Canadian economy while,

as much as possible, preserving Canada as a predominantly white nation (see Avery 1979; Basran 1983). The current Act, which came into effect in 1978, seems fairly straightforward at first glance. It divides immigrants into three categories: independent immigrants, including 'assisted relatives', whose entry into Canada is subject to economic requirements and criteria measured by a point system; 'sponsored' or 'family class' immigrants, who do not accrue enough points by themselves and who are sponsored into Canada by a close relative; and business-class immigrants who have capital to invest in Canadian industries and businesses. In addition, immigrants can apply for refugee status, and be assessed by a different set of criteria. The 'family class' category is the one crucial to our discussion.

This classification of immigrants, as such, does not distinguish between the gender, ethnic origin, or class position of individuals. But when we take into account the indexes for determining entry of 'independent immigrants' (based on language proficiency, educational attainment, investment potential, and the labour requirements of Canada, ranked according to a point system), then the sexist, racist, and class biases of the immigration policy become visible.

The majority of the people entering Canada as 'sponsored immigrants' are the elderly, children, and women from Third World or industrially less developed countries, who do not have the education, skills, and economic resources seen to be adequate for or relevant to the requirements of the Canadian economy. They are permitted to enter the country under the sponsorship of the man, seen to be the main wage earner, or close relatives (e.g., spouse, parents, adult children) already residing in Canada. Women, in particular, are frequently considered their husbands' dependants, and are classified as 'family class', even when they have been working in the paid labour force in their home countries (see Estable 1986). According to the philosophy of the policy, family class immigrants are to provide emotional and other support for the wage earner and are not destined for the labour market. In reality, due to financial necessity, many sponsored immigrants, especially the women, do engage in waged work (see Ng and Ramirez 1981, esp. 46–9).

These immigrant categories are not merely legal definitions. They have real social and economic consequences for people's lives. For example, a sponsored immigrant is not entitled to public assistance of any kind, such as training subsidies, welfare, etc., available to independent immigrants and other Canadians. They are seen to be the dependants of the sponsor, who is legally responsible for their financial welfare for a period of five to ten years (see Ng and Ramirez 1981: 49–55; Ng and Das Gupta 1981; Estable 1986). They can be deported if they are deemed to be a financial burden to the Canadian state. This forces women to be completely dependent on their sponsor and contributes to their isolation and captivity in unpleasant and abusive family situations. The lack of access to government subsidized language- and job-training programs means that women are forced to seek jobs which are low paid and marginal.

Many factors in the labour market restrict immigrant women's occupational mobility: the segregated nature of the Canadian labour force (see Armstrong and Armstrong 1978; Connelly 1979); the lack of recognition of education, skills, and work experience from non-English and non-European countries; the lack of appropriate language and re-training programs (see IWS 1985); pressures exerted by professional associations and labour unions to restrict membership (see Campbell 1980; IWS 1985), and so on. Thus, when they join the paid labour force, immigrant women are forced into certain labour pools at the lower end of the occupational hierarchy, frequently taking jobs that other Canadians would not take because of low wages and poor working conditions. Due to the nature of their paid employment (e.g., part-time, seasonal,

or piece work), labour standard legislation is not rigidly enforced in many cases, which further exacerbates the poor conditions of their work. Meanwhile, their domestic responsibilities, including child care, and lack of educational opportunities mean that their mobility in the wage labour market is severely curtailed. As a result, most non-English-speaking immigrant women, if they enter the labour force, become members of the most exploited sectors of the working population.[1]

This is the social context within which the work of the employment agency was situated. In order to improve the situation of immigrant women, employment counsellors had to enter into relations with employers and with the state, which ultimately curtailed their effectiveness. In our analysis, we will see how their work also played a part in the organization of immigrant women into an ethnic and gender segregated labour force, and contributed to determining their class positions.

* * *

To make sense of the tensions and contradictions I witnessed at the employment agency, I followed a line of inquiry in sociology adapted from Marx's method of political economy (Sayer 1979; Smith 1981a; 1981b). This approach has been called 'institutional ethnography' by Smith (1981b). Unlike standard ethnographic research, which describes a local setting as if it was a self-contained unit of analysis, institutional ethnography seeks to locate the dynamics of a local setting in the complex institutional relations organizing the local dynamics.

In terms of my study, the employment agency was taken to be one component of a larger work process in the highly complex division of labour characteristic of an advanced capitalist social formation; the interactions within the agency could not be understood without reference to the organizational context within which it was situated.

Thus, in addition to recording the routine daily work of employment counsellors, I paid particular attention to the historical development of the agency and its linkages to other organizations and relations. My own participation in the agency and my increasing competence as a counsellor was central to my subsequent analysis of the workings of the employment agency. It was through participating as a competent member of the setting that I was able to acquire an understanding of the institutional processes to which the agency was linked.

What came into view, when I adopted this approach, was that the act of counselling did not begin or end in the agency. It was connected to a set of social relations which had to do with the way in which the state attempted to regulate and rationalize labour market demands through contracting out some of its functions to community groups with closer ties to the grassroots. The counselling and placement process thus constituted one component in a set of social actions which organized the relation between immigrant women and employers in the labour market.

Once we develop this understanding and grasp this set of connections, we then see that although the counsellors' individual 'style' might be idiosyncratic, the relations underpinning that activity were not. They (the social relations of the labour market) could not be reduced to a simple set of transactions. The agency was also shaped by its relationship to the state. The funding procedures which organized its operation were not peculiar to this agency. They had been elaborated over time as the *general* forms of such relations. To fulfill the agency's funding obligations to the state, the counsellors necessarily entered their work into this social course of action which gave the counselling process its determinate character. This had very little to do with the intention of the counsellors vis-à-vis their clients. Thus, my analysis of the counselling process must not be construed as a critique of the counsellors' style. It is intended to illuminate the labour market relations

to which the counselling process was inevitably tied, which are at the same time the class relations of contemporary capitalist societies.

Obviously, this concept of class deviates from its standard treatment in stratification theory, which measures class in terms of economic and social indicators (e.g., income, merit, social background). My understanding follows a recent revival in Marxist analyses which focus on class as a set of social relations: relations between people (see Sayer 1979; Smith 1983; Cockburn 1983).

Marx and Engels, in *The German Ideology* (1970) and *The Communist Manifesto* (1967), view all forms of societies and change in society as arising out of the struggles between different groups/classes of people in terms of their relation to the means of production. In capitalist societies, the two major classes are the bourgeoisie (or capitalists), who own and control the means of production, and the proletariat (the working class), who must sell their labour power in exchange for a wage because they do not own the means of production. However, Marx and Engels hasten to add that these classes are not homogeneous apart from this broadest definition of their respective relationship to the means of production. Each class emerges and is given cohesion and definition in relation to the other; it is also internally fragmented. This is what they say of wage labour: 'Wage labour rests exclusively on competition between labourers' (Marx and Engels 1967: 93).

Furthermore, the exploitation of the labourers by the capitalists is not a simple, one-way relation. It is a contradictory process. In bringing workers together into a factory to maximize the generation and augmentation of production for capital, and educating workers to use new machinery and equipment (albeit for the purpose of eliminating some workers to cut costs in the long run), the bourgeoisie also brings workers together, revealing their common conditions of exploitation. This process in fact facilitates the formation of the proletariat as a class (Marx and

Engels 1967; Marx 1954). Thus, the concept of 'class' is not just a delineation of a set of social and economic indicators. It is fundamentally a relation between two groups of people (albeit internally fragmented) who are engaged in a process of mutual definition and re-definition over time (Marx and Engels 1967; Thompson 1963; Cockburn 1983).

Contemporary theorists, Smith in particular, draw attention to class relations as practical activities. That is, in order for class to be an objective feature of contemporary societies, it must be *accomplished* by people (see Smith 1981c; 1983). In her investigation of women and class, Smith examines the activities of bourgeois women in organizing the transgenerational relations of the bourgeoisie, and the fragmentation of gender (women in her case) along class lines (Smith 1983). Dehli's study of home–school relations in early twentieth-century Toronto shows the dominant role played by upper-middle-class mothers in developing 'proper mothering practices' which were antithetical to the interests of working-class (immigrant) women (Dehli 1984).

My analysis follows this tradition in Marxist thought and develops the notion of class as a set of practices which organize relations among people. This [study] focuses on the practices of employment counsellors in organizing immigrant women's relation to the paid labour force, and the organization of the internal relations of the employment agency. These changing relations will be described to throw light on how class is created by a set of routine activities in everyday life.

Central to the (re)organization of class relations in contemporary societies is the state. In advanced capitalist societies, 'the state' has increasingly taken on the role of mediating and intervening in the economy, augmenting the infrastructure essential for the continuous accumulation of capital. It actively organizes and manages the economy and the workforce through special grants and tax shelters to busi-

nesses and industries, monitoring the workforce by developing educational and training programs, and facilitating and regulating labour supply through legislation, including immigration policy and unemployment insurance. In this way, the state plays a major part in the constitution and organization of the working class through various intervention and control mechanisms.

The progressive expansion of the functions of the state and its formal organization is the central debate in Marxist scholarship.[2] This [study] does not take up this debate directly. Instead, it makes use of a more general understanding of the state (see, for example, Miliband 1969; Poulantzas 1978; 1980; Therborn 1980; Corrigan and Sayer 1985; London-Edinburgh Weekend Return Group 1979). Simply put, the state is not a monolithic structure, composed of different apparatuses, which perform different functions for the dominant classes on behalf of capital. It is also the focus and embodiment of struggles between classes. My purpose is to discover 'how the state in concrete ways organizes the hegemony of dominant classes' (Findlay 1982: 14); or, put in another way, 'what does the ruling class do when it rules?' (Therborn 1980). In order not to distract the reader from the empirical examination of the workings of the state, I will use the common sense usage of the term as short-hand to refer to the multiplicity of levels, functions, and activities of the government. At the end of the [study], I will re-examine this usage, to see whether in fact it is adequate in accounting for the relations analyzed.

One central aspect of ruling and the coordination of the complex functions of the state are documents. Documents, in various shapes and forms, provide for organizational action in the state apparatus and other large bureaucratic organizations: in records and files, legislation, press releases, Orders-in-Council, memoranda, and various kinds of information systems (see Garfinkel 1967; Wheeler 1969; Smith 1974; 1984; Jackson 1980; Campbell 1984). The documentary process is crucial for organizing the complex division of labour within the state and ensuring its reproduction, because people move in and out of, and have a limited 'lifespan' relative to this structure. It is through documents of various kinds, from interdepartmental memoranda to job descriptions to statistical data, that the multitude of the seemingly disparate activities of the state apparatus is coordinated and given coherence. This documentary mode of action concretizes and binds departments and individuals to a legal course of action.

Indeed, through this process, the employment agency became connected to the state apparatus, although in appearance it remained an independent community agency. My study shows that in actual fact its functions were an extension of the coordinated activities of the state. . . . [I]t was through documents that employment counsellors organized and produced groups of women (in this case immigrant women) as particular kinds of workers (particular 'commodities') for the labour market.

* * *

Notes

This [study] is based on my doctoral dissertation completed in September 1984. In revising it for the Network Basic Series, I have omitted many technical details (e.g., textual analyses of contracts and forms) and the literature review (e.g., the theoretical debates on class, and a review of studies of immigrant women). The reader who seeks these details may turn to my dissertation, 'Immigrant Women and the State: A Study in the Social Organization of Knowledge', [Department of Education (OISE), University of Toronto, 1984], for fuller discussions.

1. For fuller discussions of immigrant women in the labour force, see Arnopoulos (1979), Boyd (1975; 1986), Jenke and Yaron (1979), Ng and Das Gupta (1980; 1981), Ng and Ramirez (1981), Estable (1986).

2. For a long time, Marxist theorization of the state has been stuck in the 'instrumentalist' versus the 'structuralist' debate which centred around Miliband's refinement of and quarrel with the earlier works of Poulantzas. (For a summary of this debate, see Holloway and Picciotto 1978.) Recently, the 'state derivation' debate has gained popularity in Britain and western Europe (see Holloway and Picciotto 1978; Jessop 1982). I tend to agree with Poulantzas's suggestion in his later work that there can be no general theory of the state (Poulantzas 1980). Although we can map out certain elements of the capitalist state, a theory of the state has to undergo constant revision in accordance with the actual state of affairs and the particular configuration of class struggle in a social formation. Some of the usefulness of Poulantzas's later conceptualization has been critically assessed by Jessop (1982).

Chapter 10

Theorizing Connections: Gender, Race, Ethnicity, and Class

Daiva K. Stasiulis

This chapter explores the possibilities and problems inherent in analyses that seek to conceptualize the links among relations organized by gender, race, ethnicity, and class.[1] In Canada, as in all multiracial, multi-ethnic societies, all social relations have class, gendered, racial, and ethnic elements. Within any given context and for any given population, however, one of these social constructions or identities may be perceived to be more salient than the others.

There is a growing body of literature that illustrates the many levels (economic, political, and ideological) and modalities (discourses, practices, institutional mechanisms) through which race, ethnicity, gender, and class are intermeshed. This chapter critically examines selected theoretical debates in the international and Canadian literature[2] that seek to integrate notions of 'class' and 'gender' with 'race' and 'ethnicity'.

In it I will discuss both the strengths and the weaknesses of some of the recent efforts to theorize the connections among class, race, ethnicity, and gender. Given the immense size, richness, and diversity of this literature, I can adequately address only a few major debates. . . . The chapter concludes with a few remarks about the implications for political practice of multidimensional theories of oppression.

* * *

Feminist Incorporations of Race, Ethnicity, and Class

The necessity of coming to grips with racism and racial/ethnic divisions, both within and outside the women's movement, has posed one of the greatest challenges to contemporary feminist theory and practice in Canada, the United States, and Britain. The task of developing an adequate anti-racist perspective and adopting authentic anti-racist strategies for all segments of the feminist movement is a direct response to the growing collective strength and public voice among Aboriginal, immigrant, and racial-minority women (Das Gupta 1986; Hernandez 1988; Native Women's Association of Canada 1988; Silman 1987; Wallis, Giles, and Hernandez 1988). It also reflects growing international contact among feminists and growing exposure to analyses by and about women in developing countries (Broom 1987: 273; Hill 1987). One effect of this exposure has been to reveal the ethnocentric Western assumptions about women's roles in much North American and European feminist writing.

In Canada and elsewhere, the definition given by socialist feminists in the 1980s to their understanding of the power relations within which women are embedded frequently, if not routinely, includes the category of 'race'. For instance, one recent study of the contemporary women's movement in Canada gives as the framework for analyzing women's oppression 'four intertwining categories: gender, class, race, and sexual orientation' (Adamson, Briskin, and McPhail 1988; see also Bhavnani and Coulson 1986; Harriss 1989).

Within a few short years, socialist-feminist theories have moved from a position providing dismissive or only cursory treatment of racial and ethnic identities and divisions[3] to one claiming to treat 'race' and racism as integral to feminist analysis. The inclusion of race and ethnic identities as lenses through which to understand the diverse experiences of women reflects a serious intent to represent, and free from oppression, *all* women. It is important to inquire, however, whether feminist theories have in the process been transformed, or, alternatively, whether the issue of racism and the categories of race and ethnicity have simply been 'grafted' onto existing analyses of sex and class. In other words, are feminist analyses of connections among gender, race, ethnicity, and class merely a matter of 'bland intersectionism', or are they real theoretical advances that might fruitfully serve to inform not only feminist politics but those of labour and other social movements? These questions will be pursued through an examination of the critiques of white feminism made by black feminists, the alternative formulations offered, and some recent efforts to theorize the experiences of Native, migrant, and racial-minority women in the Canadian context.

Both the labels 'white feminism' and 'black feminism' are vast simplifications of the diversity —of priorities, epistemologies, politics, levels of abstraction, and incorporation of class analysis and other social categories such as sexual orientation—within feminist scholarship. These admittedly problematic terms will be adopted in this paper in order to show how the omission of analyses of racism in feminist historiography and social science undermines both the analytical strength of these fields and their potential for building political solidarity.

By 'white feminism' I mean the vast majority of Western feminist writing that has been produced by white women and either ignores race and ethnicity or treats these social divisions and identities as accessories to the basic definition of 'woman'. Because it is socialist feminism that most consistently addresses the articulation between gender (or sex) and class, and the relationship between capitalist production and human reproduction,[4] the following discussion will focus on the socialist-feminist writing of white feminists.

By 'black feminism' I mean the growing body of literature, in the United States, Britain, and, increasingly, Canada, that conveys and conceptualizes the historical and contemporary circumstances of black women and other women of colour. The vehicles of expression of black feminist thought and emotions are frequently richly evocative, experiential literature—poetry, short stories, and essays, 'the interweaving of protests and laments from women who come from the farm and the ghetto; the factory and the university' (Jones 1985: 315)—as well as more analytical writings. Although fed by diverse national and group-specific histories and cultures of resistance, black feminists frequently draw inspiration from the same sources (e.g., the writings of Frantz Fanon and Angela Davis) and from anti-imperialist and black liberation struggles led and supported by women around the globe. The recent proliferation of analytical black feminist writings offers a more precise and pointed critique of the Eurocentric bias common to white feminist writings. Black feminist writings also suggest elements for alternative theories sensitive to the differing material circumstances and experiences among women differentiated by race and ethnicity.

The omission of women of colour from white feminist analysis has in itself been regarded as reflective of the racism and ethnic exclusivity of the white women's movement. Minh-ha (1989: 99) has argued that the labels by which feminists refer to racial differences among women—such as 'Western', 'non-Western', or 'Third World'—

'take the dominant group as point of reference, and they reflect well the West's ideology of dominance', adding, for dramatic illustration, that 'it is as if we were to use the term "non-Afro-Asian" . . . to designate all white people'.

Equally important, however, is black feminism's insistence on an adequate incorporation of anti-racism into feminist theory and politics. This task necessitates that white women acknowledge the 'material basis of their power in relation to black people, both women and men' (Bhavnani and Coulson 1986).

In other words, white feminists must come to terms with the complexities and contradictions of power relations involving the intersection of gender, class, and race, where white women may simultaneously be privileged *and* oppressed. The Janus-faced position that white women have held vis-à-vis women and men of colour is apparent in the legacy of racism within white feminist politics (hooks 1981; 1984). Racist strategies were evident in the first wave of feminism, when American suffragettes broke their alliance with blacks and co-operated with avowed racists in order to gain the southern vote for female suffrage (King 1988). More recently, white British feminists involved in anti-rape campaigns have managed to ignore the way their marches through black areas have reinforced racist stereotypes of the violent sexuality of black men and legitimized the greater policing of black communities (Bhavnani and Coulson 1986).

Black feminists have challenged the hegemony of white feminism and critiqued the tendency of white feminists to generalize from the experiences of Anglo-Celtic women to those of all women, regardless of their respective positions within structures of racial and/or ethnic oppression. In political struggles as well as theoretical debates, black feminists have expressed their concern over the tendency within white feminism to a priori privilege gender divisions and sexism (or, in socialist feminism, gender and class divisions) over race divisions and racism.

Black feminism rejects the claims to universality of the central categories and assumptions of white feminist analyses. The major disagreements centre on the theorized construction of women's oppression in the matrix of social relations formed by the state, the private family household, and the wage-labour system. White feminism's treatment of ideological discourses and symbolic representations (motherhood, sexuality, feminity) that uphold women's dependent and subordinate status as wives, mothers, and workers has also been critiqued for failing to consider the intersection of these ideologies with racist ones.

In addition, black feminists criticize the treatment of the family by white feminists. Both socialist- and radical-feminist approaches have taken the family to be a significant, if not the primary, source of women's oppression (Barrett 1980; McIntosh 1978: 254–90). As Marshall (1988: 211) has observed, 'Whether viewed primarily as the locus of domestic labour, the site of human reproduction and socialization, or as a hegemonic ideology, the family, and women's roles as wives and mothers within it, is central to feminist theory.' The major emphasis given to the family in much feminist theorizing is likely connected to women's role in child-bearing, which cuts across class, time, and space, and the major significance for women (far greater than for men) of domestic and kinship relationships.

Given the salience of the family in white feminist explanations of women's subordination, it has often followed that the predominant role assigned to the state under capitalism is that of upholding a particular form of private family household, characterized by a male breadwinner and a financially dependent housewife (McIntosh 1978; but see Jenson 1986 for a critique). The major role of women is then viewed as that of performing domestic labour, especially the bearing and raising of children.

The attention given to the family as a site for women's oppression and its particular conceptualization in white feminism are regarded by black feminists as highly problematic. They argue that first, in racist societies, the family is commonly experienced by black women as the *least* oppressive institution; rather, it functions as a site for shelter and resistance, and offers opportunities for egalitarian relations between oppressed minority women and men that are denied in major societal institutions, imbued as they are with racism (Carby 1982: 214; Davis 1971; 1983: 15–18; Jones 1985: 12–13; but for an opposing view, see White 1984: 7–26).

In defending the black family, many black feminists do not deny that domestic violence and struggles over the sexism of black men are significant issues within the black community. In order to deal with such painful domestic realities as assaults on women and child sexual abuse, black women have organized shelters and self-support groups (Bogle 1988: 132; Mama 1989). Their reluctance to speak publicly about sexism and domestic violence within the black community, however, is based on their fear that such disclosure will feed into popular perceptions of the violence of black males (long represented as dangerous to white women) and the broader criminalization of the black community (Mama 1989; Pettman 1989: 14).

A second and related critique by black feminists centres on the concept of female financial dependence on male wage-earners, which they regard as racially and culturally bound. In both historical and contemporary contexts, the rates of labour-force participation have generally been higher for black and minority women than for their white counterparts in Canada, the United States, and Britain. In addition, black women more often have had the *sole* responsibility for earning an income and supporting dependants than have white women (Brand 1984; Bruegel 1989; Davis 1983; Dill 1983; Jones 1985; King 1988; Wallace 1980).

Third, the assumption of the 'normal' male-led, female-dependent family household has

been absorbed into much social science in a manner that has pathologized both the black family and black women's roles in the family household and labour force. A notorious instance of this occurred in 1965, when Daniel Moynihan, as advisor to the American government, argued that Afro-American oppression could be attributed primarily to the matriarchal structure of the black family and community (Bhavnani 1989: 69–70). The 'displacement' of black men from the position of household head and the relative deprivation of the black community were attributed to black women, who were represented as emasculating matriarchs. Among the structural processes Moynihan ignored were the effects of the capitalist labour market and state social welfare policies in marginalizing black men into the waged economy and propelling black women into adopting strategies geared toward maintaining the financial survival of black families.

Somewhat different renditions of the 'black matriarch' thesis are encapsulated in white social scientists' analyses of Aboriginal societies in both Canada and Australia (for Australia, see Pettman 1989; Langton 1981). For instance, on the basis of very little evidence and rather speculative reasoning, LaPrairie argues that the disproportionately heavy involvement of Native women with the Canadian criminal justice system is attributable to a cycle in which the severe role strain and feelings of impotence experienced by Indian men as a result of the failure of traditional economies resulted in aggressive male violence against Indian women and subsequent criminal activity by Indian women (1987: 106–7). Thus, in analysis of female Aboriginal criminality, similar emphasis is placed on the links between female household heads, male impotence, and deviance as in the 'black matriarch' thesis.

Fourth, the central role accorded by white feminism to the family in enforcing women's oppression ignores the effects on black families of racially restrictive immigration and citizenship laws. Such laws—in Canada, Britain, Australia, and, above all, South Africa—have historically served to *destroy* rather than to maintain black families by separating husbands from wives, wives from husbands, and parents from children.[5] Moreover, the critical stance adopted by white feminists toward 'the family' assumes a nuclear family and neglects the range of kinship and household structures in different cultures. The destructive influence of immigration policies that disallow the preservation of family forms other than nuclear families (forms that are important sources for women's strength and solidarity) is similarly ignored within white feminism (Ramazanoglu 1989: 148).

The failure of white feminists to define immigration and citizenship issues as 'women's issues' is linked to the inadequate theorization of the state within white feminist writings. In specifying the contradictory roles played by the state in mediating relations between gender and class, capitalist production and biological reproduction, socialist feminists neglect the role of the state in organizing the political and ideological conditions under which the nation-state is reproduced (Miles 1988: 438). Central to this process is the way racism becomes intertwined with issues of nationalism in defining the parameters of the nation-state and what Benedict Anderson (1983) has called 'the imagined community' (see also Anthias 1988; Gilroy 1987: 26). It is the combination of patriarchal logic with principles of racial and ethnic exclusivity embedded in immigration and citizenship laws that is particularly devastating for minority women. Immigration policy establishes the parameters for the 'legitimate' entry, settlement, and access to social services and paid work of immigrant women. Citizenship policies (in combination with social welfare policies) severely limit their access and entitlement to the fruits of liberal democratic, feminist, and class struggles (Baptiste 1988; Boyd 1989; Pettman 1989; Sondhi 1987; Yuval-Davis and Anthias 1989).

Thus what is at issue in the critiques of white feminism by black feminists is not merely the conceptualization of women's role in the family, but the role of racism in differentiating the material circumstances of white and black women in relations of both production and reproduction. This point is elegantly brought forth in a study by Carby (1987) of nineteenth-century literary representations of black and white women by female Afro-American novelists. Carby begins by delineating the distinct and antagonistic positions held by white mistresses and black female slaves in the plantations of the southern United States. White women were viewed as the means of consolidating property through the institution of 'marriages of alliance' between plantation families and through their role as bearers of the inheritors of that property. In contrast, 'black women, as slaves, had their reproductive destiny bound to capital accumulation; black women gave birth to property, and directly to capital itself in the form of slaves, and all slaves inherited their status from their mothers' (1987: 24–5).

In addition, renewed attention has been given in feminist writings to the role of symbolic representation in the reproduction of women's subordination (Marshall 1988: 213). Much black feminist work has been directed at bringing out the race- and class-specific character of ideologies and images of feminity, domesticity, and female sexuality. Carby's study of the nineteenth-century American discourses and literary conventions of 'true womanhood' sheds light on how ideologies of 'true' (i.e., white) womanhood and black womanhood in the antebellum South were polarized yet interdependent images of each other: the fragility, modesty, and repressed sexuality of white plantation mistresses existed in sharp contrast to the 'masculine' strength and unbridled sexuality of black slave women. The cult of true womanhood and the antithetical ideology of black womanhood were built upon a hierarchical differential in the positions that black women and white women occupied in the social formation of slavery. Carby's approach is both historical–materialist and dialectic. She argues that the discourses of white and black womanhood were *not* simply reflective of lived sets of material and social relations, but themselves played a role in resolving the contradictions in the sets of social relations in which white women, in particular, were located.

Images of sturdy, asexual, and subservient black domestics and of exotic, sexually dextrous, and compliant Asian women are pervasive in Western popular culture and mass-media advertising, whereas the images of white women, while sexist, are both different and at least somewhat more diverse (Brand 1984; Hull, Scott, and Smith 1982; Parmar 1982). Such racially and culturally specific notions of feminity play an important role in relegating women of different 'races' and ethnicities to specific occupations, in barring them from entry into others, and in conditioning managerial strategies of control (Glenn 1980). In addition, state practices such as the nature of policing and social services delivered to particular communities frequently capitalize on differential racial/ethnic images of women. Thus Mama accounts for the allocation of far fewer refuges for battered women in Britain to the black than to Asian communities in terms of the different racial stereotypes of Asian and Afro-Caribbean women: 'If the former are passive, exotic, quiet, and inspire paternalism, then the latter are aggressive, promiscuous, violent like their men, and more threatening than mysteriously silent' (1989: 43).

Race-specific ideologies of womanhood are also important in directing women's reproductive activities toward meeting race (e.g., eugenic) as well as class ends. For instance, black women and other women of colour have at various times been encouraged to limit their family size and to aid in the reproduction of *white* children through the provision of domestic service to white families. This contrasts with the periodic drives to encourage Anglo-Celtic women in Britain and 'white settler colonies' such as Canada and Australia to have more babies. Such racially exclusive pro-natalist policies have been legitimated through recourse to nationalist and imperialist objectives (Klug 1989; de Lepervanche 1989).[6] The fear of 'miscegenation', or sexual relations between white women and black men, and the birth of 'mixed race' children has also led to legislation restricting the entry, settlement, and many rights of black men (Carby 1987: 31; Rich 1986: 30).

In sum, black feminism maintains that by ignoring race, the analytical formulations of white feminism are impoverished. Because it treats 'women' as a homogeneous racial category, white feminism is unable to account for the differences and hierarchical structuring in material and discursive conditions that govern black and white women's lives. Black feminist analyses reveal how, for *both* white women and women of colour, the relationship to the family, state, production, and reproduction has been mediated simultaneously by class interests, gender divisions, and white supremacist logics, in a way that has constructed barriers to sisterhood across racial lines. Finally, black feminism discloses the important role played by racially specific gender ideologies and images—part of popular 'common sense'—in 'naturalizing' the suitability of black women and women of colour for jobs in the lowest stratum of a labour market already segmented along gender lines, in aiding (as nannies and domestics) the reproduction of white families, and in justifying differential entitlement and administration of social services.

The challenge posed by black feminism, then, goes beyond that of merely rendering visible the differential experiences of gender across racial and ethnic lines. It calls for nothing less than the incorporation of systematic analyses of racism into feminism, and a subsequent reconsideration and reformulation of some of the accepted concepts within feminist writings. Central concepts within feminism such as 'reproduction', 'the state', and 'the family' all currently embody white, racist logics. Indeed, the recognition that race and ethnicity, in addition to class, play a central role in defining the nature and extent of relative privilege and oppression of women, renders simplistic and misleading the very notion of 'women's oppression' (Lamoureux 1987: 64).

Black Feminism in the Canadian Context

Leaving aside for the moment the question of defining 'black women' or 'women of colour' in the Canadian context, black feminist arguments appear to strike a deep chord of resonance with the historical and contemporary experiences of several groups of Aboriginal and non-European migrant women. Canadian feminist politics incorporate a history of racial and ethnic exclusion. An instance of this occurred in the early twentieth century, when Anglo-Celtic suffragettes sought the vote for British-Canadian women on the grounds that it would enable them to influence immigration policy to ensure the exclusion of undesirable eastern Europeans (Palmer 1982).

Aboriginal women have echoed many black feminist writers in insisting that racism, rather than sexism, is the primary source of their oppression; that solidarity with the men of their community is critical in ameliorating their oppression; and that the concerns of the white, middle-class women's movement are far removed from their own concerns for physical and communal survival (LaChapelle 1982; Silman 1987; for a similar position among Aboriginal women in Australia, see Pettman 1989: 26). Far from acting to preserve the family, the Canadian state has followed coercive paternalistic policies in seizing Native children and placing them in white foster homes or boarding schools. The consequences of these state policies vis-à-vis Native families and education include a tendency for young people to leave school altogether, destruction of Native culture, and a tragic pattern of Native youth suicides.

The process of migration of Asians and blacks into Canada has been mediated by two often competing objectives in immigration policy: the desire to populate Canada with white British people and the demands of the capitalist labour market. This has meant that prior to the explicit expunging of racist criteria in Canadian admissions policy in 1967, non-white migrants were accepted into Canada only if they met pressing needs for cheap, exploitable labour. In each case—for instance, the importation of 15,000 Chinese male labourers to construct the transcontinental railway, and the more recent migration of Caribbean women to perform domestic work—state regulations were designed to actively discourage settlement in Canada (Adilman 1984; Li 1988: 60). Indeed, a distinctive and subordinate relationship of non-white, non-European women to the state has been encoded in a patchwork of racist immigration policies that actively restricted the entry into Canada of dependants of either male or female non-white migrant workers. This had the effect of severely limiting family size and thus controlling the growth of resident non-white populations.

Thus black feminism places on the agenda of Canadian feminist historiography a number of important questions. These questions pertain to the race, gender, and class specificity of mechanisms circumscribing the lives of black women and women of colour in Canada, and the activities of the Canadian women's movement. Black feminism also opens up analyses of the discursive operations that have justified the treatment of black women and other women of colour as 'alien' and undesirable. Yet there are limits to the capacity of black feminism to comprehend the experiences and incorporation of different 'racial' and ethnic groups of women into Canada's economy, class structure, and political and symbolic orders.

Chief among these limitations is the implicit black/white dichotomy that is frequently assumed to structure the racist and gendered oppression of women. Indeed, some American and British black feminist works explicitly state that whatever the degraded conditions of the work and home lives of other women of colour or European immigrant women, black women 'shouldered unique burdens at home and endured unique forms of discrimination in the workplace' (Jones 1985: 9; for Britain, see Mama 1989; Murphy and Livingstone 1985).

The arguments most commonly expounded by black feminism and taken up by black Canadian feminists such as Brand (1984) have the effect of linking racism to skin colour, rather than to the structural location of particular groups of women in concrete and historically specific social relations and to the accompanying discourses that aid in the processes of denigration, subordination, and exploitation. The insistence on the enduring and unique liability of race or skin colour for black women (and possibly other women of colour) draws attention to the origins of racism in colonial and imperial relationships, from which white Western women have benefited. But it would be equally important to point out the distinctive and protracted burdens within Canadian colonialism that have been borne by Aboriginal women (*Fireweed* 1986; LaChapelle 1982; Silman 1987).

The Native Women's Association of Canada has noted the inordinately slow pace at which Bill C-31 (the 1985 amendments to the Indian Act) has been implemented, through which Indian women and their families are having their rights to First Nationhood restored.[7] The organization has attributed the 'tardiness, the inefficiency, and the inhuman procedures' of Indian Affairs in administering applications for reinstatement to the fact that 'the applicants are Aboriginal people' (Native Women's Association of Canada 1988: 128).

The unique histories both of the class, racial, and gender oppression of Native women and of their resistance to that oppression are nurturing grounds for such distinctive political concerns as land claims and self-government. Frequently, however, white feminists, far removed from Native peoples' battles over sovereignty, are quick to recognize the sexist character of the old Indian Act, but are less comprehending of the role of women in Aboriginal self-determination. The unique kinds of oppression experienced by Native women may result in flat stereotypes, useful for categorization of Aboriginal women as a special group. One Native woman related how the organizers of a feminist conference were discomfited by the decision of two Native participants to attend the workshop on 'empowerment' rather than the one on 'poverty' to which they had been assigned (Silman 1987).

To apply black feminist arguments in the Canadian context would also require consideration of the impact of French–English divisions and Quebec nationalism. The context for immigration to Canada was not one but two linguistically and culturally defined nations or imagined communities. The elevation of the role of Quebec French women in the home and reproduction (i.e., through the 'revenge of the cradle') was deemed necessary to resist the pressures of external encroachment by the English and other non-French immigrant groups and to maintain the specificity of the Quebec nation (Lamoureux 1987; Dumont et al. 1987). The extent to which the contradictions involving the role of nationalism in the Quebec women's movement have affected the experiences and well-being of racial-minority and non-French migrant women in Quebec is an important issue.

The fact that a long history of European and non-European immigration has brought to Canada, in different waves, people who have departed from the English model of physical appearance and cultural desirability has led to the development of many different racisms. Racisms built upon language, religion, and other cultural markers have historically been directed at white as well as non-white groups who were regarded as threatening to the British and Protestant character of English Canada (Iacovetta 1986: 209). One effect of structural racism in Canada is that in a multiracial, multi-ethnic female workforce, particular groups of European immigrant women have historically shared disadvantages similar to those of black working-class women, and continue to do so.

The flowering of ethnic feminist historiography in Canada has made it possible to replace such clumsy and misleading concepts as 'double (or triple) oppression (or jeopardy)' with an increasingly detailed portrait of the social structures, social relations, institutional mechanisms, and discourses that affect the lives of immigrant and minority women (Abele and Stasiulis 1989: 267–8). Analyses of the multiple disadvantages faced by immigrant women have centred on two related factors: (1) entry statuses within immigration policy that make women dependent on husbands, fathers, and other male relatives; and (2) restricted opportunities to learn the official languages (see Boyd 1986; 1984; Estable 1986; Ng and Ramirez 1981; Stasiulis 1987). But detailed case studies that take as their setting the workplace (Gannage 1987; Johnson 1982), trade unions (Lipsig-Mumme 1987), the household (Iacovetta 1986), or the employment agency (Ng 1986; 1988) reveal many other situations in which immigrant and racial/ethnic-minority women constitute distinct groups facing circumstances that are sometimes unique and sometimes shared with other women. Such histories also document the spirited and creative resistance of these women to male, capitalist, racist, and bureaucratic forms of domination, and thus undercut the image of them as hapless victims of a seamless web of oppression.

The capacity of black feminism to inform analyses of racial- and ethnic-minority women in Canada is limited by a second inherent tendency: namely, its treatment of 'black women' or 'women of colour' as homogeneous, thus avoid-

ing the issue of how class has mediated the effects of race and gender.[8] This is a critical issue in Canada, where significant class differences have emerged within black, Asian, and other racial categories of women as the result of a selective post-war immigration policy.

Since the early 1960s, Canadian immigration policy has sought to recruit Third World immigrants with high levels of education and professional and technical skills, yet has also brought in many less-skilled and -educated family members of primarily male immigrants. More recently, Canadian immigration has included large numbers of refugees from Southeast Asia, whose skills frequently do not match the demands of the Canadian labour market, and who carry a formidable liability in that market: lack of fluency in one of the official languages. The Mulroney government has also aggressively recruited capital via the Immigration Department's Entrepreneur and Investor programs, through which wealthy individuals, including many Hong Kong capitalists seeking solutions to the '1997 jitters',[9] have gained immigration status.

This latter migration of Asians to Canada is guaranteed to foster racism, particularly in British Columbia, which has a long history of anti-Asian hostility, and whose resource-based economy has been rocked by current movements and state policies of capital restructuring (including free trade with the United States) and heightened assaults on the labour movement. But it is important to distinguish between the forms and effects of racism experienced by wealthy female immigrants from Hong Kong and those experienced by Indo-Chinese refugee women who have few income and job options apart from the highly exploitive needle trades. The very different circumstances of these two groups of 'visible minority' women offer but one example where connections among gender, race, and class in the Canadian context defy analyses based on essentialist conceptions of 'women', or indeed 'black women' or 'women of colour'.

Conclusion: Political Implications

At both the theoretical and political levels, these heated debates about race and class reflect one aspect of the crisis in Marxism. Not only has orthodox Marxism's focus on production and class relations been seen by some academics as incomplete; it has also been widely regarded as inadequate to the task of informing social movements based on other social identities (gay, ecological, anti-militaristic, as well as feminist and anti-racist). Most recently, the task of analyzing the interconnections between these social divisions and identities has been taken up by these movements as well as by many Left and socialist parties, particularly in western Europe.

The era of the 'new social movements' provided the political context for the development of black feminism and feminisms of other women of colour (American-Asian feminism, Chicana feminism, etc.) (Garcia 1989). By the late 1980s, the assessments of the political efficacy of black feminism are mixed. For instance, the black British feminist Mama (1989) emphasizes the continuing need for separate forums for the empowerment of black women and specialist services for those women who face racism from both state agencies and white feminist organizations. The impact of black feminism was also felt in the shift in the British feminist politics of reproduction, from emphasis on the single issue of abortion rights to a more inclusive focus on women's reproductive rights in general (Amos and Parmar 1984: 13).

Reflecting upon the organizational rise and disintegration of the black women's movement in Britain, Parmar (1989) confirms the historical necessity of such autonomous organization as both empowering and strengthening for the participants. Ultimately, however, the British black women's movement foundered over a number of conflicts and ended in theoretical and political paralysis. Parmar argues that this immobilization resulted from, on the one hand, 'accumulating a collection of oppressed identities which in turn have given rise to a [destructive] hierarchy of oppression', and on the other, constructing a notion of blackness that reflected forms of essentialism such as 'cryptic nationalistic sentiments [relying on] biologistic definitions of race' (1989: 58–9).

Other assessments of politics based on a general notion of race/gender/class have critiqued the mechanistic manner in which women are labelled 'as "doubly oppressed" or "triply oppressed" without recognizing that oppressive systems work in highly contextualized ways' (Harriss 1989: 38). Both black feminism and the recent debates on race and class have contributed significantly to a clearer understanding of various forms and dimensions of racism. In the rush to embrace a form of politics that incorporates different social divisions and dynamics of power, the women's movement and other progressive movements need to resist the superficial and even rhetorical inclusion of race/class/gender axes of domination. This danger is apparent in the concept of 'classism' adopted by some feminists, which 'served to reduce the whole issue of class exploitation to a set of attitudes or prejudices' (Harriss 1989: 39).

The need to comprehend the class character of all oppressions is particularly clear when one considers the time-worn strategies of state agencies to use pluralism—the recognition of discrete (and intersecting) social identities such as gender, race, and ethnicity—to divide people into special interest groups and ignore and obfuscate shared class interests.[10] Versions of feminism whose major preoccupation is incorporating 'difference' risk losing sight of class issues such as the growing power of transnational capital—even in areas, such as China and eastern Europe, that have long been avowedly anti-capitalist—and the reign of conservative governments in the majority of Western democracies. The post-modernist feminist project of exploring 'gender, race, and class as sites of difference' is, as Barrett points out, in danger of failing to recognize that these are also sites of power, exploitation, and oppression (1989: 42). As a guide to politics, organizing around 'difference'—in the sense of taking as a starting point only the personal and experiential modes of being—can lead to a form of closure, a directing of energy inward, leaving the sources of oppression unchallenged.

Since the 1970s, in Canada and many other Western democracies, the state has developed several specialist programs, advisers, commissions, and bodies to represent women's, Aboriginal, racial-minority, and other sectional interests. During the same decade, conservative governments have been elected whose overall economic and social agendas emphasize principles of 'freeing the market', cost-effectiveness and profitability in the restructuring of the labour market, and delivery of services. As Frigga Haug (1989: 112–13) states, for these conservative governments

meeting or palliating women's demands were no part of their policy. On the contrary, cutbacks in social spending, shifting the burden to private households and so partic-

ularly to women, privatization, and the glorification of old feminine virtues are typical of the policies of Western conservative governments.

The raising of these stark economic and political realities is not meant to obviate the task of understanding the impact of these larger processes for specific racial- and ethnic-minority women. Nor is it an argument for subordinating all struggles against race/gender/class to a larger class struggle. Totalizing politics are unrealistic and less effective than alliances based upon grassroots activism, whose social configuration is determined by the specific issue. Rather, what I mean to underscore are the inevitable intrusions of capitalist relations within the construction of intersecting forms of oppression. It is only by keeping in view the larger context of global and national economic and political realities that any movement seeking to understand the complex intersections between gender, race, ethnicity, and class can avoid becoming inward-looking and blandly pluralistic, and develop a politics of social transformation that truly moves beyond the fragments.[11]

Notes

1. I have dispensed with the convention, adopted by many social scientists, of placing 'race' within quotation marks to signify that 'race' is a social construction rather than a biological division within humankind, and as a reminder that biologically there exists only the one (i.e., human) race. Marxists also frequently follow this convention in order to differentiate the (epi)phenomenal or ideological character of 'race' from the materialist foundations of class, rooted in the respective relations of individuals and groups to a historically specific mode of production. While I fully support the assump-

tion that within any given society and historical era, the process of racial categorization is social, political, and ideological, and profoundly affected by economic relations of exploitation rather than simply found in nature, it remains that race, like gender, has biological referents and is most commonly associated with physiognomically based differences such as skin colour. Moreover, the emphasis that is rightly placed on the social nature of [the] constitution of races is also applicable to gender, ethnicity, and class, all of which have specific and intermeshed material and ideological modes of reproduction.

2. The following discussion of race, ethnicity, gender, and class in Canada draws almost entirely on English-Canadian literature and treats only tangentially the very important issue of French–English divisions and nationalism among Quebec women.

3. Typical in this regard is Armstrong and Armstrong's (1986) relegation of race, ethnicity, and religion to the sidelines within the socialist-feminist project: 'While the working class may or may not be differentiated by race, ethnicity, religion, occupation, industry, or whatever, it is invariably differentiated by sex' (212).

4. Socialist feminists diverge, however, on the theorized integration of the capitalist mode of production and the sexual or gendered division of labour. While Armstrong and Armstrong (1986) regard the sexual division of labour, premised on the biological role of women in having babies, to be essential to capitalism, forming one integrated system, Barrett (1980) and Connelly (1986) argue that gender divisions are a historically constituted integral part of, but not a necessary condition for, the development of capitalism.

5. Black feminists in Britain have categorically stated that 'even though the family may be a major site of women's oppression and subordination, it is not for the state to divide families against their wishes. Furthermore, in a racist society, the family can also be a source of support and strength for those under attack by the state' (WING 1985: 7; see also Amos and Parmar 1984: 15; Baptiste 1988; Sondhi 1987).

6. Francesca Klug argues that the 1906 social welfare reforms of the Liberal government in Britain were motivated by two concerns: a genuine commitment to boosting the living standards of the poor, and a desire to improve the physical well-being of the British population as defenders of the Empire (1989: 23).

7. Under the old Indian Act, Indian women who married non-status Indian or non-Indian men were removed from the Indian Register by the Department of Indian and Northern Affairs. Aided by the new Canadian Constitution, and after a protracted process of protest and lobbying (detailed in Silman 1987), the Canadian government moved to amend the Indian Act. Bill C-31 removed the sexually discriminatory sections of the Indian Act and allowed individuals who had lost their status to be reinstated.

8. 'A middle-class, black American woman who can have a career and employ a cleaning woman may experience the social impact of racism but she is not in the same structural position as an unemployed Bangladeshi woman worker in Britain who is treated by the state as dependent on her husband even if he is refused entry to Britain. In the West, black women are disadvantaged by racism in relation to white women, but black is not a static or universal category of disadvantage that transcends all other sources of social difference which determine the quality of people's lives' (Ramazanoglu 1989: 134).

9. In that year, China formally takes back the British colony into its fold (Malarek 1987: 215).

10. This point is persuasively made in Kathryn Harriss's (1989) study of the left-wing municipal socialism of the Greater London Council. The GLC experimented with welding socialist aims with a consciousness of the needs of autonomously organized groups such as blacks, gays, the disabled, etc. Harriss argues that the identities of race, gender, sexual orientation, etc., provided the GLC with a 'set of convenient pegs upon which to hang [its] policies, insofar as the borough population becomes classified according to what people have in common with their "identity group" rather than with others of the local working-class population' (48). Thus, beset by the pressures of accountability to central government, and finally to capital, the local council, *notwithstanding its socialist philosophy*, attempted to contain the demands of various sectional populations. By focusing on such issues as discrimination, it was able to avoid the fundamental class issues of poverty and decent

housing and thus obscure the class-bound character of the local state within capitalism which makes it 'governed by constraints . . . placing it at odds with its working-class population' (51).

11. *Beyond the Fragments* is the title of a British book that addressed many of the difficulties of developing a form of socialist-feminist organizing that simultaneously avoided the limitations and fracturing consequences of autonomous struggles while respecting the integrity of autonomous organization (Rowbotham, Segal, and Wainwright 1979).

Chapter 11

The Ideology of Racism

Frances Henry, Carol Tator, Winston Mattis, and Tim Rees

We are at one of those critical junctures where two ideals are in conflict. There's the principle of the legal equality of all. There's the fact that there are serious inequalities in our society, many of which can only be remedied by treating people unequally. Which puts liberals like myself at war with ourselves. (Gwyn 1993)

This chapter examines the ideology of racism in Canada today. It begins with a brief examination of the function of ideology as the basis of social behaviour and then explores the nature of racist ideology. This ideology provides the foundation for understanding the racist attitudes and behaviours of individuals, the maintenance of racist policies and practices in Canadian institutions, and the promulgation of racist doctrines and laws by the state. The chapter analyzes the role and functions of racist ideology and introduces the concept of democratic racism. The last section of this chapter examines the discourse of democratic racism and some of the myths that support and reinforce racism as ideology and praxis.

Democratic racism is an ideology that permits and sustains people's ability to maintain two apparently conflicting sets of values. One set consists of a commitment to a liberal, democratic society motivated by the egalitarian values of fairness, justice, and equality. Conflicting with these values are attitudes and behaviours that include negative feelings about people of colour and that

result in differential treatment of them, or discrimination against them. Democratic racism, in its simplest form, is an ideology that reduces the conflict between maintaining a commitment to both egalitarian and non-egalitarian values.

Introduction

What Is Ideology?

Ideology is a set of beliefs, perceptions, assumptions, and values that provide members of a group with an understanding and an explanation of their world. At another level, ideology provides a framework for 'organizing, maintaining, and transforming relations of power and dominance in society' (Fleras and Elliott 1992: 54).

Ideology influences the ways in which people interpret social, cultural, political, and economic systems and structures, and it is linked to their perceived needs, hopes, and fears. Ideological formations are not static but organic and constantly evolving, often as a result of contradictory experiences (Hall 1983).

People are often unaware of their ideologies:

It is indeed a peculiarity of ideology that it imposes (without appearing to do so) obviousness as obviousness which we cannot fail to recognize and before which we have the inevitable and natural reaction of crying out (aloud or in the still small voice of conscience): 'That's obvious! That's right! That's true!' (Althusser 1971: 127)

Within these everyday ideological constructs, ideas about race, gender, and class are produced, preserved, and promoted. These ideas form the basis for social behaviour. Therefore, understanding ideology is crucial to an understanding of the marginalization, exclusion, and domination of people of colour in Canadian society.

The Definition and Function of Racist Ideology

Racist ideology provides the conceptual framework for the political, social, and cultural structures of inequality and systems of dominance based on race, as well as the processes of exclusion and marginalization of people of colour that characterize Canadian society.

The cognitive dimensions of racism are located in collective patterns of thought, knowledge, and beliefs as well as individual attitudes, perceptions, and behaviours. 'Racism as ideology includes the whole range of concepts, ideas, images, and institutions that provide the framework of interpretation and meaning for racial thought in society' (Essed 1990: 44). Racist ideology therefore organizes, preserves, and perpetuates the power structures in a society. It creates and preserves a system of dominance based on race and is communicated and reproduced through agencies of socialization and cultural transmission, such as the mass media, schools and universities, religious doctrines, symbols and images, art, music, and literature. It is reflected and regenerated in the very language we read, write, and speak.

The Elusive Nature of Racism

One of the most complex aspects of racism is its elusive and changing nature. The most com-

monly accepted concept of racism in Canada is one that refers to the individual expression of overt feelings or actions. Racism is generally understood to refer to physical assaults that have been perpetrated by bigoted individuals, racial slurs and harassment in schools or in the workplace, defacing property with racial graffiti, and similar overt acts. There seems to be an extremely limited understanding of racism in public discourse. Racism manifests itself not only within individuals but also in groups, organizations, institutions, at the state level, and in the value system of society. In each arena, racism assumes a different form. It has 'a geographic, social, and historical specificity. In any country, at any point of time, the realization of racist practice will be of a specific nature' (Brandt 1986: 67–8).

Racism is not a natural element in society, just waiting for a series of events to trigger its manifestations:

It has no natural and universal law of development. It does not always assume the same shape. There have been many significantly different *racisms*—each historically specific and articulated in a different way. Racism is always historically specific in this way, whatever common features it may appear to share with other similar social phenomena. It always assumes specific forms which arise out of the *present*—not the past—conditions and organization of society. (Hall 1978: 26)

Thus the ways in which racism manifests itself at any particular time are fluid, dynamic, and ever-changing. They are affected by the social contexts in which racism develops.

In a similar vein, the study of racism provides 'a picture . . . of historically variant racism both continuously and discontinuously transformed from one period to another. Subject, objects, and modes alter. Developments and changes in racist discourse are demonstrated to be functions of dominant inter-ests, aims, and purposes' (Goldberg 1990: xiii).

Another important dimension of racism is its ability to be so subtly expressed or indirectly implied that its targets are not even aware of it. Conversely, racism is sometimes visible only to its victims. It remains indiscernible to others, who therefore deny its existence.

The subtle and ever-changing nature of racism helps to explain both its persistence over time and the difficulties of defining and measuring it. However, although many are confused by the term, racism rests on this mystification of social relations—the necessary illusions that secure the order of public authority (Gilroy 1987).

Racist ideology forms part of 'common sense'. Racist thinking, according to this view, is natural and forms part of the ways in which ordinary people view the world—they do not need to have specialized knowledge about minority groups to be racist. 'Common sense' racism is not based on theory, nor does it have a unified body of knowledge to support it; it contains a 'storehouse of knowledge' that guides the think-ing of 'the practical struggle of everyday life of the popular masses' (Lawrence 1982: 49).

The construction of and belief in a racist ideol-ogy helps people to understand the increasingly complex societies in which they live. Thus, re-cently unemployed people can easily blame the new immigrants who have taken their jobs away. People who are fearful in their homes and on the streets can now blame all those black or Asian people who commit crimes. Teachers whose black students are underachieving can believe that it has nothing to do with their racial atti-tudes or classroom practices. The corporate man-ager is able to justify a refusal to hire those who are racially 'different' on the basis of not wanting to disrupt the harmony of the workforce.

Racist assumptions and beliefs provide a ready explanation for the stress experienced by people who live in a country undergoing rapid social and cultural change:

Racism is not a set of false pleas which swim around in the head. They're not a set of mis-taken perceptions. They have their basis in real material conditions of existence. They arise because of concrete problems of differ-ent classes and groups in society. Racism represents the attempt ideologically to con-struct those conditions, contradictions, and problems in such a way that they can be dealt with and deflected in the same mo-ment. (Hall 1978: 35)

Ideology may go far beyond individual beliefs and attitudes; it carries with it a predisposition to behave in negative, derogatory, or discrimina-tory ways toward members of the targeted group. An ideology of racism therefore is more powerful than mere attitudes or beliefs (Hall et al. 1978). Ideology denotes a set of ideas and values that legitimate particular economic and social conditions. It penetrates and saturates everyday discourses in the form of common sense and provides codes of meaning (Hebridge 1993: 363).

The Concept of Democratic Racism

The primary characteristic of democratic racism—the most appropriate model for under-standing how and why racism continues in Canada—is the justification of the inherent con-flict between the egalitarian values of justice and fairness and the racist ideologies reflected in the collective mass-belief system as well as the racist attitudes, perceptions, and assumptions of indi-viduals.

Racist beliefs and practices continue to per-vade Canadian society. Attitude surveys have found that many Canadians hold racist views. In the first such survey carried out in Canada, about 16 per cent of Canadian adults were found to be confirmed bigots, while a further 35 per cent held somewhat intolerant views. Another 30 per cent leaned toward tolerance, and the remaining 20 per cent were extremely tolerant (Henry 1978). Later surveys and polls support these findings. . . . Most Canadians therefore hold some degree of racist attitudes. But, living in a society that believes in democracy, most Canadians also recognize that these attitudes are socially unacceptable. In order to maintain their racist beliefs while championing democratic values, Canadians have developed the ideology of democratic racism—a set of justificatory arguments and mechanisms that permit these contradictory ideologies to coexist.

Democratic racism, therefore, results from the retention of racist beliefs and behaviours in a 'democratic' society. The obfuscation and justificatory arguments of democratic racism are deployed to demonstrate continuing faith in the principles of an egalitarian society while at the same time undermining and sabotaging those ideals.

Before discussing this ideology as it pertains to Canada, it is useful to analyze it in the context of the United Kingdom and the United States. In the former the concept of 'new racism' has been elaborated, while in the latter 'aversive racism' has appeared in the literature. These aspects of racism, identified by critical theorists in the United Kingdom, are also relevant to Canada and are included in democratic racism.

New Racism in the United Kingdom

Distancing themselves from the crude ideas of biological inferiority and superiority, 'new racists' have defined a national British culture that is homogeneously white. It is concerned with

> mechanisms of inclusion and exclusion. It specifies who may legitimately belong to the national community and simultaneously advances reasons for the segregation or banishment of those whose 'origin'. . . assigns them elsewhere. [West Indians, and Asians,

> for different reasons] are judged to be incompatible with authentic forms of Englishness. Alien cultures come to embody a threat which, in turn, invites the conclusion that national decline and weakness have been precipitated by the arrival of blacks. (Gilroy 1987: 45–6)

Scholars in the United Kingdom have analyzed the trend toward the increasing racialization of state policies 'in all areas of social life' (CCCS 1982: 19). For at least the past two decades, observers have noted the central government's lack of sympathy and support for racial-equality initiatives (Ball and Solomos 1990). The policy interventions of the central government have tended to affirm a deep-seated commitment to the rights of the white majority rather than those of minority communities. Herman Ouseley notes that the failure 'to implement radical race equality policies was the result of inadequate attempts by national and local politicians' (Ball and Solomos 1990). Such state policies reinforce the racist thinking of much of the population.

Lawrence (1982) identified a number of racial ideologies characteristic of the Conservative-run state in Great Britain. At their heart is a definition of 'British' that clearly excludes people of colour who come from former (and present) commonwealth countries. This definition affirms the 'naturalness' of British values, British culture, and especially British family life. Within the politics of nationalism, sovereignty, and cultural identity, it defines the nation as a unified *cultural* community (Gilroy 1987). Thus, white anti-racists are regarded as having been influenced by 'alien' ideas.

Although new racism no longer espouses doctrines of racial superiority (there are exceptions, particularly in academia and the extreme Right), it nevertheless denigrates people of colour. The myths that fuel new racism often derive from a negative evaluation of other cultures rather than from a focus on race. This ideology, for example, expresses itself in a negative evaluation of black culture, particularly the 'deviant' black family and the 'aberrant' behaviour of black youth. Thus, although police officials do not consider themselves racist, they believe that blacks are culturally disposed to criminal behaviour. Further, the media, while not admitting racism, publish report after report in which derogatory cultural characteristics are highlighted.

New racism cites pathological cultural patterns as major reasons for criminal behaviour, poverty, poor achievement in school, and an assortment of other social problems. Blacks show their inferiority by having a propensity for loud music and raucous conversation. New racists therefore cloak their negative attitudes toward other groups by claiming that while they do not believe in racial superiority, not all cultures are equally valid. The cultural behaviour of the 'others', such as blacks, demonstrates that they are not the same as whites and cannot be part of the national culture.

When race is identified with identity and culture, careful language enables people to 'speak about race without mentioning the word' (Gilroy 1987: 53). The crude and overtly racist labels of the far Right are avoided, but the new racism can be articulated by the choice of carefully coded language: '"They", despite the good qualities of some of "them", are held to be different from "us" and would, on the whole, be better off back in "their" countries' (Billig et al. 1988: 107).

Another form of discourse in which overt racism is avoided occurs in the 'two-handedness of the "on the one hand, on the other hand" formulation. Having stated an opposition to racism or to prejudice, the way is then opened for an expression of racist or prejudiced views' (Billig et al. 1988: 109). These formulations appear in an ideology in which traditional racism is eschewed but a newer, masked, and more subtle form is allowed expression. Modern racism is expressed in a rhetorical context, demonstrated in comments such as 'I'm not a racist, but . . .', which are followed by an overtly racist statement.

Aversive Racism in the United States

In the United States, a new form of democratic racism has been explored by social psychologists, who analyze the individual's attitudes. Gaertner and Dovidio (1986) present the results of studies of racism among the 'well intentioned':

> Our work has focused on those white Americans, who, in terms of racism and public policy, seem 'well intentioned'. That is, they genuinely profess egalitarianism, as well as the desire to ameliorate the consequences of racism and poverty. However, we believe that the racial attitudes of many of these well-intentioned people may be characterized by a special type of ambivalence: aversiveness. (Gaertner and Dovidio 1981: 208)

Their analysis builds on what was earlier identified as 'aversive racism' (Kovel 1970). In this pioneering work, Kovel distinguished 'dominative' racists—strong hard-core bigots who are prepared to act on their attitudes—from 'aversive' racists. The latter also believe in white supremacy, but do nothing about it. Aversive racists are prejudiced but do not act in discriminatory ways. Some avoid contact with blacks and other minorities, but when contact is unavoidable, they are polite.

Other aversive racists, however, 'are impelled by a strong social conscience, consider themselves liberals, and despite their sense of aversion (which may not be admitted inwardly) do their best within the given structure of society to ameliorate the conditions of the Negro' (Kovel 1970: 55). They believe in fairness and equality for all and pride themselves on their strong social conscience. They may not be aware of their aversion to blacks (or other minorities) and appear to have a positive racial attitude. Gaertner and Dovidio note that this attitude is superficial, ambiguous, and complex.

Their studies have identified a number of characteristics of aversive racists, including the following:

- Aversive racists consider themselves prejudice-free but attempt to avoid contact with the minority group to which they are averse.
- Aversive racists think of themselves as politically liberal and non-discriminatory. In a situation in which clearly prescribed norms call for tolerant behaviour, they will behave appropriately. However, in situations in which there are no clear prescriptive norms, they may indulge in discriminatory behaviour because it would not be obvious.
- Aversive racists' positive actions toward minority groups relate less to a genuine effort to help minorities or to implement egalitarian values than to reaffirm their own lack of prejudice. This attitude may result in tokenism: aversive racists affirm that they are prejudice-free by making trivial gestures that preclude the necessity for extensive, costly action. (Gaertner 1976: 208)

Aversive racism therefore 'represents a particular type of ambivalence in which the conflict is between feelings and beliefs associated with a sincerely egalitarian value system and unacknowledged negative feelings and beliefs about blacks' (Gaertner and Dovidio 1986: 62). Moreover, this type of racism does not necessarily include feelings of hate or hostility, nor will it usually express itself in hostile or discriminatory behaviour. Aversive racism involves 'discomfort, uneasiness, disgust, and sometimes fear, which tend to motivate avoidance rather than intentionally destructive behaviours' (Gaertner and Dovidio 1986: 63).

Aversive racism stems from socialization and is reinforced by social and cultural factors. In the United States, for example, the denigration of black culture, black stereotypes, and the constant association of black people with poverty, crime, and delinquency reinforces negative racial attitudes. Moreover, the differential distribution of social, economic, and political power between blacks and whites further reinforces these attitudes.

Symbolic Racism

Closely aligned to the aversive form, symbolic racism is an attitude in which 'abstract moral assertions are made about blacks' behaviour as a group, concerning what blacks deserve, how they ought to act, whether or not they are treated equitably, and so on' (Sears and McConahay 1973: 138). Symbolic racism manifests itself in 'acts that are rationalized on a non-racial basis but that actually maintain the racial status quo by continuing discrimination against blacks' (Sears and McConahay 1973: 24). In the United States, these acts include voting for white rather than black candidates, opposing affirmative-action programs, and opposing desegregation in housing and education. In Canada, opposing affirmative action and employment equity is an act of symbolic racism.

Other aspects of symbolic racism have relevance for Canada. For example, unlike the older 'redneck' bigotry, which denied equal rights and opportunities for people of colour, symbolic racism allows a person to uphold these values but still believe that blacks are 'too pushy' because they are making too many demands for equality too quickly. Moreover, whites who hold these views may not feel personally threatened by black claims to equality but feel that their values are endangered: black assertiveness may be regarded as a threat to the very fabric of society. Another important component of symbolic racism is that, as its name implies, it operates through symbols rather than overt discrimination. Thus, there is opposition to welfare, black politicians, and fair housing laws because they symbolize the unreasonable demands being made by blacks. In sum, then, symbolic racism is the expression in terms of abstract ideological symbols and symbolic behaviours of the feeling that blacks are violating cherished values and making illegitimate demands for changes in the racial status quo (McConahay and Hough 1976: 38).

Democratic Racism

Although democratic racism pertains largely to ideology and stresses the role of value differences as these are reflected in systems and institutions, individuals are largely responsible for the development of policies and the implementation of procedures that regulate systems and institutions. Thus democratic racism is related to new racism, aversive racism, and symbolic racism. It differs from them by positing a value conflict.

Democratic racism is an ideology in which two conflicting sets of values are made congruent to each other. Commitments to democratic principles such as justice, equality, and fairness conflict but coexist with attitudes and behaviours that include negative feelings about minority groups, differential treatment, and discrimination against them.

One of the consequences of the conflict is a lack of support for policies and practices that might ameliorate the low status of people of colour. These policies and practices tend to require changes in the existing social, economic, and political order, usually by state intervention. The intervention, however, is perceived to be in conflict with and a threat to liberal democracy. Thus democratic racism holds that the spread of racism should only be dealt with—if at all—by leaving basic economic structures and societal relations essentially unchanged (Gilroy 1987). Efforts to combat racism that require intervention to change the cultural, social, economic, and political order will lack political support. More

importantly, they will lack legitimacy, according to the egalitarian principles of liberal democracy.

The Discourse of Democratic Racism

How is democratic racism manifested in the daily lives, opinions, and feelings of people? What are the values, assumptions, and arguments of democratic racism? As Wellman (1977) noted, the maintenance of a wide array of myths and misconceptions about racism has permitted a pattern of denial that has led to a wholly inadequate response to racism.

Democratic racism in its ideological and discursive form is deeply embedded in popular culture and popular discourse. It is located within what has been called society's frames of reference (Hebridge 1993). These frames of reference are a largely unacknowledged set of beliefs, assumptions, feelings, stories, and quasi-memories that underlie, sustain, and inform perceptions, thoughts, and actions. Democratic racism as racist discourse begins in the families that nurture us, the communities that socialize us, the schools and universities that educate us, the media that communicate ideas and images to us, and the popular culture that entertains us.

Goldberg (1993) contends that racist discourse covers a wide spectrum of expressions and representations, including a nation's recorded history; scientific forms of racist explanations (such as Rushton's theory of racial differences); economic, legal, and bureaucratic forms of doctrine; cultural representations in the form of national narratives, images, and symbols, and so on. Social power is reflected in racist discourse.

The conflict between the ideology of democratic liberalism and the racist ideology present in the collective belief system of the dominant culture is reflected in the racist discourse that operates in the schools, the media, the courts, law enforcement agencies, arts organizations and cultural institutions, human services, government bureaucracies, and political authorities.

The school, the university, the newspaper and the television station, the courtroom, police headquarters, the hospital, and the government office are discursive spaces. Within these spaces, controlled mainly by a dominant white culture, there exists a constant moral tension: the everyday experiences of people of colour, juxtaposed with the perceptions and responses of those who have the power to redefine that reality.

Many people resist anti-racism and equality initiatives because they are unwilling to question *their* own belief and value systems and discursive practices, *their* organizational and professional norms, *their* positions of power and privilege within the workplace and society. Thus, they are unable to examine the relation between cultural and racial differences and the power dynamics constructed around ideas about those differences. Acknowledging that ethno-racial differences make a difference in the lives of people is to concede that Euro-Canadian hegemony continues to function and organize the structures within which the delivery of mainstream programs and services operates (Dei 1996). In each of these discursive spaces we see tension and resistance in relation to how multicultural and anti-racism ideologies and policies are 'imagined, internalized, and acted upon' (Yon 1995: 315).

Resistance may manifest itself as active opposition, expressed openly, but it is more commonly articulated in more subtle forms of discourse. Discourses on race and racism converge with concerns about Canadian identity, national unity, ethnicity, multiculturalism, and so on. Discourse provides the conceptual models for mapping the world around us and incorporates both social relationships and power relations (Goldberg 1993), but as Yon (1995) demonstrates in his ethnographic study of students and teachers in a Toronto high school, discourse about identity and nation that never mentions the word 'race' can also be considered racist discourse.

Increasingly, the discourse of liberalism is juxtaposed with popular conservative ideology, and individuals slide ambivalently between the two. As Yon (1995) points out:

> Resistance and accommodation can be present in the same moment. Discourse often reveals ambivalence, contradiction, and subtleties in relation to the issues of difference. For example, discussions about culture are often framed in the context of being 'tolerant', 'sensitive', and sufficiently enlightened to appreciate and respect the diverse cultures of the 'others'.

Cultural discourse tends to cover up the 'unpleasantness' of domination and inequity (Wetherell and Potter 1992). . . .

The paradox of a postmodern liberal society is that as modernity commits itself to these liberal ideals and to the moral irrelevance of race, there is a proliferation of racial identities and an assortment of exclusions they support and sustain. Making a similar point, Mackey contends that 'liberal principles are the very language and conceptual framework through which intolerance and exclusion are enabled, reinforced, defined, and defended' (Mackey 1996: 305).

The elusive nature of the dominant discourse allows it to mask its racialized ideas (Fiske 1994). Within it are unchallenged assumptions, or myths. These myths attempt to explain, rationalize, and resolve unsupportable contradictions and problems in society. Myths arise at particular historical moments in response to a perceived need within society. They function as a guideline for new ideas and behaviours. The final section of this chapter explores some of the prevailing myths that underpin democratic racism.

* * *

The Discourse of Denial

Within this discourse the principle assumption is that racism simply does not exist in a democratic society. There is a refusal to accept the reality of racism, despite the evidence of racial prejudice and discrimination in, and the effects of racism on, the lives of people of colour. The assumption here is that because Canada is a society that upholds the ideals of a liberal democracy, it could not possibly be racist. When racism is shown to exist, it tends to be identified as an isolated phenomenon relating to a limited number of social deviants, economic instability, or the consequence of 'undemocratic' traditions that are disappearing from the Canadian scene. This discourse resists the notion that racism is systemic and inherently embedded in Canada's cultural values and democratic institutions.

* * *

The Discourse of Equal Opportunity

This discourse suggests that all we need to do is treat everyone the same, and fairness will be ensured. This notion is based on an ahistorical premise, that is, we all begin from the same starting point; everyone competes on a level playing field. Society merely provides the conditions within which individuals differentially endowed can make their mark. All have an equal opportunity to succeed and the same rights. Thus, individual merit determines who will succeed in the workplace, school, politics, the arts.

This view ignores the social construction of race, in which power and privilege belongs to those who are white (among other social markers of privilege, including gender, class, sexual orientation, and able-bodiedness). Equal opportunity represents a passive approach and does not require the dismantling of white institutional power or the redistribution of white social capital (Crenshaw 1997). This paradigm demands no form of proactive institutional or state intervention such as employment equity or anti-racism policies.

The Discourse of Blaming the Victim

If equal opportunity and racial equality are assumed to exist, then a minority population's lack of success must be attributed to some other set of conditions. One explanation used by the dominant culture is the notion that certain minority communities themselves are culturally deficient—they may be lacking intellectual prowess or be more prone to aggressive behaviour or other forms of 'deviant behaviour'. In this form of dominant discourse, it is assumed that certain communities (such as African Canadians) lack the motivation, education, or skills to participate fully in the workplace, educational system, and other arenas of Canadian society.

Alternatively, it is argued that the failure of certain groups to succeed and integrate into the mainstream dominant culture is largely due to recalcitrant members of these groups refusing to adapt their 'traditional', 'different' cultural values and norms to fit into Canadian society and making unreasonable demands on the 'host' society.

* * *

The Discourse of Reverse Racism

In a semantic reversal, those associated with the dominant culture contend that they are *now* the victims of a new form of oppression and exclusion. Anti-racism and equity policies are discredited by suggesting in strong, emotive language that they are nothing more than 'apartheid in reverse', a 'new inquisition', or 'McCarthyite witch hunts'.

Positive and proactive policies and programs are thus aligned with creeping totalitarianism and accused of incorporating the anti-democratic, authoritarian methods of the extreme Right. 'These are fertile times for hate-mongers and reactionaries. The defenders of the status quo have discovered a wonderful refuge in their opposition to the excesses of political correctness' (DiManno 1993).

Those concerned with addressing racial inequalities have frequently been accused of belonging to radical, extremist groups. The implication of these reproaches is that the issue of race is being used as a cover for promoting conflict in pursuit of other questionable political ends. Those concerned with racial injustice have been labelled as radicals who are using an anti-racism platform to subvert Canada's fundamental institutions, values, and beliefs.

* * *

The Discourse of Multiculturalism: Tolerance, Accommodation, Harmony, and Diversity

The concepts of tolerance, accommodation, sensitivity, harmony, and diversity lie at the core of multicultural ideology and are firmly embedded in multicultural policy and discourse. . . . The emphasis on tolerance and sensitivity suggests that while one must accept the idiosyncrasies of the 'others', the underlying premise is that the dominant way is superior.

Within this minimal form of recognition of difference, the dominant culture creates a ceiling on tolerance, that is, it stipulates what differences are tolerable. This ceiling is reflected in responses in public opinion polls and in surveys dealing with multiculturalism (Mirchandani and Tastsoglou 1998), in which a significant number of respondents take a position that 'we' cannot tolerate too much difference because it generates dissent, disruption, and conflict. According to this view, paying unnecessary attention to 'differences' leads to division, disharmony, and disorder in society. Where possible, the dominant culture attempts to accommodate *their* idiosyncratic cultural differences.

Declarations of the need for tolerance and harmony tend to conceal the messy business of structural and systemic inequality and the unequal relations of power that continue to exist in a democratic liberal society. Mohanty contends that 'differences defined as asymmetrical and incommensurate cultural spheres situated within hierarchies of domination and resistance cannot be accommodated with a discourse of "harmony in diversity"' (1993: 72).

The Discourse of Liberal Values: Individualism, Truth, Tradition, Universalism, and Freedom of Expression

Democratic liberalism is distinguished by [a] set of beliefs that include: the primacy of individual rights over collective or group rights; the power of (one) truth, tradition, and history; an appeal to universalism; the sacredness of the principle of freedom of expression; and a commitment to human rights and equality, among many other ideals. But as many scholars observe, liberalism is full of paradoxes and contradictions and assumes different meanings, depending on one's social location and angle of vision (Hall 1986; Goldberg 1993; Apple 1993; Winant 1997). As Parekh argues, 'Liberalism is both egalitarian and inegalitarian.' It simultaneously supports the unity of humankind and the hierarchy of cultures. It is both tolerant and intolerant (1986: 82). Ignatieff claims, 'We live by liberal fictions'; despite the fact that human beings are 'incorrigibly different . . . equality is a moral story which governs our hypotheses' (1998: 19).

From the perspective of the marginalized and excluded, traditional liberal values have been found wanting. In the interests of expanding liberal democratic principles and extending the promises of liberalism to those who have not enjoyed its benefits, minority communities are demanding an 'affirmative' correction of historical injustices (Stam 1993).

However, those individuals and groups who invoke the validity of alternative voices, experiences, traditions, perspectives, and histories are seen to be violating a sacred body of principles, values, and beliefs. There is only one truth, a single 'authentic' history, a noble Euro-American tradition, a universal form of human understanding and expression that includes and transcends all cultural and racial boundaries.

The Discourse of National Identity

The discourse of national identity is marked by erasures, omissions, and silences. Ethno-racial minorities have been placed outside the 'national project' of Canada and excluded from the 'imagined community' (Anderson 1983) of Canadian society. From Canada's earliest history, the idea of 'hyphenated' Canadians has been a fundamental part of the national discourse, but it has been limited to two identities: English Canada and French Canada. The Fathers of Confederation ignored the cultural plurality that existed even at that time. Aboriginal and other cultures were omitted from the national discourse and thereby rendered invisible. Later, a category of 'others' was added—but only two of these had constitutional rights.

National discourse constructs meanings and influences 'our actions and our conceptions of ourselves' (Hall 1992a: 292). National culture defines identity by 'producing meanings about the nation with which we can identify; these are contained in the stories which are told about it, memories which connect it with its past, and the images which are constructed of it' (Hall 1992a: 282).

The debate over national identity is fundamental to Canadian discourse. Canada's search for national unity is really a search for cultural stability. The question of cultural identity is influenced by the politics of difference, a politics shaped by the interplay of history, culture, race, and power. In the struggle over national identity, the dominant culture is reluctant to include identities of 'others' that it has constructed, perpetuated, and used to its advantage. To discard 'otherness' would in a sense be to abandon the vehicles through which inequalities and imbalances are legitimized.

Many Canadians see themselves as egalitarian and have little difficulty in rejecting the more overt expressions of racism. They may make symbolic gestures of inclusivity. However, beyond these token efforts, the struggles of people of colour are met with the arbitrary use of political, economic, and cultural institutional power in the interests of 'maintaining democracy'. . . .

Chapter 12

Geopolitics, Culture Clash, and Gender after September 11

Sherene Razack

Culture clashes were essential to the success of racial myths, for throughout history the foreigner outside the tribe has never been truly welcome.

　　　　　—George L. Mosse (1985: xxvii)

[. . .] the imperialist feminist desire to emancipate the Muslim woman is part of a system based on the disciplining and normalizing gaze of modern colonial disciplinary power.

　　　　　—Meyda Yegenoglu (1998: 111)

The modern woman is first and foremost an imperialist.

　　　　　—Rosemary M. George (1993–94: 97)

The attacks on the World Trade Center and Pentagon on September 11, 2001, have resulted in 'anti-terrorism' measures that have included surveillance, stigmatization, and the actual incarceration of men considered 'Muslim looking or Arab looking'. In this climate, to write about violent Muslim men guarantees royalties and the prestige of being on bestseller lists. When the writing is done by Western feminists, both Muslim and non-Muslim, it provides ideological justifications for the 'War on Terror' and the US bid for empire. The post-September 11 climate has also enabled Western feminists to use the Israeli–Palestinian conflict as evidence of the violence of Muslim and Arab men. In recent years, there has been a steady stream of books and articles announcing that the current Israeli administration is entirely justified in its treatment of Palestinians and that those who criticize Israel are simply being anti-Semitic.[1] In many of these texts, the violence Muslim women endure at the hands of Muslim men becomes a marker of Muslim men's barbarism and a reason why the claims of Palestinians, who are mainly Muslims, are unacceptable. This logic is available at a glance in subway posters in San Francisco in which a blond woman announces that she has just been to Israel, a land where women have equal rights.

In this article, I argue that the convergence of the US 'War on Terror' and its inextricable links to US support of Israel has produced a particular geopolitical terrain in the post-September 11 period that has enabled blatant racism to be articulated in the name of feminism. As I will show, the seemingly disparate strands of this political position are bound together and given coherency by the notion of 'culture clash' in that the West, Jews included, are caught up in a violent clash with the Islamic world. The clash is cultural in origin: Islam is everything the West is not. Furthermore, as fatally pre-modern, tribal, non-democratic, and religious, the barbarism of Islam is principally evident in the treatment of women in Muslim communities.

Of course, this approach is not new. As Edward Said (1992: 25) pointed out long ago in

The Question of Palestine, the argument that turns colonial dispossession of a people into a story of an empty land awaiting European improvement draws on 'the picture of a handful of European Jews hewing a civilization of sweetness and light out of the Black Islamic sea'. Yet if the notion of a Black Islamic sea has long been marshalled in support of the state of Israel's oppressive policies toward Palestinians, today it has gained greater currency and the bodies of Muslim women have been useful to the argument.

What are the implications for feminists of these two geopolitical conditions, in which the Muslim woman's body is constituted as simply a marker of a community's place in modernity? First, the pervasiveness of violence against women in the West is eclipsed. Additionally, saving Muslim women from the excesses of their society marks Western men and women as more civilized. Observing that 'the declaration of an emancipated status for the Western woman is contingent upon the representation of the Oriental woman as her devalued other', Yegen-oglu (1998: 105) reminds us that women can only enter the privileged space of the universal through 'a masculine gesture'. Just as men claim the universal for themselves by confining women outside of it as non-rational subjects, so the Western woman requires the culturally different body to make her own claim of universality. Unveiling the Muslim woman, making her body visible, and hence knowable and available for possession, renders the Western woman as the colonial, observing, possessing subject. Thus, old colonial technologies enjoy renewed vigour at a time when the hegemonic framing of the New World Order centres on Islam versus the West.

This examination was prompted in part by my own experiences as a secular feminist with a Muslim name. Whereas the 'marking' that identifies me as Muslim seldom drew attention before, my body, my feminist commitments, and my scholarship became suspect in the post-September 11 environment. In 2002, for instance, I became the target of an e-mail campaign that vilified me for distributing a petition that denounced the military activities of the Israeli state in Jenin. Predictably, this campaign featured threatening, violent, and misogynist language of the kind familiar to any woman who takes strong anti-sexist and anti-racist positions. This time, however, I was also reminded of the barbarities of the treatment of women in Muslim–Arab cultures. Often in these messages, 'the oppression of women, religious intolerance, lack of freedoms, lack of democracy, absence of free press, and honour killings of family members in the Arab countries' were put against Israel as a 'free country with tolerance of all religions and equality for women'.[2] To criticize Israel, my correspondents insisted, was not only to be anti-Semitic and anti-American but also to be on the side of patriarchy. Since these messages specifically targeted me, I knew that my body had become something of a global sign and that a strange nexus had emerged in contemporary geopolitics between Western feminism and racism.

A similar confluence between Western feminism and racism was taking place in popular culture. Between 2002 and 2003, three books appeared that did very well in sales and were almost without exception positively reviewed in the press: Orianna Fallaci's *The Rage and the Pride* (2002), Phyllis Chesler's *The New Anti-Semitism* (2003), and Irshad Manji's *The Trouble with Islam* (2003). Each book advances the idea of a culture clash of epic proportions between the West and Islam. They outline the need to defend the West generally, and Israel in particular, against an Islamic threat, a threat reinforced by the idea of misogynist Muslim men. Implicitly or explicitly, each book suggests that to take a political position critical of the then-current US and Israeli administrations (George W. Bush and Ariel Sharon) is at best being callous toward Muslim women and at worst supportive of profoundly misogynist political regimes. . . .

Although I am addressing myself to feminists, my task is not to explore what I consider to be an imperialist feminism. . . . Instead, I wish to closely examine the racial logic that structures so much of this geopolitical terrain, gesturing to gender as one of its principal technologies, but remaining focused on the overall thrust of these books: a message of European superiority in which both the US bid for empire and the contemporary politics of Israeli occupation are defended and legitimized. My aim is to take stock of a geopolitics that has begun to profoundly alter the conditions under which feminists can address issues of violence in communities of colour. . . .

Culture Clash

Mosse's observation that racial myths depend upon the language of culture (our culture is more developed than theirs) is an important reminder of why it is dangerous to consider culture apart from racism. The close connection between assertions of cultural difference and racism has meant that in white societies the smallest reference to cultural differences between the European majority and Third World peoples (Muslims in particular) triggers an instant chain of associations (the veil, female genital mutilation, arranged marriages, etc.). This chain ends with the declared superiority of European culture, imagined as a homogeneous composite of values, including a unique commitment to democracy and human rights, and to the human rights of women in particular. Culture clash, in which the West has values and modernity and the non-West has culture, consolidates membership in the dominant group; it provides belonging by enabling dominant groups to imagine that they share something in common that marks them as superior.

Today in the West, culture clash as the means of expressing European superiority is often organized around the Muslim Other, whose presence on European and North American soil has been increasing. An Internet search of the key words 'Muslims and gender equality' readily produces this popular articulation of culture clash, as in the following statement by Barbara Walker (2002):

> The newcomer Muslims bring an ancient social structure that is authoritarian and misogynist, where knowledge is an inherited commodity rather than derived through rational inquiry. Western culture, on the other hand, has built upon its Greek, Roman, and Renaissance traditions to value *democracy, gender equality, individual rights, and rational thought.* [emphasis added]

Apart from the decontextualization and dehistoricization that underpin the explanation of culture clash, in which 'the West and the Rest' exist as discrete and unrelated entities forever frozen at different levels of development, a disturbing spatializing of morality occurs in the story of culture clash and its underpinning Enlightenment narrative of progress that facilitates the use of force. We have reason; they do not. We are located in modernity; they are not. Significantly, because *they* have not advanced as we have, it is our moral obligation to correct, discipline, and keep them in line. In doing so, the West has often denied the benefits of modernity to those it considers to be outside its bounds. Evicted from the universal, and thus from civilization and progress, the non-West occupies a zone outside the law. Violence may be directed at it with impunity.[3]

Examining the premises of Samuel P. Huntington's widely cited book *Clash of Civilizations* (1997) reveals the importance of the notion of culture clash to the contemporary making of empire. Huntington argued that the primary source of conflict in the world today is the cultural difference between the West and non-West, a culture clash in which Islam figures

prominently as the antithesis of Western civilization. People who are alike culturally co-operate
with each other; dislike or fear of the foreigner
and accompanying feelings of superiority are
present in all cultures. From such simple premises, Huntington explains a wide range of complex phenomena, such as the Rwandan genocide,
the massacre of Muslims in Bosnia, the triumph
of political Islam, and so on. Islam has been at
war with the West for 1,400 years, a conflict that
flows from the differences between the two civilizations, he declares.

For Huntington, cultures are distinct entities
with values and practices that form an unchanging essence. Indeed, he explicitly rejects histori-
cizing. The cause of this ongoing pattern of conflict lies in the 'flow from the nature of the two
religions and the civilizations based on them'
(Huntington 1997: 210). Today, because of the
West's attempts to universalize its own values of
democracy and human rights, the West faces
considerable challenge from the Islamic world.
To add fuel to the fire, large numbers of Muslims
now live in close proximity to non-Muslims
(Europe being a prime example) and this,
Huntington reports, has an innate 'propensity
toward violent conflict' (Ibid.: 264).

Critics of Huntington's thesis of a clash of civilization have all observed that the cultural line
ignores historical processes and works handily to
foster what Said (2001) called 'defensive self-
pride' and an ensuing 'War of the Worlds'.
However, few scholars have expanded on the role
of gender in culture clash. Huntington himself
merely warned cursorily that under the banner of
multiculturalism, Muslims attempt to dislodge
'American' values; we should thus be vigilant
about calls to respect diverse cultural practices,
many of which involve women (Ibid.: 318). He
sets up a classic dichotomy between multicultur-
alists, who foolishly respect Muslim cultural
practices with respect to women, and those who
understand the menace it poses, a polarization I
discuss below.

Some of Huntington's admirers have had
rather more to say about culture clash and gender in the New World Order. Echoing
Huntington, Ronald Inglehart and Pippa Norris
have sought to show that a fatal cultural flaw
plagues the Muslim world. In their estimation,
the issue of gender gives rise to the 'True Clash of
Civilizations' [emphasis added]. Gender is the
reason 'freedom' will never grow in the Middle
East (2003a). Their book Rising Tide (2003b:
154) argues that regardless of the degree of economic modernization, an Islamic religious heritage remains one of the most powerful barriers
to 'self-expression, subjective well-being, and
quality of life concerns'. Because the Islamic
world lacks the core self-expression values of
individual autonomy, tolerance, personal freedom, and interpersonal trust, they exhibit a weak
commitment to gender equality and democracy.
Inglehart and Norris's claims are based empirically on data from value surveys. For example,
the survey includes the question: 'Do men make
better political leaders than women?' Those who
disagreed that men made better political leaders
also scored highest on the self-expression scale
and came from the most democratic societies
(2003b: 158). Gender, they conclude, is the single most important value change in post-indus-
trial societies, a predictor of all other values.

Analyses like that of Inglehart and Norris,
which abstract culture from history, depend
heavily on the logic of culture clash. The aim is
to show that Islam is unchanging and untouched
by politics or economics. It is claimed that patriotism and nationalism are characteristics of traditional societies, not of secular–rational ones
such as the United States. The rise of the
Christian Right and President George W. Bush's
repeated reliance on the notion that God is on
America's side (Didion 2003) is not, according to
this line of argument, comparable to the religious
rhetoric of al-Qaeda. The West's valuing of quality of life is a straightforward sign of progress and
the mark of a superior civilization, a condition

unrelated to the economic coercion required to achieve this state.

Inglehart and Norris anticipate several arguments found in . . . Manji, as well as those used by most reviewers. . . . As in *Rising Tide*, these arguments naturalize free-market capitalism, making it a feature of modern civilizations. Trapped in the pre-modern, Muslims fail in the economic realm and remain locked into tribal cultures in which women are treated particularly badly. As with all explanations based on culture clash, the modern and pre-modern exist as discrete realms, with the latter stuck in culture and the former having progressed to the age of enlightenment.

* * *

The View from Inside the Harem

Irshad Manji, a young, openly lesbian Canadian of Muslim origin, published a book, *The Trouble with Islam* (2003), that soon became a bestseller in Canada. . . . Though addressed to 'my fellow Muslims', and ostensibly about calling Muslims to account for their own backwardness, the book is from the beginning an invitation to consider the merits of Jews, Judaism, and the current Israeli government. Culture clash is the principal means she employs to invite readers to recognize Israel's claims, specifically the notion that Islam, and the Arabs who practise it, are a fatally pre-modern, misogynist, and tribal community whose shortcomings reveal why Jews must occupy the land and defend themselves against the ever-present barbarism of the Arabs who surround them.

The Trouble with Islam is marketed as a view from inside the harem, continuing a long tradition of Western fascination with a forbidden world (Kaplan 1995; Yegenoglu 1998). Manji begins with her childhood and the story of her family's flight from Idi Amin's Uganda to the place where Manji was able to learn democratic

values. Life in Vancouver was nevertheless bleak and violent. Her father's violence toward her and her mother (graphically conveyed by the story of Manji spending the night on the roof of her family's house to avoid his beatings) comes to stand in the text for the violence of Islam and the non-West. Her lot, Manji speculates, would have been one of 'unyielding hierarchy' had she remained in Muslim Uganda and, as the rest of the book makes clear, the same would have applied had she not fled her home, culture, and community (Manji 2003: 11). Calling to mind Samuel Huntington, hers was a 'personal clash of civilizations' (Ibid.: 12).

Manji was compelled to attend fundamentalist religious schools. There, she learned truths about Islam, such as that it does not permit excessive laughter. In the Sunday school she was also permitted to attend since her father saw it as babysitting, she heard stories and histories. The fundamentalist schools never made such offerings; what she did learn provided the basis of Manji's awareness that there is trouble with Islam. The trouble did not crystallize until Manji's boss, Moses Znaimer, the owner of an important television station, sent her a memo in which he demanded to know whether she could reconcile her faith as a Muslim with female genital mutilation or with the public lashing of a 17-year-old Nigerian girl who was sexually assaulted by three men, but who was punished for having sex outside marriage. Brushing aside the aggressive nature of the question—could she have asked her boss to defend Israeli policies toward Palestinians?—Manji only sees the reasonableness of the question, which launches her on a journey that concludes with her decision that the fault lies with Islam.

'Pick a Muslim country, any Muslim country, and the most brutal humiliations will grab you by the vitals' (Ibid.: 31). Manji adds that such humiliations particularly affect women and girls. A 'cruel, crude Islam' thrives even in Toronto, where, in reaction to Manji's local broadcasts of brutalities, Muslims denounce homosexuals as Jews. She grants that Christians and Jews of this ilk may exist (though Jews encourage debate, while Muslims slavishly rely on the Quran), but in contemporary Islam, such figures are mainstream. The Quran provides support for fundamentalist views, even as it occasionally provides the opposite. Moving quickly through Jewish–Christian relations in Moorish Spain to the Taliban, the history of Muslims confirms Manji's hypothesis that Muslim brutalities originate in Islam. If no moderate Muslims are to be found, it is because so few exist. To historicize and suggest, for example, that US support for the Taliban effectively destroyed any moderate opposition is to blame the United States unfairly. Muslims, Manji declares, must begin to be self-critical; the first step would be to acknowledge that 'being self-critical means coming clear about the nasty side of the Koran, and how it informs terrorism' (Ibid.: 47). Outraged that the Muslims she meets have refused to acknowledge any complicity in the events of September 11, Manji insists that we recognize that Osama bin Laden is 'scripturally supported' (Ibid.: 48).

The Trouble with Islam reaches the heart of its argument when Manji accepts a six-day trip to Israel that was funded by 'Zionists'. The Israelis we meet in the second half of the book are self-critical, democratic, and tolerant toward Palestinians. However, Israel is plagued by the kind of Muslims Manji had come to know during her childhood. She meets leering fundamentalist Muslim men, who insist that she wear a 'girdle' over her outer garments when visiting a sacred Muslim site and are unwelcoming and relentlessly misogynist. Palestinians who are not fundamentalists are welfare cheats. Manji relates with pride her blistering response to a Palestinian woman who pleads with her to employ Palestinians as a camera crew because Palestinians are desperate for work:

'But what about all the foreign aid the Palestinian Authority gets from the West?' I counter. I don't bother to bring up additional monies from a United Nations relief agency that's been devoted to Palestinian refugees for three generations now. 'We're talking millions of dollars that can be used for labs and hospitals and schools and business enterprise zones. Why do you still have refugee camps? Where does all the aid go?' (Ibid.: 90)

Chastened, the Palestinian woman must finally admit that her people are corrupt and care more for symbolism than they do for people.

In the West Bank, Manji finds Palestinians who mouth 'the script'—the line of argument that Israel has occupied Palestine. Recognizing that this claim requires a complicated historical counterclaim, Manji argues . . . that Palestine belonged to Jews anyway and, in any event, Jews needed a refuge from anti-Semitism. If there are Palestinian refugees, it is only because of the 'disruptions of war—a conflict initiated by Arab countries that couldn't accept Israel's existence in their midst' (Ibid.: 106). The UN has deepened the crisis by acknowledging that the descendants of the originally displaced people are also refugees. Not really refugees to begin with, Palestinians face the added disadvantage that their fellow Arabs will not help them and they themselves keep refusing reasonable deals. Only Israel has been prepared to help Palestinian refugees. Israel, Manji concludes, 'brings more compassion to "colonization" than its adversaries have ever brought to "liberation". The Jewish state negotiates tensions openly. That's the stuff of genuine democracy' (Ibid.: 123).

Lest we are tempted to conflate Israel with the United States, Manji ends her book with a catalogue of Arab sins to make the point that US power cannot be blamed for most of the world's ills. Instead, these may be blamed on Muslims themselves. 'The cancer begins with us', Manji writes, not with the US, a country that has the courage to acknowledge its own corruption, as it did with Enron! By the end of *The Trouble with Islam*, it is not clear what will redeem Muslims from their fatally pre-modern cultures. Manji offers one small suggestion: 'God-conscious, female-fuelled capitalism' (Ibid.: 173). This is in line with *Vogue* magazine's suggestions that beauty schools will save Afghanistan (Reed 2003). Manji is hopeful about small, income-generating projects for women in Muslim countries—along with continued vigilance toward Muslims.

. . . [R]eviewers who praise Manji quickly bypass the book's evident lack of scholarship, conceding that *The Trouble with Islam* is not the 'most learned or scholarly treatise on the history or theology of Islam' and that Manji is a little 'naive' and 'haphazard' in her geopolitics, as well as 'a mite attention-seeking'. Reviewers generally conclude: 'Its spirit is undeniable, and long, long overdue.' Manji is lauded for bravery in daring to criticize people well known for their murderous tendencies toward critics. Thus Manji, who considers herself one and the same as Salmon Rushdie and Taslima Nasreen, is admired for having dared to write a book that apparently endangers her life (Reed 2003). Reviewers comment that Manji has installed bulletproof windows in her home and is accompanied by bodyguards (Donnelly 2003; Posner 2003). Itemizing these measures in his review, Daniel Pipes observes: 'And non-Muslims wonder why anti-Islamist Muslims in western Europe and North America are so quiet' (Pipes 2003). Not unaware of the currency of these images, on the eve of publication Manji's publisher announced that it was possible that she might be the subject of a fatwa, as Salmon Rushdie had been. They approached the federal solicitor general to grant 'international protected person' status to Manji, a request the Canadian government denied.

Manji, whose reviewers maintain that she is 'fearless and intrepid' (Posner 2003), was recognized by *Maclean's*, Canada's national magazine, when it named her 'Leader for Tomorrow', and by *Ms Magazine*, where she was named a 'Feminist for the 21st Century'. She is 'a spiky-haired spitfire' (Remsen 2004), and the 'smartest, hippest, most eloquent lesbian feminist Muslim you could ever hope to meet' (Kalman 2004). In its first ever 'Chutzpah Awards' given to women who have 'pushed, pulled, prodded, and persevered through thick and thin, poverty and wealth, hope and hopelessness, past naysayers and yes-men', *Oprah Magazine* (2004) saluted Manji for standing up to 'Islamic bullies and terrorists'. These accolades, and the fact that *The Trouble with Islam* has been on bestseller lists for several months and is being translated into several languages, suggest that the journey thus far has not been, as one reviewer sympathetically predicted, 'a rough ride' (Sullivan 2004), but rather, highly rewarded. Only one reviewer, Justin Podur (2003), notices the irony of Manji's claim that she is likely to be targeted by Muslim extremists and to pay dearly for daring to criticize the Islamic world. Despite Manji's self-styling as a Muslim refusenik, Podur observes, she profits handsomely from her position while genuine Israeli refuseniks—conscientious objectors who refuse to serve in the West Bank and Gaza, actions Manji fails to mention—are jailed for theirs. Indeed, Podur notes, dissent in the Islamic world or among Palestinians goes entirely unmentioned throughout Manji's book. If the Revolutionary Association of the Women of Afghanistan (RAWA) were mentioned, Afghanistan could not so easily be characterized as filled only with the Taliban and victimized women. For RAWA is part of the Islamic world.

Despite—and because of—it's obvious appeal to notions of Western superiority, *The Trouble with Islam* reaches young Muslims in the West (which I have corroborated through personal conversations). Manji succeeds in giving voice to the exclusion young Muslims experience from *within*, which is especially directed at gay and lesbian Muslims, feminists, and, increasingly, at anyone progressive. She confronts head on the fundamentalist turn of political Islam and despite her misleading explanations of the phenomenon, she notes the takeover of Islam by Wahhabi Muslims.[4] . . . As a place in which a single woman can make a difference and a dollar, the West is marked as inherently civilized because free-market capitalism underwrites the freedom to act. It is no accident that the 'bravery' ascribed to . . . Manji rests on ideas of intrepid individuals who make it despite tribe and clan, a capitalist message that depends upon the notion that anyone with defining links to the community occupies the pre-modern.

A Conclusion for Feminists

The easy alliance . . . between racism, neo-liberalism, the US politics of empire, and the Israeli politics of occupation reveals the tie that binds them: a wilful inattention to history. In culture clash explanations, if fundamentalism has arisen in Muslim parts of the world, it is because that is how they are. We cannot begin to consider, as Yegenoglu (1998: 135) does with respect to veiling in *Colonial Fantasies*, how colonial policies in Algeria, for example, so denigrated everything Islamic that anti-colonial movements won popular support by proposing a return to Islamic tradition that was understood largely as the opposite of the foreigners. Within the Manichean world created by colonialism, women's bodies remained the terrain on which men sought to articulate their desires and fears. Moderate Algerians who advocated improving the status of women (in the name of strengthening the Indigenous) were compelled to distinguish their political policies from colonial ones. In such an environment, it was far easier for those making the case for a return to Indigenous traditions to advocate a kind of 'reverse Orientalism'. That is, what the French sought to suppress in the name of penetrating Native culture was the very thing the nationalists would seek to revitalize. Drawing

on Marnia Lazreg's conclusion that before colonial conquest the Algerians perceived their Muslimness not too differently from the way the French perceived of themselves as Christians, Yegenoglu reminds us of Gayatri Spivak's observation that the figure of the woman disappears here in 'the violent shuttling' between tradition and modernization (Ibid.: 144). Muslim women and men lack a history, content, or specificity and all we ever know of them from culture clash explanations is that they are stuck in pre-history.

Western feminists have relied on culture clash logic when analyzing violence against women. As illustrated in one recent book on feminist responses to fundamentalism, the feminist story also begins with the claim that new relations of equality became possible in modernity:

> As women became better educated, went out to work, and won more rights, as families became smaller and less tied to the land, as information flowed more freely, scientific and technical knowledge became more widely disseminated, and thrones and dynasties crumbled in favour of representative democracy, the natural similarity of the sexes was supposed to stand revealed, making possible new, more equal, and companionable relationships between them. The same forces of progress, this view held, would cause organized religion to wither away or at any rate modulate away from dogma and authority and reaction toward a kind of vague, kindly, non-denominational spiritual uplift whose politics, if it had any, would be liberal. (Pollitt 2002: ix)

While Europe modernized, however, the rest of the world strangely did not. Tradition and religion 'tightened its grip' in non-European regions, and a religious fundamentalism took hold that has resulted in tremendous violence against women.

The story that 'we' modernized and 'they' did not sets the stage for a clash between multiculturalism and feminism. Many feminists have understood the reluctance of Western states to condemn practices of violence against Muslim women, including female genital mutilation, forced marriages, and honour killings, as due to the triumph of multiculturalism over universal values. The logic is this: in liberal democracies, all citizens are treated equally. This means that minority cultures must be respected (multiculturalism). However, minority cultures include practices that are harmful to women. States often choose to respect culture over women's human rights. As Beckett and Macey (2001: 111) put it:

Multiculturalism does not cause domestic violence, but it does facilitate its continuation through its creed of respect for cultural differences, its emphasis on non-interference in minority lifestyles, and its insistence on community consultation (with male, self-defined community leaders).

Reinforcing the idea of the West as a realm beyond culture and the place of universal values, the stage is set for the neo-liberal world imagined by . . . Manji, with its civilized Europeans, imperilled Muslim women, and dangerous Muslim men. In the words of Rosemary George, the modern woman is first and foremost an imperialist. Western women achieve their own subject status through claims that they are the same as, but culturally different from, Muslim women—women that must be rescued. Gender, unmoored from class, race, and culture, facilitates this imperialist move, as does culture equally removed from history and context. As Lila Abu-Lughod discovered when she was repeatedly sought out as an anthropologist of women in Muslim societies to provide the cultural explanations that would help Americans to understand the terrorist attacks on the World Trade Center, the turn to culture frozen in time and outside history helped Americans to feel innocent. As she writes (2003), it was as though:

knowing something about women and Islam or the meaning of a religious ritual would help one understand the tragic attack on New York's World Trade Center and the US Pentagon, or how Afghanistan had come to be ruled by the Taliban, or what interests might have fuelled US and other interventions in the region over the past 25 years, or what the history of American support for conservative groups funded to undermine the Soviets might have been, or why the caves and bunkers out of which bin Laden was to have been smoked 'dead or alive', as President Bush announced on television, were paid for and built by the CIA.

Abu-Lughod itemizes what the cultural and the feminist explanation so neatly dislodges. A cultural framing 'prevented the serious exploration of the roots and nature of human suffering in this part of the world'. Of the West's insistence that its values represent progress, Abu-Lughod (2003) insightfully asks:

Might other desires be more meaningful for different groups of people? Living in close families? Living in a godly way? Living without war? Why presume that our way, whatever that is, is best? The historical record of the secular humanist West is far from unblemished, with genocides, colonialism, world wars, slavery, and other forms of inequality [in] deep parts of it.

Post-September 11, to place gender and culture back into context, to see Muslim women less as sisters awaiting our help into modernity and more as subjects whose lives are profoundly affected by the West's bid for empire, Western feminists will need to be deeply aware of the historical record. We must also refuse to come into being as subjects against women constituted as culturally different. This exploration of the geopolitical terrain in which we find ourselves illustrates the dire need to reject explanations that locate patriarchy in pre-modernity and posi- tion Western feminists as poised to help their Muslim sisters into modernity.

Notes

1. In addition to Fallaci (2002), Chesler (2003), and Manji (2003), there were: A. Dershowitz, *The Case for Israel* (2003), A. Foxman, *Never Again? The Threat of the New Anti-Semitism* (2003), and P. Iganski and B. Kosmin, *A New Anti-Semitism? Debating Judeophobia in 21st Century Britain* (2003).

2. Anonymous e-mail from isalit@rogers.com, personal communication (11 Aug. 2002).

3. For a brilliant illustration of this concept, see Ferreira da Silva (2001).

4. Wahhabism is an ultra-orthodox, eighth-century strain of Islam that has recently gained considerable prominence. Osama bin Laden subscribes to Wahhabism. See T. Ali (2002).

Questions

1. How does the Canadian state socially construct 'immigrant women'?
2. How have the Left and feminists generally analyzed the family? How would you analyze the family using an integrated analysis of race, class, and gender?
3. How is democratic racism articulated in Canada? Give two examples.
4. After the attacks in New York on September 11, 2001, how are modern-day imperialist actions legitimized?

Websites

Canadian Council of Muslim Women: http://www.ccmw.com
Canadian Race Relations Foundation: http://www.crr.ca
Native Youth Media: http://www.redwiremag.com

Suggested Readings

Bolaria, B. Singh, and Peter S. Li. 1985. *Racial Oppression in Canada* (Toronto: Garamond Press).

Daniels, Ronald J., Patrick Macklem, and Kent Roach. 2001. *The Security of Freedom: Essays on Canada's Anti-terrorism Bill* (Toronto: University of Toronto Press).

Estable, Alma. 1986. *Immigrant Women in Canada, Current Issues: A Background Paper*, prepared for the Canadian Advisory Council on the Status of Women (Ottawa: Canadian Advisory Council on the Status of Women).

Folson, Rose Baaba. 2004. *Calculated Kindness: Globalization, Immigration and Settlement in Canada* (Black Point, NS: Fernwood).

Hamilton, Roberta. 1996. *Gendering the Vertical Mosaic: Feminist Perspectives on Canadian Society* (Toronto: Copp Clark).

Jiwani, Yasmin. 2006. *Discourses of Denial: Mediations of Race, Gender, and Violence* (Vancouver: University of British Columbia Press).

Lee, J., and J.S. Lutz. 2005. *Situating 'Race' and Racisms in Space, Time, and Theory: Critical Essays for Activists and Scholars* (Montreal: McGill-Queen's University Press).

Satzewich, Victor N. 1998. *Racism and Social Inequality in Canada: Concepts, Controversies and Strategies of Resistance* (Toronto: Thompson Educational).

Racialization: From Theorizing Race to Racializing Practices

The politics of race in Canada confirm what many have long suspected: race as social location not only constitutes an indicator of success and failure, but also represents a key variable in shaping people's identities and outcomes. Despite its centrality in informing the human condition, reference to race as an empirically based biological reality is widely dismissed as scientifically invalid and morally bankrupt. Predictably, few will openly admit that people can be slotted into fixed and permanent categories on the basis of innate characteristics, with a corresponding capacity to determine thought or action. Even fewer will endorse a system that ranks some differences higher than others along a stratified scale of worth. Not surprisingly, those who continue to uphold this 'fiction' are generally reduced to the status of knuckle-dragging Neanderthals.

But the status of 'real' versus 'reality' plays out differently with race. First, the reality of race is not grounded on the existence of something tangible or empirical—a fixed and measurable biological entity (Modood 2007). Rather than something existing in the world, race constitutes a way of seeing, interpreting, organizing, and responding to social reality. Second, something like race does not have to be real (i.e., reflect reality) to be thought of as real or experienced as such. That is, people implicitly assume the reality of race for evaluating others, for organizing their world, and for conducting themselves accordingly. Third, race does not have to be real to be real in its consequences. The proliferation of racial myths has exerted—and continues to exert—incalculable damage to racialized minorities.

Clearly, then, race is neither an objective reality nor is it a fictionalized fabrication divorced from reality. This realization has prompted a discursive shift in how race is theorized. Attention is moving away from studying the physical attributes of minority groups and their presumed inferiority, including the pre-slotting of individuals into unproblematic racial categories in which all members are thought to think and act in the same way. Emphasis instead is shifting from race to racialization—from race as a thing or noun to race as a process or verb, from race as a biological entity to race as a social construct, from race as a naturally existing category to the politics of naming the 'others', involving a stigma imposed on others by those with the power to make such labels stick

(Fleras 2008). Race is now conceptualized as a 'negotiated reality' by which intergroup relations are racially coded and socially constructed within contexts of power and inequality. This shift is consistent with postmodernist philosophies about social reality; that is, in our mind-dependent world, there is no such thing as an objective reality or absolute truth, only discourses about reality reflecting people's social location (standpoint) and relations of power.

This discursive shift in theorizing race is not inconsequential. No longer is it accurate to talk about race relations as a set of relationships between two racially distinct groups. More accurately, what exists are relationships between groups who have been defined (racialized) by attributing social significance to racial properties to one or both groups (Smith 2007). To the extent that the race concept has no empirical justification except in the perceptual sense, it is more accurate to speak of relationships that have been 'racialized' rather than race relations per se (Bonilla-Silva 1996). Even the concept of racial minorities is a misnomer. Existing instead are groups who have been colour-coded and devalued by association with often negative racial attributes. For example, consider the social processes which construct and label certain groups and assign them negative qualities so that certain crimes are associated with minorities ('criminalizing race'), while certain minorities are linked with excessive criminality ('racializing crime') (Webster 2007). To the extent that racialization involves a process that attributes biological determinism and racial consciousness to previously unclassified group relations, the status of race bolsters white power while suppressing minority resistance (Dei 2007).

But while racialization may have emerged as a central dynamic in the study of race and racism, the concept remains poorly theorized and indiscriminately bandied about (Goldberg 2002: 12; Murji and Solomos 2005). For some, racialization refers to contexts in which racial meanings and negative implications are attributed to social conditions or arrangements (according to Goldberg [2002] the concept was first used by Fanon [1968] to contrast 'to racialize' with 'to humanize'). For example, poverty continues to be a racialized issue in Canada, disproportionately affecting minority groups because of race-induced barriers (Keung 2007). For others, racialization refers to those cultural/political processes that invoke race to explain or excuse; that is, groups come to be designated as different and inferior and on that basis subjected to unequal treatment (Amin and Dei 2006). With racialization, minorities are not only stigmatized as inferior or irrelevant by linking their activities with race or with negative racial attributes. Racialization also entails a process by which minority women and men are defined as a self-evident category that exhaustively encompasses the essence of that group (Jiwani 2006; Fleras 2008).

In short, the concept of racialization approaches race ('visibility') as socially constructed, internally diverse, sharply contested, and fluid and evolving—unlike race essentialism which claims that an innate set of properties defines all group members, resulting in a series of generalizations that can be applied to members of the racial group. In that it signals an activity by which ideas about race are constructed, regarded as meaningful, and acted upon (Murji and Solomos 2005), racialization reflects the process by which the powerful assign race-based meanings to issues or activities or, conversely, impose social significance on racial differences (James 2005; Agnew 2007). Not surprisingly, the politics of racialization may say more about those constructing and imposing race labels than those who are racialized.

That makes it more imperative than ever to understand the 'how' and the 'why' behind the 'what' and the 'who'.

Part III begins with an article by Levitt and Shaffir that draws attention to something most Canadians would like to forget, namely, the intensity of anti-Semitism in Toronto prior to the Second World War. The article describes how the anti-Semitic activity of blatantly pro-Nazi groups came to a boil in 1933 with the unfurling of a swastika flag during a ball game at Toronto's Christie Pits. The article also provides two critical insights: first, in contrast to public perceptions of Jewish passivity in the face of external threats, young Jewish Canadians actively resisted threats to their status and security; second, the decision by the Toronto mayor to abolish public displays of swastikas foreshadows later moves to impose justifiable restrictions on individual rights as ground rules for living together safely.

In his historical description of the Chinese in Canada, Peter Li reminds us that the Chinese too were racialized as a despised race—a racialization that he argues persists into the present but in more coded forms. Why do Chinese Canadians—despite their occupational achievements and economic success—continue to be regarded by some as an inferior race and by others as a cause of social problems? Peter Li argues that public discourses on immigration—how many, where from, and what kind—are often (mis)informed by notions of race, especially when immigrants arrive from non-traditional sources whose racialized characteristics are seen as problematic.

The excerpt from David Tanovich's book *The Colour of Justice* provides a timely reminder that racialization by way of racial profiling is not something relegated to the dustbin of Canadian history. Racial profiling remains a problem in those contexts where racialized minorities and state authorities come into contact—no more so than in the domain of the criminal justice system (Tator and Henry 2006; Smith 2007). While many believe justice is or should be colour-blind, Tanovich contests this belief by demonstrating the persistence of racial profiling in Canada. He also demonstrates how racial profiling involves a process whereby authorities single out racialized minorities as suspects for discriminatory treatment because of prevailing stereotypes. For Tanovich, then, justice is distorted by stereotypical assumptions about crime and criminals, in effect racializing crime while criminalizing race.

The article by Minelle Mahtani on performing race provides an important insight: race is not just an abstraction for analysis, but a negotiated process involving different dimensions of people's lived experiences. Drawing on a series of interviews with mixed race women, Mahtani demonstrates how race is played out through everyday performances by racialized women that challenge conventional notions and mono-racial gazes, disrupt oppressive readings of their racialized identities, and create new meanings out of ambiguous and multiple racialized spaces. Mahtani's article also reminds readers that race can never be painted out of the picture, especially for women of mixed race backgrounds, but must be incorporated in ways that reinforce how race intersects with gender to create both challenges and opportunities.

In an original article for this volume, Augie Fleras analyzes a famous experiment that demonstrates how arbitrarily selected physical features can be racialized in ways that benefit some, but exclude others. When Jane Elliot divided her third-grade class into blue eyes and brown eyes to demonstrate the arbitrariness of the rationale behind prejudice and racism, few could have predicted the repercussions. The 1970 video *Eye of the Storm* (on which the article is based) remains a powerful and moving indictment of how punishing consequences can flow from imagined realities. The article further reinforces the validity of the self-fulfilling prophecy; that is, those racialized as superior (either by design or by default) will tend to act successfully because success often breeds yet more success, whereas those racialized as inferior will act subordinately if only to conform with public expectations.

Carl James points out that participation in sports in Canada is highly racialized—not in the sense of race as determinative of skills or talents but because perceptions of race influence those social, cultural, and economic conditions that foster participation. By reproducing an acceptable definition of athletic superiority regarding race ('self-fulfilling prophecy'), the structures of schools are shown to racialize minority (black) students in terms of their abilities and success. Emphasis on the social constructedness of identities also challenges much of the essentialism that continues to be associated with the process of racialization.

The fact sheet 'Understanding the Racialization of Poverty in Ontario' provides an excellent overview of the relationship between race and inequality. Nowhere is the impact of inequality on racialized minorities more evident than in the degree to which poverty and race overlap. To be sure, race per se does not determine poverty; more accurately, it's people's perceptions of race that create barriers for opportunity and success.

The final article provides insights into how racialized groups may be doubly victimized. The article demonstrates how Japanese-Canadian fishers were racialized and victimized by arbitrarily imposed racial distinctions within the BC fishing industry. (By contrast, see Chapter 7 for an article by Fleras on Aboriginal fishing allocation as race or rights.) By drawing attention to the numerous acts of racial discrimination directed at Japanese-Canadian fishers, two conclusions follow: first, Canada's discriminatory treatment of racialized minorities reflected and reinforced the embeddedness of racism in what virtually amounted to a 'white man's' country; second, few should be surprised by the subsequent World War II internment of Japanese Canadians into camps across Canada, together with the confiscation of their property and rights. Efforts by the Japanese-Canadian Fishermen's Association to challenge conventional notions of fishing allocation were rejected by the Supreme Court of Canada in June of 2008.

Chapter 13

The Swastika as Dramatic Symbol: A Case Study of Ethnic Violence in Canada

Cyril Levitt and William Shaffir

A review of the literature on social unrest reveals that many scholars attribute rebellious or riotous behaviour to the actualization of predispositions rooted either in the personality of the individual or in the social structure.[1] Thus, as Herbert Blumer notes, 'they assert that social unrest is but a reflection of personality instability or an expression of acute structural strains on the existing social order'.[2] While such analyses have identified the important determinants of collective behaviour, they have only paid limited attention to the process by which such behaviour is shaped. Attention to this process necessitates an examination of how people define and interpret the stream of events unfolding in their experience. As the literature has shown, social unrest does not suddenly emerge fully formed, but undergoes a process of growth and development.[3]

In identifying the more vital features affecting the maturation of social unrest, Herbert Blumer draws attention to the role of dramatic events which serve as the nucleating points in their formation:[4]

It is the dramatic event which incites and focalizes predispositions, and brings them to bear on a concrete situation; which shocks, arouses, enlivens, and shakes people loose from their routines of thought and action; which catches collective attention and stirs imagination; . . . which incites heated discussions and initiates intense interaction; and which stimulates the novel proposals and the impulsive tendencies that are so characteristic of social unrest.

The centrality of the dramatic event in the unfolding of social unrest is, of course, not unique to Blumer's formulation of collective behaviour. Others have also emphasized its significance. For example, Smelser claims that 'it is nearly always a dramatic event which precipitates the outburst of violence',[5] and provides the generalized beliefs with concrete and immediate substance.

The significance of the dramatic event lies in the fact that it serves as a central turning point affecting the career route of the social unrest. It brings into sharper focus the existing social arrangements, arouses passions of moral indignation, and rallies persons to redress some perceived injustice collectively. The object recognized as the turning point must be defined by the participants as something qualitatively different from what has occurred up to that point in the unfolding of events.

This paper examines the role of the swastika emblem in fomenting the virulent antagonism between Canadian Jews and Gentiles which culminated in the Christie Pits riot in the summer of 1933.[6] It focuses specifically on the dramatic event in the development of the riot—the sudden appearance of the swastika symbol along Toronto's eastern Beaches and, about two weeks later, at a baseball game in Willowvale Park (commonly known as Christie Pits). Toronto's Jews had been made fully aware by both the city's English-language newspapers and the Yiddish daily (*Der Yiddisher Zhurnal*) of the savage Nazi persecution of Jews in Germany and of the symbolism of the swastika. They were also aware of overt anti-Semitic prejudices in Canada but had not considered such manifestations to be a serious threat to their safety or to their very existence, until the swastika was displayed provocatively in Toronto.

In referring to those objects which are the focal points of 'the impulses, feelings, and imagery of . . . people',[7] Blumer fails to distinguish between those objects which have passive symbolic value and those which have a highly-charged meaning for some groups. We suggest that dramatic symbols are best understood as objects which denote beliefs, ideas, or ideals that are capable of arousing intense feeling, emotion, passion, or energy. Admittedly, a merely formal symbol may become dramatized under certain conditions, just as a dramatic symbol may be demoted to passive status or even, under extreme conditions, robbed of its symbolic value completely.[8] For instance, the Japanese flag, once a dramatic symbol of treachery in the United States, is now trotted out and flaunted in public as a symbol of technological, scientific, and economic achievement. The symbols of the Civil Rights Movement in the United States, which occasioned riots in the American South during the early 1960s, are now looked upon with indifference or occasionally only with passive disapproval. The dramatic symbol is highly contextual in nature, a lightning rod of collective sentiments and shared emotions not for all time, but in specific circumstances and particular conditions. New dramatic symbols come into being and pass away quickly. Others, such as the German swastika, break dramatically upon the world historical stage and remain

charged for long periods with strong collective sentiments.

In their well-known study of the so-called 'Zoot-suit' riots in Los Angeles in 1943, Turner and Surace claim that most symbols, even those we call dramatic ones, are ambiguous; that is, they evoke conflicting images.[9] It is precisely such ambiguity which serves as an inhibiting feature in collective behaviour. It is as if the countervailing images act as a brake upon that behaviour which is not generally sanctioned by the community at large. It follows, therefore, that if the symbol's ambiguity is resolved, then an important restraining feature on extreme collective behaviour will have been removed. As the authors assert: 'symbols which are unambiguous in their connotations permit immoderate behaviour toward the object in question. In the absence of ambivalence toward an object there is no internal conflict to restrict action.'[10]

In our case study of ethnic violence, the swastika became stripped of its ambiguity, in part by the collective action surrounding its appearance in public in the weeks preceding the outbreak of the riot at Christie Pits. As an alarmed Jewish community confronted the new and heightened significance assumed by the swastika as a dramatic symbol of Nazi anti-Semitic persecutions, it unmasked the weak cover adopted by members of a swastika-bearing organization who had claimed that the emblem was nothing more than a good-luck charm associated with Indian tribes who had once lived in the area.[11]

In this paper, we first give a brief description of the prevailing anti-Semitism in Toronto which had alerted the Jewish community to be on guard against victimization. We then show how the city's English-language newspapers and the Yiddish daily published detailed reports about the plight of German Jews at the hands of Nazis, whose emblem was the swastika. . . . We then describe how the unfurling of a white large blanket displaying a black swastika at a baseball match (where one of the teams was predominantly Jewish) triggered off a riot, and we conclude with an examination of the other factors which incited the rioters.

According to the Canadian Census of 1931, there were 45,305 Jews in Toronto in that year; they accounted for 7.2 per cent of the total population of the city, excluding the suburbs. In no area of Toronto did the Jews constitute a majority of the residents, but 30.5 per cent of the inhabitants in Ward 4 were Jewish, as were 18.6 per cent of those who lived in Ward 5 (where Christie Pits was situated). On the other hand, the number of Jews in Ward 8 (which included the eastern Beaches area) was very small, accounting for under 1 per cent (0.08 per cent) of the ward's residents. Only 18,612 of Toronto's total Jewish population of 45,305 were born in Canada. Most of the Jewish immigrants had come from Poland and Russia and Yiddish was the mother tongue of the overwhelming majority (95.54 per cent) of Jews in Canada in 1931. The majority of those gainfully occupied in Toronto were wage earners in small factories and shops producing and selling articles of clothing or furs while others were mainly retailers of dry goods or street hawkers.

Toronto Jews were often treated as undesirables. Stephen Speisman has shown that in contrast to earlier anti-Semitism in Toronto, which was typically expressed in actions against individuals, by 1933 a blanket condemnation of Jews had emerged.[12] There were restrictive covenants prohibiting the sale of some plots of land or houses to prospective Jewish buyers and the fact that the courts upheld such practices was ready confirmation for Canadian Jews that they could be discriminated against with impunity.[13] They were also unwelcome in some summer resorts where hotels had signboards boldly stating: 'Patronage exclusively Gentile'.[14] Indeed, a number of people we interviewed specifically recalled signs, located in various parts of Toronto and its outskirts, stating: 'No Jews or Dogs Allowed'. The effects of anti-Semitism were most severely

felt in employment. It was practically impossible for Jews to get jobs as sales staff in any of the big department stores, and very few Jews were hired by the banks and financial institutions (it was standard practice in those days to ask for the applicant's religion on the employment form). Very few Jews worked for Ontario or Toronto Hydro or for government departments. One interviewee told us that a relative of his obtained a job in a company known for its discriminatory hiring practices by writing 'Protestant' in the space reserved for religion on the application form. Her boss discovered that she was Jewish (she was absent on the major Jewish holidays), and she was summarily dismissed. Another recounted that, after applying for a job at one of the major department stores in Toronto, he saw the personnel manager crumple his application form and throw it in the waste bin only moments after assuring the applicant that this application would be given 'careful attention'. The relative absence of Jews in specific professional and occupational groupings in Toronto has been explained in part by the restrictions placed upon Jewish applicants, candidates, students, and professionals. Speisman stated in his study of Toronto Jewry:[15]

From the 1930s through the Second World War, Jews found it difficult to enter certain professions. . . . Jews could study law, medicine, and dentistry only on a *numerus clausus* basis, and many a worthy Jewish student had to seek his livelihood in other pursuits. At the University of Toronto School of Dentistry, a dexterity requirement was a favourite ploy for keeping Jewish students out; the small number who made it into the program often found themselves subjected to open abuse by anti-Semitic professors. Graduates of the University of Toronto Medical School found that their prestigious diplomas could not obtain internships for them, so an entire generation of Jewish medical students emigrated to the United States seeking hospital posts to hone their craft. Canada did not want them.

The difficulties encountered by Jews in the professions were not confined to any particular region of Canada. In Regina, Saskatchewan, for instance, the General Hospital was informed in 1934 by the superintendent that a Jewish radiologist was unacceptable to the staff and to the public, and that physicians with Anglo-Saxon sounding names were preferable, even at a higher salary, to Drs Teitlebaum and Friedman. Indeed, any analysis of anti-Semitism in Canada during the early 1930s must emphasize both its scope and intensity. Although frequently camouflaged as nationalism, particularly in the province of Quebec, and disguised and justified in terms of rising unemployment and economic uncertainties, the effects of the anti-Semitism for the Jews were unmistakably clear. Increasingly stereotyped as 'radical, disloyal, unbelieving, domineering, cosmopolitan, and otherwise as being a danger to Canadian society',[16] Jews encountered growing prejudice and discrimination because of their religion or ethnicity. The consequences of this had their most serious impact during the 1930s, as officials in the highest reaches of Canadian government, succumbing to various internal pressures, pursued a systematic policy of barring Jewish refugees from entry into Canada, thus ensuring their deaths at the hands of the Nazis. More than ever, Jews had reason to believe that anti-Semitism was stitched into the very fabric of Canadian society.[17]

The summer of 1933 revealed to Toronto Jews that some of their Gentile fellow inhabitants felt profound hatred and contempt for them when the swastika emblem was publicly displayed and those who sported it shouted 'Heil Hitler' along the eastern Beaches and later in Willowvale Park. Although the swastika symbol was not unknown in the city (for example, Rudyard Kipling's books in the public library bore the swastika on the title pages), by the middle of 1933 the hooked-cross emblem had acquired notoriety as the badge of the Nazis and sinister connotations for Jews.

The Newspapers: Toronto Learns about the Swastika in Germany

In 1933, the newspaper was the prime source of national and international news for the majority of people. News broadcasts on the radio consisted of little more than newspaper items read verbatim. There were four daily English-language newspapers in Toronto in 1933: two morning papers, *The Daily Mail and Empire* and *The Globe*, and two afternoon/evening papers, *The Toronto Daily Star* and *The Evening Telegram*. In addition to these mass circulation dailies, the Jewish community of Toronto had its own daily Yiddish paper, *Der Yiddisher Zhurnal*. Other Yiddish daily newspapers, published in New York and Montreal, were on sale in Toronto and reported on matters affecting Jews in Canada and other parts of the world. *The Toronto Daily Star* had the largest sale of all the English-language dailies in the city (its circulation was about 215,000) and it was also the newspaper most frequently read by Jews. Together with the *Zhurnal*, it supplied Toronto Jews with horrifying reports of Nazi atrocities and frequent references to the swastika emblem which became invested with connotations of degradation, terror, and physical violence against Jews.

In a front-page story of its 13 February 1933 edition, the *Zhurnal* reported a speech by a Nazi deputy and stated: 'Kube, deputy in the Prussian parliament, says that Jews have polluted Germany like bedbugs. The only way to smoke them out is to drive them out.' No great leap of imagination was required to reach the conclusion that if Jews were 'like bedbugs' then the most efficient remedy was extermination. The editorial in that same issue stated that German Jews who believed Hitler's promise to punish those who insulted any recognized religion were naïve and indulging in wishful thinking. It pointed out that on the very day that Hitler publicly proclaimed his determination to protect established religious groups, the Nazis were staging a pogrom against Jews in Gresfeld and it recommended:[18]

> The Central Verein of German Jews should stand by its former resolution to deploy self-defence organizations over the whole country, wherever there are Jewish centres. This would be more effective than all the decrees which Hitler might publish taken together.

A few days later, on 24 February, the *Zhurnal* published a report from Germany under the headline: 'Jews Will Hang from Lampposts, Promises Nazi Leader if a Hair on Hitler's Head is Touched' and quoted the threat: 'If a hair is touched of any leader of the Nazi government, we will give a signal for a general massacre of Jews which will only be halted when not a single Jew is left alive.'[19] The Jewish Telegraphic Agency and German Jews fleeing the Nazi terror and seeking refuge abroad provided further evidence of anti-Semitic outrages. The *Zhurnal* of 23 March reported harrowing details under a prominent headline which stated: 'Nazi Atrocities Beyond Human Imagination. Murderers, Torturers Unhindered. Jews Kidnapped and Beaten to Death. Every Night a Tortured Jew Abandoned in Berlin Cemeteries. Those Left Behind Alive Forced to Sign Statement that They Were Well Treated'.[20]

Reports of atrocities in the *Zhurnal* were not as numerous in April as they had been in February and March, largely owing to the newspaper's pre-occupation with reports of protests against the Nazi terror and of the efforts of Toronto Jewry to aid their German-Jewish brethren. Nevertheless, some incidents of physical violence against Jews in Germany were reported throughout the month. On 7 April a *Zhurnal* headline stated: 'German Jew and His Wife Dead Fleeing

Kidnappers'.[21] Later that month the *Zhurnal* reported more cases of kidnapping as well as instances of German Jews who had abandoned all hope and had committed suicide. It also revealed that German Nazis were organizing pogroms in Poland and Romania while the violence was unabated in Germany. A man who sought refuge in Holland revealed that Nazis had entered a synagogue in Gelsenkirchen looking for any concealed weapons and arrested Jews whom they took to prison and severely tortured, according to a report in the *Zhurnal* of 20 April. Four days later, it published the account of a Jewish Telegraphic Agency correspondent who had witnessed the plight of the German Jews at first hand after secretly going to Berlin:[22]

> Not Berlin proper, not America, and not even the countries which border on Germany can have an exact notion and paint for themselves a complete picture of what is truly happening in Germany. The insults, the tortures, the awful hopelessness, the absolute helplessness of the Jews in Germany today are indescribable. I personally have found the Jewish situation far worse, infinitely more horrible than I imagined, far worse than even the worst reports, and I've just arrived here. Everything which was shocking in the very first days of Hitler's coup d'état remains absolutely true to this very day. . . . Jews are continuing to disappear all the time and the whereabouts of their remains is unknown. Often they are found in the morgues.

There were further reports of violent attacks against Jews in Germany during the following months and on the first day of August the *Zhurnal* reported a 'bloody pogrom' in Berlin and quoted proclamations that described Jews as 'poisonous snakes'. The swastika was now the official emblem of the Nazi Party and a leaflet was distributed in Berlin stating:[23]

The swastika, the official government emblem . . . 'Kill the Jews. Free yourselves from them once and for all!' There are two kinds of anti-Semitism. One, of a higher kind, limits Jewish power through laws. The other, lower kind, kills Jews. The latter is perhaps a dreadful kind, but it brings the best results because it ends for all time the Jewish question by exterminating them.

Some months earlier, in March 1933, *The Toronto Daily Star* had already carried reports of the swastika's association with Nazi anti-Semitic actions. One of its correspondents in Germany described how he saw 'a parade of hundreds of children, between the ages of seven and 16, carrying the swastika and the old imperial colours, and shouting at intervals: "The Jews must be destroyed."'[24] Two days later, the same newspaper had a front-page story under a headline which stated: 'Nazism Embodies Ideal Followed by Ku Klux Klan: Extreme Nationalism, Hatred of All Aliens Common to Both Orders: Nordics Superior'. Its reporter commented:[25]

Curiously enough, the Swastika or Hooked Cross, Hakenkreuz, the Nazi symbol, was an emblem much in evidence in the Ku Klux Klan lodges and in the parades of the order in days gone by. . . . A man without a program save hatred, ignorance, and vulgarity is driving a great and disillusioned people to perdition. This is a pessimistic prognosis, yet I am afraid, although I hope not, that history will bear me out in this assertion.

A few days later, and again on its front page, *The Toronto Daily Star* published a report from Germany which stated that Pastor Dr Mieneke of Soldin had declared to his congregation: 'Christ himself was a Hitlerite. The Christian cross and the swastika belong together.'[26] On 15 April the newspaper published a photograph of Nazi Brownshirts wearing swastika badges. On 28 April, the front page of the same daily claimed that Jews who had fainted under torture were 'revived for further torture' in Germany and that a Polish Jew, whose name was printed in full, 'was carried into a cellar by uniformed men and beaten. They pulled the hair of his beard out and shaved a swastika on his head. He was then beaten again in time to the music of a piano.'[27]

There can be no doubt that by midsummer 1933 the swastika was seen by Toronto Jews as the symbol of infamous and inhuman Nazi anti-Semitism and it is not surprising that when it was publicly flaunted in the city, they were incensed. On the other hand, the members of Toronto's newly formed Swastika Clubs were still claiming with pretended innocence that the emblem was merely a good-luck sign and that it was openly displayed on Rudyard Kipling's books which could not be said to be in any way associated with Nazism.

* * *

The Swastika at Christie Pits

The swastika, which had disappeared entirely from the eastern Beaches district by 11 August, reappeared suddenly at Willowvale Park (Christie Pits) on the evening of 14 August. During a junior softball quarter-final game, in which Harbord Playground (a predominantly Jewish team) met St Peter's (a predominantly Catholic team), a huge swastika sewn in white cloth on a black pullover was unfurled in the final innings. According to *The Daily Mail and Empire* of 15 August, only small sections of the emblem had been unfurled from time to time 'amid much wisecracking, cheering, and yelling of pointed remarks'. But according to both that paper and *The Evening Telegram*, when the Harbord team tied the score in the ninth inning, St Peter's fans unfurled the whole pullover with the emblazoned swastika—hoping thereby to spur their team to victory. On the other hand, according to

The Toronto Daily Star of the same day, those who hoisted the swastika flag to the accompaniment of 'Heil Hitler' were a local gang. Whether the wavers of the banner were or were not local hooligans, the appearance of the swastika was seen as a deliberate attempt to provoke the Jewish supporters of the Harbord team, by displaying the Nazi emblem. After the end of the game, which was won by Harbord Playground, those holding the swastika flag raised it high and members of the gang swarmed onto the field, chanting their 'club yell' again and surrounding members of the Jewish team, according to the same newspaper. Though spectators expected that the situation on the playing field would result in fisticuffs, between supporters of the two teams, an uneasy calm prevailed.

At some time during the night of 14 August, a large swastika and the words 'Heil Hitler' were painted on the roof of the Willowvale Park clubhouse, after the attendants had left the grounds at ten o'clock—so that the vandals could not be identified. On the following morning, the Parks Commissioner announced that the swastika and the words 'Heil Hitler' would be obliterated and the matter turned over to the police. (*The Toronto Daily Star* of 15 August supplied more details of the incident and revealed that those guilty were a few members of the Pit gang, the gang that frequented Willowvale Park.)

On Wednesday evening, 16 August, Toronto experienced one of the worst non-labour riots in its history;[28] it was triggered by the flaunting of the swastika, according to *The Daily Mail and Empire*:[29]

Widespread disorder raged over the vast area of Toronto streets for hours last night when rioting broke out following the display of the swastika emblem on a white quilt at a baseball game in Willowvale Park.

The disturbance became largely racial in character, bands of Gentiles and of Jews apparently taking up opposing sides in the battle. As far as could be deemed, no arrests took place arising from the disorders, the police apparently devoting their major attention to breaking up the several serious mêlées which developed, in which hundreds appeared to be fighting at once.

Cries of 'The Swastika! The Swastika!' rose in various parts of the park as soon as the taunting emblem made its appearance.

In one confused mass, in sections of the crowd, more than 3,000 surged across the park and over the hill toward the emblem. Fighting broke out as Jews recognized Gentiles.

The Toronto Daily Star reported:[30]

While groups of Jewish and Gentile youths wielded fists and clubs in a series of violent scraps for possession of a white flag bearing a Swastika symbol at Willowvale Park last night, a crowd of more than 10,000 citizens, excited by cries of 'Heil Hitler!' became suddenly a disorderly mob and surged wildly about the park and surrounding streets, trying to gain a view of the actual combats, which soon developed in violence and intensity of racial feeling into one of the worst free-for-alls ever seen in the city.

Scores were injured, many requiring medical and hospital attention. . . . Heads were opened, eyes blackened, and bodies thumped and battered as literally dozens of persons, young and old, many of them non-combatant spectators, were injured more or less seriously by a variety of ugly weapons in the hands of wild-eyed and irresponsible young hoodlums, both Jewish and Gentile.

Der Yiddisher Zhurnal's account was more moderate and put the blame for the violence squarely upon the swastika bearers, calling them Nazis:[31]

Greater police detachments were called upon last evening in Willowvale Park on account of a fight which erupted between young Nazis and young Jews, and which threatened to assume a serious character. It was expected that the same gang which on the previous Monday incensed the Jewish players by displaying a swastika along with shouts of 'Heil Hitler' would once again attempt to cause trouble. And so it was . . .

All was quiet until the end of the game, which the Gentile team won. As the crowd was dispersing, a group of Gentile boys celebrated the victory by yelling insults at the Jews and they unfurled an old blanket, on which was painted a swastika.

After the Monday game, supporters of the Harbord Playground team had announced that they would be back in force for the return match on the following Wednesday. One Harbord fan reportedly told *The Toronto Daily Star*: 'We are not going to make trouble, but if anything happens we will be there to support our players'; the 'Willowvale Swastikas' (as that newspaper referred to the swastika bearers) were aware of that intention and they also mustered their supporters.[32] The predicted trouble was not long in erupting. Even before the game began, one Gentile spectator was reported to have required medical attention. The 'Swastika supporters' claimed that while they were cheering for the St Peter's team, a crowd of Jewish youths arrived and ordered them to be silent. 'Whatever the cause', *The Toronto Daily Star* of 17 August reported, there followed

a swiftly ending free-for-all, with an unidentified swastika supporter requiring medical attention, the result, it is claimed, of a blow from a club, while one of the Jewish leaders was thrown down the hill into a cage back of the batter's box.

In the second inning, a second fracas occurred. It started in a section where a Jewish group was seated on the rising ground above the northwest diamond on which the game was being played; about 30 'Willowvale Swastikas' yelled in unison 'Heil Hitler' close to where about a thousand Jewish supporters of the Harbord Playground team were positioned on the elevated site. Infuriated, the latter rushed toward those who had provoked them and a fight ensued in the course of which a spectator was struck with a sawn-off piece of lead pipe. A newspaper report the following day stated: 'Batons, lead pipes, and other weapons were swinging freely'.[33]

The game was temporarily suspended while many of the spectators gathered around the battling groups. When play resumed, there were more yells of 'Heil Hitler' during the third inning and again violence erupted with supporters rushing to [the] assistance of both sets of combatants. The police restored order and the game proceeded without further serious unrest until the end, when the St Peter's team won by 6–5. It was almost dark by then and before the crowd had dispersed there suddenly appeared at the top of the hill a large white blanket bearing a startling black swastika. *The Toronto Daily Star* reported that when the emblem was flaunted, 'a mild form of pandemonium broke loose'[34] and *The Evening Telegram* stated: 'In a moment all was turmoil'[35] and added that 'the sign stood out visible to the entire crowd and acted like a red rag to a bull';[36] the Jewish supporters immediately raced toward the hill, intent on capturing the hated Nazi banner and 'the swastika, the swastika' could be heard 'for blocks away'.[37] The 'Willowvale Swastikas' tried to repel the attack and very quickly the battle intensified. *The Globe* reported:[38]

The assault upon the swastika wielder was the signal for a general inrush of Gentile youths, who plied baseball bats and fists in a wild riot. By the time police reserves arrived the battle had gradually moved over to Bloor and Clinton Streets, where some serious casualties occurred, and where, it is alleged, bottles for the first time became legitimate weapons. From this battlefront, it is said, many injured limped away or were assisted to their various homes.

All four English-language newspapers and the Yiddish daily gave a great deal of space the next day (17 August) to their reports of the riot under alarming headlines. Those of *The Daily Mail and Empire* stated:

Scores Hurt as Swastika Mobs Riot at
    Willowvale
Mayor Promises Immediate Probe of
    Disturbance
Thousands Caught Up in Park Mêlée
Gang Wielding Lead Pipes and Bats Sweep
    Streets, Bludgeoning Victims

The Globe was more restrained:

Swastika Feud Battles in Toronto Injures 5
Fists, Boots, Piping Used in Bloor Street War
'Heil Hitler' Is Youth's Cry
City in Turmoil

The Toronto Daily Star claimed that Dennis Draper, Chief of the Toronto Police Department, had been advised earlier by the Parks Department that the baseball game would merit special police attention (but Mr Draper denied being warned that anything resembling a riot might occur):

Draper Admits Receiving Riot Warning
Six Hours of Rioting Follow Hitler Shout
Scores Hurt, Two Held

The Evening Telegram's headline stated:

Report Gunmen Here to Slay Swazis
Communists Incite Riot Police Authority
    States
Jewish Toughs Began Trouble Says Witness

while *Der Yiddisher Zhurnal* stated:

Swastika Attacks Give Rise to Great Panic in
    the City
Mayor Stewart Agrees to Take Swift Steps
    Against Nazis
Draper Asked to Report

If the swastika had not been flaunted at Willowvale Park, the Christie Pits riots would probably not have occurred. The deliberate display of a Nazi symbol was an irresistible provocation to the Jewish contingent because it was the final straw which broke the comparative restraint of those who had been subjected to less strident forms of anti-Semitism.

Conclusion

In his article entitled 'Civil Disorder Participation: A Critical Examination of Recent Research', McPhail successfully argues that in focusing on the 'states' or attitudes of individuals as causal variables in collective disorder, insufficient emphasis is placed on the conditions in the immediate surroundings which may contribute to the violence of a confrontation. In the Christie Pits riot, there were several factors which contributed to the affray apart from the flaunting of the swastika. First, whereas the police were present in considerable numbers at the Beaches, and were thus able to keep the crowds moving, they were conspicuously absent at Willowvale Park when the riot started despite warnings that trouble was anticipated. Second, in the earlier disturbances at the Beaches, young Jews could not quickly summon reinforcements since the Jewish area of the town was at that time some distance away; by contrast, Christie Pits was then on the edge of a Jewish enclave in Toronto. Third, as McPhail and Miller have noted,[39] an important condition for the initiation of civil disorder is the presence of a large number of people with a period of uncommitted time at their disposal;[40] the first baseball game drew large numbers of supporters of both the Jewish and Gentile teams. Fourth, after describing the violence at that game, the newspapers publicized the intention of the Jewish supporters to return in force for the second game in anticipation of trouble; that report must have spurred the leaders of the Gentile faction to muster their own reinforcements. Fifth, the attitudinal difference between the Jewish immigrant generation and their offspring in terms of reacting to the rising tide of anti-Semitism meant that the latter were less likely to be as accommodating as their parents to anti-Jewish sentiments and behaviour. Lacking their parents' memories and experiences of the anti-Semitism in eastern Europe, the young Jews who reacted physically to the swastika provocation considered their response to be entirely appropriate. By contrast, their parents' generation generally believed that the Gentile authorities, including elected officials and the police, could be entrusted to deal with the problems posed by the swastika and that they would responsibly fulfill their official duties. Negotiation with the Mayor's office as well as with representatives of the Swastika Clubs was the chosen route of Jewish officialdom, an approach which was judged decidedly unattractive by young Jewish men who relied instead on physical confrontation.

It was evident that the display of the swastika in Toronto in the summer of 1933 was a deliberate attempt by some young Gentiles to insult and provoke their Jewish contemporaries. Their pretence that the swastika was merely a good-luck symbol might have been more credible if its display had not been often accompanied with chants of 'Heil Hitler'. After the Christie Pits riot, Mayor Stewart banned the display of the swastika in public in the interest of 'peace, order, and good government'.[41] The riot provided ample evidence that the younger generation of Toronto's Jewry would not meekly tolerate excessive forms of anti-Semitic abuse without resorting to violence. David Rome has commented[42] that a refugee from tsarist Russia, who was

accustomed to the hostile glance of the passerby and the official, is not as likely to be injured by a similar meeting in Montreal. But his son who was taught in school and by his juvenile reading the decent expectations of western European and American equality, whose life is less tightly limited even by the invisible ghetto walls—this generation is likely to be stunned even by a static measure of hostility, especially when sensitized by shocking happenings overseas which can be readily transposed to his country.

Mayor Stewart's ban on the public display of the swastika in Toronto might have seemed an infringement of the civil liberties of the individual but there is a Canadian tradition of taking quick and firm action to avert the likelihood of collective violence and Mayor Stewart's decision accorded with that tradition.[43]

Notes

1. See, for example, Richard A. Berk, 'The Controversy Surrounding Analyses of Collective Violence: Some Methodological Notes', in *Collective Violence*, eds James F. Short Jr and Marvin E. Wolfgang (Chicago, 1972): 112–18; Nathan S. Caplan and Jeffrey M. Paige, 'A Study of Ghetto Rioters', *Scientific American* 219, 2 (1968): 15–21; Kenneth B. Clark and James Barker, 'The Zoot Effect in Personality: A Race Riot Participant', *Journal of Abnormal and Social*

Psychology 40, 2 (Apr. 1945): 143–8; L. Festinger, A. Pepitone, and T. Newcomb, 'Some Consequences of De-individuation in a Group', *Journal of Abnormal and Social Psychology* 47, 1 (Apr. 1952): 382–9; Kerner Commission, *Report of the National Advisory Commission on Civil Disorder* (Washington, DC, 1968); G. LeBon, *The Crowd* (London, 1952); Stanley Lieberson and Arnold R. Silverman, 'The Precipitants and Underlying Conditions of Race Riots', *American Sociological Review* 30, 6 (Dec. 1965): 887–98; William R. Morgan and Terry Nichols Clark, 'The Cause of Racial Disorders: A Grievance Level Explanation', *American Sociological Review* 38, 5 (Oct. 1973): 611–24; A. Oberschall, *Social Conflict and Social Movements* (Englewood Cliffs, NJ, 1973); Jerome H. Skolniek, *The Politics of Protest* (New York, 1971); and Seymour Spilerman, 'The Causes of Racial Disturbances: Tests of an Explanation', *American Sociological Review* 36, 3 (June 1971): 427–42.

2. Herbert Blumer, 'Collective Behavior', in *Review of Sociology: Analysis of a Decade*, ed. Joseph B. Gitler (New York, 1959): 127–58.

3. See Herbert Blumer, 'Social Unrest and Collective Behavior', in *Studies in Symbolic Interaction: An Annual Compilation of Research*, ed. Norman K. Denzin (Greenwich, CT, 1978): 1–54; Carl Couch, 'Collective Behavior: An Examination of Some Stereotypes', *Social Problems* 3 (Winter 1971): 310–22; Kurt Lang and Gladys Engel Lang, 'Collective Behavior Theory and the Escalated Riots of the Sixties', in *Human Nature and Collective Behavior: Papers in Honor of Herbert Blumer*, ed. Tamotsu Shibutani (Englewood Cliffs, NJ, 1970): 94–110; Clark McPhail, 'Civil Disorder Participation: A Critical Examination of Recent Research', *American Sociological Review* 36, 6 (Dec. 1970): 1058–73; Clark McPhail and David Miller, 'The Assembling Process: A Theoretical and Empirical Examination', *American Sociological Review* 38 (Dec. 1971): 721–35; Enrico L. Quarantelli, 'Emergent Accommodation Groups: Beyond Current

Collective Behaviour Typologies', ed. Tamotsu Shibutani, op. cit.: 111–23; Neil J. Smelser, *Theory of Collective Behavior* (New York, 1963); Ralph H. Turner and Lewis K. Killian, *Collective Behavior* (New York, 1972); Ralph H. Turner and Samuel J. Surace, 'Zoot-Suiters and Mexicans: Symbols in Crowd Behavior', *American Journal of Sociology* 62 (1956): 14–20; and S. Wright, *Crowds and Riots: A Study in Social Organization* (Beverly Hills, 1978).

4. Blumer, op. cit.: 17.

5. Smelser, op. cit.: 16.

6. This paper is based on research for a wider study which has been published in book form: Cyril Levitt and William Shaffir, *The Riot at Christie Pits* (Toronto, 1987).

7. Blumer, op. cit.: 17.

8. Turner and Killian, op. cit.: 48, come close to drawing this distinction in explaining the difference between cognitive and mystical symbols. In their view, 'the symbols most likely to gain currency in collective behavior are mystical rather than cognitive. They invest the object of the crowd action with an aura of infamy, of tragedy, or of nobility.'

9. See Turner and Surace, op. cit.: 50.

10. Ibid.

11. According to the 1988 edition of *The New Encyclopaedia Britannica*, the 'swastika as a symbol of prosperity and good fortune is widely distributed throughout the ancient and modern world. The word is derived from the Sanskrit *svastika*, meaning "conducive to well-being". . . . In 1910 a poet and nationalist ideologist Guido von List had suggested the swastika as a symbol for all anti-Semitic organizations; and when the National Socialist Party was formed in 1919–20, it adopted it. On 15 September 1935, the black swastika on a white circle with a crimson background became the national flag of Germany.'

12. See Stephen A. Speisman, *The Jews of Toronto: A History to 1937* (Toronto, 1979): 318–19.

13. See Lita-Rose Betcherman, *The Little Band* (Ottawa, 1982): 50–1.

14. See Arnold Ages, 'Antisemitism: The Uneasy Calm', in *The Canadian Jewish Mosaic*, eds Morton Weinfeld, William Shaffir, and Irwin Cotler (Toronto, 1981): 387.

15. See Speisman, op. cit.: 318–19.

16. See Yaacov Glickman, 'Anti-Semitism and Jewish Social Cohesion in Canada', in *Ethnicity and Ethnic Relations in Canada: A Book of Readings*, 2nd edn, eds Rita M. Bienvenue and Jay E. Goldstein (Toronto, 1985): 267.

17. For an extensive discussion of anti-Semitism in Canada during the 1930s, consult the following sources: Irving Abella and Harold Troper, *None Is Too Many* (Toronto, 1933); Ages, op. cit., N. 14 above: 383–95; Lita-Rose Betcherman, *The Swastika and the Maple Leaf* (Toronto, 1975) and *The Little Band*, op. cit.; Glickman, op. cit., N. 16 above: 263–84; David Rome, *Clouds in the Thirties: Antisemitism in Canada 1929–1939*, Sections 1–13 (Montreal, 1977); and Speisman, op. cit.

18. *Der Yiddisher Zhurnal*, 13 Feb. 1933: 1.

19. Ibid., 24 Feb. 1933: 1.

20. Ibid., 3 Mar. 1933: 1.

21. Ibid., 7 Apr. 1933: 1.

22. Ibid., 24 Apr. 1933: 1.

23. Ibid., 1 Aug. 1933: 1.

24. *The Toronto Daily Star*, 27 Mar. 1933: 1.

25. Ibid., 29 Mar. 1933: 1.

26. Ibid., 5 Apr. 1933: 1.

27. Ibid., 28 Apr. 1933: 1.

28. Estimates of the size of the crowd in the Pits that evening ranged from 600–15,000 as reported by *Der Yiddisher Zhurnal* of 18 Aug.; *The Toronto Daily Star* of 17 Aug. reported that 10,000 people were in the park on the night of the riot, while *The Daily Mail and Empire* placed the figure at 'more than 8,000' in its 17 Aug. edition. Realistically, it is likely that at least 2,000 to 3,000 were in the park when the riot broke out. Of these, probably no more than several hundred actively participated in the physical violence, although many others undoubtedly shouted encouragement to one side or the other.

29. *The Daily Mail and Empire*, 17 Aug. 1933: 1.

30. *The Toronto Daily Star*, 17 Aug. 1933: 1.

31. *Der Yiddisher Zhurnal*, 17 Aug. 1933: 1.

32. *The Toronto Daily Star*, 17 Aug. 1933: 1.

33. Ibid.: 3.

34. Ibid.: 1.

35. *The Evening Telegram*, 17 Aug. 1933: 1.

36. Ibid.

37. Ibid.

38. *The Globe*, 17 Aug. 1933: 1.

39. Clark McPhail and David Miller, op. cit.: 725.

40. Ibid.: 726.

41. See *The Daily Mail and Empire*, 17 Aug. 1933: 1. This resulted in some embarrassment for a number of the city's organizations. In a story entitled 'Must Not Flaunt Swastika Is Warning Of Boy Scouts', *The Toronto Daily Star* reported on 18 Aug., on its front page, that Toronto Boy Scouts' headquarters warned all recipients of the Scouts' 'Thank You Badge'—a swastika cross surmounted by the fleur-de-lys, given to friends of scouting for some exceptional deed—'against flaunting the badge in public until the current feeling against the Hitler symbol has died down'. The Toronto Library Board had to decide what to do about the swastika emblems decorating the thousands of Kipling volumes in their public libraries. It was decided not to remove the emblem. Toronto motorcycle police unwittingly defied the Mayor's ban on the emblem since they were unaware that the swastika was stamped on the keys to the lockers at the police motorcycle depot.

42. See David Rome, op. cit., Section 3: 10.

43. See Kenneth McNaught, 'Violence in Canadian History', in *Character and Circumstance*, ed. John S. Moir (Toronto, 1970): 66–84.

Chapter 14

Thorny Questions and Conceptual Biases

Peter S. Li

When the 1991 Canadian census was taken, 633,933 persons, or about 2.4 per cent of Canada's population, claimed 'Chinese' as an origin (Statistics Canada 1994c). About 46 per cent of them resided in Ontario and 31 per cent in British Columbia; Toronto and Vancouver accounted for 66 per cent of those of Chinese origin in Canada (ibid.). Until 1981, this group of Canadians represented no more than half of 1 per cent of the country's population, and possibly less. Since the 1970s the numbers of Chinese immigrants to Canada have increased, and their arrival has substantially increased the population of persons of Chinese origin—from 124,600 in 1971 to 285,800 in 1981 to well over 600,000 in 1991 (Statistics Canada 1976; 1984; 1994c). Thus within 20 years the Chinese-Canadian population had increased five times. Without doubt, immigration in the 1970s and 1980s has played a major role in sustaining the growth of the Chinese community in Canada.

The image of the Chinese as recent additions to the Canadian mosaic is not incorrect: as many as 73 per cent of Chinese Canadians in 1991 were born outside Canada, and 63 per cent of them immigrated only after 1970 (Statistics Canada 1994c). However, these statistics can be misleading, since they do not reveal the social and political reasons why so many current Chinese Canadians remain foreign-born even though their predecessors first immigrated to

British Columbia in 1858—nine years before the Canadian Confederation was formed.

There are other discrepancies between statistical facts about Chinese Canadians and sociological explanations of their position as a racial minority in Canada. Throughout most of their history in Canada, they made up less than 1 per cent of the country's population, and in the nineteenth century were concentrated mainly in British Columbia. Yet this numerically small racial minority became the object of anti-Orientalism throughout the latter part of the nineteenth century and the early twentieth. Today it seems almost incomprehensible that people first brought to the country to alleviate labour shortages could have been seen as so threatening that municipal, provincial, and federal governments would pass extensive laws to restrict their rights and single them out for exclusion. The severity with which the question of Chinese people and Chinese immigration was treated in Canada was out of all proportion to any threat they could have posed.

In light of the harsh conditions that they endured in the past, the social mobility of Chinese Canadians today, which first became evident in the 1980s, appears remarkable. The emergence of the Chinese middle class, the affluence of the Chinese consumer market, and the movement of Chinese Canadians into professional, technical, and managerial occupations are only some indications of how far they have come from the Chinatown enclave and the second-class status to which they were once confined. Various explanations have been suggested to account for this spectacular social mobility, including the opportunities available in post-war Canada, transplanted Chinese values, and changes in immigration policies, which encouraged the migration of those with professional and technical skills.

Yet despite the occupational achievements and financial security of many Chinese Canadians today, they are periodically singled out as causing racial tension and social stress in urban centres. Hence their residential concentration in established middle-class neighbourhoods, their superficial foreign appearance, the alleged incompatibility of their values with Canadian traditions, their linguistic profile, and their consumer patterns become the subject of public scrutiny. It would appear that it is not so much their cultural characteristics or urban concentration in themselves that are perceived as being at odds with Canada's Occidental traditions, but rather the fact that, historically and culturally, racial minorities such as the Chinese have always appeared foreign to white Canadians.

The simple facts raise many hard questions. Why were the Chinese legally discriminated against and denied the rights and opportunities that other groups enjoyed in Canada when their labour was instrumental in building many industries, especially in the West? Why was there a sex imbalance in the Chinese-Canadian community before the war, and why does a large proportion of the Chinese-Canadian community remain foreign-born after a history in Canada of 140 years? Why are Chinese Canadians still regarded by some as members of a foreign race? Why, despite their social mobility, are they not fully accepted as genuine Canadians?

These are difficult questions, and they call for careful analyses of historical data and contemporary statistics, as well as sociological explana-tions. In the pages to follow, a wide range of material is used to show why institutional racism developed against the Chinese in the nineteenth century, how the Chinese-Canadian community survived the period of exclusion before 1947, and what demographic and social forces transformed it in the decades after the Second World War.

Finding a Term for 'the Chinese'

It is difficult to find a satisfactory term to refer to the Chinese minority in Canada without misrepresenting its members in some way. Ethnically, their ancestral roots can be traced to China, although some left China a few generations ago and others migrated elsewhere before coming to Canada. It would be misleading to refer to them simply as 'Chinese', since there are some 1.2 billion people in mainland China who are known as Chinese, and another 30 million ethnic Chinese distributed in 134 countries outside mainland China, Hong Kong, and Taiwan (Poston, Mao, and Yu 1992). Culturally, it is difficult to justify treating all the people of China and the Chinese diaspora as one entity, since historical conditions and social realities have produced many cultural differences and linguistic variations among the Chinese around the world. Thus a semantic distinction must be maintained when referring to Chinese in China and Chinese in Canada, even though many of the Chinese in Canada originated, whether in their own generation or in their ancestral past, in China.

Many Chinese in Canada are Canadian citizens, either by birth or by naturalization. They participate in the same educational, political, and economic institutions as other Canadians, and they share with other Canadians the rights and entitlements of citizens or residents of Canada. Hence the term 'Chinese Canadians' is appropriate to stress the fact that they are Canadians of ethnic Chinese origin. The term is not without problems, however. It suggests a class of what are sometimes referred to as 'hyphenated' or 'ethnic' Canadians, with the implication that the prefix indicates a status lower than that of unhyphenated Canadians. The sensitivity toward the term 'hyphenated Canadian' is well justified given the historical dominance of European culture and tradition in Canadian society and the tendency to view people of non-European origin and their cultures and traditions as foreign. In this book [*The Chinese in Canada*], the term 'Chinese Canadians' is used to stress that fact that they are not foreigners in Canada but Canadians with a history that precedes Confederation and to distinguish them from Chinese in mainland China and in the Chinese diaspora around the world. The term 'Chinese in Canada' is used interchangeably with 'Chinese Canadians', despite its subtle suggestion of an alienated status or a sense of marginalization among members of an Oriental minority in an Occidental country. Such alienation and marginalization have been part of the history of Chinese Canadians, and the term 'Chinese in Canada' is a quiet reminder that the notion of the Chinese as belonging to a foreign race in Canada is part of the country's history and tradition.

A History Reconsidered

Aside from the Indigenous people, no racial or ethnic group in Canada has experienced such harsh treatment as the Chinese. Anti-Chinese sentiments were widespread in British Columbia in the nineteenth century, and except for a few years after the arrival of the Chinese in 1858, the province's history was marred by a long-lasting anti-Chinese movement. Anti-Orientalism was common among politicians, union leaders, white workers, and employers, even though all these groups benefited, directly or indirectly, from the presence of the Chinese. In this sense the Chinese in Canada, like those in the United States, were the 'indispensable enemy' (Saxton 1971) of the state.

The same social and economic forces that had led many Europeans to settle in North America earlier in the nineteenth century also led many Chinese to immigrate during the latter half of the century. These waves of migration were propelled, on the one hand, by poverty at home and drawn, on the other, by opportunities abroad—a classic case of disparity between rich and poor nations. But unlike the European immigrants, who were generally accepted into Canadian society either as homesteaders on the Prairies or as workers in the urban labour force, the Chinese were not considered a permanent feature of Canada. They were simply recruited as cheap labour to fill the shortage of white workers here. It was no accident that the Canadian government passed the first anti-Chinese bill in 1885, the same year the transcontinental Canadian Pacific Railway was completed. Earlier, the federal government had been so concerned about the shortage of labour in the West that it was unwilling to restrict Chinese immigration, despite requests from British Columbia. Between 1875 and 1923 British Columbia passed numerous bills to restrict the civil rights of the Chinese. Finally, in 1923 the federal government passed the Chinese Immigration Act, which prohibited Chinese from entering Canada for 24 years before it was repealed.

The Chinese gained the right to vote in the first few years after the Second World War. With the repeal of the Chinese Immigration Act in 1947, and subsequent changes in Canada's immigration policy, they were allowed to immigrate on a limited basis. The volume of immigration was small in the two decades after the war, as Canada maintained its traditional policy of favouring immigrants from Europe and the United States over those from the Third World. But with the changes in immigration policy introduced in 1967, a larger volume of Chinese immigrants began to enter Canada. Further policy changes that broadened the admission categories for business immigrants, together with the changing political situation in Hong Kong, triggered another wave of Chinese immigration to Canada in the 1980s. By 1994 over half a million Chinese were estimated to have immigrated to Canada after the Second World War, about 92 per cent of them after 1967.

The experiences of the Chinese in Canada may be grouped in three distinct periods. During the exclusion era, from 1923 to 1947, no Chinese were allowed to immigrate to Canada, and those already here were denied many civil rights. The period before exclusion, between 1858 and 1923, had witnessed the emergence of institutional racism, which made the Chinese in Canada frequent targets of racial antagonism and attacks. The end of the Second World War marked a new epoch as the Chinese gained their civil rights and began to build a new post-war community. Such a schematic periodization is only a crude way to think about a history that spans almost one and a half centuries. Many changes occurred even within the same period; for example, the Chinese-Canadian community in the 1980s and 1990s differs occupationally, financially, and politically from the one that existed in the 1950s and 1960s.

The development of the Chinese community in Canada before the Second World War was largely constrained by exogenous factors over which the Chinese had little control. By the turn of the century they had been virtually reduced to second-class citizens in Canada. Subjected to social, economic, and residential segregation, they responded by retreating into their own ethnic enclaves to avoid competition and hostility from white Canadians. Ironically, these unfavourable external conditions enabled ethnic businesses and community organizations to thrive in the Chinese community. Thus in many ways the emergence of these ethnic institutions had more to do with institutional racism in Canada than with whatever traditional culture might have been transplanted from China.

The Chinese community in Canada before the war displayed several characteristics that were largely produced by government policies. The restriction on immigration after 1885 in the form of a head tax, and the total exclusion of Chinese after 1923, further distorted the sex ratio in the Chinese-Canadian community, which remained a predominantly male society made up of married bachelors separated from their wives and children in China. With few women, the growth of a second generation of Chinese Canadians was severely inhibited. As a result the Chinese population in Canada shrank drastically from 1931 to 1951. It was not until after the war, when changes in immigration policy enabled many Chinese to reunite with their families, that conjugal family life was gradually restored. In addition, the occupational opportunities available to the Chinese were limited to the service sector or ethnic businesses.

The Chinese who immigrated to Canada after the Second World War were very different socially and occupationally from their predecessors who came in the last century. Immigrating in a different era, these new arrivals came from more heterogeneous backgrounds. Many had professional and technical qualifications, and together with an emergent second generation of Chinese Canadians they began to form a new middle class. At the same time, the large volume of post-war immigrants increased the foreign-born segment of the Chinese community. Consequently, despite a history in Canada dating back to 1858, the Chinese-Canadian community in the 1980s and 1990s was largely made up of first-generation immigrants.

By the 1980s there were many indications that Chinese Canadians were doing well in Canadian society. By 1991 over half of all employed Chinese Canadians worked in white-collar occupations, as many as 28 per cent of them in managerial, professional, and technical jobs. Chinese Canadians were moving into exclusive neighbourhoods in urban centres, and the growth of an affluent consumer market led to a proliferation of Chinese businesses in suburbs and other parts of urban Canada. No doubt the affluence and social mobility of contemporary Chinese Canadians reflect in part the wave of immigration from Hong Kong and Taiwan in the 1980s and 1990s, which brought additional offshore capital and human resources to the already thriving community.

Despite the occupational mobility of Chinese Canadians and their financial achievements and business success, the prevailing mentality in Canadian society has viewed the Chinese race as foreign, and their implied cultural differences as incompatible with Canada's entrenched Occidental values and traditions. Thus the residential concentration of Chinese Canadians in traditionally white neighbourhoods, the prosperity of Chinese businesses in suburban malls, and the affluence of the rapidly expanding Chinese consumer market, among other changes, have often become targets of public concern, primarily on the grounds that these changes have been produced by a 'foreign-looking' racial minority.

The Chinese-Canadian community will continue to grow as a result of immigration as well as natural increase. As the Chinese middle class becomes more firmly established in Canadian society, it can be expected that Chinese Canadians will play a greater role in Canadian politics. Chinese Canadians are now increasingly active both in grassroots community organizations and in formal electoral politics. Their continuing involvement in Canadian politics and their growing awareness of issues of racial equality will likely give Chinese Canadians a stronger voice in asserting their rights, and in time secure their status in the Canadian mosaic.

Theoretical Tools

Although this book [*The Chinese in Canada*] focuses on the Chinese in Canada, it is in many ways a reflection of Canadian society and how it treats a racial minority. If, in retrospect, Canadians find it absurd to have imposed such extreme treatment on a racial minority that made many contributions to the building of Canada, particularly in the West, without posing any actual threat to Canadian society, they must find it equally difficult to accept the internment of Japanese Canadians during the Second World War, or the unequal life chances that Native people continue to face. These absurdities have occurred too frequently to be dismissed as historical accidents, and in the search for explanations it is often tempting to attribute them to the idiosyncrasies of the groups discriminated against. After all, the victims are visibly different from white Canadians. Thus the historical perception that the Chinese were physically different and the belief that they were culturally inferior made it possible for the average Canadian of the time to accept the injustices that were imposed on them; thus too, the behaviours, habits, and living conditions of the Chinese were used to show their unassimilable character and justify their mistreatment. In fact, however, the injustices done to racial minorities cannot be understood outside the context of social and economic developments in Canada and the structural contradictions that are inherent in such developments.

In the nineteenth century, the Chinese were not assimilated into Canadian society because they were not allowed to assimilate. Their marginal position was a consequence of institutional racism, not an alien culture. If Chinese Canadians appeared foreign to white Canadians in the nineteenth century, it was because their social isolation, vice activities, and poor living conditions contravened middle-class standards. These features of Chinese-Canadian life had nothing to do with traditional Chinese culture; they were the products of racial oppression and societal alienation.

Throughout the history of the Chinese in Canada, their oppression and survival have had little directly to do with either their race or their culture. The racial background of the Chinese cannot be held responsible for the menial jobs they held in the nineteenth century. Rather, the racial factor was used as a convenient justification for unequal treatment once Canada had become dependent on the Chinese as a cheap source of labour. Likewise, the structure of the Chinese community in Canada had much less to do with the persistence of Confucian culture than with discriminatory Canadian policies. In the process of adapting to a hostile social environment, Chinese Canadians mobilized whatever resources were available to them, including elements that might otherwise have become dormant in their cultural repertoire, such as the reliance on remote kinship ties used in building ethnic businesses. If their culture played a part in Chinese people's adaptation and survival in Canada, it was not their ancient culture that was at work. Rather, it was a new Chinese-Canadian culture that reflected both the experiences of the past and the challenges of the present. In this sense, the key to understanding the Chinese in Canada lies in the structure of Canadian society, not in a primordial culture that somehow was transplanted to a foreign land.

It is sometimes tempting to romanticize the social mobility of Chinese Canadians in recent decades as the product of remote cultural elements that encourage diligence, perseverance, and education. Such an explanation is untenable because it fails to explain why those elements should have remained dormant for most of the history of the Chinese in Canada, reviving only in the 1980s and 1990s. Much of the mobility of the Chinese Canadians has to do with selective immigration and changing employment opportunities in Canada. Once again, Canada's restructuring of industrial demands and corresponding changes in policies governing the inward flow of international labour and capital have played a major part in facilitating the entry of Chinese immigrants, many equipped with skills and capital. In addition, the economic growth and capital accumulation that have been taking place in the parts of Asia where many recent Chinese immigrants come from have enlarged the pool of human capital from which Canada has been able to choose skilled immigrants and capital-rich business immigrants. Consequently, many recent Chinese immigrants have come to Canada with previously acquired qualifications and capital that enable them to do well in Canadian society. These global and domestic structural factors do far more than remote cultural elements to explain the social mobility of Chinese Canadians in recent decades.

Conceptual Biases

It is difficult to tell the story of the Chinese in Canada without making some reference to the notions of 'race' and 'culture'. Academics have treated 'race' as a primordial characteristic explaining why people differ in the way they construct their societies and adapt to new social environments (Li 1990: 3–17). Racial differences are taken for granted since superficial phenotypic differences such as skin colour provide convenient but false grounds for believing that racial groups are biologically different from birth and that such 'natural' differences automatically explain subsequent cultural and social variations among people.

From this vantage point, the history and development of racial minorities in Canada is often seen as reflecting the traditional cultures transplanted by immigrants from their homelands. It is true that racial minorities look different from the Canadian majority, and these superficial physical features are widely accepted as naturally connected to cultural and other differences. The primordial view of 'race' gives rise to a narrow theoretical perspective on minorities such as the Chinese in Canada. They become an important subject of academic inquiry largely because they are believed to be culturally distinct, and this distinction provides both novelty and contrast to what is known about the majority.

This conceptual bias means that virtually every aspect of the lives of the Chinese in Canada is viewed through a tinted cultural lens that finds them worthy of study only because they are culturally and racially different from the majority. At the extreme, what is supposed to be a scientific endeavour becomes a peculiar journey in search of the exotic, and the Chinese in Canada present themselves as little more than representatives of a remote and ancient culture, the nature of which can be deduced from the way Chinese immigrants adapt to a new land. Again, the superficial racial distinction between the Chinese and the Canadian majority becomes the 'natural cause' to which social differences between them can be attributed.

It is from this limited theoretical viewpoint that the topic of voluntary associations among the early Chinese immigrants to Canada has captured disproportionate attention from academics. Largely influenced by social anthropological writings about how the Chinese in Southeast Asia preserved their lineage and kinship networks, scholars have focused on voluntary associations in the belief that communities in the Chinese diaspora have developed unique social organizations that can be traced to their distinct cultural origins.[1] There is nothing particularly wrong with this approach, and it has produced many sound academic studies. Taken together, however, they provide a distorted view of the history and development of the Chinese in Canada, since the focus is primarily on the cultural adaptation of the Chinese as a racial minority coming from an ancient culture. The consequence is a serious academic omission and a failure to address the thorny question of how the 'Chinese race' was socially constructed in Canadian society in the context of unequal power relations between the dominant majority and a subordinate minority. To do so would require that academics abandon the limited cultural perspective

in which the Chinese in Canada are seen as merely an extension of a foreign culture, detached from the structures and opportunities of Canada, and instead adopt a sharper theoretical tool to examine the history and development of the Chinese-Canadian community as an integral component of Canadian society.

The question of how 'race' should be studied has given rise to vehement disagreements between social constructionists and primordists (Li 1990: 3–17). Instead of treating 'race' as something ascribed at birth, social constructionists are interested in understanding how superficial physical and social features are used to construct differences among people, with the result that the fundamentally irrational notion of 'race' takes on real social significance. In other words, superficial physical and cultural features are important in the social construction of 'race' to the extent that they are used as social criteria to organize, process, reward, or penalize people. In this way, the fundamentally irrational concept of 'race' is given an artificial meaning as it is used as a tool and a justification for social segregation (Bolaria and Li 1988: 13–40).

The theoretical argument over 'race' is more than just an intellectual exercise, for it affects the kinds of questions that are framed. For example, if 'race' is treated as a social construct, it becomes logical to ask how anti-Orientalism developed against the Chinese in the nineteenth century, and how the notion of the Chinese race was constructed in Canadian society. In short, the question focuses on how Canadian society dealt with a racial minority, and how the treatment led the Chinese to become stigmatized as a racial minority with an inferior status in Canadian society. From this point of view, the treatment of racial minorities and their responses to it are parts of the same reality and cannot be understood in isolation from each other.

Much of the history of the Chinese in Canada has to do with how the community survived under externally imposed constraints. Its growth and development in the decades after the Second World War have been closely related to the changing structural conditions in Canadian society and the country's policies concerning Chinese Canadians and Chinese immigration; in the process, Canada continues to redefine its racial minorities and to construct new cultural symbols and racial images that affect the way a new generation of Chinese Canadians is incorporated into Canadian society. To take this perspective on race is not by any means to suggest that Chinese Canadians themselves are merely the passive objects of such construction, without social actions or cultural responses of their own; rather, Chinese Canadians respond to societal opportunities and constraints as members of a racial minority, and in turn their living experiences and actions help to shape Canada and its future.

Although this book [*The Chinese in Canada*] is a case study of the Chinese, it has much larger implications for Canadian society. Policies concerning racial minorities frequently reflect more the internal contradictions of the state that engineers them than the groups to which the policies are applied. These policies in turn are determined by other social and political forces. Ultimately, the success of a theoretical perspective depends on its heuristic value in explaining the empirical reality. The case of the Chinese offers an excellent opportunity for academics to sharpen their theoretical tools and for Canadians generally to broaden their cultural perceptions in unravelling the tangled maze of historical and contemporary facts underlying the relations between Chinese Canadians and Canada.

Note

1. Classic examples of such social anthropological studies are the works of Freedman (1958, 1961–62). A good example of academic interest in the social organizations of overseas Chinese can be found in Crissman (1967).

Chapter 15

What Is It?

David M. Tanovich

A Rite of Passage

In the early morning hours of 22 October 1993, Dwight Drummond, a popular CityTV assignment editor, and his friend, Ron Allen, were driving home in Drummond's blue Volkswagen Passat. They were young black men and about to experience, as Drummond would later call it, a 'rite of passage'—an unwarranted encounter with the police. This time, the stakes were particularly high. Before they knew it, their vehicle was boxed in by two police cruisers near the intersection of Dundas and Sherbourne streets in Toronto. With the officers assuming a defensive position behind their vehicles, one of the officers used his loudspeaker to order Drummond and Allen to raise their hands and exit the vehicle. A high-risk takedown had begun. The two men were ordered to take three steps back, go down on their knees, and lie on their stomachs with their arms stretched out. As Allen was exiting, one officer thought he heard a metal sound, reinforcing his opinion that there was a gun in the vehicle. This assumption immediately made a tense situation even more tense.[1] With one of the officers 'covering' Drummond and then Allen, two other officers approached and handcuffed them. They were searched and placed in the cruiser.[2] When no gun was found, the officers let them go. What was a routine ride home from work and a meeting of friends suddenly escalated into a situation where Drummond and Allen faced the very real possibility of joining the many other young black men who have been shot by the Toronto police under troubling circumstances.

Drummond filed a complaint with the police against the two officers who had initiated the takedown. Allen refused to do so because he felt the 'outcome was predetermined'[3]—a sentiment shared by many in the black community. As Cecil Foster, one of Canada's most highly regarded writers on race relations, put it in his book *A Place Called Heaven: The Meaning of Being Black in Canada*, 'the complaint would amount to a case of the word of a black man against a white policeman, and everyone knew the likely outcome'.[4] The complaint was dismissed.[5] Deputy Chief Robert Kerr was troubled by the incident and intervened. He took the unusual step of having the officers charged with discreditable conduct under the Police Services Act.[6] Kerr's decision sparked a controversy at 51 Division, where the officers worked.[7] On 26 January 1995, Constable Craig Bromell, who would later become president of the Toronto Police Association, advised his superiors that the division's 50 officers would not be going on patrol that day and that the station doors would be locked. For the next eight hours, Toronto witnessed the first police strike in its history.[8]

Why were Drummond and Allen singled out? At their disciplinary hearing, the officers testified that there had been two 911 calls reporting gunshots in the area. Although they were in that neighbourhood, the officers had not heard any gunshots.[9] They felt that Drummond and Allen were acting suspiciously. When their vehicle passed the officers' cruiser, it appeared to slow and, as Drummond put it, 'we broke the unwritten rule and made eye contact'.[10] The officers felt that the men were looking at them 'intently' and as if they were going to 'bolt'. They also saw Allen bending down to put something under his seat, as if to hide it.[11] What they likely thought was a gun turned out to be chicken that Allen had just bought at George's BBQ, a well-known restaurant in downtown Toronto.[12]

Finally, the officers claimed to be acting on a tip they had received from someone they thought was a prostitute. Apparently, a woman had approached them out of nowhere and asked, 'Are you guys looking for the guys with a gun? They are getting into a blue car from the parking lot of George's [BBQ].' She even used police lingo in describing them as 'two male blacks'.[13] The officers were unable to provide a name for this mysterious woman, and, when they advised dispatch that they were planning on stopping two 'male black' suspects in relation to the gun incident, they failed to mention the 'tip'. Moreover, they provided no description of her to the other officers on the scene, made no attempt to locate her, and, ultimately, she never surfaced.[14] In her cross-examination of the officers, Jean Iu, counsel for Ontario's police complaints commissioner, suggested that the tip was a fabrication: 'You never got any information from a woman', she said. 'You were acting on hunch, only a hunch.' The officers rejected this version of events.[15] In her closing submissions, Iu 'made it clear that she thought the officers and their supervisor had lied about an alleged prostitute informant'.[16]

The three-member civilian Board of Inquiry, which included one black member, dismissed the disciplinary charges.[17] It held that while it was aware of the 'perception held by some mem-bers of the public that black motorists are randomly and arbitrarily stopped by police officers for no reason other than the colour of their skin', this was 'not a case for such a determination'.[18] It was satisfied that the officers' conduct was warranted in light of the 'suspicious activity' of Drummond's vehicle, the lateness of the hour, and the lack of vehicular traffic.[19] In addition, the board observed that '[w]e would be hard pressed to presume that these officers would go through such a complex, military, precise technique as the high-risk takedown, involving several police officers, *with the motivation of racial bias or harassment.*'[20]

In so concluding, the board gave no weight to its own observations that this purported chance meeting with a mysterious informant was 'puzzling' and 'intriguing'.[21] It simply concluded that it was 'not necessary to enter into the speculation as to whether the streetwalker did in fact exist' because the officers' conduct was justified even in the absence of the tip.[22] But surely this issue was relevant to the credibility of the officers? Moreover, was the board as sensitive to systemic racism as it believed itself to be?[23] It did not, for example, address the issue of whether the officers had unconsciously or unintentionally relied on race to convert innocent into suspicious conduct.

Drummond was angered by the decision: 'Throughout my life,' he said, 'I've been going through this thing, day in–day out. It's been a rite of passage for me. It's not the first time I was stopped and it probably won't be the last time. . . . I think it's open season on young black men in this city.'[24] The notion that racial profiling is a rite of passage for young black men in Toronto is a common refrain.[25] Hamlin Grange, for example, a current member of the Toronto Police Services Board, observed in recounting his own experience with profiling that '[i]t is a rite of passage that most young black people in this city have been through.'[26] The decision of the board was upheld on appeal.[27]

A Definition

Until recently, there was no generally accepted definition of racial profiling in Canada.[28] This deficiency has proved to be a problem in seeking a remedy and in otherwise moving forward. As University of Toronto law professor Kent Roach has observed, '[a]ny debate about profiling that is not guided by a clear definition is bound to be a recipe for frustration and bitterness.'[29] We saw first hand in the Drummond case the problems of not having a clear definition. What we need is a concise definition that captures the issues that make this practice discriminatory. It is not good enough to claim 'I know it when I see it' because not all of us are looking at it with the same lens. Racial profiling occurs when law enforcement or security officials, consciously or unconsciously, subject individuals at any location to heightened scrutiny based solely or in part on race, ethnicity, Aboriginality, place of origin, ancestry, or religion, or on stereotypes associated with any of these factors rather than on objectively reasonable grounds to suspect that the individual is implicated in criminal activity.[30] Racial profiling operates as a system of surveillance and control. It 'creates racial inequities by denying people of colour privacy, identity, place, security, and control over [their] daily life'.[31] It shares many similarities with previous systems of control such as slavery and segregation, both of which had a long history in Canada.[32] As one scholar has pointed out, '[r]acial profiling is best understood as a current manifestation of the historical stigma of blackness as an indicator of criminal tendencies.'[33]

Defined in this way, racial profiling is both unlawful and unconstitutional. It violates our constitutional right to be free from arbitrary detention as guaranteed in section 9 of the Canadian Charter of Rights and Freedoms.[34] It also violates our section 15(1) Charter right to equal protection of the law, a right that serves to protect against 'the violation of essential human dignity and freedom through the imposition of disadvantage, stereotyping, or political or social prejudice'.[35] Finally, racial profiling is a violation of human rights.[36]

Systemic Racism and Stereotyping

The day-to-day racial profiling that occurs in Canada today is primarily about stereotyping rather than the expression of animus or overt racism. Those few that target out of hate, such as officers who target Aboriginals and leave them for dead in the middle of winter in the outskirts of town, are truly the 'bad apples'. But we need to be equally concerned about the much larger group of police officers who use racialized stereotypes consciously or unconsciously on a daily basis. Overt racism, the intent to treat individuals differently based on a belief in the superiority of one's own racial group, has been largely overshadowed in Canada by a more subtle and yet equally pervasive form of racism known as systemic racism.[37] Systemic racism is the 'social production of racial inequality in decisions about people and the treatment they receive'.[38] It occurs through a process called racialization:

> Racialization is the process by which societies construct races as real, different, and unequal in ways that matter to economic, political, and social life. It involves:
> - selecting some human characteristics as meaningful signs of racial difference;
> - sorting people into races on the basis of variations in these characteristics;
> - attributing personality traits, behaviours, and social characteristics to people classified as members of particular races; and
> - acting as if race indicates socially significant differences among people.[39]

For the most part, racialization is largely unintentional. As the Ontario Human Rights Commission observed in its 2003 racial profiling inquiry report, '[p]ractical experience and psychology both confirm that anyone can stereotype, even people who are well meaning and not overtly biased.'[40] In other words, most police officers probably do not even realize that they are engaging in inappropriate conduct when they conduct race-based stops and searches.

Where does this racialized 'usual offender' stereotype come from? In part it comes from our history of overt racism, a history that has made us far less likely to be critical of the suggestion that crime can be linked to certain racialized groups. It also comes from the people the police see most often in court or in high-crime areas. As Jacques Lelièvre, assistant director of the Montreal Police, candidly admitted: 'Officers see street gangs . . . [t]hey see some black people doing wrong. They get used to that, and myths develop. So when they see a black guy in a Lexus, they assume he's in a gang.'[41] A similar admission came from Ottawa's Deputy Police Chief Larry Hill: 'Do stereotypes exist? Yes. Do things happen because we stereotype people? Yes. So if we're going to call that racial profiling, then, yes, it certainly occurs in our police force as well as [in] other police services.'[42] Racialized 'usual offender' stereotypes also come from 'the misinformed anecdotal musings of associates, inaccurate media information, or a misunderstanding of information, reports, and studies, etc., disseminated by police or governmental agencies'.[43]

A Misnomer?

Alan Young, a law professor at Osgoode Hall Law School and author of the provocative book *Justice Defiled: Perverts, Potheads, Serial Killers & Lawyers*,[44] has argued in a *Toronto Star* commentary that it is a 'misnomer' to use the term 'racial profiling' to identify what is going on when the police improperly use race as a proxy for criminality. He believes that we have mischaracterized the problem. 'We are not dealing with racial pro-

filing,' he writes, 'we are dealing with racism, the same racism that infects our schools, our courts, our legislatures, and our homes.'[45] What is the basis for Young's misnomer argument? He argues that 'properly understood . . . [racial profiling] is not an established police practice. . . . Such a practice would mean there exists some training manual instructing officers to consider racial features in determining whether to investigate an individual.' He goes on to state: 'If our police have been secretly relying on an express racial profile for criminal investigations, then the only solution would be armed insurrection.' But rebellion need not occur, he concludes, because 'we have mischaracterized the problem'.[46]

But does Young's misnomer argument withstand closer scrutiny? As a factual matter, there are official police and government materials in Canada that racialize crime and, in doing so, fuel the targeting of racialized groups. For example, some intelligence reports explicitly link drug trafficking and gang activity to particular racialized groups. The 2004/2005 Annual Report of Criminal Intelligence Service Alberta provided quite detailed information to Alberta police officers:[47]

Jamaican Organized Crime

In 1999/2000, a CISA funded Joint Forces Operation in Edmonton, Project Kalcium, revealed that groups of Jamaican males were bringing cocaine from Jamaica to sell in the city.

Asian Criminal Groups

There are a large number of groups comprised of Asian criminals who, collectively, dominate the distribution of cocaine and marijuana.

Self-identified Criminal Groups

The Indian Posse and Redd Alert are comprised largely of Aboriginal males who carry out criminal activities relating to drug trafficking and violence at the street level. These groups cause considerable harm to rural and First Nation communities. . . .

According to statistics, single-parent families (with children under 18 years of age) in Canada are earning 40 per cent less than two-parent families. This is disproportionately impacting Aboriginal children where 32 per cent on reserves live in single-parent families and 46 per cent in urban areas. Forty-one per cent of Aboriginal children in Canada live in poverty (as do 42.4 per cent of immigrant children).

Aboriginal people are disproportionately impacted in the criminal justice system. They represent 3 per cent of the population but 18 per cent of the federally incarcerated population—an increase of 9 per cent in 20 years. They are more likely than the average Canadian offender to be incarcerated for violent crimes. The Aboriginal 'baby boom' will have a profound impact on gang activity and incarceration rates. Aboriginal people are targeted by organized crime and many Aboriginal youth are feeding organized crime groups in Alberta.[48]

In addition to racializing crime, these intelligence reports emphasize that racialized groups are predominantly involved in street-level crime, and it is on the streets that racial profiling largely occurs. It's enlightening to compare the treatment of Aboriginal, Italian, and eastern European groups in the 2003 Annual Report of Criminal Intelligence Service Canada (CISC):[49]

Aboriginal-based gangs are generally involved in street-level trafficking of marijuana, cocaine, crack cocaine, and methamphetamine as well as other criminal activities. . . .

While eastern European-based organized crime (EEOC) groups participate in most types of criminal activity, they are notable for their ability to plan and carry out sophisticated fraud schemes. . . . The most powerful traditional (Italian-based) Organized Crime (TOC) groups continue to be based in Ontario and Quebec; however TOC groups either directly or indirectly exploit criminal activities across the country. TOC continues to increase their wealth and influence through criminal activities, such as illicit drug importation/distribution, money laundering, illegal gaming/bookmaking, and their subsequent investment of illicit profits in legitimate businesses.[50]

While these materials may not explicitly instruct officers to target racialized communities on the street, the implicit message is there. Indeed, CISC has felt the need to include the following disclaimer in its annual reports:

References to organized criminal activity associated with particular ethnic-based organizations in this report are not meant to suggest that all members of that specific ethnic group are involved in organized crime or that the government of the country of origin or its authorized agencies permits or participates in illegal activities. These references allude to the illegal activities of particular criminal organizations, the majority of whose members share ethnic origins.[51]

This disclaimer arguably makes profiling even more likely. By suggesting that the link between race and crime does not target all members of the group, this statement suggests that it will be appropriate to target individuals where race plus some other distinguishing factor such as age, gender, or clothing is present. However, as noted earlier, this is racial profiling because what is being targeted is appearance, not behaviour. In addition, on a practical level, it is difficult to understand how the official linking of crime with racialized groups is of any assistance to the day-to-day policing of our streets. While some internal tracking may be relevant to the establishment of undercover operations where it seems advisable to have an officer who shares a similar background to a known group of criminals, it's unclear how this information assists officers conducting routine street patrols unless they use it as part of a generalized profile.

This official racialization of street crime explains, in part, why black police officers are just as likely as their white counterparts to engage in racial profiling and why there is no 'armed insurrection', as Young puts it. For example, in *Singh*, a case involving an allegation of racial profiling against a black police officer, the trial judge observed: 'It seems that any person of any race could consciously or unconsciously believe that persons of a particular race, his own or others, have a propensity toward criminal activity and thus should be targeted for attention by the police.'[52] While we do not have any data on this issue in Canada, the evidence from the United States confirms that African Americans experience differential stops and searches 'at the hands of white *and* black officers alike'.[53] As David Harris, one of the leading racial-profiling scholars in the United States and author of *Profiles in Injustice: Why Racial Profiling Cannot Work*, has observed:

If both black and white officers seem to use traffic stops and searches disproportionately against blacks and other minorities, this implies that profiling is about more than the racism of a few racist whites with badges. Rather it is an institutional problem, and an institutional practice.[54]

There is also an official document that invites racial profiling in the national security context. One week after the 11 September 2001 terrorist attacks, the Royal Canadian Mounted Police (RCMP) issued the following profile of the 'adversary', to use their words, in a Criminal Intelligence Brief:

Law Enforcement Requirement to Combat Terrorism

The second phase is to develop a longer term strategy to deal with future potential attacks. This longer term strategy will have to take into account the type of adversary we are up against. By all accounts the hijackers of the four planes were men who lived in the United States for some time, did not act conspicuously, were well spoken, well dressed, educated, and blended in well with the North American lifestyle. Similar subjects live in Canada and some have been identified. . . . These identified individuals travel internationally with ease, use the Internet and technology to their advantage, know how to exploit our social and legal situation and are involved in criminal activities. Indications from investigative leads in the past week have given us a glimpse that there are many more potential terrorists in Canada.[55]

By specifically identifying the adversary as the men who flew the planes, the profile implicitly includes their ethnic and religious characteristics. In addition, the profile is so general that it requires the reader to add these elements if it is to have any practical use at all. When Superintendent Michel Cabana, the former command officer of Project AO Canada, an RCMP-led anti-terrorist probe that had a number of Ottawa Arab men including Maher Arar under surveillance,[56] testified at the Arar Inquiry, he confirmed that this document was an express invitation to use racial profiling.[57] And so, after 11 September, the RCMP effectively warned all security officials that any young, educated, well-dressed Arab or Muslim male living in Canada could be a terrorist and, therefore, must be investigated.

As a normative matter, most Canadians understand what is alleged when a claim of racial profiling is made and recognize that the practice is unjust and fundamentally wrong. Although there is no question that the policing of race is the product of both overt and systemic racism, we should not fear giving it a more precise identifying marker. Young appears concerned that 'our choice of language'[58] has contributed to the resistance of the police to recognize the disparate treatment faced by racialized groups. However, will labelling it as racist further the dialogue? 'Racial profiling' is a term that focuses on the underlying conduct that gives rise to the differential treatment of racialized groups, rather than explicitly labelling an officer as a racist as the term 'racist' does. It also focuses on institutional beliefs and norms, not on the individual officer.

To that extent, the phrase is consistent with the view of the Ontario Human Rights Commission's *Policy and Guidelines on Racism and Racial Discrimination* which states: 'except in the most obvious circumstances, such as where individuals clearly intend to engage in racist behaviour, it is preferable that actions rather than individuals be described as racist'.[59] While the commission's position has come under attack as 'soft' or as shifting responsibility away from the individual,[60] this approach may increase the likelihood of an open dialogue—something that is often missing when it comes to the issue of race and policing. For example, it allows reform-minded police officers like Kingston Police Chief Bill Closs to undertake measures to address racism within his force and yet attempt to maintain morale and internal legitimacy by publicly stating that his officers are not racists. As he puts it:

I believe racial profiling exists. I believe biased policing exists. Because we're human, we all come into a police department with our own experiences and values and beliefs and I've learned that when police officers engage in racial profiling or biased policing, it can be intentional, unintentional, or subconscious . . . [but] I don't believe for a moment that I have racist officers.[61]

* * *

Notes

1. See *Board of Inquiry Decision* (26 Sept. 1995) (Ontario) [on file with the author], 1–6 [*Board of Inquiry Decision*]. See also *Ontario (Police Complaints Commissioner) v. Hannah* [1997], OJ No. 1411 at para. 2 (Gen. Div., Div. Ct.) [*Hannah*]. See also Philip Mascoll, 'Police Cleared in "Take Down"', *Toronto Star* (27 Sept. 1995) ['Police Cleared'].

2. See *Board of Inquiry Decision*, 6.

3. See 'Young Black Men', *Toronto Star* (2 Oct. 1995): A16 ['Young Black Men'].

4. Cecil Foster, *A Place Called Heaven: The Meaning of Being Black in Canada* (Toronto: Harper-Collins, 1996), 7. See also Cecil Foster, 'Blacks Learn Futility of Complaint', *Toronto Star* (3 Oct. 1995): A19.

5. See Clayton Ruby, 'Police Complaints a Monster We Can't Control', *Toronto Star* (4 Oct. 1995): A21.

6. RSO 1990, c. P-15.

7. See Rosie DiManno, 'Attacks on Kerr a Punishment for Breaking Ranks', *Toronto Star* (30 Jan. 1995): A6, discussing the police union's motion of non-confidence.

8. See Rosie DiManno, 'Scary Rogue Police Law unto Themselves', *Toronto Star* (27 Jan. 1995): A6; Philip Mascoll, 'Police Only Had "Hunch"', *Toronto Star* (28 Jan. 2005): A4 ['Police Only

Had "Hunch'"]; and John Duncanson and Michelle Shephard, 'Police Union Chief Calling It
Quits', *Toronto Star* (11 Sept. 2002): A2.

9. See *Board of Inquiry Decision*, 3–4.

10. Philip Mascoll, 'Skin Color Reason for "Take-
Down"', *Toronto Star* (31 Mar. 1995): A22 ['Reason for "Take-Down"'].

11. As quoted in Rosie DiManno, 'TV Editor Fears
"Open Season" on Black Men', *Toronto Star* (27
Sept. 1995): A7 ['Open Season']. See also *Han-
nah*, para. 10.

12. See 'Police Only Had "Hunch"'; and *Board of Inquiry Decision*, 7–8.

13. 'Police Only Had "Hunch"'; and *Board of Inquiry
Decision*, 4.

14. See *Board of Inquiry Decision*, 5–7.

15. Ibid. See also Bruce DeMara, 'Officer Never
Sought Witness', *Toronto Star* (30 Mar. 1995):
A7; 'Open Season'; and 'Young Black Men'.

16. As reported in the *Toronto Star*. See 'Reason for
"Take Down"'.

17. The board consisted of Fernando Costa (a lawyer), Edward Clarke (founding director of the
National Black Coalition), and Keith Aiken (re-
tired police officer). See 'Police Cleared'.

18. *Board of Inquiry Decision*, 11.

19. Ibid., 10. See also *Hannah*, para. 15.

20. *Board of Inquiry Decision*, 11 (emphasis added).

21. Ibid., 10–11.

22. Ibid., 10.

23. For example, in its reasons, the board noted
that it 'shares a special sensitivity to subtle and
covert racism'. See *Board of Inquiry Decision*, 11.

24. As quoted in 'Police Cleared', and 'Open
Season'.

25. See Carl James, '"Up to No Good": Black on the
Streets and Encountering Police', in *Racism and
Social Inequality in Canada: Concepts, Controver-
sies and Strategies of Resistance*, ed. Vic Satzewich
(Toronto: Thompson Education, 1998), 157.

26. Jennifer Lewington, 'Councillor's Racial Remark
Sparks Furor', *Globe and Mail* (17 Aug. 2005):
A15.

27. See *Hannah*.

28. See, generally, the discussion in Sujit Choudhry,
'Protecting Equality in the Face of Terror: Ethnic
and Racial Profiling and s. 15 of the Charter', in
*The Security of Freedom: Essays on Canada's Anti-
terrorism Bill*, eds Ronald J. Daniels et al.
(Toronto: University of Toronto Press, 2001),
368–70 ['Protecting Equality'].

29. Kent Roach, 'Making Progress on Understanding and Remedying Racial Profiling', *Alberta
Law Review* 41 (2003): 896.

30. See also *Paying the Price: The Human Cost of
Racial Profiling* (21 Oct. 2003), online: Ontario
Human Rights Commission <http://www.ohrc.
on.ca/english/consultations/racial-profiling-
report.pdf> (date accessed 21 June 2005), 6
[*Paying the Price*]; and Canadian Bar Association, 'Resolution 04-07-A, Racial Profiling and
Law Enforcement', online: Canadian Bar
Association <http://www.cba.org/CBA/resolu-
tions/pdf/04-07-A.pdf> (date accessed 10 June
2005).

31. Beverly Cross, 'A Time for Action', in *Racial Profiling and Punishment in US Public Schools: How
Zero Tolerance Policies and High Stakes Testing
Subvert Academic Excellence and Racial Equity*,
eds Tammy Johnson, Jennifer E. Boyden, and
William J. Pittz (Applied Research Centre,
2001), 5, online: Applied Research Centre
<http://www.arc.org/erase/downloads/profil
ing.pdf> (date accessed 26 Sept. 2005).

32. See Chief Justice Beverley McLachlin, 'Racism
and the Law: The Canadian Experience', *Journal
of Law & Equality* 1 (2002): 10–14; 'Policy and
Guidelines on Racism and Racial Discrimination' (9 June 2005), 5–8, online: Ontario Human Rights Commission <http://www.ohrc.on.
ca/english/publications/racism-and-racial-dis-
crimination-policy.pdf> (date accessed 11 Aug.
2005) ['Policy and Guidelines on Racism']; San-
jeev S. Anand, 'Expressions of Racial Hatred
and Racism in Canada: An Historical Perspective', *The Canadian Bar Review* 77 (1998): 187–
92; Carol A. Aylward, *Canadian Critical Race
Theory: Racism and the Law* (Halifax: Fernwood,

1999), 39–49; Barry Cahill, 'Slavery and the Judges of Loyalist Nova Scotia', *University of New Brunswick Law Journal* 43 (1994): 73; H.T. Holman, ed., 'Slaves and Servants on Prince Edward Island: The Case of Jupiter Wise', *Acadiensis* 12 (1982): 100; James Walker, *Race, Rights and the Law in the Supreme Court of Canada* (Waterloo: Wilfrid Laurier University Press, 1997); Constance Backhouse, *Colour-coded: A Legal History of Racism in Canada, 1900–1950* (Toronto: University of Toronto Press, 1999); Robin Winks, *The Blacks in Canada* (New Haven, CT: Yale University Press, 1971); Constance Backhouse, 'Racial Segregation in Canadian Legal History: Viola Desmond's Challenge, Nova Scotia, 1946', *Dalhousie Law Journal* 17 (1994): 299; 'Looking Forward, Looking Back', in *People to People, Nation to Nation: Highlights from the Report of the Royal Commission on Aboriginal Peoples* (1996), online: Indian and Northern Affairs Canada <http://www.ainc-inac.gc.ca/ch/rcap/rpt/lk_e.html> (date accessed 20 Nov. 2004); John S. Milloy, *A National Crime: The Canadian Government and the Residential School System, 1879 to 1986* (Winnipeg: University of Manitoba Press, 1999); and 'The Residential School System Historical Overview', online: Indian Residential Schools Resolution Canada <http://www.irsr-rqpi.gc.ca/english/history.html> (date accessed 21 Nov. 2004).

33. William M. Carter Jr, 'A Thirteenth Amendment Framework for Combating Racial Profiling', *Harvard Civil Rights—Civil Liberties Law Review* 39 (2004): 20. See also N. Jeremi Duru, 'The Central Park Five, the Scottsboro Boys, and the Myth of the Bestial Black Man', *Cardozo Law Review* 25 (2004): 1322–43.

34. It is now generally accepted that targeting an individual for investigation based on race is contrary to section 9 of the Charter. See, for example, *Brown v. Durham Regional Police Force* (1998), 131 CCC (3d) 1 at 17 (Ont. CA) ('[o]fficers who stop persons intending to conduct unauthorized searches, or who select persons to be stopped based on their . . . colour . . . all act for an improper purpose'); and *R. v. Richards* (1999), 26 CR (5th) 286 at 293–5 (Ont. CA) ('if the demand for the appellant's driver's licence and identification was racially motivated the demand was unlawful . . .'). In *R. v. Smith* (2004), 26 CR (6th) 375 at 384–5 (Ont. SCJ), the Court held that racial profiling also violates section 7 of the Charter, which guarantees that the state will not deprive someone of life, liberty, or security of the person except in accordance with principles of fundamental justice.

35. *Law v. Canada (Minister of Employment and Immigration)* [1999], 1 SCR 497 at para. 51, Iacobucci J. See 'Protecting Equality' for a discussion of the section 15(1) analysis.

36. See, for example, the *International Convention on the Elimination of All Forms of Racial Discrimination* (21 Dec. 1965), 660 United Nations Treaty Series (UNTS) 195 (entered into force 4 Jan. 1969, accession by Canada 14 Oct. 1970); and the *International Covenant on Civil and Political Rights* (16 Dec. 1966), 999 UNTS 171 (entered into force 23 Mar. 1976, accession by Canada 19 May 1976).

37. Systemic racism is present in every social institution in Canadian society. See the discussion in *Anti-black Racism in Canada: A Report on the Canadian Government's Compliance with the International Convention on the Elimination of All Forms of Racial Discrimination* (Toronto: African Canadian Legal Clinic, 2002) [on file with the author]; *Report of the Commission on Systemic Racism in the Ontario Criminal Justice System* (Toronto: Queen's Printer for Ontario, 1995), Ch. 3 [*Ontario Systemic Racism Report*]; Multiculturalism and Citizenship Canada, *Eliminating Racial Discrimination in Canada* (Ottawa: Minister of Supply and Services Canada, 1989), 3–7; W. Head and D.H. Clairmont, *Discrimination against Blacks in Nova Scotia* (Halifax: Royal Commission on the Donald Marshall Jr Prosecution, 1989); Canada, *Findings and*

Recommendations, The Royal Commission on the Donald Marshall Jr Prosecution, Vol. 1 (Halifax: Royal Commission on the Donald Marshall Jr Prosecution, 1989) (Chair: T.A. Hickman); Law Reform Commission of Canada, *Report on Aboriginal Peoples and Criminal Justice: Equality, Respect and the Search for Justice* (Ottawa: Law Reform Commission of Canada, 1991); and Royal Commission on Aboriginal Peoples, *Bridging the Cultural Divide: A Report on Aboriginal People and Criminal Justice in Canada* (Ottawa: Minister of Supply and Services Canada, 1996). See also the discussion in *R. v. Williams* [1998], 1 SCR 1128 at paras 20–31; *R. v. Gladue* [1999], 1 SCR 688 at paras 58–74; and *R. v. Parks* (1993), 84 CCC (3d) 353 (Ont. CA).

38. *Ontario Systemic Racism Report*, 39.

39. Ibid., 40. See also Anthony C. Thompson, 'Stopping the Usual Suspects: Race and the Fourth Amendment', *New York University Law Review* 74 (1999): 983–6 ['Stopping the Usual Suspects']. See further Alan W. Mewett, 'Secondary Facts, Prejudice and Stereotyping', *Criminal Law Quarterly* 42 (1999): 319; and Marilyn MacCrimmon, 'Developments in the Law of Evidence: The 1995–96 Term: Regulating Fact Determination and CommonsenseReasoning', *Supreme Court Law Review* 8 (2d) (1997): 368–74.

40. *Paying the Price*, 6.

41. Miro Cernetig, 'Looking Over Their Shoulders', *Toronto Star* (13 Feb. 2005): A8; and Roberto Rocha, 'Police Admit to Racial Profiling', *Montreal Gazette* (29 Jan. 2005): A1.

42. Chris Sorensen, 'Ottawa Police, Deputy Chief at Odds Over Racial Profiling', *Toronto Star* (2 Mar. 2003): A1.

43. *R. v. Singh* (2003), 15 CR (6th) 288 at 295–6 (Ont. SCJ) [*Singh*].

44. Alan Young, *Justice Defiled: Perverts, Potheads, Serial Killers & Lawyers* (Toronto: Key Porter Books, 2003).

45. Alan Young, '"Racial Profiling" a Misnomer for Racism', *Toronto Star* (26 Sept. 2004): F7 ['Misnomer for Racism'].

46. Ibid.

47. The Criminal Intelligence Service Alberta (CISA) is described on its website as follows:

> CISA exists to facilitate the exchange of criminal intelligence between intelligence units, enforcement units and CISC Provincial Bureau where collection, evaluation, collation, analysis, re-evaluation, and dissemination can be made to effectively combat the spread of organized crime in Canada. CISA and its Alberta *regular member police agencies* are also responsible for implementing the Provincial Organized and Serious Crime strategy to combat the spread of organized and serious crime in Alberta.

In carrying out its mandate, CISA is involved in intelligence sharing, strategic analysis, operational support, and training. CISA's Executive Committee is made up of the chiefs of police from cities across the province. 'About CISA', online: Criminal Intelligence Service Canada <http://www.cisalberta.ca/faq.asp>; and <http://www.cisalberta.ca/mandate.htm> (date accessed 18 Oct. 2005).

48. The Annual Report of Criminal Intelligence Service Alberta, 2004/2005, 9–10, online: Criminal Intelligence Service Alberta <http://www.cisalberta.ca/Annual%20&%20Semi%20Annual%20Reports/2004-2005%20annual%20report.pdf> (date accessed 20 Sept. 2005).

49. The Criminal Intelligence Service Canada (CISC) is an organization that 'provides facilities to unite the criminal intelligence units of Canadian law enforcement agencies in the fight against organized crime and other serious crime in Canada'. CISC consists of a Central Bureau, in Ottawa, and ten provincial bureaus, with one located in each province. CISC is funded by the RCMP through its National Police Services. The Executive Committee of CISC is headed by the

commissioner of the RCMP and is composed of 22 leaders from Canadian law enforcement. See 'About CISC', online: Criminal Intelligence Service Canada <http://www.cisc.gc.ca/about/about_CISC_e.htm> (date accessed 21 Sept. 2005).

50. Annual Report of Criminal Intelligence Service Canada, 2003, 5, 8, 15, online: Criminal Intelligence Service Canada <http://www.cisc.gc.ca/annual_reports/AnnualReport2003/Document/CISC_annual_report_ 2003.pdf> (date accessed 20 Sept. 2005).

51. Ibid., 2.

52. *Singh*, 295–6. The trial judge ultimately concluded that no racial profiling had occurred.

53. David A. Harris, *Profiles in Injustice: Why Racial Profiling Cannot Work* (New York: The New Press, 2002), 101.

54. Ibid.

55. RCMP Criminal Intelligence Brief (Vol. 8, No. 25) (18 Sept. 2001), 2 [on file with the author]. This document was filed at the Arar Inquiry as part of Exhibit P-85. See Transcript of Proceedings (30 June 2005), 8184–6, online: Commission of Inquiry into the Actions of Canadian Officials in Relation to Maher Arar <http://www.stenotran.com/commission/maherarar/2005-06-30%20volume%2033.pdf> (date accessed 23 Aug. 2005) [Transcript of Arar Proceedings].

56. See James Gordon, 'A-O Canada: The RCMP's Hunt for al-Qaida', *Regina Leader-Post* (2 Aug. 2005): A5; Jim Bronskill, 'RCMP Targeted Another Engineer', *Toronto Star* (10 Aug. 2005): A8 ['RCMP Targeted Another Engineer']; and Michelle Shephard, 'Arar Deportation Surprised RCMP', *Toronto Star* (27 Nov. 2004): A4.

57. See Transcript of Arar Proceedings, 8187, 1.3–8.

58. 'Misnomer for Racism'.

59. 'Policy and Guidelines on Racism', 13–14.

60. See 'A Racist Is a Racist', editorial, *Ottawa Citizen* (30 June 2005): C4; Nicholas Keung, 'New Rights Guide Targets Racism Not Racists', *Toronto Star* (29 June 2005): A11; and Avvy Go and Michael Kerr, 'New Racism Policy Falls Short', *Toronto Star* (7 July 2005): A20.

61. Tamsin McMahon and Frank Armstrong, 'Police Chief "Sorry" for Racial Profiling', *Kingston Whig-Standard* (27 May 2005): 1. But see Frank Armstrong, 'Officers Suffering in Wake of Racial-profiling Study', *Kingston Whig-Standard* (17 June 2005): 3; and Tamsin McMahon, 'Officers "Wounded" by Publicity Given to Racial-profiling Study', *Kingston Whig-Standard* (31 May 2005): 1.

Chapter 16

Tricking the Border Guards: Performing Race

Minelle Mahtani

Introduction

We all skinwalk—change shapes, identities, from time to time, during the course of a day, during the course of our lives. I think about how we create these identities, how they are created for us, how they change, and how we reconcile these changes as we go along.
—Scales-Trent (1995: 127)

I try all different sorts of ethnicities to identify myself. I'll just tell people I'm certain things, just to see what they say . . . sometimes, they'll be like, 'Oh let me guess, you're Pilipino, right?' And I'll go 'yeah' but then I'll tell them the truth. I kinda make fun of them to their face. Which is fun. Sometimes I like to make up whatever ethnic mix I can!
—from an interview with a 'mixed race' woman of self-identified Japanese and European descent

In this paper I interrogate the complex relationship that emerges between performativity and racialization by grounding a Butlerian approach to performativity. Drawing from qualitative, open-ended interviews . . . , I suggest that some women of 'mixed race' enact complicated racialized performances in order to disrupt oppressive and dichotomous readings of their racialized identities. Some women of 'mixed race' challenge

and contest racialized labels by putting into practice a varied set of racialized performances, revealing their ability to intervene and disrupt racialized social scripts. They adopt identities which are, all at once, 'strategic, tactical, mobile, multi-faceted, blurred, awkward, and ambivalent' (Pile 1997: 27). I outline the situated practices through which many 'mixed race' women in this study not only contest but also produce their own racialized and gendered locations, challenging racialized readings of their bodies.

I begin by drawing attention to examinations of performativity in geography, pointing out that recent forays have displayed a particular racial blindness. Then, I explore the parallels between the performative nature of gendered identities and racialized identities by focusing on the relationship between performativity and the 'mixed race' woman. I examine the gaze placed upon 'mixed race' women and explore participants' varied responses to that sexualized and racialized gaze. Last, through interviews with some 'mixed race' women, I suggest that the experience of 'mixed race' identity can offer a site for the performance of potentially enabling political identities.[1]

Performance, Gender, and Geography

I draw largely from Butler's notion of performativity in order to develop my argument. It is worthwhile here to outline briefly Butler's model of performativity as it relates to gender in order to explicate my reasoning for drawing this comparison between Butler's work and the stories of my informants. I employ Butler's theory of performativity inasmuch as it relates to processes of racialization. I choose not to explore the resonances between other definitions of performativity and performance as related to the work of Austin (1955) or Goffman (1959). I leave that task to other geographers (see Gregson and Rose 2000; Rose 1996). Instead, I wish to extend only Butler's notion of performativity by examining the relationship between performativity and race. It is, of course, challenging to translate a text-based theory into practice. However, I draw from Butler's work because I believe it is imperative to consider the linkages between the real-life worlds of 'mixed race' women and our theoretical developments in feminist theory. The exploration of the links between Butler's model of performance and the lives of some 'mixed race' women may help bridge 'the comfort of the abstract and the relevance of the empirical, the seduction of the ivory tower, and the romance of the street' (Keith 1991: 182). I hope that the reader will discover some unexpected resonances between the day-to-day worlds of participants in this study and the writing wor(l)ds in the academy.

Butler asserts that gender is constructed through various performances, suggesting that some performances can, in fact, challenge gender. Thus, gender is read as a kind of cultural performance, which results from the effect of contested power relations. Relying upon a theory of the performative, taken from speech-act theory and involving gendered meanings in the day-to-day, Butler argues against the fixity of gender identity. Acts and gestures are seen to be performative in the sense that:

> the essence or identity that they otherwise purport to express are fabrications manufac-

tured and sustained through corporeal signs and other discursive means. That the gendered body is performative suggests that it has no . . . status apart from the various acts which constitute its reality. (1990: 136)

By revealing how a parodic act like drag offers opportunities to destabilize and denaturalize gendered subject positions, Butler insists that gender is merely an elaborate, socially constructed fabrication:

> If the inner truth of gender is a fabrication and if a true gender is a fantasy instituted and inscribed on the surface of bodies, then it seems that genders can be neither true nor false but are only produced as the truth effects of a discourse of primary and stable identity . . . the body is not a 'being', but a variable boundary, a surface whose permeability is politically regulated, a signifying practice within a cultural field. (1990: 126–39)

Gender is seen to be a significatory practice through which acts are to be understood as linguistic concepts, where gendered subjectivities and identities are produced discursively. To imagine gender in this way positions gender within the arena of continual cultural (re)production.

To summarize this very brief discussion of Butler's notion of performativity: first, Butler insists that gender can be created through performances; second, she claims that gendered performances are repeated through a series of stylized acts. The making of these claims shift gender from being substantively foundational to socially temporal. The idea of gender as performative—an act, a style, a fabrication, involved in a dramatic construction of meaning—is a crucial element of her argument.

I turn now to a brief account of geographers' engagement with performativity. Performativity has not been neglected among geographers—as Nelson points out, Butler's non-foundational approach to identity has been embraced among geographers with increasing interest (Nelson 1999). The concept has been employed in relation to geographers' studies on workplaces (see Crang 1994; McDowell and Court 1994), bodily practices (Longhurst 2000; Nelson 1999), research processes (Gregson and Rose 2000; Pratt 2000), and gender and sexuality (Bell and Valentine 1995; Cream 1995; Lewis and Pile 1996; Rose 1996). Most recently, performativity has been explored in greater detail in a special issue of this journal [*Environment and Planning D: Society and Space* 2000, 18 (4 and 5)]. Clearly, Butler's model of performativity has provided food for thought for many geographers. Her notion of performativity has 'had a long and deservedly successful journey' (Thrift and Dewsbury 2000: 413). However, I am primarily concerned with exploring two aspects of Butler's theory: namely, Butler's tendency to ignore space and race in her discussion of performativity. I draw upon this critique in order to bring energy to Butler's largely theoretical discussion, and to ground racialized meanings in the spatial.

Geographers have pointed out that Butler's work is highly theoretical and displays a disturbingly metaphysical quality (Rose 1995a; 1995b). Beyond her discussion on drag, Butler provides little practical idea of what her new gendered configurations might look like in our day-to-day realities. Rose has noted wryly: 'Butler is just about the only major social theorist writing at the moment who has virtually nothing to say about space . . . with her linguistic definition of performance, the social becomes irrelevant to her argument' (Rose 1995a: 546; 1995b: 373). Similarly, Thrift and Dewsbury explain that Butler seems reluctant to give concrete examples within the social. They put it succinctly: 'Butler makes very little room for space, period. The space within which performance occurs is implied, not implicated' (2000: 414). In her

lucid critique of the potentials and pitfalls of performativity in geography, Nelson (1999) also suggests the need for a more careful translation of performativity, proposing that a more nuanced use of Butler's model would map out how subjects 'do' identity in real time and space, and the role of subjects in that process. Nelson is concerned that performativity uncritically assumes an abstracted subject, leaving little leeway for the possibility of theorizing agency in the processes of 'doing' identity. The analysis that follows provides an opportunity to consider the spatiality of performed identities, and, more specifically, where and when racialized performances take place, and contributes toward understanding subjects as critical and conscious identities on the ground. I will suggest that by enacting racial performances participants recognize their complex role in a sea of social meanings, in such a way that they grasp and take control of racialized readings of their identities in real time and space.

Processes of racialization are often also remarkably absent from discussions of performativity. Butler's model of performance has proven useful in theorizing and validating gay and lesbian experiences and performances in particular. But Butler does not move beyond this analysis to provide a detailed analysis of the interconnectedness of gendered identities with race. I find this ironic, as many have insisted that race, gender, and space are co-constructed and mutually constitutive (see Kearns 1997; McKittrick 2000; Ruddick 1997, among others), yet Butler chooses not to investigate the interconnections between race, gender, and her model of performativity.

Geographers have also suggested that the relationship between gender, race, and performativity is worthy of further attention. The introductory essay in the recent special issue on performativity in *Environment and Planning D: Society and Space* makes a passing reference to the potential link between gender, race, and performativity (Thrift and Dewsbury 2000: 430). Some authors in critical race theory have provided an initial navigation of this terrain (see Alexander 1996; Rahier 1999; Ugwu 1995), but studies have yet to explore the complicated relationship between performativity and 'mixed race' people. In this paper I attempt to contemplate that relationship by grounding geographers' insistence that performativity may well provide an important conceptual tool for a critical geography concerned with the denaturalization of social processes (Gregson and Rose 2000; Nelson 1999).

Taking my cue from Butler, I want to complicate the notion of performativity by suggesting that narratives from some women of 'mixed race' provide an avenue through which to explore the relationship between performativity and race. I read Butler's theorization of performativity through a racialized lens in order to demonstrate that racialized categories, like gendered categories, may also be viewed as regulatory fictions that can be produced through varied performances among 'mixed race' women, if we take performances to suggest 'dramatic and contingent construction[s] of meaning' (Butler 1990: 139). I will ground the notion that racialized productions, like gendered productions, are culturally constructed, rather than biological, imperatives.[2] Some of the stories that I am about to unveil reveal the very malleable nature of social identities. Race, not unlike gender, is a permanently contested concept and both these 'terms of cultural engagement, whether antagonistic or affiliative, are produced performatively' (Bhabha 1994: 2). This concept has not been neglected by researchers working in Ethnic Studies. Di Leonardo, for example, has pointed out that culture and ethnicity can be something that individuals can possess or lose (1984) and Back (1996) has explored how youth inhabit and vacate particular ethnic identities (see also Alexander 1996). In the empirical work that follows, I demonstrate a series of 'parodic proliferations' (Butler 1990: 138), enacted by some women of 'mixed race' identity, in order to draw upon the

language of performativity more critically. I believe we must connect the discursive practices of performativity with thinking and speaking subjects located in real time and space (Nelson 1999: 332). I show how race is actively performed and masqueraded among participants, rendering it ephemeral, such that racial categories are subtly, and not so subtly, displaced and disrupted. The unveiling of particular performances of some 'mixed race' women as they reinvent impressions of their racialized identities provides a practical way of grounding the notion of performativity, and also helps to explain how racial categories are regulatory fictions, much like gendered categories of identity.

I want to delineate the boundaries of my exploration of performativity here, as I acknowledge that it remains limited in an empirical sense. My interest is more in terms of the expressivity of the performance; it is less upon performance as display than as an articulation of a bodily practice which creates a self and space. The interview excerpts that follow provide examples among participants who choose to perform particular strategies in order to enact difference. Based upon narratives, and my desire to demonstrate how racial categories are socially constructed in different ways and in different places, I will show how participants strategically employ identity, with a view to understanding the contextual causes and effects of various performances. I highlight the theory of performativity in order to contextualize racialized performance; to make it less fixed and multiple; to emphasize its social production and reproduction, rather than focus upon contestations at a microscale. My concern lies more with the moment of the performance, which, 'like a landscape, is only a small part of a mysterious narrative' (Michaels 1996: 107). I am interested in the various personas these women cloak themselves in, where we may be able to locate the significance of the performance through the relationship that is intended with the audience, as Rose suggests:

the question of the politics of the masquerade might then become, how does the audience interpret the performance: *who are you?* and the answer *how about you?* This performative context is crucial in thinking about the subversive possibilities. (1996: 73)

Performance and the 'Mixed Race' Woman

In this section, I introduce the relationship that emerges between performance and the narratives from 'mixed race' women in Toronto, Canada. Racial performance is one avenue open to some 'mixed race' women because of the shifting ways they are racialized. Readings of their bodies are complex and multi-faceted. Their racialized identities do not necessarily fit in socially constructed categories of race. Many 'mixed race' women explained that their racial identity is defined differently over time and space because of the shifting spaces of racialization. There is a considerable literature in this arena (see Azoulay 1997; Ifekwunigwe 1999; Parker and Song 2001; Twine 1998, among others) that examines the experience of 'mixed race' identity, demonstrating how processes of racialization for multiracial people vary over time and space considerably. In some spaces, they might be seen as white; in others, they may be seen as people of colour (Mahtani 1996), but often these readings are unstable and constantly changing. This theme laced through many transcripts among the women I interviewed, but, it is important to note, it would be wrong to presume that all the women in this study experience racial ambiguity. This is a crucial point. To assume all women of 'mixed race' experience a freedom to perform racialized identities is to essentialize the very diverse population of women interviewed. I draw upon those experiences of certain 'mixed race' women who do experience racial ambiguity regarding others' perceptions of their racial

appearance in order to demonstrate the links between performativity and race. However, I emphasize that not all 'mixed race' women experience this freedom, as their racial identity will be framed for them regardless of their own intentions and desires (Trinh 1992). The constraints and conventions of their racialized circumstances should not be ignored. These women will be positioned as particular subjects by their framers and, as a result, often experience limited flexibility to subvert those socially constructed framings of their racialized identities. My interests lie in exploring some 'mixed race' women's responses to that experience of racialization.

Racial performance relies upon an understanding that informants often actively respond—as opposed to accept passively—the ways their racialized selves are perceived by others. Many women in this study told me that they felt hypervisible, constantly judged and evaluated, weighed down by the stresses of having to explain why they look the way they do, over and over again. This is not an unusual experience for 'mixed race' people, and it is particularly heightened among participants in this study, as 'mixed race' women are often marked as sexually deviant or exotic and subsequently turned into an object of scrutiny. Some researchers have suggested that 'mixed race' women, more so than 'mixed race' men, may be more vulnerable to society's reactions to their ambiguous features (Root 1996). These gendered, sexualized, and racialized myths derive from the popular discourse about the 'mixed race' person which pronounces her as being 'out of place'. Cresswell has effectively demonstrated how the notion of being 'out of place' brings to mind images of isolation, fear, dread, loneliness, or despair (1996). Historically, 'mixed race' people have been stigmatized by representations derived from discussions in nineteenth-century racial theory, where racial differences were read as biological classifications, and used to rationalize human deprivation. The collusion of scientific racism, or what

Ifekwunigwe calls 'race as science fiction' (1999), plays a key role in the historical genealogies of 'mixed race' identities.

Interracial relations, and the existence of multiracial people, were criminalized (see Tyner and Houston 2000) because they challenged the supposed sanctity of racial categories. Distinct categories of races were firmly established, and those who did not fit clearly into those racial boundaries disrupted the well-drawn borders by 'illegally' crossing them. 'Mixed race' people directly challenged mainstream categories of race and fuelled the fear that something sacred or pure was in danger of losing its racial authenticity—as if such a thing existed. Therefore, 'mixed race' people were seen as a threat to racial purity. In no small part influenced by this insidious underpinning, several clinical psychological evaluations of the experience of 'mixed race' identity in the late 1800s concluded that 'mixed race' people suffer from social maladjustment, anxiety, and confusion related to identity development. 'Mixed race' individuals were also seen as infertile and as a 'nuisance to others' (Davenport 1917). Clearly, 'mixed race' people have been made intelligible in ways that reinforce and maintain the racialized hierarchy (Mahtani 1996; 2001).

Because some 'mixed race' women blur socially constructed racial boundaries, they do not fit neatly into the observer's schema of reality and can be seen as 'abnormal'. This often results in stares and scrutiny—a sort of racial voyeurism. Even self-identified 'mixed race' researchers are not immune to this tendency, as Marin admits:

[While] I discount any biologistic fact of pure race and therefore racial difference . . . I [nevertheless] find myself staring—to a degree that I have to consciously control it— at all persons of mixed race heritage. In fact the way I determine that they are mixed race is because I am staring, unable to stop looking until I can put ambiguity to rest, know what race is, call it something. And of course

that's the problem. If race rests on the concept that racial difference is absolute, then to be mixed race is not really possible. So I keep staring . . . [knowing] that even as I look, I don't see them. (1996: 113)

Some of the women interviewed talked intensely about this gaze, explaining that they are continually being analyzed for clues to their racial backgrounds. Farideh is a 17-year-old student whose mother is Chinese and whose father is European. She explained how she feels when she is being watched: reminiscent of 'an aggressive plastic lens pushing on her' (Rose 1993: 143):

When I'm involved in political stuff, a seminar, or a march or a rally, like even International Women's Day, I feel like it's not me who's watching everyone else? I feel like my eyes reflect other people's eyes watching me? Not my own eyes watching people?

Farideh describes the gaze which accentuates a self-consciousness which results from being the object of the other. The situational context affects what Farideh sees in herself, what she sees in others, and how she perceives others read her racialized identity. She communicates a sense of being 'otherized' and objectified. Farideh was careful to point out that she experiences this disease when she is in certain sites: in this case, at political events, where her status as a 'woman of colour' is scrutinized. Some political groups of colour have narrow criteria for group membership and thus many 'mixed race' individuals can experience feelings of exclusion simply because they do not look 'coloured enough' (Root 1997).

Makeda expressed similar feelings of being scrutinized for clues as to her racial place in society. Makeda is a 26-year-old graduate student whose mother is Japanese and whose father is European. Although Makeda is secure in her own sense of ethnic identity, she is aware of others' perceptions of her racial background:

I think it's a little bit that feels off to people, that's what they can't place, that is what allows for that slipperiness to occur? They feel like 'Well, she LOOKS something, but what is it?' Right? And it's that kind of category crisis. But it's not my crisis. It's theirs, usually. And they're going, 'Hmmm'. And that is why I think that people always try to second guess what a mixed race person is when their features, or their physical appearance is kinda in any way, slippery? You know? Or ill-defined or something? People are anxious to define me. I get that every day any time I meet someone new.

By stating that 'it's their crisis, not mine', Makeda insists that she knows who she is, whereas others are floundering in their attempt to classify her racially. For some 'mixed race' women, particular places offer, because of their racially ambiguous appearance, sites where racial codes cannot be easily read. Farideh also hints at some of the shifting nature of space in how others interpret her racially and, in turn, how she decides how she will interpret others' readings of her racialized identity:

It's always changing. I'm always getting certain reactions from people, and having to deal with different situations, sort of thing. Like work out in my head and the room and what the vibe is before I enter it.

Within that moment of the others' ambiguity, spaces are created which are ambivalent and fraught with tension. The only stability in other people's interpretations of Farideh's ethnicity is the precariousness of the situation. Farideh never knows how others will read her racial identity. She reveals how her perceptions of herself through the eyes of others are 'informed by conceptions of space that recognize place, position, location, and so on as created, as produced' (Bondi 1993: 99).

In the next section, I wish to document what happens after that process of racialization occurs, exploring those actions that follow, which set off, like a crazed pinball machine, the possibilities for performances. Choosing *what* performance *where*, depends upon a myriad of conditions—a complex exchange among a variety of characters, where everyday interactions occur across gendered and racialized terrains. These exchanges are complex because places are not 'inert, fixed backdrops' (Moore 1997: 87) where racialized meanings are consistent. The ground upon which these performances are enacted are not permanent, fixed, nor stable. Rather, it is continually shifting and changing. Spaces of interrelations where performances are employed cannot be compared to multicoloured splatters of paint upon a blank canvas. Everyday spaces are rife with diverse social dynamics, power, and subjectivity, much like Gregson and Rose suggest: 'performed spaces are not discreet, bounded spaces, but threatened, contaminated, stained, enriched by other spaces' (2000: 442). In the next section, I suggest how some women of 'mixed race' in this study choose among a multiplicity of invented identities that accommodate various situations, dependent upon their reading of their encounter, and their temperament at the time. I document these performances, where participants attempt to transform the constraining cages of racialized categories. I do this in part to demonstrate that women of 'mixed race' are actively creating places to call home, effectively dispelling notions of them as 'out of place', and also to try and bring agency to Butler's model of performativity.

Mapping Racialized Performance in the Social Landscape

We are what we pretend to be, so we must be very careful who we pretend to be.
            —from Vonnegut's novel *Cat's Cradle*

A starting place for a cartography of identity could be to map how individuals and/or collective subjects do identity in relation to various discursive processes (e.g., class, race, gender, and sexuality), to other subjects, and to layers of institutions and practices—all located concretely in time and space.
— Nelson (1999: 349)

I have previously explored how Farideh feels as if she is continually under scrutiny through others' perceptions of her racialized identity. In this section of the paper, I demonstrate that Farideh does not just idly 'take on' the gaze of others without appropriating a stance to counteract their readings. Farideh explains how she puts into play a performance in order to create alliances among others. The gaze demands a response that enables her to reconstitute herself as someone in control of how she views herself and how others look at her:

I play different roles with different people. I won't be exactly the same, within, like in Chinese circles. For example, I started playing on this basketball team with other Chinese women, it's called Lady Dragons. It's an all-Chinese team. And there was a big thing about whether or not I could play. Because they weren't sure if the rules permitted it because I'm only half-Chinese. So it's OK, so I'm playing. I went to the first practice, and I realized that I consciously started trying to prove my Chineseness to them. And I make jokes a lot, about myself. It's the only time I do really feel in a group like I have to prove myself, is when I'm with Chinese friends who all speak Cantonese. And who are all very proud of being Chinese. And so, yeah, it's still fun but I sorta play like the joker role. I just notice. I try to prove myself by like showing how well I can write Chinese characters, and talking about Chinese food that others might not know about.

Farideh relays an experience where she feels she has to prove her ethnicity. Tests of ethnic legitimacy are power struggles, often serving purposes of increasing fragmentation around ethnicity and questions of authenticity (Root 1996). In this situation, Farideh enacts a performance in order to prove her ethnicity to others on her basketball team by exaggerating certain ethnic gestures. She masters a series of 'repetitive stylized acts' (Butler 1990: 140) around Chineseness, which she hopes will be familiar to her Chinese peers, while at the same time hoping to disrupt their readings of her perceived whiteness. Given the precarious nature of the situation, where her mere presence on the team was in fact debated, she feels she must prove her ethnic identifications to others.

Although Farideh adopts particular forms of performance in order to create and maintain alliances with a particular ethnic community, in contrast, Katya's performance is employed in order to subvert socially constructed ideas associated with racial categories. Katya is a 30-year-old filmmaker whose father identifies himself as West Indian and whose mother identifies as Irish. Katya tells me how she deliberately dislodges particular stereotypes associated with her phenotype, explaining how she moves away from stereotypes associated with the racialized categories of whiteness and blackness:

Katya: I spend time challenging what people think I am. And being able to bring more information into the situation than they expected, or, in some cases, desire.

Question: Can you give me some examples of that?

Katya: Well growing up. High school, university. I was very acutely aware that people would look at me, and say, 'OK. A black woman, therefore she must be into reggae and funk. And she is a really good dancer. She's got rhythm, naturally!' I think that I was sparked, or spurred into appreciating, a music that was not particularly black music. And I did not delve into black music. I mean I was familiar with it. But I made some effort to, I was into punk and new wave, and all this kinda stuff. I mean this is what my friends were into. And sure, some of them were into reggae, and stuff like that. But I didn't know as much about reggae as they did. As some of my white friends.

Me: Was that a conscious decision on your part?

Katya: I'd say pretty close to conscious. I know I did certain things, I mean, if I just met you, and I got the impression that you would assume that I knew everything about funk and reggae, I would let you know that I had every Japan album that has ever been made, or I'm an AC/DC fan, which I'm not actually, but I'll just say that I'm a Led Zeppelin fan. So, yeah. I would let them know that, or if people would, I guess it was a desire to be unique in a way. I would let them know that my mother's white. 'You think I'm just a plain black person? Well, it's a little bit more than that. It's not what you think. You THINK this. But this is not what you're thinking.' So it was my little way, a strange, convoluted, demented way of telling people, 'Don't assume. Don't be so ignorant as to assume.'

Katya's decision to tell others about her music preferences reflects her desire to provide a local intervention which can shift racist discourses, disrupting a smooth reproduction of dominant imaginaries of race. Katya is pointing out the limitations of race as a defining concept about a person's identity. A preliminary reading of the narrative might suggest that Katya is identifying with other sorts of music in order to be seen as unique, articulating a politics of teen angst or

dissent through the notion of refusing to conform, or that Katya may practise internal racism by self-consciously positioning herself outside of reified notions of blackness. However, I suggest that Katya's decision to define herself outside of socially constructed stereotypes illustrates a deliberate ploy which refuses to conform to reductionist or essentialist notions of race. Katya employs a strategy of paradox, of serious play, debunking the constructedness of qualities associated with racial categories. Katya interrupts others' impressions about her based upon her phenotype and stereotypes surrounding the 'mixed race' woman as passive and 'out of place'.

Katya may well adopt the role of the *new mestiza*[3] by demonstrating her pluralized sense of self. Katya explains that she was frustrated when others were unable to see through the external appearances of a collective racialized identity to the internal reality of her own individualized identity. In refusing to collude with insidious colour biases and categories, she decides to contradict the stereotype. . . .

Conclusion: Troubling Racialized Categories

I have attempted to demonstrate how we might more fully read, interpret, and understand the various racialized performances employed among some 'mixed race' women. I have unveiled narratives from some women of 'mixed race' identity who explained how they enacted various racialized performances in different spaces. Butler has asserted that gender is a regulatory fiction (1990), and in juxtaposing that idea through these narratives, I assert that race is also a regulatory fiction. This phrase resonates with me because of its paradoxical nature. On the one hand, race is utterly fictional, a story, and a social construction (see Omi and Winant 1994; Radhakrishnan 1996). On the other hand, the very real limits of racial performance are unveiled by the term *regulatory*, meaning that performances take place in constrained places, the vigilant racial border guards constantly on patrol. Such roles rely upon how individuals have been rendered as subjects within the oppressive framework of racialized meanings. I have also suggested that some women rework their identities and disrupt social values associated with the seeing of race. These performances can trouble racialized lines—participants are wittingly creating 'emotional and psychic earthquakes with emotional reverberations' (Root 1996: 9). Interviewees like Katya and Farideh challenged the notion of naturalized categories and of singular and stable identities.

Although particular meanings associated with racial representations can be challenged and contested by some of these performances, it is crucial to note that some of the examples cited here may actually reinvest racist ideals by re-idealizing them and re-consolidating their hegemonic status—far from what anti-racist practitioners would see as a progressive move. It would be ignorant to assume that *all* performances can in fact challenge binary and oppositional modes of racial identification. In fact, some seemingly subversive actions enacted by informants are constituted out of, and actively maintain, racialized boundaries. The intentions and meanings of these performative strategies are clearly not straightforward, primarily because the consequences of negotiating various racialized positions are not open to simple or transparent readings. Participants acknowledged to me that they are not able to alter systematic racism through racialized performances alone. What is at stake is the hope that their interventions, in some small way, will sometimes generate reverberations that do matter. The articulation of an 'unnatural discourse' (Kobayashi and Peake 1994) may create unpredictable dissonances, but there is no certainty that this will be the inevitable result. Therefore, the total effects of these performances are incalculable. These narratives provide an opportunity to challenge any notion of a pristine or fixed model of resistance or opposition, as if such a thing were possible, as Sharp et al. may well remind us (2000). The voices of these women open up the possibilities for an analysis that ascribes critical power to the subject, and contributes toward examining the construction of complex and shifting 'mixed race' identities. I echo the words of Gregson and Rose: '[it] is not to say that certain performances elude power relations, but rather to suggest that power operates in a rather different, although less predictable manner' (2000: 442). I have explored examples of racial performance because they provide an opportunity to examine how many women of 'mixed race' actively recombine conventionally racialized elements into new and often unexpected ways that disrupt racial binaries. Many of these strategies shake things up a little, unveiling new possibilities of identity configuration. Participants sometimes radically recontextualize stereotypes in ways that reconstitute a rethinking of racial categories.

I was initially reluctant to develop a model of racialized performativity among participants for fear of perpetuating the myth of the 'mixed race' woman as cunning or deceitful. As Bell and Valentine have noted, the actor is often seen as a con artist (1995). Upon reflection, however, I recognized the critical importance of documenting the various aspects of the cultural game being played by these women, through which a sense of self becomes not a stable essence but, rather, a kind of a positioning (Hall 1992b: 226). Their many performances make up various aspects of their identity. I was also curious as to why some women chose to narrate these particular examples of racialized performance to me as a researcher. At times, these stories were told to me after the formal interview questioning was over, at which point some women told me that there were a 'few other things' that they wanted to tell me. Although 'mixed race' women have often been read as a marginal, stigmatized, psychologically maladjusted, and oppressed group (Root 1996), I discovered that during the interviews participants challenged these fixed readings of themselves, often accompanied by anger and indignation. They found these stereotypes degrading, and, through their stories, they refused rehearsed social scripts about the experience of multiraciality, defying racialized interpretations of their selves based upon pervasive cultural stereotypes of the 'mixed race' woman. However, as Pratt has suggested, it may well be that the interview itself might be envisioned as a site of performance (2000). It is possible that participants might have projected a positive representation of the experience of 'mixed race' identity in order to contest the systematic dominant representations of themselves as weak or as in positions of relative powerlessness. Their responses may have been further complicated by my own status as a self-identified 'mixed race' woman; participants may well have expected me to want to hear a more 'positive take' on the experience of 'mixed race' identity—as both a researcher studying 'mixed race' identity and as a 'mixed race' woman myself. Critical 'mixed race' theory and geography may well contribute to debates about the situationality of performativity and 'mixed race' identity by examining the relationship between the research process and performances as employed among both interviewer and interviewee.

In this paper I have considered the implications of Butler's concept of performativity in relation to racialization. Processes of racialization and performance combine to play unusual roles for women of 'mixed race' in this study. The unveiling of the performative strategies among participants reveals these women's understanding of racialized processes—and their own acknowledgement of their ability to intervene and disrupt racialized social scripts. To end, I want to ask how these stories about performance from 'mixed race' women complicate contemporary discussions of performance in geography. I believe that this analysis of identity narratives speaks to issues of space and performativity by spatializing and grounding performed racialized identities. My research has contested the highly theoretical explorations on performance and identity by reminding us about the extraordinary complexity of the everyday. I do not read participants as passive spectators who are simply racialized. Instead, I emphasize how women of 'mixed race' may be envisioned as embodied actors who engage with their life-worlds in imaginative and innovative ways, employing particular stances within the grids of racist and sexist containment. 'Mixed race' women in this study are actively redrawing lines on the battlefield. They are effectively tricking the racial border guards and redefining the terrain upon which racial contestation occurs.

Notes

1. It is important to delineate the difference between performance and performativity. I borrow from Gregson and Rose here, who explain performance as 'what individuals do, say, act out' and performativity as 'the citational practices which reproduce and/or subvert discourse and which enable and discipline subjects and their performances' (2000: 434). My interests lie in exploring the agency employed among some 'mixed race' women in this study rather than focusing upon the citational practices.

2. However, it is imperative to note that race is not a cultural construction in the same way as gender. For although both are predicated on real or manufactured biological differences, the former (race) is a 'science fiction', whereas sex (of

which gender is derivative) is not. For further analyses, see Butler's work (for example, 1993), as well as Ifekwunigwe (1999) and Stolcke (1993), among others.

3. Anzaldua's *new mestiza* provides a framework from which to deconstruct binary either–or identities and reconstruct a truly multiplicitous self. The *new mestiza* is one who: 'Copes by developing a tolerance for contradictions, a tolerance for ambiguity . . . learns to juggle cultures . . . [and] operates in a pluralistic mode' (1987: 54).

Chapter 17

An Optical Delusion: 'Racializing Eye Colour'

Augie Fleras

Anti-racism can be defined as the process that isolates and challenges racism through direct action (see also Dei 1996; Bonnett 2000). Anti-racism entails any active involvement in changing those cultural values, personal prejudices, discriminatory behaviour, and institutional structures of society that perpetuate racism. Two styles of anti-racist strategy can be discerned: interpersonal and institutional. Interpersonal anti-racism is concerned with modifying individual behaviour through law, education, or interaction; institutional anti-racism focuses on removing discriminatory barriers and the structural roots of racism.

Taken at its most obvious level, racism is normally envisaged as a personal problem of hatred or ignorance. There is an element of truth to this assertion. Racism is often expressed through the thoughts and actions of individuals who dislike others because they are different or appear threatening. Thus anti-racist strategies tend to focus on changing people's behaviour by modifying defective attitudes related to prejudice, ethnocentrism, and stereotyping. One of the most popular personal anti-racist strategies involves *education*. According to this line of thinking, racism arises when individuals are locked into ignorance or irrational beliefs. Once informed of the error of their ways, people are deemed sufficiently rational to make the appropriate adjustments. This commitment to enlightenment

through learning has put multicultural education in the vanguard for 'e-racing' racism.

Patterns of multicultural education can vary (Fleras 2002). Milder versions propose modifying individual attitudes through exposure to diversity. Special days are set aside to celebrate other cultures or religious holidays, while students are encouraged to be more tolerant toward those who are racially and culturally different. Harder versions of multicultural education encourage individuals to look inside themselves, to examine their own racism and privileged positions, to critically reflect on how the dominant sector exercises power over racialized minorities, and to take responsibility for the disempowerment of others (McIntosh 1988). But while most whites sympathize with victims of racism, many are incapable of linking their privilege with the disempowerment and exploitation of others (Bishop 2005).

Clearly, then, conventional forms of multicultural education are subject to criticism. In failing to address the issue of white racism and the complicity of whites in preserving white privilege, a 'happy face' multicultural education fails to get to the root of the problem. Furthermore, there are dangers in intellectualizing diversity under a celebratory multicultural education, resulting in a lack of urgency to do something about the problem out there. Proposed instead of a passive educational experience are anti-racist initiatives whose commitments challenge the status quo through direct involvement. Such a commitment was put to the test in a way that shocked, and continues to shock, the world.

The Eye of the Storm

In the wake of Martin Luther King's assassination in 1968, Jane Elliot, a third-grade teacher in Riceville, Iowa, conducted a simple but effective exercise within the context of an all-white classroom. To explore the nature of prejudice, bigotry, and discrimination, while conveying Martin Luther King's notion that the content of a person's character should be more important than the colour of his or her skin, Elliot wanted to impress on her students how easy it is for people to (1) assign a social worth on the basis of seemingly irrelevant characteristics over which they have no control, (2) explain behaviour in terms of a physical attribute, and (3) construct a reward system around a baseless distinction. But rather than simply telling the children that prejudice and discrimination are wrong—after all we have been told it's wrong and yet still continue to tolerate it—she wanted her students to find out personally and painfully about the meaning of discrimination, its experience in everyday life, and the impact it could have on those most vulnerable (PBS 1970).

On the first day of the exercise, Elliot divided her third-grade pupils into two groups on the basis of eye colour (blue versus brown), and rewarded them accordingly. The blue-eyed children were defined as superior to the brown-eyed children. They received extra privileges both in class and during recess, while privileges were withheld from the brown-eyed children who quickly developed a sense of self-loathing and fear. As Elliot points out, the blue-eyed children relished their new empowerment and enthusiastically played along by sharply enforcing the penalties against the brown-eyed children. During recess, children resorted to name-calling

on the basis of eye colour. Some children even got into fights when teased about their 'brown-eyedness'. Within the span of 15 minutes, Elliot observed, 'these marvellous, co-operative, wonderful, thoughtful children turned into nasty, vicious, discriminating little third graders'. More importantly, the distinction appeared to influence test scores. The blue-eyed children scored much higher than usual on daily quizzes; conversely, the scores of brown-eyed children plummeted.

The brilliance of Elliot's experiment did not end there. The next day Elliot reversed the exercise by announcing that she had made a 'mistake': it was the brown-eyed children who were superior to the blue-eyed children. Accordingly, it would be the brown-eyed children who would have all the privileges, while the blue-eyed children's privileges were withheld. This role reversal had the 'desired effect': for the brown-eyed children it was payback time and they eagerly pounced on the opportunity to punish the blue-eyed children for the previous day's inflictions. The same children who had been oppressed the day before quickly assumed the oppressor role, and vice versa. Predictably, the brown-eyed children did much better on classroom quizzes; the scores of the blue-eyed children declined accordingly.

What can we learn from this experiment? First, when social reality is involved, phenomena do not have to be real to be real in their consequences. The notion that the world can be arbitrarily racialized into fixed and bounded categories ('races') with each possessing an assemblage of physical and biological attributes that determine thought and behaviour has long been discredited by all but a handful of social scientists. And yet although the concept of race has no empirical or scientific validity, people continue to act as if it does, with negative consequences (from slavery to genocide) for those racialized. Similarly, there is no scientific justification for racializing the world into blue and brown eyes and claiming one is superior to the other. Nevertheless, this lack of reality did not preclude having very real consequences on the children. Second, the concept of self-fulfilling prophecy is expressed: blue-eyed children who were defined as superior excelled on class quizzes unlike the brown-eyed children who did poorly. The next day the brown-eyed children who were re-racialized as superior dramatically improved their scores. Therefore, if people are labelled as inferior, they will act accordingly; conversely, if defined as superior, people will act successfully. Applied to the real world where this labelling is routinely and constantly enforced, racialized minorities who are deemed to be inferior will assume patterns of inferiority. Third, Elliot's exercise exposes the subliminality of racism. While Elliot had hoped to teach the children a lesson, it was clear that they had already internalized notions of prejudice and discrimination, that some people had privilege and others didn't, and that some possessed the power to define what counts as difference, what differences count. Their ability to quickly adapt to and play the role of 'master/slave' is not only a testimony to the power of socialization but also a warning that erasing deeply embedded patterns of prejudice and racism is easier said than done.

The story doesn't end here. According to Elliott, the exercise in racializing eye colour may have proven a wake-up call for her students (in a follow-up documentary in 1985, the now-adults of the 1970 class acknowledged how profoundly the experiment had changed their lives); however, the residents of this predominantly white Christian town of 1,000 were less enchanted. Elliot and her students were harassed, even called 'nigger lovers', and a family-owned business was boycotted by community dissidents. Elliot moved to another city but, once her father died, was asked by her mother never to return because of continued town antagonism. Rather than being deterred by this hostility, Jane Elliot went on to conduct these exercises in corporations and university settings. As with her school children, participants are labelled as inferior or superior on the basis of eye colour and then exposed to the experiences of being a minority, often with an equally powerful impact. In 2004 she brought this exercise to Canada by way of a documentary entitled *Indecently Exposed*, which explored the racist attitudes toward Aboriginal peoples. And this racism persists. Jane Elliot, now in her mid-70s, continues to crusade against the injustices that classify, rank, and evaluate people on the basis of arbitrary traits.

Chapter 18

Race and the Social/Cultural Worlds of Student Athletes

Carl E. James

Hi Carl,

A quick glance through the pages of my old high-school yearbook paints a picture of a school with a student population representing a variety of cultures. Page after page, the yearbook displays photographs showing a multitude of white, black, and brown faces. That is, of course, until you get to the sports teams' photos, where quite a different picture begins to emerge. If one were to randomly open my school yearbook at boys' basketball team's photograph, one would see a group of almost exclusively black faces. By contrast, the school's hockey team photo is filled with white faces. Why such an obvious racial divide along sporting lines in a school with such a racially mixed student population? What follows is a short reflection about my experiences as a white male high-school student athlete, and some possible answers to these questions.

I went to school in Montreal, where high school begins in Grade 7 and lasts until Grade 11 (from 12 until about 17 years). By the time I got to high school, I was already serious about playing baseball (which I did during the summers), and I wanted to get serious about playing basketball, a sport that I had only played recreationally up until then. Although I don't remember much about my first day of high school, I do remember that on that day my most important concern was finding out when the school basketball tryouts were. The same was true for many of my friends, who themselves were representative of our school in the diversity of their collective backgrounds. When the day of basketball tryouts finally did arrive several weeks later, our coach made a surprise announcement. In an effort to increase enrolment for volleyball, which he was also coaching, he announced that any student who would agree to play volleyball would get an automatic spot on the basketball team. For that reason alone, several players, myself included, decided to play volleyball. Never mind that many of us had never even played the sport. It was worth learning if it could get us a spot on the basketball team.

That first year and the following year as well, I played both basketball and volleyball for my school team. Both teams were quite mixed racially, and we enjoyed a lot of success, particularly in my second year, when we won the Greater Montreal Athletic Association city championships in both sports. However, as the years went on, the racial demographics of both teams began to change significantly. To put it simply, the volleyball team started to get a lot 'whiter' and the basketball team a lot 'blacker'. By my senior year of high school, only two black players remained on the volleyball team. Conversely, on the basketball team the number of white players decreased to zero. My own choices regarding the sports I played reflected this pattern. Ironically, while I had only joined the volleyball team to ensure a spot on the basketball team, I decided to quit playing basketball after my second year of high school. As for volleyball, I continued playing throughout my five years of school.

Why did I choose to stop playing basketball? One reason had to do with my skill level. Although I had been one of the better players on the team during my eighth-grade year, I can remember coming back to school from summer vacation the next year and playing a game of pick-up basketball with my teammates. I had been playing baseball all summer and hadn't even touched a basketball during those months. It was obvious that many of my teammates had. As we played, I can remember getting the sense that others had caught up to me and, in some cases, surpassed me in skill level. That year I made the decision to stop playing basketball competitively in order to concentrate on my other two sports of choice, baseball and volleyball.

In retrospect, I can see that my motivation for playing the sports I chose as a youth was correlated to my perceived skill level. In other words, I came to enjoy playing baseball and volleyball because I felt I was good at it. Likewise, I enjoyed playing basketball early on for the same reasons. However, once others started to surpass me in skill level, I lost motivation. Perhaps this all has something to do with my own psychology, but I do believe that many youth make decisions about the sports they play based on similar factors. We play sports because we

want to participate in something that we are good at, or that we aspire to become good at. When those aspirations toward a particular sport leave us, we often leave the sport.

So the question then remains, why did so many of us move toward or away from specific sports, based on what looks like predictable patterns based on race? While I do not feel equipped to completely answer that question, I can offer insight from my own experience: even during my first few years of basketball, I can remember feeling that while I was not at a disadvantage in terms of my talent, many of my teammates and I, both black and white, all shared in a sort of acceptance that black basketball players in general were far superior to whites. Whether it was true or not, we all believed it on the basketball court, and spent a good deal of time joking about it. On the other hand, we never joked about that on the baseball field or volleyball court. We never operated under a notion of black athletic superiority in playing those sports. What was different about basketball? Well for one, from all of the television and media images of professional basketball players, the reason for this perception seems rather obvious. At elite levels, black basketball players are undoubtedly the top performers. And while the chances of anyone being good enough to play sports professionally are extremely remote, most young athletes will admit to spending a great deal of time thinking about and often working toward collegial or professional sports aspirations. In reality, those aspirations are a big motivating factor in the reason we are so passionate about playing our sports in the first place. With that in mind, it doesn't seem so far-fetched that certain groups gravitate toward certain sports based on ideas and beliefs about race, when the images they see point them in certain directions. Perhaps I too made my own unconscious choices based on related factors. Incidentally, I never did play hockey, but I wonder if there is a reverse mentality given that at the elite level, white players dominate. Similarly, I wonder if the fact that blacks and whites often choose to play certain sports based on accepted notions of athletic superiority with regard to race has created a self-fulfilling prophecy. If this were true, one could easily see the evolution of a cycle in which different groups would favour participation in different sports.

Despite this seeming divide among races, I find it interesting that participation in sports can accomplish the opposite as well. For example, when I look back at my own experiences as a sports-playing youth, some of my best memories are of the lasting friendships that I made (and kept). Ten years after leaving high school, some of my closest friends are former coaches and teammates from my high-school basketball, volleyball, and baseball years, whose backgrounds are very different from my own. If I had not participated in sports, I might never have enjoyed those friendships. On the other hand, this personal observation brings up a very troubling issue: if sports participation provides such important socializing benefits, what does it say about our society that now sports are so highly segregated among students?

A final note: in my senior year of high school, I tried out for the boys' basketball team again after staying away from playing competitive level for about three years. During the tryouts, I was the only white player in attendance. Although I was by no means one of the better players, I did make the team, only to later decline. In the end, I just did not feel like playing basketball on a competitive level. As had been the case several years earlier, the sport no longer appealed to me. And yet, in thinking back on it, my decision always seems somewhat peculiar: given that I had once been so passionate about basketball, why the lack of interest? Did I simply decide to stop playing for personal and unrelated reasons, or did other societal factors contribute? Although I would like to believe the former, those pictures in my high-school yearbook tell a different story.

David

Indeed, the photographs in David's high-school yearbook show a disconnection between the diversity of his high-school population and the makeup of the hockey and basketball teams. These photographs provide clues to David's 'sudden lack of interest in playing basketball' even though he had been playing on his school teams in the earlier years. He remembers having good relationships with his coaches, and he even now says that some of his 'closest friends' are his former basketball teammates, some of whom 'have backgrounds that are different from his' (i.e., black). Evidently, skill level aside (something that could be improved with practice), lack of friendship or having difficulties with coaches were not the only reasons for David's lack of interest in playing basketball in his senior year of high school. In fact, as he implies, his disinterest in basketball likely had something to do with race. That he was going to be the only white player on the basketball team in his senior year was probably a situation for which David was not quite ready, particularly when in his early years playing basketball, he and his teammates, as he discloses, 'black and white, all shared in a sort of acceptance that black basketball players in general were far superior to whites'.

In this chapter, I take up this idea that participation in sports is related to 'race'. I reason that the 'self-fulfilling prophecy' that David mentions, may indeed be so, but that a significant factor here is how the structures of schools produce and reproduce the 'accepted notions of athletic superiority with regard to race'—in other words, racialize students. With reference to comments from young male athletes, I examine how race is used to explain students' interests, abilities, and skills in particular sports, as well as to account for their 'political and cultural decisions about what to play and who to play with and against' (Booth and Tatz 2000: 8; see also Hatchell 2004). I concur with Booth and Tatz (2000) that it is important to scrutinize preferences in sport as related to race (as well as class, gender, ethnicity, religion, and sexuality) in order to determine 'what a group represents, how it lives, its priorities, and its values', and how this reinforces the group's 'sense of exclusiveness and distinctiveness so as to enable groups to regulate their membership. Often this prevents the mobility of others who may want to join in and participate in the privileges they have built up over time' (Booth and Tatz 2000: 8).

An important aspect of this discussion is the deployment of race to explain such things as the abilities, skills, habits, interests, behaviours, practices, aspirations, and outcomes of some students and not others. In the context of Canadian 'colour-blind' multicultural discourse, people who 'have' race (more appropriately, those who are raced) are those considered 'visibly different' (that is, different from the 'white norm') in terms of skin colour—in Canada, officially referred to as 'visible minorities'. These groups are also those that are constructed as having 'culture'. . . . And educational and athletic activities, in which particular ethno-racial minority and/or immigrant group members excel, are perceived to be a product or characteristic of their 'race culture'.[1] I maintain that athletes' preferences, concentration, or dominance in a particular sport have more to do with the economic, political, cultural, and social conditions that promote or make possible their participation in a sport rather than any inherent talent they may possess based on ethno-racial characteristics (see Kell 2000). In this regard, David and his teammates' (including

blacks) 'sort of acceptance' that blacks are superior to whites in basketball reflects how race is used to explain the athletic interests, talent, and capabilities of some athletes (in this case, blacks) and not others (i.e., whites), and reinforces cultural beliefs, ideas, and behaviours of individuals (Harrison et al. 2004; Sailes 1991).

That they 'joked' about the superiority of black basketball players on the basketball court and not 'on the baseball field or volleyball court' reflects how spaces also become racialized and identified with particular groups (see also Abdel-Shehid 2003).[2]

Race and Sports Participation: Who Plays What and Why?

The dominance of black athletes in sports such as basketball, football, and track and field has been debated for years. In a feature article in *Sports Illustrated* (8 December 1997), S.L. Price writes that in the United States, white athletes who had dominated the American athletic scene for much of the century do not want to play any more. Distracted by other leisure-time pursuits and discouraged by the success of black athletes, who have come to dominate sports in spectacular fashion, the white athlete, unlike his black counterpart, is now less interested in playing certain mainstream games. He is increasingly drawn to sports that are primarily 'white' such as soccer, or to alternative athletic pursuits that are overwhelmingly white, such as mountain biking or rock climbing (1997: 30).

Price argues that whites are 'now tagged by the stereotypes of skin colour' (33) and as a result are choosing to compete in sports like baseball, ice hockey, and in-line hockey in which they feel they have a chance of maintaining a competitive edge. High-school coaches in urban areas complain that they can recruit white students for activities like baseball and wrestling but not basketball. The coaches also point out that in the early high-school years, basketball teams tend to be racially diverse, but in the senior years the teams become 'more black'. And when white students are asked why they do not participate on the teams, they say: 'I can't run with those guys' (Price 1997: 34).

A *Sports Illustrated* youth poll revealed that 'while many young whites are unsure of their place in athletics, young blacks, brimming with self-confidence and certain that sports are one of the few professions in which they can make it big in America, are pouring heart and soul into team sports' (Price 1997: 34).[3] But this situation is not only about race, for race intersects with social class, gender, and other demographic factors to influence the sports in which students participate and the use they make of it (see Varpalotai 1996; Kell 2000; Nakamura 2003; Paraschak 2000; Armour [and Jones] 2000). Price also points out that while affluent white urban students tend to play basketball 'for the fun of it', blacks, particularly those living in 'inner cities', look at basketball as a means of financial security. As one coach said, 'the white athlete is not as hungry as the black athlete—period' (in Price 1997: 35). From a coach's perspective, 'hungry' athletes (typically from 'inner-city projects') are more likely to be 'coachable' and hence make good basketball players (Frey 1994).[4] Frey gives the example of an occasion (at a Nike basketball camp in Indianapolis) when he heard a coach, after enumerating the various life circumstances of an athlete—'orphaned at a young age, living in a foster home, searching endlessly for authority figures'—said 'with enthusiasm', 'Bet he's *extremely* coachable' (67; italics in original).

Linked to social class and race is immigrant status or citizenship. In my study (James 1990) of African-Canadian youth (mostly of Caribbean immigrant background, either born there or of parents born there), sports helped them negotiate educational structures that were culturally new to many of them (see also Solomon 1992). Capitalizing on the opportunities and possi-bilities that came through basketball and track and field (since soccer[5] and cricket, to which they were accustomed, are not popular sports in Canada), these first- and second-generation African Canadians quickly learned the rules and skills of these athletic activities to fit in; in the process, they were recognized, valued, and respected in the school community. This would, in part, account for such notable players such as Denham Brown, Jamaal Magloire, Tammy Sutton Brown, and many others making it to the NCAA, NBA, and WNBA, and for track and field stars such as Ben Johnson, Donovan Bailey, Angela Bailey, Angela Taylor-Issajenko, and Bruny Surin, who have represented Canada in the Olympics. Members of other immigrant groups have also used sports to make their way in Canadian society. For instance, in a longitudinal study of the 1973 and 1974 Ontario high-school graduating class, my colleagues and I identified three study participants of working-class Italian-born parents, who used sports to serve their needs and interests through high school. One participant, Ray, who was a chartered accountant when he was interviewed in 1995, was involved in football and basketball during his high-school years, and credited his athletic involvement with making his school years among 'the best time of his life'. Sam, another participant in the study, had an MBA. He had obtained an athletic scholarship to an American university after he completed high school in Toronto, but he completed only one semester at the scholarship university. With reference to these study participants, we wrote that 'sports operated as a cultural resource, whereby they were able to learn the norms and values of Canadian society. It also provided an emotional benefit, in that it helped them to relieve their tensions and stresses' (Anisef et al. 2000: 168).

Members of recent immigrant groups in Canada, as in the United States and Britain, have used sports to negotiate the economic, cultural, and social structures of society, and ultimately to better their lives. In other words, they tend to capitalize on the space provided by athletics and establish themselves in the 'mainstream' of the society, believing they will eventually attain their educational and occupational goals. But there is also a perception—if not a belief—among many, including blacks, that their dominance in certain sports is much more than an attempt to advance in society. In fact, what Price (1997) says of African Americans could be applied to Canadians:

> many people find it hard to believe that economic incentives alone account for black athletic dominance. These observers offer a simple theory: blacks dominate sports because they are faster, quicker, better . . . , they possess superior athletic skills and have thus transformed the way sports are played.' (36)

Individuals, including coaches and, in some cases parents, who subscribe to this belief cite the black athlete's 'mobility, toughness, and physical ability' to run fast and jump (most of us know of the movie *White Men Can't Jump*) (see also Kell 2000). These individuals ignore the many factors (socialization, role models, stereotyping, provision of opportunities, etc.) that channel black students into athletic activities and play positions (i.e., 'positional segregation' *à la* Lapchick in Price 1997: 38); instead they claim that it is a result of genetics. In such a context, then, it is understandable that blacks would, as Isiah Thomas said, 'always want to keep the stereotype that we're better than whites; it's an advantage' (in Price 1997: 37). And as Price further points out, 'mix the notion of white athletic inferiority with the comfortable suburban culture in which many young white males live, and the result is an atmosphere in which commitment to a sport such as basketball or football become ever rarer'.

While conducting research . . . , I asked a number of white male university students and former high-school student athletes to read Price's (1997) *Sports Illustrated* article: 'Whatever Happened to the White Athlete?' I asked them, on the basis of their experiences as student athletes, to comment on the points that Price raises about white athletes. Did they agree with his representation? Did they see themselves in his representations? I will share two of the responses I received. The first is from David, whose reflections we read in the introduction to this chapter, and the second is from Craig.[6] These responses also came to me via e-mail after our conversations.

David: I just read the article you gave me, 'Whatever Happened to the White Athlete?' I was completely fascinated by it. The author brought up a lot of issues about a subject that I think a lot of athletes and former athletes have been captivated by for quite some time. Perhaps most interesting to me is the question of whether black athletes seem to be outperforming whites because of innate ability or outside influences, and how that affects the choices that young athletes make in choosing what sports to participate in.

I can see how socio-economic and cultural differences have an effect on the choices that youth make regarding what sports to play. The article points this out very effectively. However, I really do believe that there is something to be said for the 'innate' argument. From my own observations as a former student athlete and as an avid professional sports fan, there is absolutely a difference in the way blacks and whites 'play' certain sports (and not just at the professional level but at amateur levels as well).

'You play white' has become a common term in basketball vernacular. When someone says it to you, it of course implies that you're probably not a very good leaper, you're probably a little on the slow side, and your overall set of skills is not all that exciting. There's a basketball player in the NBA right now named Jason Williams. His nickname is 'White Chocolate'. His teammates (predominantly black) gave him the nickname because he's a white player who plays a 'black' style of play.

But is playing a 'black' brand of basketball or playing a 'white' brand innate? Let me argue both sides for a second. If I watch a basketball game at any level I am quite confident that I can pick out each player and with some level of success determine whether that player learned to play basketball in an urban environment or in the suburbs. I've seen black players who play 'white' and white players who play 'black'. Really, the more appropriate term would be, 'He is a city player', or 'He is a suburban player.' I think people just use the terms 'he plays black' or 'he plays white' because that's what they see—and it so happens that most black players come from and learn the 'city' game and vice versa for the white players.

Now let me refute what I just said. Despite the effects of culture on the way we play sports (and ultimately on the sports we choose to participate in), there is quite obviously a superiority among blacks in many sports where culture and geography might not have anything to do with it. I think culture definitely enters the equation in this debate, but it does not exist alone. There is something to be said for innate athletic ability (as much as I hate the term 'innate', I have yet to be convinced that environment acts alone here. I'm open to the fact that it might, but like I said I have yet to hear a convincing argument . . .).

Craig: During my 16 years of playing organized and competitive hockey, I have never worn the same jersey as a black person. I did, however, play on a team with a girl for a few years. . . . She was the most talented player on the team. Aside from hockey, baseball is the only sport I have played outside of the school context. I played one year of 'rep' baseball and there was only one black player on the team. He was the most talented. . . . The rest of my sporting career took place on school teams.

Before I respond to the issues raised in the *Sports Illustrated* article, it is necessary that I share my own background and experiences. I attended [one of Canada's prestigious high schools] in Toronto.[7] During my high-school [years], I played on the volleyball, rugby, football, hockey, and baseball teams. When I was in my senior years, I focused on athletic endeavours on the varsity football and baseball teams. There was only one [black] player on the varsity team; he was also the only player on the team who was faster than me. My sporting experience at [high school] epitomizes the notion that blacks are simply better athletes than whites.[8] The few black students that there were in the school did excel in their respective sporting careers. . . .

It is a virtual impossibility to find an area in the life of any athlete that is not shaped or influenced by socio-economic factors. The harsh reality in North America is that . . . competing in sports costs money. Of course, different sports require different amounts of money in order to participate. When understanding school sports, it becomes a question of which sports certain school boards are willing to pay for in terms of equipment and insurance for their students. For example, traditionally hockey is a sport for which school boards in North America are not willing to pay for students' equipment. Football, however, is. . . . All one needs to play soccer and basketball are the appropriate footwear and balls, while hockey skates alone cost in excess of $200. It is inevitable that these types of socio-economic circumstances will influence who plays which sports. When I was in high school, there was a prevalent belief that blacks were 'better' athletes than whites. . . . When I was an active athlete, I was certainly more comfortable playing on an ice surface than on a basketball court. The main reason for this was due to my mastery of hockey as compared to basketball. . . . While I was growing up in an affluent and white context in Toronto, hockey was a central part of mainstream life. . . . As a white Canadian male, instilled in me was a desire to play hockey, not basketball. The majority of black friends growing up did not play hockey. Either they could not afford to, or did not have the desire to strap on a pair of skates. . . .

Part of my reason for not picking basketball as a child was influenced by my country's obsession with hockey, but this does not completely account for my not wanting to play basketball. In my childhood, when I watched the NBA slam-dunk competition on the television, I did set up a trash can on a shelf with an ottoman positioned beneath it to play the role of a launching pad. I rented the ever-so-popular video game, 'NBA Jam'. I occasionally watched games. I had friends, mostly black friends, who played basketball. I could have joined in the hoop action with my friends had I wanted to, and I did have white friends who played basketball. . . . However, there was an invisible and mysterious barrier that kept me and the majority of my white friends from stepping onto the basketball court with any substantial amount of confidence. . . .

However, this does not answer the question of whether whites are intimidated by black prowess on the basketball court. I have no credible answer to this question other than 'probably'. Is this intimidation supported by biological evidence? Are black people more genetically predisposed to excel in athletic pursuits? . . . Could it be that

throughout these centuries of physically demanding lives that blacks genetically adapted to their environment in order to cope with the demands put on them? It is impossible to say with certainty what the answer to this question is. However, it is something that should be considered in this debate over racial dominance in athleticism.

I share at length David's and Craig's reflections to indicate the process they used to assess the sociology versus biology debate. Interestingly, while both of them agreed that sociology has something to do with blacks' athleticism, they both insist that biology cannot be ruled out. Their reasoning probably has to do with their exposure to black athletes—both have played with 'very good' black athletes. For example, Craig relates that there was one black player on his baseball team and that he was 'the most talented'. And the only black player on his football team was the one who was 'faster than him'. It seems that participating on teams with black players, as Craig did, or attending racially diverse schools, as David did, contributes to their beliefs about the superiority of black athletes. In fact, according to a *Sports Illustrated* poll, whites in the US who attended racially diverse schools were found to be more inclined to believe the athletic stereotypes, while blacks in similarly diverse schools (compared to 'all-black' schools) also believed that blacks are athletically superior to whites (Price 1997). The same could be said of African-Canadian students.

In my earlier study of the experiences and perceptions of black student athletes in the Toronto area, although most attended racially diverse schools, I found a tendency to believe that participating in sports was 'natural'. For instance, when one participant, Brian, was asked about his involvement in school sports, he responded:

Do you believe in God? Do you believe that everybody is here for a reason? I believe that everyone has a talent and I believe that my talent is sports. So when I was born I was naturally an athlete. So it would be pretty dumb for me to go into science. (James 1995: 28)

I wrote then that the problem with this logic is that

it contributes to the self-fulfilling prophecy . . . ; and ignores the complex social mechanisms that are responsible for his participation and success in sports in the first place. In fact, this social construction of blacks as naturally superior in sports is a stereotype based on racism.' (James 1995: 28)

However, it should also be pointed out that other participants reasoned that sporting success was due more to practice than to genetics. For instance, one participant asserted that 'blacks are good because they spend many hours a day playing basketball. The more you do something, the better you get at it. It's not a natural thing. It is something they work at. . . . They've been running for a long time, so it accumulates' (James 1995: 28; see also Sailes 1991).

Beliefs about the types of athletic activities that best suit particular ethno-racial group members are part of the racist discourses and practices found in Canadian society in general and schools in particular. This sports discourse also tends to polarize and compare whites and blacks. Whites are represented as people whose skills in athletics come through learning, interest, motivation, talent (not 'raw talent', a term that is often used with reference to blacks), and exposure to a particular sport: they 'choose' to participate in sports, suggesting that they have alternative means of participation and paths to success in society. Blacks, on the other hand, are represented as people whose athletic skills, abilities, and interests are integral to who they are: they participate in sports because of their physical-

ity/biology. For instance, in a study of race broadcasting at US college basketball games, Billings et al. (2002) noted that white athletes were frequently praised for their perceived 'intellect' and 'leadership capacity', and black athletes were often praised for being 'naturally talented'. It was also observed that 'black athletes are expected to succeed athletically; conversely, white athletes are expected to have an innate ability to overcome seemingly insurmountable odds to accomplish their "athletic stature"' (1). So for blacks, sports are perceived to be an 'easy' means for them to participate in society and ensure their success. For other racial minority groups, their athleticism is related to perceptions of their physicality, their intellectual abilities, and the historical and contemporary roles that they have played, or are expected to play, in society.[9] This paradigm of athleticism can be seen in the raced culture of, for example, basketball and hockey, and manifested in the values, behaviours, habits, aspirations, and activities of student athletes. In the following [section], using newspaper and magazine articles, and data from in-person and e-mail interviews, I discuss the experiences, socially constructed images, identifications, material and athletic interests, and aspirations of minority youth in . . . hockey.

* * *

Experiences of Minority Athletes in Hockey: A Sport 'Central to Mainstream Life'

In his account (above) of choosing hockey over basketball, Craig explains that he was much better at hockey. But probably more significant is what is implied in his further statement about hockey being 'a central part of mainstream life' and that as a 'white Canadian male' he was instilled with the desire to play hockey (see Abdel-Shehid 2000). In this statement, Craig gestures toward the significance of 'mainstream' and how much hockey helps him build confidence and affirm his status as a white middle-class male. So, we might say that what hockey does for Craig and his white male friends, basketball does for racial minority youth: it builds confidence and a sense of community. But if hockey is a sport of the 'mainstream', as Craig indicates, why don't racial minority student athletes seek economic and social privileges by getting involved in hockey? By extension, if through hockey racial minority (and immigrant) youth might be acculturated or integrated into the mainstream, and in the process establish networks that will enable them to negotiate the white structures, why not choose hockey instead of basketball? Or is their preference for basketball and basketball culture evidence of minority youth's resistance to the 'mainstream', and a counterculture where they can exercise agency, assert their presence, and take control of their sporting lives in ways that best represent their interests and aspirations? In considering these questions, I discuss below some of the experiences of racial minority youth in hockey, noting how issues they faced as players may account for their low participation in hockey, even though in some cases they grew up loving the game and wishing to some day make it to the NHL (National Hockey League).

Access to Hockey—'A Sport that Fewer People Can Afford'

More telling is that hockey is a middle-class sport. It costs serious cash to play. You need to buy the equipment (about $1,000); plus most games are all over the city—you need a car. This makes the sport one that fewer people can afford to play. Kids are no longer happy or able to become NHL stars by just owning skates and a stick playing on the outdoor rink. . . . Whereas basketball games are organized by schools, hockey, for the most part, is organized in private civil society leagues. This means that parents hang around more with hockey but let l'école [school] deal with basketball. This has an impact on access to the game. (Howard Ramos, e-mail communication, July 2003)

In the above comment, my colleague Ramos draws attention to the cost of hockey as one of the factors that makes it inaccessible to economically deprived youth and families. Many of them are recent immigrants or mainly racial and ethnic minorities who live in large metropolitan areas like Montreal and Toronto. It follows, therefore, that those racial minority youth who get the opportunity to play hockey beyond their neighbourhood streets will be those who can afford the necessary costs of playing (including equipment costs, team and league fees, etc.), as well as having access to teams and transportation. Furthermore, for youth of working-class backgrounds, their opportunities to play hockey are likely to be attained through sponsorship—i.e., obtaining financial support from interested individuals, organizations, or businesses—based on recognition of their potential, skill, and ability. Anthony Stewart of Scarborough, Ontario, is one example. According to the *Toronto Star* newspaper, he was a 'Florida draft pick who overcame poverty to realize [his] dream'—a realization made possible by his 'parents and important mentor' (Campbell 2003: E8). That mentor, according to Campbell, 'saw enough talent and nobility in the young man to pay the minor hockey registration and equipment expenses that Stewart's parents couldn't pay' (E8).[10] By way of illustrating the significance of Stewart's achievement, or as it was put, 'Stewart's tough journey to NHL', Campbell writes: 'After all it's a long way from the strip of seedy motels on Kingston Road [where Stewart's financially strapped family stayed at times] and long subway rides to the arena to the cusp of the NHL, but Stewart made the journey . . .' (E8). It was a journey that 'made him stronger' and instilled in him a desire 'to help his family out by playing hard and with the hope that one day he would be drafted' (Campbell 2003: E8).

Stewart's story demonstrates the salience of economics in shaping and influencing the sporting activities and outcomes of youth. . . . Accordingly, when parents are unable to provide the resources to participate in sports, young people, particularly those of working-class backgrounds, will have to look for these opportunities in schools, community recreation centres, and youth service organizations. And given the significance and role of school in young people's lives, it is logical to think that it is not only the social and economic situation of families that determines the sports in which they engage but the situation of the school as well. In other words, the sports to which students will have access depend on the finances and willingness of school boards and/or particular schools to provide equipment and insurance for students. They also depend on having teachers who are willing and able to be coaches. In this regard, based on cost alone, hockey, which is much more expensive to play than basketball, baseball, and soccer, is a sport that is less likely to be found in many of today's urban schools, administered by cash-strapped school boards. But at schools in which parents are willing and able to finance such sports, hockey is likely to be a sport to which students will have access. By comparison, in urban area schools (often referred to as 'inner city'), with youth of immigrant, racial minority, and working-class backgrounds, sports activities tend to be mostly basketball and baseball. Hence, it is in these sports that we often see a significant proportion of minority student athletes. But inaccessibility to hockey through school does not fully explain the low participation of racial minorities in the sport; it is, as some youth indicate, 'the cruelty and meanness' that they experience that operate to keep them away from the sport.

'. . . Being a Visible Minority Requires You to Be Extra Special'

In talking about their experiences playing hockey during their high-school years, brothers Gary and Troy,[11] of Chinese-Canadian background, said that in their early years of playing hockey they were treated like every other hockey player, but that was not the case in their later years.

> Gary: As a hockey player, I never felt discriminated in any way until last year [Grade 11]. Before, I was treated like every other kid that played hockey with me. Hockey did not have such a big meaning until last year, which was the year you either go on (to the provincial or junior level) or not. In my last year of competitive hockey, I realized that my colour and size really mattered; I realized that I wasn't 6'2" and scouts look for size first. I felt my dreams crushed because of the reality that I would never be able to fulfill my hockey dream. . . . I know this is happening to a lot of talented people as well. I wish I didn't have to go through this, but it has helped me become who I am today. (April 2003)

> Troy: Early on, it seemed that it didn't matter that I was Chinese, my skills in sports were sufficient enough for me to gain respect. This was true in high school. Even though I was shorter than most, I was working out, which allowed me to excel in football and rugby. My hockey experience was a little different. After playing competitively on a winning team (we were first in the league), I was released, so I went out and tried out for other sports teams. I wasn't the best goalie in the league but certainly had a lot to offer to a team. In the end, I was not chosen. . . . What I conclude is that being a visible minority requires you to be extra spe-

cial. . . . I don't think I was ever meant to play in the NHL, but I was certainly capable of playing competitively. (April 2003)

It is likely that the decision not to invite Gary and Troy to participate on their hockey teams, from the coach's perspective, might have had to do with their skills and abilities. Nevertheless, we must consider Gary's and Troy's perception that their colour and size were factors—by inference, their race. Their comments imply that the decision of who plays hockey competitively is based not only on talent, skill, and dedication but also on physicality and race (see Abdel-Shehid 2000; Carnegie 1997).

The ways in which race and racism operate to limit and eventually discourage racial minority youth participation (see Fernández-Balboa 2000; Schempp and Oliver 2000) in hockey is captured in Rav Johal's (2003) reflections on his experiences growing up as a South Asian in a suburban area of Toronto. Johal explains that his immigrant father, who had grown to enjoy hockey from watching *Hockey Night in Canada*, enrolled him in hockey school at the age of six years ('much to the chagrin of my mother, who was worried sick that I would get injured'). Johal recalls that he was one of three racial minorities (himself, a black, and an Asian) in hockey school, and one of 'a handful of ethnic minority kids' playing in the community league. This continued to be the case during the seven years (1982–1989) that Johal played organized hockey. And while he remembers most of his ice hockey coaches as supportive, he says that his 'dad still reckons that my first coach was a jerk—I don't really remember' (he did not give Johal equal playing time, and this did not change until the coach was confronted by his father). Of his teammates, Johal says that for the most part they were 'okay', but he remembers being occasionally ostracized:

I do remember being called a 'Paki' in the eyes of opposing players—that was their way of targeting me, trying to either identify me or get under my skin. I hated that term—like many other South Asians who have been labelled as such, I knew my family was from India, not Pakistan. I was born in England, so I had no clue why I was being called a 'Paki'. It really used to hurt at times, but I had my own way of coping. I remember being called a 'Paki' when I first went to school and defending myself. It worked. Other times, I just ignored it, and that's what I usually did in hockey, hoping to hurt them by putting the puck in the net instead. (Johal 2003: 3)

He loved the game ('It was a fun sport—I really enjoyed it, and I was pretty good too. I always played every day . . . on our street with other kids') and his father tried hard to make him a successful player by following 'Walter Gretzky's model of building a rink for me a couple of times in the backyard'; however, by the time he entered Grade 10, he 'stopped playing hockey all together—playing soccer instead, as well as basketball' (3). Johal (2003) suggests that his disinterest in hockey had to do with his development of a consciousness of ethnic identification:

I remember going through a lot of issues regarding my ethnic identity. I began to feel somewhat distant from the white friends I had grown up with, choosing to hang around kids that were South Asian, West Indian, and black. . . . I felt that hockey was a 'white man's sport', and that as an ethnic minority, I should be playing sports that coloured kids played. For about 3–4 years, I rarely picked up a hockey stick, and hardly watched the sport on TV. (4)

Like Johal, Montreal-born Sean (July 2003), who identifies himself as 'mixed-race black' (because of his African-Jamaican, Chinese, and South Asian ancestry), started playing hockey at an early age. As he says: 'At five, I was playing organized hockey. Everybody on my street played hockey. Everybody in my school played hockey. Everybody talked about hockey and everyone watched hockey. So not once did I ever think it was strange to play hockey.' At school Sean would wear his hockey jacket to register that he played hockey, and to 'show off his team affiliation' (his team was known for winning), but nevertheless his teachers questioned his skating ability. And during hockey games where he 'played hard', Sean reports receiving 'taunts' from other team members. But, he recalls,

> I was not surprised. What was strange, however, was the names I had only previously heard on the playground were now becoming part of the game I lived and breathed. It got to me, but I never said a word about it. I just hit them harder and often. My mother said I was impossible to talk to when I came home after a game.

However, despite his determination and best efforts, by the end of high school, while he was 'still playing good hockey', Sean admits that his 'dreams of the NHL were far away'. This was because he had switched from playing hockey competitively to playing football. It was not because he preferred football, but because it seemed that he was better accepted as a football player. Sean recalls, 'Other than the coach once calling us the "running blacks", the thing I liked was in the four seasons I played at high school, I did not hear the "nigger this" and "monkey that", or the host of other ridiculously sad stereotypical comments that came with me playing hockey.'

Toronto-born Ramish, of South Asian background, captures well the sentiments and experiences of these former hockey players who, despite their efforts, skills, and abilities, found racism so demoralizing that they chose to stop playing competitive hockey:

I love hockey and have been playing the game since I was young. I remember the name calling and repeatedly being told that I couldn't play hockey because I was not white. I was [made] fun of and laughed at, and I was the last one picked for teams. I grew up in a white neighbourhood, and as all the kids played hockey, I began practising the game in the hope that one day I could play with everyone else. After a couple of months of practise I became a better player as I was faster and much smarter than the rest of the guys. I was asked to play for higher calibre teams because I excelled in the sport. I was always working hard, but was still made fun of by the opposing teams. My teammates learned to accept me. However, when another minority played on another team they taunted him with the same names used against me by the other teams. All I wanted was the opportunity to play and to be treated like everybody else. I finally learned to work harder and shield myself from the comments. Unfortunately, I would go home and feel the effect of the cruelty and meanness of some people. (in James 2003: 131)

While youth like Ramish, Sean, Rav, Gary, and Troy were willing to pursue playing hockey, there are others, like Devin . . . , who did not go beyond playing street hockey with their neighbourhood friends. For Devin, this was because of the cost of playing, and because at a young age growing up in his working-class, immigrant community, he did not see hockey as 'fitting who he thought he was':

I couldn't identify with anybody in that sport. There were no role models for me because they were different cultures . . . different backgrounds . . . ; things that I couldn't myself relate to. . . . Even the players that I played with had difficulty relating to, you know, some of the players. . . . None of my black friends who were equally skilled . . . were playing ice hockey. . . . We'd all play together on the street, but never on ice.

Conclusion

I have argued here that the preference, concentration, and/or dominance of particular ethnoracial group student athletes in specific sports is a product of the educational, economic, social, cultural, and political conditions in society and school that encourage their participation in a sport rather than any innate abilities. So the fact that black youth often prefer basketball is not entirely a situation of their own making; instead, it reflects the opportunities available to them in a society where sports, in conjunction with other social structures, help to create and perpetuate inequalities. Indeed, as Armour [and Jones] (2000) declare: 'Simply put, sport, in most manifestations, is not a "classless" [or raceless] activity offering equal opportunities for all' (79). In this context, therefore, the 'basketball culture' that evolves reflects minority athletes' particular interests, priorities, values, and aspirations—a culture that represents their lived experiences as minorities, and their related social mobility ambitions. On the other hand, in a society where the discourse of athleticism represents particular minority groups as having 'natural athletic abilities', sports such as hockey, which are dominated by white European players, will understandably be policed (just like basketball is) to ensure that its ethnic and racial membership and program remain consistent with the values, priorities, and aspirations of players. Further, there are mythologies within both cultures that serve to maintain exclusivity in memberships. For example, mythologies such as 'white men can't run or jump', and 'blacks have weak ankles that prevent them from skating' (as Craig heard from his parent), have operated to restrict access to these sports. Fortunately, change is inevitable, and with every 'different' athlete that joins a team or sport, we will see not only a change in the physical characteristics of players but also corresponding changes in the cultures of the sports.

Notes

1. Space restricts me from including the complex situation of Aboriginal peoples. However, it is important to note that in spite of some key differences, their situation is also in many ways similar to that of racial minority student athletes (see Gabor et al. 1996; Paraschak 2000).

2. While the reference here is to David's high school, it is possible that in other schools, depending on the racial composition, social class, and school facilities, the racial makeup of the sports teams will be different. Nevertheless, the general discourse related to the social construction of one racial group's superiority in a particular sport will be in evidence. In 1997, Eitzen and Sage found that only 18 per cent of professional baseball players were black, while 77 per cent and 65 per cent of the basketball and football players, respectively, were black. And more recently Dimmons identified a similar representation in the percentage of black and white players on professional teams. And the presentations on divisional teams were as follows: basketball (34 per cent whites, 56 per cent blacks, and 1 per cent Latinos); football (64 per cent whites, 46 per cent blacks, and 2 per cent Latinos); and baseball (88 per cent whites, 3 per cent blacks, and 5 per cent Latinos) (*Toronto Sun*, 8 Dec. 2002: S14–15).

3. The study found that young black athletes, compared to whites, were three times more likely to say that being successful in sports could earn them 'a lot of money'. And 51 per cent agreed that blacks cared more about sports because it was one of the few ways that they could make the money (Price 1997). In a more recent national survey of 865 high-school students, Lou Harris found that 'many African Americans still harboured unrealistic aspirations to stardom. Fifty-one per cent of them compared to 18 per cent of white student athletes believed that they would make the pros' (cited in Lapchick 2001: 235).

4. Similarly, in her discussion of coaches' perceptions of what makes good football players, Armour (2000) makes reference to what her son's football coach said of the group of eight-year-old boys: 'they were a joy to teach', but they would 'never make "real" footballers', which Armour took to mean 'they were too middle class for football' (77).

5. Today, soccer is one of the fastest growing sports in North America and is played in many schools.

6. David and Craig were both in one of my classes, and I spoke with them individually. They were told that their e-mail responses would be published; they received a copy of the chapter in its draft form.

7. The school is a privately owned and funded institution with tuition fees of approximately $15,000 annually, and a student population that is largely white Anglo-Saxon.

8. Craig notes that during his five years in his private high school, there were three black students in the school and two of them played on the football team.

9. Within this paradigmatic context then we come to hear of the academically gifted model minority students (Pon 2000; Lee 2003; Nakamura 2003).

10. With reference to the support he received from his 'mentor', Stewart said, 'I wouldn't be here today if it weren't for him. There were families that took me in when my family wasn't in a great situation. I can't tell you how grateful I am to be here today' (E8).

11. Gary, a high-school student, and Troy, a third-year university student, were participants in a discussion group on the subject.

Chapter 19

Understanding the Racialization of Poverty in Ontario: An Introduction in 2007

The Colour of Poverty Campaign

Did You Know That . . .

- Ethno-racial minority group members (people of colour) make up over 13 per cent of Canada's population; by the year 2017, this number will rise to 20 per cent;
- By the year 2017, more than half of Toronto's population will be people of colour;
- Nearly one in five immigrants experiences a state of chronic low income, which is more than twice the rate for Canadian-born individuals;
- Ethno-racial minority (i.e., non-European) families make up 37 per cent of all families in Toronto, but account for 59 per cent of poor families;
- Between 1980 and 2000, while the poverty rate for the non-racialized (i.e., European heritage) population fell by 28 per cent, the poverty among racialized families rose by 361 per cent; and
- Thirty-two per cent of children in racialized families and 47 per cent of children in recent immigrant families in Ontario live in poverty.

What Does This Mean?

More and more people in Ontario come from racialized group backgrounds (i.e., communities of colour). These persons face a much higher risk of being poor and are differentially impacted by the factors linked to it, like unstable and unsafe work conditions and poor health. While poverty can be a concern for nearly anyone, its causes, forms, and consequences aren't the same. Racialized group members face specific and particular hurdles and challenges.

What Is Meant by Poverty?

Canada most often uses the Low Income Cut-off (LICO) to measure financial hardship. The LICO is based on how much of a family's income is spent on basic needs like food and shelter. It also considers family size and community size. For example, a family of four living in a city of 300,000 people would fall just below the LICO with an annual income of $32,000 before tax. So, when a family is only making this much money, they are likely to spend a disproportionate share of their income on basic needs when compared with the average family.

What Is Meant by the Racialization of Poverty?

Racialized communities experience ongoing, disproportionate levels of poverty. In other words, people from ethno-racial minority groups (communities of colour) are more likely to fall below the LICO and to have related problems like poor health, lower education, and fewer job opportunities than those from European backgrounds. While it is possible for anyone to experience low income and reduced opportunities, individual and systemic racism plays a large role in creating such problems. Discrimination means that they are less likely to get jobs when equally qualified and are likely to make less income than their white peers. It means they are more likely to live and work in poor conditions, to have less access to health care, and to be victims of police violence.

* * *

Who Do We Mean by Racialized Groups?

. . . We are aware of Aboriginal realities and lived experience as well as advocacy efforts to redress their racialized exclusion. We very much believe there are many links between such struggles and those of other racialized groups in Ontario and Canada. However, we also acknowledge and respect that Aboriginal claims to justice are distinct and require a different set of strategies and policy responses due to First Peoples' specific historical relationship with Canada. For this reason, we do not include or address Aboriginal issues and circumstances. . . .

How Do We Understand Racism?

In 'western' societies dominated by people of white, European backgrounds, different ethno-racial groups have always been targets of discrimination and social exclusion. These groups can be said to be *racialized* or *marked* by the dominant group as inferior. Racism refers not only to individual, negative beliefs and attitudes toward specific ethno-racial groups in society; beyond that, racism is systemic and is a built-in feature of our society, embedded in our social institutions—like the education, health, social services, and justice systems.

Racism has existed in many different forms throughout history. In Canada and other 'western' countries, for example, white people have discriminated against racialized groups through the practice of slavery, the destruction of communities, racial segregation of schools and neighbourhoods, selective and punitive immigration policies, exploitation of certain groups' labour, over-policing in communities of colour, racial slurs, hate crimes, and so on. Assorted behaviours and policies change over time, but the facts of inequality and unequal treatment have not gone away.

Chapter 20

Japanese-Canadian Fishermen's Association: Seeking to Intervene before the Supreme Court of Canada in *R. v. Kapp*

Canadian Constitution Foundation

Legal and Historical Background Information

History of the Japanese-Canadian Fishermen's Association

The objective of the Japanese-Canadian Fishermen's Association (JCFA) is to recognize, promote, and protect the heritage of Canadians of Japanese ancestry in the British Columbia fishing industry and ensure that commercial fisheries in British Columbia are open equally to all Canadians without regard to race, colour, ethnicity, or ancestry.

The JCFA was legally incorporated as a non-profit society under the Society Act of British Columbia in 2007, and has existed in various forms since the late 1800s. Japanese-Canadian fishermen organized the Fraser River Fishermen's Association in 1897 with mandates to negotiate labour disputes with fishing companies and to provide social security services for its members. This association was registered as the Japanese Fishermen's Benevolent Society in 1900, with these same objectives plus an additional one to counter racial discrimination.

The federal government's race-based policies during the 1920s expelled approximately one half of Japanese-Canadian fishermen engaged in BC's commercial fisheries, forcing the unemployed fishermen to seek work in other indus-

tries. Federal fisheries policy in the 1920s mandated that Japanese Canadians were only eligible for certain licences, confined to fishing in specified districts, and prohibited from using gasoline-powered boats. In addition to expelling one half of Japanese-Canadian fishermen from the commercial fisheries, these policies also severely limited the earning power of those who remained.

In response to these racially discriminatory policies during the 1920s, Japanese-Canadian fishermen formed the Skeena River Fishermen's Association. This association lobbied for the removal of regulations requiring Japanese Canadians to use sail- and oar-powered boats when Caucasians and Natives were allowed to use gasoline engine–powered boats on the Skeena River, which is BC's second largest salmon river after the Fraser. Japanese-Canadian commercial fishermen also formed the Amalgamated Association of Fishermen of BC to raise money to challenge race-based fisheries policies in court.

Japanese-Canadian fishermen intervened in the Supreme Court of Canada in the 1928 case of *Reference Re: Fisheries Act 1914* to argue that the Minister of Marine and Fisheries (as he was then called) did not have a discretionary authority to grant or refuse fishing licences on the basis of race. The federal government argued that racial discrimination was necessary for the effective management of the commercial fishery in BC. The Supreme Court of Canada ruled in favour of the Japanese-Canadian fishermen, and this decision was later affirmed by the Judicial Committee of the Privy Council, which was then Canada's highest court.

During the Second World War, Japanese Canadians suffered many injustices, including the seizure of their homes, fishing boats, and other property, all taken without compensation. In 1942 the federal government ordered Japanese Canadians to be removed from the BC coast, and forced them to live in internment camps in the interior of BC and east of the Rockies. It was not until 1949, more than three years after the war had ended, that Japanese Canadians were permitted to return to the BC coast and resume their livelihood in the commercial fishery.

From 1949 until the present, the JCFA and its predecessor organizations remained dormant in the absence of racially discriminatory policies in BC's commercial fishery. In the context of one single racially diverse and racially integrated commercial fishery from 1949 to 1992, where rules applied equally to all Canadians regardless of ancestry, it was not necessary for Japanese-Canadian fishermen to maintain their own organization.

Early History of Japanese Canadians in BC

Immigrants from Japan were relative latecomers to British Columbia, with Manzo Nagano the first confirmed arrival in 1877. His first job was rowing the boat for an Italian skipper in the Fraser River sockeye fishery, in the same waters where the 1998 protest fishery occurred that gives rise to the *R. v. Kapp* court case.

In the late 1800s, the Fraser River was one of the largest producers of sockeye salmon in the world. The village of Steveston, located at the entrance to the Fraser River, became the world capital for salmon canneries. The Japanese

arrived at Steveston—today part of the city of Richmond—after Marshall English built the English Cannery in 1882. They fished for the English Cannery during the two-month sockeye salmon season, and sought work in the off-season in the larger centres of Victoria, Vancouver, and New Westminster.

From 1891 to 1901, the number of canneries in the Steveston area increased from four to fifteen, with a corresponding increase in labourers, fishermen, and businesses to serve the industry. Attracted by open access to the fishery, Japanese fishermen had become a large force in the Fraser River salmon fishery by 1900, holding more than 1,700 licences. In return for housing and pre-season loans to finance their fishing activities, the fishermen sold all their catch to the canneries, and their wives generally worked on the canning lines. As a result, the Japanese-Canadian population increased steadily and accounted for 66 per cent to 75 per cent of Steveston's population prior to the Second World War.

With few other job opportunities, Japanese-Canadian fishermen had no choice but to work harder and longer hours in the fishery, because it was one of the few sources of employment available to them. Historical records kept by the federal fisheries department recorded licences and catch data by the race of the fisherman, and indicated exceptional productivity amongst Japanese-Canadian fishermen. Because Japanese Canadians were not on the federal voters list until 1948 and the provincial voters list until 1949, they were prohibited from various forms of employment. Without actually writing discriminatory provisions into the law, government and other bodies made the franchise a qualification for many fields of employment. For example, the Law Society of British Columbia required that the name of a student be entered on the voters list at the age of 21. Japanese Canadians were also prohibited from logging on public lands and from working on contracts issued by the Department of Public Works. Japanese Canadians were excluded from careers in law, education, pharmacy, the civil service, the police, forestry, the post office, and public health nursing. Some of these discriminatory practices continued until the franchise was granted, but other practices ended sooner, in response to changes in government or a court decision.

Given the above noted employment restrictions, Japanese Canadians looked to expand their fishing activities beyond the salmon season. The commercial herring fishery was first started by Japanese fishermen in the late 1890s with a two boat purse-seine fishery in Burrard Inlet. The fish were salted in Steveston using practices adapted from the sardine fishery in Japan, and exported to China, Japan, and elsewhere.

Government Imposed Discrimination against Japanese-Canadian Fishermen

The early decades of the twentieth century were marked by racial intolerance and industrial strife, with violent disputes over the price of fish. Because few other jobs were available to Canadians of Japanese ancestry, Japanese fishermen were less able to stay on strike for a season. Cannery owners often set Japanese fishermen against fishermen of other races in an effort to reduce fish prices.

The insatiable demand for resources during the First World War ignited an economic boom in British Columbia, which greatly benefited Japanese fishermen. However, with the end of the war, demand for resources declined and a recession ensued, resulting in few job opportunities for the returning veterans. Members of Parliament from British Columbia, the unions, and the press lobbied for an increase in Caucasian and Native participation in BC's commercial fisheries through the exclusion of Japanese-Canadian fishermen. Caucasian and Aboriginal fishermen also used the pretext of the returning veterans to try and eliminate their biggest competitor in the fishery.

The federal government responded to these demands with a series of policies aimed at eliminating Japanese Canadians from the commercial fishery. In 1920, the minister capped the number of salmon and herring licences issued to Japanese-Canadian fishermen at 1919 levels, while increasing the number of fishing licences issued to Caucasians and Aboriginals.

Prior to the opening of the 1922 salmon season, the federal fisheries department imposed a one-third reduction in the number of troll licences issued to Japanese-Canadian fishermen. Further, Japanese Canadians who fished the west coast of Vancouver Island were henceforth required to reside on the west coast of Vancouver Island. This cut the Japanese presence in the troll fleet from about 400 to about 90 fishermen. Fifty Japanese fishermen moved to Ucluelet, 30 to Tofino, and 10 to Bamfield. Some fishermen fished despite the residence requirement, but the boats of Japanese fishermen who did not reside in the area were seized. In contrast, Aboriginal and Caucasian fishermen did not have residency requirements attached to their fishing licences; they could live where they pleased and fish where they pleased.

In 1922, the federal government established the British Columbia Fisheries Commission, headed by Nova Scotia Member of Parliament William Duff. It came to be known as the Duff Commission, and four of its six MPs were from BC. The Commission convened hearings with fishermen, fishing company personnel, government officials, and the general public at numerous fishing villages along the BC coast. The Commission recommended that Japanese fishing licences for all major fisheries be reduced by 40 per cent in 1923.

In its 1924–25 annual report, the federal fisheries department noted that its policies had resulted in a 40 per cent decline in the number of gillnet licences issued to Japanese-Canadian fishermen. The annual report also noted that the east and west coasts of Vancouver Island were the only areas left for salmon trolling for Japanese fishermen, with the exception of one single licence issued for the north coast. The east coast of Vancouver Island saw a 51.3 per cent reduction in 'Japanese' licences, with a corresponding increase in 'white' and 'Indian' licences of 39.1 per cent and 58.5 per cent respectively.

The annual report also noted that the number of Japanese-Canadian fishermen in the seining and salting of herring was reduced by 25 per cent, and that an additional 25 per cent reduction would be imposed in subsequent years, so the 'industry will then be in the hands of white men and Canadian Indians only'. Additional restrictions on Japanese fishermen following the Duff Commission included:

- Limiting Japanese Canadians to only one salmon gillnet licence for either the Fraser River (District 1) or the north coast (District 2), while there were no such gear or geographic restrictions for other fishermen;
- Expelling Japanese Canadians from the purse-seine fishery for salmon, which subsequently became the largest harvester in the salmon fishery;
- Prohibiting Japanese Canadians from using motorized fishing vessels in the north coast (District 2) while allowing Caucasian and Aboriginal fishermen to use gas-powered boats;
- Restricting Japanese Canadians trolling the west coast of Vancouver Island to the area between Estevan and Pachena points, thereby prohibiting them from the productive Kyuquot fishing grounds; and
- Reducing Japanese-Canadian representation in the salt-herring fishery, which they had started in the 1890s and dominated since that time, by requiring that 50 per cent of the workforce be comprised of Caucasians and Aboriginals.

Japanese Canadians were uniquely affected by these policies. The federal government has never imposed rules or policies that discriminated against Aboriginal Canadians or members of any other ethnic, cultural, or linguistic group wishing to participate in BC's commercial fishery.

Japanese Fishermen's Efforts to Oppose Government Discrimination

In 1920, Japanese Canadians did not object overtly when the number of fishing licences issued to them remained frozen at 1919 levels. But they realized the seriousness of the problem when the federal government reduced the number of Japanese west coast trolling licences by one third in 1922, followed by a reduction in almost all the other major fisheries licences in 1923 through 1926. In 1926, the department announced further reductions in the number of licences to be issued in 1927 and in subsequent years, until Japanese Canadians were completely eliminated from BC's commercial fisheries.

These expulsions prompted all the Japanese fishing associations to come together and organize the Amalgamated Association of Fishermen of BC to lobby from a unified front and also to raise money necessary for retaining counsel to challenge the minister's policy of discriminating against British subjects of Japanese ancestry.

In response to lower court rulings that the federal government lacked jurisdiction to license fish canneries, the federal government submitted a reference to the Supreme Court of Canada to deal with this jurisdictional question, as well as the issue raised by counsel for the Japanese fishermen: whether ministerial discretion to issue fishing licences could be exercised on the basis of race. Japanese-Canadian fishermen were successful as interveners in the Supreme Court of Canada in *Re: Fisheries Act 1914 (Canada)*. In May of 1928, the Supreme Court of Canada struck down the fisheries department's discriminatory licensing practices, ruling that 'any British subject resident in the province of British Columbia, who is not otherwise legally disqualified, has . . .

the right to receive a licence'. The federal government appealed this decision to the Judicial Committee of the Privy Council, which in October of 1929 dismissed the appeal and awarded costs in favour of the Japanese-Canadian fishermen.

Prior to the Privy Council's decision, Japanese fishermen on the Skeena River continued to suffer under the policy which allowed only Caucasian and Aboriginal fishermen to use motorized fishing vessels. Japanese fishermen had to row or use sails, which was extremely difficult due to tides, river currents, and unpredictable winds.

Japanese-Canadian fishermen raised money to enable Jun Kisawa, a young bachelor willing to risk jail, to hold a protest fishery on the Skeena River. They helped him to buy a motorized vessel with which he fished alongside Caucasian and Aboriginal fishermen, who were also using gas-powered vessels. Jun Kisawa was promptly prosecuted, and his licence was suspended. In the local court in Prince Rupert, he admitted to having broken the law for the purpose of challenging racial discrimination, and successfully asserted his right to be treated equally with other Canadians. On 3 July 1929, Chief Inspector Motherwell advised the Deputy Minister that Kisawa's fishing licence had been returned.

The federal government's Oriental exclusion policy became entirely moot after the bombing of Pearl Harbour by Imperial Japan in December of 1941. All fishing vessels owned by Japanese Canadians were seized, along with their homes and other property, without any compensation to the owners. In February of 1942, the federal cabinet passed an Order-in-Council mandating the expulsion of the Japanese from a 100-mile strip of the BC coast. Canadians of Japanese ancestry living in coastal fishing and logging villages were rounded up and interned at an exhibition ground in Vancouver for shipment to camps in the interior of British Columbia and east of the Rockies. They were allowed to take only 150 pounds of personal effects per person. Their remaining chattels and properties were left in trust with the Custodian of Enemy Alien Property, which later sold the property to allay the costs of its owners' internment.

The restrictions banning Japanese Canadians from the BC coast were not lifted until April of 1949, more than three years after the war had ended.

Starting from scratch, Japanese Canadians re-entered the fisheries from which they had been excluded for seven long years. Upon return to the coast, Canadians of Japanese ancestry chose to move past the events of World War II and rebuild their lives by looking to the future. The cultural values of the Japanese-Canadian community were evident in the qualities of *gamen* (patience and perseverance), *enryo* (reserve or restraint), and *shikataga-nai* (acceptance, resignation, or 'nothing can be done'), which enabled the Japanese-Canadian community to move past the rejection, abuse, and loss of property to achieve both economic and social success.

From 1949 to 1992, all commercial fishermen in British Columbia fished under the same rules and regulations regardless of race, culture, language, ethnicity, or bloodline ties. Ethnic minorities in BC's commercial fishery included, and still include, Canadians of Vietnamese, Aboriginal, Croatian, Norwegian, and Japanese origin, and a large number of other ethnicities.

In 1988, Prime Minister Brian Mulroney issued a formal apology to Japanese Canadians and the government also provided some financial compensation. Most important was the Prime Minister's promise:

As a people, Canadians commit themselves to the creation of a society that ensures justice and equality for all, regardless of race or ethnic origin . . . The acknowledgement of these injustices serves notice to all Canadians that the excesses of the past are condemned and that the principles of justice and equality in Canada are reaffirmed. Therefore, the Government of Canada, on behalf of all Canadians, does hereby . . . *pledge to ensure, to the full extent that its powers allow, that such events will not happen again* . . . (emphasis added)

Partially in response to demands by groups interned during World War II, the federal government in 1988 replaced the War Measures Act, which had enabled the 1940s uprooting, expulsion, exile, and dispossession of Japanese Canadians, with the Emergencies Act. Of particular significance to Japanese Canadians, the Emergencies Act states that the government cannot take any action against Canadians 'on the basis of race, national or ethnic origin, colour, religion, sex, age, or mental or physical disability'.

After the passage of the Canadian Charter of Rights and Freedoms, the apology from the prime minister, and the new Emergencies Act, Japanese Canadians believed that no government would ever again use their race to exclude them from BC's commercial fishery. And yet in 1992 the Department of Fisheries and Oceans created a private, race-based commercial fishery that is now being challenged before the Supreme Court of Canada in *R. v. Kapp*. This time, however, Japanese Canadians take comfort in the fact that they are joined by Canadians of diverse races—including some Aboriginal Canadians—in this attempt to ensure that a fisherman's race, ethnicity, ancestry, or bloodline ties will not decide who gets to go to work on any given day in the BC commercial fishery.

The JCFA's Interest in *R. v. Kapp*

Since 1877, commercial fishing has been—and remains today—an integral component of the culture, heritage, history, and identity of Japanese Canadians. Since the late 1800s, Canadians of Japanese ancestry have fought for racial equality, especially in respect of the rules and policies

governing BC's commercial fishery. The JCFA is a successor to previous associations of Japanese-Canadian fishermen whose members were subjected to racially discriminatory fisheries policies during the 1920s, followed by expulsion, exile, and dispossession during the Second World War. The JCFA includes members who were born in the 1920s and have personally suffered property confiscation, internment, and other injustices in the 1940s. Their children and grandchildren fish in today's commercial fishery, or have investments in the fishery in licences and vessels. JCFA members are very concerned about the future of BC's commercial fishery because their history and heritage are directly tied to it.

Members of the JCFA recognize that Aboriginals enjoy a constitutionally enshrined right to a non-commercial 'food fishery'. While respecting this non-commercial fishery, members of the JCFA are deeply offended by the current federal policy of a racially segregated commercial fishery, which is restricted to individuals with bloodline ties to select Aboriginal groups. This federal policy has reintroduced racial conflict into the BC commercial fishery, which has not been seen for decades. Numerous racial incidents have taken place since 1992, including name-calling and, in some cases, physical violence.

The Japanese-Canadian community is acutely and personally aware of the loss of dignity and racial antagonism caused by government-imposed racial distinctions. While preferring to forget the events of the past, they cannot ignore the tragedy of history repeating itself. This time it is the majority of Canadians who are being excluded, but the racial distinction is no less offensive.

The perspective of the members of the JCFA differs immensely from those who have only an intellectual or philosophical understanding of the impact of race-based policies on individuals, and on their dignity and self-respect. The race-based commercial fishery introduced in 1992 has opened old wounds that were uniquely suffered by Japanese Canadians. Consisting of Canadians whose families have fished commercially in BC for several generations, the JCFA hopes to bring its unique social, cultural, and historical perspective to the Supreme Court of Canada [in] *R. v. Kapp*.

Questions

1. According to Peter Li, why and how do Chinese Canadians continue to experience negative racialization?
2. What is the relationship between racial profiling and racialization as described by Tanovich in his article on policing race in Canada?
3. Define racialization. Provide an example that is not derived from the text.
4. How is the sociological axiom 'phenomena do not have to be real to be real in their consequences' played out in Fleras's article on racializing eye colour?
5. According to Carl James, what role does race play for young people in Canadian sports participation?
6. Perceptions of race continue to be a key factor in how reality is defined, organized, and lived, as well as a central variable in people's experiences, identities, opportunities, and outcomes. Explain.
7. Compare and contrast the concepts of race-based fishing rights versus rights-based fishing rights. Utilize the articles on Aboriginal and Japanese-Canadian fishing rights to embellish your answer.

Websites

Canadian Constitution Foundation: http://www.canadianconstitutionfoundation.ca
Colour of Poverty: http://www.colourofpoverty.ca
Ontario Human Rights Commission: http://www.ohrc.on.ca

Suggested Readings

Agnew, Vijay, ed. 2007. *Interrogating Race and Racism* (Toronto: University of Toronto Press).

Chan, Wendy, and Kiran Mirchandani. 2002. *Crimes of Colour: Racialization and the Criminal Justice System in Canada* (Peterborough: Broadview Press).

Driedger, Leo, and Shiva S. Halli, eds. 2000. *Race and Racism: Canada's Challenge* (Ottawa: Carleton University Press).

Fernando, Shanti. 2006. *Race and the City: Chinese Canadian and Chinese American Political Mobilization* (Vancouver: UBC Press).

Galabuzi, Grace-Edward. 2006. *Canada's Economic Apartheid: The Social Exclusion of Racialized Groups in the New Century* (Toronto: Canadian Scholars' Press).

Smith, Charles C. 2007. *Conflict, Crisis, and Accountability: Racial Profiling and Law Enforcement in Canada* (Ottawa: Canadian Centre for Policy Alternatives), available at <http://www.policyalternatives.ca>.

Anti-racism and
Theorizing Resistance

Theorizing resistance to systemic racism in Canada is a collective project that is growing despite official-level silences and denials. In this collective project, issues of class, gender, and other salient features such as age, disability, sexual orientation, etc., hold the promise of forging a broader alliance in a bid to widen and strengthen this social movement. This selection on anti-racism and theorizing resistance could have been a whole book given the wealth of materials that exist in Canada. Here we provide only a glimpse into the collective efforts being undertaken to establish a solid body of work on anti-racism. Racial structural inequality is being actively resisted in several areas including education (Brathwaite and James 1996; Dei 1997), law (Walker 1997; Aylward 2002), and employment (Gannage 1986; Das Gupta 1996). These resistances *are* the hope for future racial justice in Canada and the end of the legitimacy of race to deny people their human rights and, fundamentally, their respect and dignity.

The first article in Part IV is from *Canadian Critical Race Theory: Racism and the Law* (1999), one of the first Canadian books to highlight how legal practitioners, lawyers, and judges, along with racialized communities, are harnessing the law to acknowledge the existence of systemic racism and to pave the way to ameliorate the legal, social, and economic consequences of discrimination in Canada. According to Carol Aylward, going beyond a rights approach, 'Critical Race Theory methodology requires a deconstruction of legal rules and principles and challenges the so-called "neutrality" and "objectivity" of laws that oppress black people and other people of colour' (1999: 82). Aylward identifies the 1994 *R.D.S.* case as the first Critical Race Litigation case to reach the Supreme Court of Canada. The case, fought by black legal professionals, with support from the black community, 'persuaded the Supreme Court of Canada to expand the "reasonable person" standard. The Court held that the "reasonable person" is aware of the social context of a case, such as the prevalence of racism in Canadian society . . .' (1999: 132). This is but one example of the battles fought on several levels by people from racialized communities and their allies every day in present-day Canada.

In the second article, 'Decolonizing Anti-racism', by Bonita Lawrence and Enakshi Dua, the authors call for enriching anti-racism theorizations and resistances by urging 'post-colonial and anti-racism theorists to begin to take Indigenous decolonization seriously' (2005: 120). Such a perspective would have to take into account Indigenous sovereignty, land claims, means of subsistence, and a unique cultural inheritance. This approach, the authors point out, would reflect the contradictory way racialized people are located in relation to the Canadian state and Indigenous peoples. Anti-racist theorizations recognizing ongoing colonization as foundational would open the way for an alliance between anti-racism and Indigenous scholars and activists that would empower both communities.

The third article, by George J. Sefa Dei, makes a strong case for addressing Canadian 'silence around race' (2007: 53). Canada's denial of systemic racism results in dire consequences for racialized communities while implicitly complying with the structural ways white supremacy and privilege continue to exist. Dei offers a critical way forward in future theorizations and resistances to racism when he states that 'Anti-racism is a political engagement and not merely an intellectual/discursive undertaking' (2007: 55). As a result, identifying racism and privilege are seen as key decolonization projects. In addition, experiential realities are to be prioritized to highlight both the material and psychic injury of exclusion and domination. Finally, Dei suggests a focus on the racialized subject to gaze at who is doing the racializing, that is, to expose the structural dynamics of whiteness (2007: 61–2). The anti-racist project of resistance is to counter official silence and denial of 'systemic neglect of our . . . communities' (2007: 62).

In the last article by Afua Cooper, we see the links between resistances to slavery in 1793–1803 and current resistances to systemic racial exclusion and norms of whiteness in Canada. In this article, Cooper reinterprets slavery in Canada and 'centres black Canadians, particularly the enslaved, as actors and agents in the making of their own, and thus a significant part of Canada's, history' (2007: 53). Cooper's documentation links individual acts of resistance to collective initiatives. As a message to those resisting in 2007 and beyond—2007 marked the bicentenary of British abolition of the Atlantic slave trade—Cooper's interpretation provides hope and inspirational role models for us today, as countless black men and women in Upper Canada were 'active agents in their own emancipation' (2007: 53).

In summary, the four articles in Part IV utilize the lens of Critical Race Theory, ongoing colonization, official silence and denial of racism to accomplish white supremacy and privilege, and historical resistance to slavery, to theorize anti-racism and resistance. Each author, in their own way, helped create the very future that is being imagined by writing resistance and providing alternative paths to accomplish individual and collective resistance. To date, this work continues and is gathering strength.

Chapter 21

Canadian Critical Race Litigation: Wedding Theory and Practice

Carol A. Aylward

Criminal and Constitutional Law: Canadian Critical Race Cases

On Monday, 4 May 1992, hundreds of Metropolitan Toronto police officers watched as an angry mob of about 1,000 black and white youths and young adults attacked bystanders and police and smashed windows at about 100 stores in downtown Toronto following a peaceful demonstration organized by the black community. This peaceful demonstration and the resulting riot came in the wake of the verdict in the Rodney King case and the ensuing Los Angeles riots and were fuelled by yet another shooting of a black man, Raymond Lawrence, on 2 May 1992, in Toronto by a white police officer (Downey 1992). Racial unrest in Canada has not been confined to Toronto or to protests over the Rodney King verdict. Rioting has also occurred in other Canadian cities over the years, including Halifax and Montreal.

There has been an ongoing and growing dissatisfaction with the state of relations between the police and racial minority communities in both Canada and the United States. These relations have resulted in numerous claims of excessive use of force against the police in many jurisdictions in Canada. Many of the claims of excessive use of force by police have involved shootings of black Canadians in Toronto and Montreal and have included accusations that these shootings were racially motivated. Claims that police use excessive force and racial slurs against blacks have also been made in Nova Scotia and other Canadian jurisdictions. While the doctrine of 'colour-blindness' has promoted the myth that racism is no longer a factor in American society, the same doctrine has promoted a prevailing myth in Canada that racism was never a factor in Canadian society.

> Many Canadians have clung to the myth that Canada is not really a racist country. The veracity of this myth is often supported by a self-serving distinction between Canada and the United States. . . . Canadian history has provided much clear evidence that belies the non-racist myth . . . [still] this myth took on a life of its own. . . . Attention should be paid to the myth of a non-racist Canada . . . it is not a harmless one . . . it has caused direct, extensive, and iniquitous consequences to individuals, groups, and society as a whole . . . hence, the really debilitating result of the pervasiveness of the myth has been the frustratingly slow and inadequate response of Canadian governments, institutions, and other organizations to racist laws, policies, and practices. (Brown and Brown 1996: 48–9)

Many commentators have recognized that the perception Canada has of itself as an egalitarian society devoid of a history of racism does not reflect reality (see, for example, Walker 1997: 3; Mendes 1995). James Walker, a social historian, looked at historical legal cases where race and law intertwined, and he explored the historical role of the Supreme Court of Canada in the perpetuation of the Canadian myth. To do this, Walker selected four Supreme Court of Canada cases that involved four separate minority groups, spanning the years 1914, 1939, 1950, and 1955. The cases he selected for examination included *Quong Wing v. The King* (1914, SCR 440 [SCC]), involving a Chinese Canadian who was charged under a Saskatchewan statute preventing Chinese men from employing white females; a case involving a black Canadian, *Christie v. York Corp.* ([1940,] SCR 139 [SCC]), who was refused service in a tavern because of colour; a case involving a Canadian Jew, *Noble and Wolfe v. Alley* ([1951,] 92 SCR 64 [SCC]), who was denied the right to purchase a cottage because of a restrictive covenant preventing owners from selling to Jews; and a case involving a Trinidadian of East Indian ancestry, *Narine-Singh v. Attorney General of Canada* ([1955,] SCR 395), who was excluded through the Immigration Act from Canada because he was of the 'Asian race'. Walker maintains that the cases present a challenge to the Canadian image of a tolerant and racism-free country:

> The four case studies suggest a startlingly different reality. Many of the restrictions in genuinely racist societies apparently had a Canadian counterpart, including features for the protection of women of the dominant class, employment and other economic disadvantages, limited access to land and services, legalized segregation and even the legal definition of citizens by 'race'. . . . Race was a legal artifact and in the process of its formulation, the Supreme Court of Canada was a significant participant, legitimating racial categories and maintaining barriers

among them. Even in *Noble and Wolf*, the Court allowed the respondents' argument—that racial discrimination was both morally and legally acceptable—to pass without contradiction, and declined to confirm the appellants' assertion that racial distinctions were contrary to public policy. None of the seven judges in the case commented on discrimination per se or its legality, so that the law already established on racial discrimination, for example by the *Quong Wing* decision, [where the discriminatory Saskatchewan statute was upheld as being within the jurisdiction of provincial powers] and [the] *Christie* [decision, where racial discrimination was found to be not immoral or damaging and the discriminatory conduct was upheld on the doctrine of freedom of commerce], was not affected. Then in *Narine-Singh* the Supreme Court positively upheld the legality of 'race' as a discernible factor in Canadian public policy. The widespread existence of a racial paradigm in Canada and a legal role in its fashioning are two of the observations one might take from the examined cases. (1997: 302)

If one could pinpoint the exact moment in legal history when the courts were most supportive of and responsible for the perpetuation of racist ideology in the United States, it would be when the United States Supreme Court handed down the *Dred Scott* decision (*Dred Scott v. Sandford*, 1857, 60 US [19 How.] 393). In Canada, it would be the moment in 1940 when the Supreme Court of Canada handed down the *Christie* decision.

The *Dred Scott* case is considered one of the most controversial decisions ever issued by the United States Supreme Court. In 1846, a Missouri slave named Dred Scott sued for his freedom in court, claiming he should be free since he had lived in a free state for a long time prior to his master's death. Dred Scott lost the case when the United States Supreme Court handed down its decision in 1857, with Chief Justice Taney declaring (at 393) that 'Dred Scott was not a citizen of Missouri within the meaning of the Constitution of the United States, and not entitled as such to sue in its courts. . . . Coloured men had no rights which the white man was bound to respect.'

The Supreme Court of Canada held in the *Christie* case in 1939 that even though blacks were discriminated against in almost all public services, including employment, housing, education, and recreation, and even though the situation of 'Jim Crow' made life no better for blacks in Canada than it did for blacks in the United States, discrimination was legal in Canada absent any 'positive' law forbidding it. Discrimination was not contrary to good morals or public order. Some would argue that the *Christie* decision was merely reflective of its times and that, although the case may somewhat tarnish the 'myth' that Canada is a tolerant country without a racist past, it has no bearing on the present time when racism has been eliminated by human rights codes and equality is guaranteed by the Canadian Constitution. Critical Race theorists and others point out, however, that 'despite these important [legal] achievements, racism is still entrenched in Canadian society' (Commission on Systemic Racism 1995: 52). . . .

Although human rights legislation had been passed in all Canadian jurisdictions by 1977, except in Quebec, the enforcement of human rights legislation in the first instance is confided to specialized tribunals and there is no recourse to the civil courts for redress. Human rights legislation . . . is problematic because the vast majority of race-based human rights complaints never reach the board of inquiry stage within the human rights process, even when the racial minority complainant would like the case to proceed. As well, the fact that jurisdiction over human rights has been confined exclusively to human rights tribunals has meant that there is no recourse to the civil courts. . . .

In Canada today, discrimination and racism exist in much more subtle forms than during the periods in which the cases considered by James Walker were decided. As the report of the Commission on Systemic Racism in the Ontario Criminal Justice System (1995: 52) has documented, today discrimination is usually found in systemic form and concealed in systems, practices, policies, and laws that may appear neutral on their face but have a serious detrimental effect on people of colour.

In the United States, black Americans who wish to challenge the constitutionality of an apparently neutral law have to prove a discriminatory intent on the part of those responsible for enacting the law or those responsible for its administration, although discriminatory effects have been recognized as a ground for relief under US federal human rights legislation (Lawrence 1987: 317). In Canada, however, an 'adverse effects' doctrine of discrimination has been adopted both in the context of the Charter and under human rights codes. . . .

Despite these significant developments, which mean that, in theory, the legal environment in Canada provides a better analytical framework for challenges to racism, the issue of systemic discrimination remains unresolved. The Charter has not been used extensively as a litigation tool to combat racism in Canadian society (Mendes 1995: 1–24). Additionally, in 1992, the only avenue open to black Canadians for redress for private acts of discrimination not covered by the Charter (in light of the *Bhadauria* case), the human rights complaints process, was found to have an 'unsettling trend' in the way it dealt with cases based on race; it was found that complaints based on race were dismissed without a hearing more often than those based on any other grounds (Mendes 1995: 2–9). Critical Race theorists and others in Canada have severely criticized human rights law and condemn it as a typically Canadian effort to maintain the myth of toleration by pretending to address intolerance while at the same time maintaining the dominant group's 'right' to discriminate.

Although Critical Race theorists condemn law as a tool of oppression, they also recognize the importance of law as a tool in the fight against oppression. When lawyers litigate race issues, they are seeking to ameliorate the legal, social, and economic conditions of their black clients and the black community in general.

Critical Race Theory methodology requires a deconstruction of legal rules and principles and challenges the so-called 'neutrality' and 'objectivity' of laws that oppress black people and other people of colour. Deconstruction is designed to confront subtle forms of discrimination perpetuated by law. The questions to be asked by the lawyer engaged in Critical Race Litigation are: Does the doctrine, legal rule, principle, or practice at issue in the particular case subordinate and discriminate against people of colour? Is race an issue? If the answers are yes, should it be litigated or should some other strategy be employed? An important stage of Critical Race Litigation, and the most crucial step in transforming theory into practice, is reconstruction. What are the alternatives, if any, to the existing doctrine, legal rule, principle, or practice? What harm or benefit to the black client and/or the black community might result from the adoption or non-adoption by the courts of this change?

Because of the historic and financial constraints on litigation by black Canadians, there is no body of jurisprudence recognizing racial equality that can compare to the extensive jurisprudence developed in the United States after the 1954 decision in *Brown* v. *Board of Education* (347 US 483). To this day, race-based litigation in Canada is impeded by the paucity of black lawyers to conduct the litigation and the unwillingness or inability of many white practitioners to make racial arguments before the courts. This unwillingness or inability may stem from a number of factors such as conscious or unconscious racism, an inability to recognize the racial implications of a particular case, a lack of knowledge about how to challenge and deconstruct legal rules and principles which foster and maintain discrimination, total acceptance of the myth of the 'objectivity' of laws, or fear that raising issues of race before the courts will disadvantage a client's case because of the courts' unacceptance or hostility toward these arguments.

For these reasons, and because the development of Critical Race Theory in Canada is very recent, there was no Critical Race Litigation in Canada until the mid-1990s. The *R.D.S.* case was the first Critical Race Litigation case in Canada to reach the Supreme Court of Canada.

Important Canadian Critical Race Cases

R.D.S. v. The Queen

On 17 October 1993, R.D.S., a black youth, was riding his bicycle home. Subsequent events would take this black youth, a black female judge, and the black community of Nova Scotia and Canada on a journey that would take four years. This journey, from the street of a predominately black neighbourhood in Halifax, would wind its way to Youth Court, through two provincial Appellate Courts and ultimately to the Supreme Court of Canada.

R.D.S. was arrested and charged with assault on a police officer in the execution of his duty, assault with intent to prevent the lawful arrest of another, and resisting arrest, after he stopped to ask his cousin, who was being arrested by a white police officer on the street, the circumstances of that arrest and whether he (R.D.S.) should call his cousin's mother.

Only two witnesses testified at the trial: R.D.S. and the white police officer, Constable Stienburg. R.D.S. testified that while he was still straddling his bicycle, he spoke only to his cousin and only asked him what happened. He denied touching the police officer with his hands or his bicycle and he also denied telling the police officer to let his cousin go. R.D.S. testified that the police officer told him to 'shut up' or he would be placed under arrest and that then the police officer had proceeded to put him in a choke hold and to handcuff him. He testified that both he and his cousin, N.R., were put in choke holds by the officer. The police officer testified that he had been assaulted by R.D.S., and that R.D.S. had been obstructing the lawful arrest of another person. He gave no testimony with regard to the handcuffing of R.D.S. or the choke holds the two youths were allegedly subjected to.

R.D.S. was subsequently tried by way of summary conviction and acquitted of all charges by a black Youth Court judge (*R. v. R.D.S.*, NS Y093-168, 2 December 1994) who, faced with making a determination based on the credibility of the witnesses, accepted the testimony of the black youth over that of the white police officer. This acquittal provoked a firestorm of controversy and litigation which uncovered the racial tensions between the black community and the criminal justice system in Nova Scotia and Canada.

The Crown appeal alleging an actual racial bias on the part of the only black judge in Nova Scotia against the white police officer, and the subsequent overturning of the acquittal of the black youth R.D.S. by the Chief Justice of the Supreme Court of Nova Scotia (*R. v. R.D.S.*, SCNS, SH No. 112404, 18 April 1995), created the 'spark' that ignited the black community. Black lawyers across the country challenged what was interpreted as an emerging legal legitimatization of a discriminatory standard with respect to the test of reasonable apprehension of bias in judicial decision-making. This standard was being applied only to black judges and, presumably, judges from other historically excluded groups.

As previously noted, in the United States, civil rights litigation has occurred since the 1960s. The resulting decisions have enhanced the civil rights of African Americans through favourable substantive and procedural outcomes on many race-related issues. However, Critical Race theorists argue the need for new strategies that go beyond the traditional rights discourse. In Canada, black lawyers and others are now beginning to take a Critical Race position for the benefit of the black community. R.D.S. was the first Critical Race Litigation case explicitly arguing a race issue before the Supreme Court of Canada in the context of section 15 of the Charter and therefore had the potential to be precedent-setting. A growing number of black lawyers and others in Canada are beginning to recognize that it is crucial to collectively and individually work in the area of race-based litigation and to identify and overcome oppressions in order to enhance the interests of blacks through substantive outcomes.

The first step in Critical Race Litigation is the ability of defence lawyers to recognize when the issue of race arises, and the ability to do so depends on an awareness and acknowledgement of the existence of racism in Canadian society. The Critical Race position taken in the *R.D.S.* case was that the existence of racial discrimination and the context of the interaction between police officers and 'non-white' groups in Canada is not a matter that requires evidence before the courts but is rather a matter of the common sense and experience of the judge which can be applied whenever the facts warrant. In this case, race was not a material fact that had to be proved but rather was a matter of societal context, and accordingly it did not require evidence nor the taking of judicial notice. The 'reasonable person' whom the court invokes to determine whether or not a reasonable apprehension of bias arises must be aware of the fact that racial discrimination exists in Canada.[1]

In the context of the *R.D.S.* case, the Critical Race Theory method of deconstruction took the form of challenging and deconstructing the doctrine of reasonable apprehension of bias, the 'reasonable person' test, the myth of 'neutrality' and 'objectivity' in the context of judicial decision-making, the concept of formal equality, and the concept of legal reasoning as ahistorical.

The Critical Race Theory approach of narrative or storytelling jurisprudence was also employed in the *R.D.S.* case. Put to practical use, narrative or storytelling can function in a number of ways. It can allow lawyers to 'tell the story' of their clients in a non-ahistorical way. In other words, in the context of the *R.D.S.* case, narrative—or storytelling—allowed the lawyers to debunk the myth of 'neutrality' and 'objectivity' by placing the encounter between the black youth and the white police officer representing the state in its social and historical context of racial discrimination. Narrative allowed the lawyers representing R.D.S. to tell the story of the racial conflict between the police and the black community of Nova Scotia, and indeed in the whole of Canada, at the time of the encounter.[2]

* * *

The Critical Race Theory Significance of the *R.D.S.* Case

The lawyer representing R.D.S. was black. The fact that R.D.S. was able to obtain a lawyer from his own community is quite remarkable, given the fact that at the time of his arrest and trial no black lawyer was on staff at Nova Scotia Legal Aid and only one was in a staff position at Dalhousie Legal Aid. Additionally, at the original trial something unique occurred: in court that day were a black female judge, a black male lawyer, a black court reporter, and the black accused. As one commentator noted, it was the kind of scene the Marshall Commissioners had hoped for. The trial was held before Corrine Sparks, Nova Scotia's only black female Youth Court judge, on 2 December 1994 (*R. v. R.D.S.*, NS Y093-168).

Historically, blacks have been excluded from the profession of law in Nova Scotia. There has

been an ongoing and continuing struggle by Nova Scotian blacks to obtain a legal education despite segregation and oppression. Throughout most of the twentieth century, blacks were legally segregated from the public school system in the province of Nova Scotia. From 1876, black communities throughout the province formally organized to combat the inferior education and racial discrimination they encountered in the provincial school system. Legal segregation of blacks in education was only officially repealed (at least on paper) in the late 1960s. In 1964 there were still four segregated school districts in the province, and differential streaming on the basis of race continues in many Nova Scotia high schools to the present day. Critical Race theorists argue that this exclusion from the educational system and the legal profession has seriously undermined the Canadian black community's ability to attack issues of racism in a legal framework and has retarded the advancement of rights doctrine in the context of race under the Canadian Charter of Rights and Freedoms. . . .

The Critical Race Theory methods of deconstruction, narrative, and reconstruction were employed in the *R.D.S.* litigation strategy. Specifically, the litigation team's strategy was to offer the argument that the allegation of a reasonable apprehension of bias arose in this case because Judge Sparks was a black female judge who, in adjudicating a trial of a black accused, explicitly recognized that the case had racial overtones.[3] And as Justice Freeman, in dissent in the Nova Scotia Court of Appeal, observed, 'Questions with racial overtones . . . are more likely than any other to subject the judge to controversy and accusations of bias.'[4] R.D.S.'s position was that the 'reasonable person', whom a court invokes to determine whether or not a reasonable apprehension of bias arises, must be aware of the fact that racial discrimination exists in Canada.

A further element of the R.D.S. team's Critical Race Litigation strategy was to use the Charter, specifically section 15 (the equality section) to challenge the formal notion of equality, that is, the proposition that judges must be colour-blind. The appellant argued that:

> To be capable of detecting racism, one must be conscious of colour, race, and racial inter-actions because s. 15 was not restricted to a formal notion of equality; it was not satisfied by the notion of equality as sameness. Judicial analysis which ignores the possible racial dynamics of a situation will perpetuate racism, while a substantive notion of equal-ity recognizes that it may be necessary to take account of race in order ultimately to discount the invidious effect of race. To be sensitive to the possible racial dynamics of a given situation, as Judge Sparks was, is not indicative of bias but rather evidence of an understanding of the real meaning of equal-ity. Given that racism is a reality in Canadian society, racism will be perpetuated if, as the majority of the Court of Appeal's analysis demands, judges studiously ignore the dynamics of race.[5]

. . . From a Critical Race perspective, the majority decisions expand the concept of the 'reasonable person' to include an awareness of the social context of a case, such as societal awareness and knowledge of the prevalence of racism or gender bias in a particular community. The Supreme Court of Canada's majority finding with respect to judges' ability to refer to social context in their decision-making and whether such references raise a reasonable apprehension of bias will depend on the individual case, as well as on the requirement that a high standard for a finding of a reasonable apprehension of bias is required. The Court's articulation that this high standard applies to all judges, regardless of their race, gender, or other characteristics, furthers the agenda of Critical Race theorists and practition-ers. It is a move away from the historical denial of the existence of racism in Canadian society,

and a move toward a recognition that the doc-trine of 'neutrality' and 'objectivity' in judicial decision-making is a myth. The Supreme Court of Canada's recognition that the 'reasonable per-son' in Canadian society is not unaware of the social reality of racism is also a significant advance for the Critical Race Theory agenda. . . .

In spite of the differences of opinion expressed by the Supreme Court justices in the *R.D.S.* case about the issue of reference to social context in the judicial decision-making process, this case can be seen as making a substantial contribution to the expansion of the 'reasonable person' stan-dard. It of course remains to be seen how the decision will affect future pronouncements on race issues before the courts, but one thing is cer-tain, *R.D.S.* v. *The Queen* will be a useful prece-dent in the Critical Race litigator's arsenal.

* * *

As difficult as Critical Race Litigation and activ-ism may sometimes be, an advocate has a duty and a responsibility under rules of professional ethics to 'ask every question, raise every issue, and advance every argument, however distasteful [or difficult], that the advocate reasonably thinks will help the client's case; and endeavour to obtain for the client the benefit of any and every right, remedy, and defence that is authorized by law' (NSBS 1990: Rule 10). A failure to take a Critical Race position in a case that warrants it should be viewed as a breach of this professional obligation, especially in light of the fact that such failures help to perpetuate the racial inequities that are pervasive in Canadian society and embedded in the Canadian legal system.

Summary
While the prevailing myth in the United States is that Americans have overcome their racist past and are no longer racist, the prevailing myth in Canada is that we are a country without a history of racism. Both myths have led to a failure by the

courts to confront the issue of 'race' and the role it plays in law. In Canada today, discrimination and racism exist in both subtle and sophisticated forms. Discrimination exists usually in systemic form and is concealed in systems, practices, policies, and laws that appear 'neutral' and 'objective' on their face but have serious detrimental and adverse effects on people of colour.

Historically, Canada did not have the constitutional or statutory mechanisms in place to enable black Canadians and other people of colour to litigate to seek civil rights and freedom from racial oppression. Human rights legislation is problematic because the vast majority of race-based human rights complaints never reach the board of inquiry stage and there is no recourse to the civil courts for redress. Although the adoption of the Charter provides a basis in theory for challenging racist legislation or practices by governments, the Charter has to date not been effectively used to combat racism. . . .

The case of *R.D.S.* v. *The Queen* can be seen as making a substantial contribution to challenges to racism in Canada. Through Critical Race Litigation, the appellants persuaded the Supreme Court of Canada to expand the 'reasonable person' standard. The Court held that the 'reasonable person' is aware of the social context of a case, such as the prevalence of racism in Canadian society and in a particular community. . . .

Notes

1. *R.D.S.* v. *The Queen*, Appellant's Factum, Supreme Court of Canada, File No. 25063, at 26 (available from the author).
2. The Critical Race Theory method of narrative has been criticized. See, for example, Rosen (1996), in which he denounces the narrative or storytelling strategy employed by Johnny Cochran in the defence of O.J. Simpson. Cochran, he says, through storytelling, set out to 'create a narrative that transformed O.J. from coddled celebrity into the civil rights martyr of a racist police force. . . . He put Mark Fuhrman's racial epithets on trial, suggesting . . . that, because reality is owed to language, hate speech can be compared to physical assault.' Rosen categorizes narrative or storytelling methodology as

   nothing more than a proposal for broadening the narratives available to judges and juries, to help them get (quite literally) to the bottom of things. . . . Instead of being limited by a legal system that 'disaggregates and atomizes' communal grievances into individual disputes, Critical Race theorists recommend that litigants think about group grievances rather than their own, and tell 'the broad story of dashed hopes and centuries-long mistreatment that afflicts an entire people and forms the historical and cultural background of your complaint'. (1996: 2)

3. *R.D.S* v. *The Queen*, Appellant's Factum, SCC, File No. 25063, 10 March 1997, at 14.
4. Ibid.
5. Ibid., at 35–6.

Chapter 22

Decolonizing Anti-racism

Bonita Lawrence and Enakshi Dua[1]

Introduction

In continuous conversations over the years, we have discussed our discomfort with the manner in which Aboriginal people and perspectives are excluded within anti-racism. We have been surprised and disturbed by how rarely this exclusion has been taken up, or even noticed. Due to this exclusion, Aboriginal people cannot see themselves in anti-racism contexts, and Aboriginal activism against settler domination takes place without people of colour as allies. Though anti-racist theorists may ignore the contemporary Indigenous presence, Canada certainly does not. Police surveillance is a reality that all racialized people face, and yet Native communities are at risk of direct military intervention in ways that no other racialized community in Canada faces.[2] This article represents a call to post-colonial and anti-racism theorists to begin to take Indigenous decolonization seriously. Because we are situated differently in relation to decolonization and anti-racism, we are beginning with our own locations.

Bonita: I first encountered anti-racism and post-colonial theory when I began attending university, in my early thirties. I looked to anti-racism, as I earlier did to feminism, to 'explain' the circumstances my family has struggled with, but ultimately both sets of perspectives have simply been part and parcel of an education system that has addressed male and white privilege, while ignoring my family's Indigeneity.

To say this is to acknowledge that several factors—notably immigration and urbanization—have already been at work in delineating relations between Aboriginal people and people of colour. In the 1960s, when Canada was overwhelmingly white, my mother, who was Mi'kmaq and Acadian, clearly felt marginalized and inferiorized by Anglo-Canadians and ostracized by many French Canadians. In the city, she welcomed the new presence of people of colour as potential friends and allies, and saw a common struggle for survival and adaptation to the dominant culture. There were not many of us, Aboriginal people or people of colour, brown islands in a white sea.

Fast forward to 2005. For many Native people in eastern Canada, the urbanization and assimilation pressures of the 1950s and 1960s meant that our parents married white people. This interval also featured large-scale immigration of people of colour, so that today urban Native people form tiny, paler islands floating in a darker 'multicultural' sea. Over the past 15 years or so since the Oka Crisis, in common with many urban mixed-bloods, I have struggled to learn about my own Indigeneity. In this context, my light skin separates me from the people of colour that my mother would have viewed as allies. There is nothing new about racial ambiguity among mixed-bloods of any background. For Aboriginal peoples in Canada, though, something else is at work: the generations of policies specifically formulated with the goal of destroying our communities and fragmenting our identities.

For years, I have witnessed the result of these policies, as my family, friends, and many of my Aboriginal students have struggled with our lack of knowledge about our heritage due to our parents' silence, the fact that our languages were beaten out of our grandparents' generation, that we may have been cut off from access to the land for generations, that we may know little of our own ceremonies, and that our Indigeneity is ultimately validated or denied by government cards that certify 'Indian' status. Neither these policies nor their repercussions are topics for discussion at anti-racism conferences. It is difficult not to conclude that there is something deeply wrong with the manner in which, in our own lands, anti-racism does not begin with, and reflect, the totality of Native peoples' lived experience— that is, with the genocide that established and maintains all of the settler states within the Americas.

Yet, even to begin to address decolonizing anti-racism, I must first acknowledge that I am one of a handful of Aboriginal scholars within academia; as such, I am routinely asked to 'speak for' and represent Indigeneity to outsiders in a manner that is inherently problematic. Because of this, I must always begin by referencing the traditional elders and community people—and other Indigenous scholars—for whom Indigenous (rather than academic) knowledge is most central. They would begin by asking: What does post-coloniality and anti-racism theory have to do with us? An academic article addressing these issues is therefore aimed primarily at anti-racism scholars and activists, who for the most part are not Indigenous. More problematically, it would use the rhythms and assumptions of academic discourse, without cultural resonance or reference to Mi'kmaw or other specific Indigenous frameworks. As such, my fear is that this article will continue to homogenize Indigenous peoples in all their diversity into a singular and meaningless entity known as 'First Nations people' to outsiders, in exactly the manner that is currently common within anti-racism discourse. The tensions between who I can claim to speak for, how I speak in arguing academic theory, and to whom I am speaking in this article thus remain ongoing.

Ena: I came to Canada as a 16 year old. I was born in India, and en route to Canada we resided in the United States. In all three contexts, I came across references to Aboriginal peoples. In India, people wondered of another place where people were also called Indian. Growing up in the United States and Canada, I was bombarded with colonialist history. From school curriculum to television programs to vacation spots, a colonialist history of conquer and erasure was continually re-enacted. I resided in a city in which the main streets were named after Aboriginal leaders and communities. As the houses that we resided in exited onto these streets, such naming of space was important as it inserted us as settlers into the geography of colonialism. Much of this made me uncomfortable. I was given a similar history of India and other Indians, and I knew that this history was not accurate. I was vaguely conscious that the same processes were shaping the lives of Aboriginal people and people of colour. I saw myself as allied with Aboriginal people. However, what I did not see was how I might be part of the ongoing project of colonization. I did not place myself in the processes that produced such representations, or relations.

As a young woman, my experiences with racism, sexism, and imperialism led me to become engaged in a project of developing anti-racist feminism. This site, I hoped, would enable us to look at the ways in which different kinds of oppressions intersected. Looking back, I realize that we failed to integrate ongoing colonization into this emerging body of knowledge. For example, in a collaborative book project I edited, anti-racist feminist scholars explored the intersections of 'race' and gender. At the time, I felt that we were doing a good task of centering Aboriginal issues. The anthology first examined the ways in which Aboriginal women had been racialized and gendered historically. Another article investigated questions of Aboriginal self-government. I now think we failed to make Aboriginality foundational. We did not ask those who wrote on work, trade unions, immigration, citizenship, family, etc., to examine how these institutions and relationships were influenced by Canada's ongoing colonization of Aboriginal peoples. More recently, I turned to cultural theory, critical race theory, and post-colonial studies, but I fear that these approaches, like my earlier work, also fail to centre the ongoing colonization of Aboriginal peoples.

My approach in this article, as someone committed to anti-racist feminist struggles, is to examine my complicity in the ongoing project of colonization. My complicity is complex. First, as an inhabitant of Canada, I live in and own land that has been appropriated from Aboriginal peoples. As a citizen of Canada, I have rights and privileges that are denied to Aboriginal peoples collectively, and that are deployed to deny Aboriginal

rights to self-government. Second, as someone involved in anti-racist and progressive struggles, I wonder about the ways in which the bodies of knowledge that I have worked to build have been framed so as to contribute to the active colonization of Aboriginal peoples. I need to read, write, teach, and be politically active differently.

Despite our different positioning, experiences, and concerns, we have reached a common conclusion: that anti-racism is premised on an ongoing colonial project. As a result, we fear that rather than challenging the ongoing colonization of Aboriginal peoples, Canadian anti-racism is furthering contemporary colonial agendas. We will argue that anti-racism theory participates in colonial agendas in two ways. First, it ignores the ongoing colonization of Aboriginal peoples in the Americas; second, it fails to integrate an understanding of Canada as a colonialist state into anti-racist frameworks. In this article, we seek ways to decolonize anti-racism theory. Our goal in writing this is to begin to lay the groundwork that might make dialogue possible among anti-racist and Aboriginal activists.

What Does It Mean to Look at Canada as Colonized Space? What Does It Mean to Ignore Indigenous Sovereignty?

Anti-racist and post-colonial theorists have not integrated an understanding of Canada as a colonialist state into their frameworks. It is therefore important to begin by elaborating on the means through which colonization in Canada as a settler society has been implemented and is being maintained. We also need to reference how Indigenous peoples resist this ongoing colonization.

Settler states in the Americas are founded on, and maintained through, policies of direct extermination, displacement, or assimilation. The premise of each is to ensure that Indigenous peoples ultimately disappear *as* peoples, so that settler nations can seamlessly take their place. Because of the intensity of genocidal[3] policies that Indigenous people have faced and continue to face, a common error on the part of anti-racist and post-colonial theorists is to assume that genocide has been virtually complete, that Indigenous peoples, however unfortunately, have been 'consigned to the dustbin of history' (Spivak 1994) and no longer need to be taken into account. Yet such assumptions are scarcely different from settler nation-building myths, whereby 'Indians' become unreal figures, rooted in the nation's prehistory, who died out and no longer need to be taken seriously.

Being consigned to a mythic past or 'the dustbin of history' means being precluded from changing and existing as real people in the present. It also means being denied even the possibility of regenerating nationhood. If Indigenous nationhood is seen as something of the past, the present becomes a site in which Indigenous peoples are reduced to small groups of racially and culturally defined and marginalized individuals drowning in a sea of settlers—who needn't be taken seriously. At the heart of Indigenous peoples' realities, then, is nationhood. Their very survival depends on it.

To speak of Indigenous nationhood is to speak of land as Indigenous, in ways that are neither rhetorical nor metaphorical. Neither Canada nor the United States—or the settler states of 'Latin' America for that matter—which claim sovereignty over the territory they occupy, have a legitimate basis to anchor their absorption of huge portions of that territory (Churchill 1992: 411). Indeed, nationhood for Indigenous peoples is acknowledged in current international law as the right of inherent sovereignty: the notion that peoples known to have occupied specific territories, who have a common language, a means of subsistence, forms of governance, legal systems, and means of deciding citizenship, are nations—

particularly if they have entered into treaties. As Churchill notes (Ibid.: 19–20), only nations enter into treaty relationships.

In contrast, the legal system in Canada, a settler state, is premised on the need to pre-empt Indigenous sovereignty. The legal system does this through the assertion of a 'rule of law' that is daily deployed to deny possibilities of sovereignty and to criminalize Indigenous dissent. Because this rule of law violates the premises on which treaties were signed with Aboriginal people, the Supreme Court occasionally is forced to acknowledge the larger framework of treaty agreements that predate assertions of Canadian sovereignty.[4] Historically, however, court decisions have been a chief instrument of the disenfranchisement of Aboriginal peoples. Recently, they have alternated between enlarging the scope of the potential for a renewed relationship between the Crown and Aboriginal peoples and drastically curtailing those possibilities.

It is important to understand how Native rights to land were legally nullified in Canada, and when this changed. In 1888, the ruling in the *St Catharines Milling and Lumber*[5] court decision was that Aboriginal peoples' rights to the land were so vague and general that they were incapable of remedy. This decision codified in law that Aboriginal peoples were on a path to extinction; the only way for 'Indians' to acquire legal rights was to assimilate into Canadian society. . . .

The immediate problem facing Aboriginal peoples in Canada is that the status quo of a colonial order continues to target them for legal and cultural extinction, while undermining the viability of communities through theft of their remaining lands and resources.[6] Aboriginal people need to re-establish control over their own communities: have their land returned to them, making communities viable and rebuilding nationhood, with a legal framework that brings Aboriginal peoples' existing and returned lands under their own authority. This requires a total rethinking of Canada; sovereignty and self-determination must be genuinely on the table as fundamental to Indigenous survival, not as lip service. If they are truly progressive, anti-racist theorists must begin to think about their personal stake in this struggle, and about where they are going to situate themselves.

We also need a better understanding of the ways in which Aboriginal peoples resist ongoing colonization. At the core of Indigenous survival and resistance is reclaiming a relationship to land. Yet, within anti-racism theory and practice, the question of land as contested space is seldom taken up. From Indigenous perspectives, it speaks to a reluctance on the part of non-Natives of any background to acknowledge that there is more to this land than being settlers on it, that there are deeper, older stories and knowledge connected to the landscapes around us. To acknowledge that we all share the same land base and yet to question the differential terms on which it is occupied is to become aware of the colonial project that is taking place around us.

Indigenous stories of the land are spiritual and political, and have tremendous longevity. For example, Mi'kmaki, the 'land of friendship', which encompasses what is now called the Atlantic provinces, was viewed by the Mi'kmaq as a sacred order, flowing from a creation story that moves seamlessly from mythical time into historical time around the end of the last Ice Age (Henderson 1997: 16). Mi'kmaki is 'owned' in a formal sense only by unborn children in the invisible sacred realm (Ibid.: 32); however, its seven regions are also traditionally governed by a Grand Council, or Mawiomi, and it has historically been part of the Wabanaki Confederacy, a larger geopolitical unit that extends into what is now the northeastern United States. At another level, to resist invasion the Mawiomi negotiated a Concordat in 1610 that consolidated Mi'kmaki formally as a Catholic republic under Rome (Ibid.: 87). All of these spiritual and geopolitical relations, past and present, connect Mi'kmaq people with Mi'kmaki.

These lands carry more than the imprint of an ancient and contemporary Indigenous presence. Focusing on the land reveals important gaps between Western and traditional knowledges that shape how we see these relationships to land. For example, land for many Native peoples is profoundly connected to language. Jeannette Armstrong (1998: 175–6, 178) explains this from her own people's perspective:

As I understand it from my Okanagan ancestors, language was given to us by the land we live within. . . . The Okanagan language, called N'silxchn by us, is one of the Salishan languages. My ancestors say that N'silxchn is formed out of an older language, some words of which are still retained in our origin stories. I have heard elders explain that the language changed as we moved and spread over the land through time. My own father told me that it was the land that changed the language because there is a special knowledge in each different place. All my elders say that it is land that holds all knowledge of life and earth and is a constant teacher. It is said in Okanagan that the land constantly speaks. It is constantly communicating. Not to learn its language is to die. We survived and thrived by listening intently to its teachings—to its language—and then inventing human words to retell its stories to our succeeding generations. . . . In this sense, all Indigenous peoples' languages are generated by a precise geography and arise from it.

This linking of land and language, of memory and history, has implications for Indigenous peoples and settlers. Part of the profound strength that has helped Indigenous peoples to maintain their identity despite five centuries of colonization derives from the fact that they have retained knowledge of who they are due to their long-standing relationship to the land. Settlers find a remapping of traditional territories to earlier names, boundaries, and stories by Indigenous peoples to be profoundly unsettling. It reveals the Canadian nation as still foreign to this land base. Even after five centuries of colonization, the names the colonizer has bestowed on the land remain irrelevant to its history. It calls into question notions of settler belonging-as-whites *or* as peoples of colour, based simply on Canadian citizenship.

Cherokee theologian Jace Weaver (1998: 20–1) has asserted that until post-colonial theory takes seriously both the collective character of Native traditional life and the importance of specific lands to the cultural identities of different Native peoples, it will have little meaning for Native peoples. In the next section, we will begin to examine how post-colonial and anti-racist theory fails to address Aboriginal people's presence and concerns.

How Has Anti-racism/Post-colonial Theory Been Constructed on a Colonizing Framework?

Our discussion will refer to a vast body of literature: critical race theory, post-colonial theory, and theories of nationalism. This diverse literature has many different arguments and has been subject to many critiques (see, for example, Ahmad 1992; Chambers and Curti 1996; Frankenberg and Mani 1992; McClintock 1997; Parry 1987). In our reading, this literature shares crucial ontological underpinnings. All of these writers fail to make Indigenous presence and ongoing colonization, particularly in the Americas, foundational to their analyses of race and racism. As a result, we fear that there is a body of work that is implicitly constructed on a colonizing framework and participates in the ongoing colonization of Aboriginal peoples.

International critical race and post-colonial theory has failed to make Indigenous presence

and colonization foundational in five areas. First, Native existence is erased through theories of race and racism that exclude them. Second, theories of Atlantic diasporic identities fail to take into account that these identities are situated in multiple projects of colonization and settlement on Indigenous lands. Third, histories of colonization are erased through writings on the history of slavery. Fourth, decolonization politics are equated with anti-racist politics. Finally, theories of nationalism contribute to the ongoing delegitimization of Indigenous nationhood. Though often theorizing the British context, these writings have been important for shaping anti-racist/post-colonial thinking throughout the West.

To illustrate the ways in which critical race theorists erase the presence of Aboriginal peoples, we have chosen Stuart Hall's essay, 'The West and the Rest' (1996a). Hall introduces a post-colonial approach to 'race', racialized identities, and racism. For him, the emergence of 'race' and racism is located in the historical appearance of the constructs of 'the West and the Rest'. Thus, the inhabitants of the Americas are central to the construction of notions of the West. He links the colonization of the Americas with Orientalism. Moreover . . . in elaborating a theory of 'race', he makes the connection between colonialism and knowledge production, between the historical construction of the idea of 'race' and the present articulations of 'race'.

Despite these strengths, Hall fails to examine the ways in which colonialism continues for Aboriginal peoples in settler nations. Indeed, he posits colonialism as having existed in the past, only to be restructured as 'post-colonial'. For example, in commenting on the last of five main phases of expansion, Hall defines 'the present, when much of the world is economically dependent on the West, even when formally independent and decolonized' (Ibid.: 191). No mention is made of parts of the world that have not been decolonized. As a result, Aboriginal peoples are relegated to a mythic past, whereby their contemporary existence and struggles for decolonization are erased from view and thus denied legitimacy. Moreover, he fails to explore how the ongoing colonization of Aboriginal peoples shapes contemporary modes of 'race' and racism in settler nations (including those in the Caribbean, where people of African and Asian descent have established political authority). Rather, the relationship between colonialism and the articulation of 'race' is limited to the ways in which the colonial past is re-articulated in the present. What are the consequences of such omissions for Aboriginal peoples in settler societies and for their struggles for nationhood? How do such omissions distort our understanding of the processes of 'race' and racism? . . .

Finally, theories of nationalism render Indigenous nationhood unviable, which has serious ramifications in a colonial context. The post-colonial emphasis on deconstructing nationhood furthers Indigenous denationalization for those targeted for centuries for physical and cultural extermination, and facing added fragmentation through identity legislation (Grewal and Kaplan 1994; Jackson and Penrose 1993; Anderson 1991; Hall 1994). Such deconstructions can ignore settler state colonization (Anderson 1991). Or they theorize, from the outside, about how communities 'become' Indigenous solely because of interactions with colonialist nationalist projects (Anderson 2003; Warren 1992). If the epistemologies and ontologies of Indigenous nations do not count, Indigeneity is evaluated through social construction theory. More problematic still are works that denigrate nationalism as representing only technologies of violence (McClintock 1997), or a reification of categories that can degenerate into fundamentalism and 'ethnic cleansing' (Penrose 1993; Nixon 1997). There is also the simple dismissal of 'ethnic absolutism' as an increasingly untenable cultural strategy (Hall 1996b: 250, quoted in Weaver 1998: 14), which calls into question the

very notion of national identity. None of these perspectives enable Indigenous peoples in the Americas to envision a future separate from continuous engulfment by the most powerful colonial order in the world, or their continuous erasure, starting with Columbus, from global international political relations (Venne 1998). In this respect, post-colonial deconstructions of nationalism appear to be premised on what Cree scholar Lorraine Le Camp calls 'terranullism', the erasure of an ongoing post-contact Indigenous presence (Le Camp 1998). Perhaps it is not surprising that from these perspectives, decolonization, nationhood, and sovereignty begin to appear ridiculous and irrelevant, impossible and futile (Cook-Lynn 1996: 88).

For Aboriginal peoples, post-colonial deconstructions of nationalism simply do not manifest any understanding of how Aboriginal peoples actualize nationhood and sovereignty given the colonial framework enveloping them. According to Oneida scholar Lina Sunseri (2005), Indigenous nationhood existed before Columbus; when contemporary Indigenous theorists on nationalism explicate traditional Indigenous concepts of nationhood, they redefine the concept of a nation by moving beyond a linkage of a nation to the state and/or modernity and other European-based ideas and values.

In summary, critical race and post-colonial theory systematically erases Aboriginal peoples and decolonization from the construction of knowledge about 'race', racism, racial subjectivities, and anti-racism. This has profound consequences. It distorts our understanding of 'race' and racism, and of the relationship of people of colour to multiple projects of settlement. It posits people of colour as innocent[7] in the colonization of Aboriginal peoples. Left unaddressed is the way in which people of colour in settler formations are settlers on stolen lands. It ignores the complex relationships people of colour have with settler projects. Although marginalized, at particular historical moments they may have been complicit with ongoing land theft and colonial domination of Aboriginal peoples. It distorts our writing of history; indeed, the exclusion of Aboriginal people from the project of anti-racism erases them from history.

Beyond Innocence: The Failure of Canadian Anti-racism to Make Colonialism Foundational

The refusal of international scholarship to address settler state colonization and Indigenous decolonization is problematic, especially since the same epistemological and ontological frameworks are reproduced in Canadian anti-racism theory, which is written on land that is still colonized. The failure of Canadian anti-racism to make colonization foundational has meant that Aboriginal peoples' histories, resistance, and current realities have been segregated from anti-racism. In this section, we will explore how this segregation is reflected in theory, as well as its implications for how we understand Canada and Canadian history. Second, we shall complicate our understandings of how people of colour are located in the settler society.

Anti-racism's segregation from the knowledge and histories of resistance of Aboriginal peoples is manifested in various ways. Aboriginal organizations are not invited to participate in organizing and shaping the focus of most anti-racism conferences. Indigeneity thus receives only token recognition. Their ceremonies feature as performances to open the conference (regardless of the meaning of these ceremonies for the elders involved). Usually, one Aboriginal person is invited as a plenary speaker. A few scattered sessions, attended primarily by the families and friends of Aboriginal presenters, may address Indigeneity, but they are not seen as intrinsic to understanding race and racism. At these sessions, Aboriginal presenters may be challenged to reshape their presentations to fit into a 'critical race' framework; failure to do

so means that the work is seen as 'simplistic'. In our classes on anti-racism, token attention—normally one week—is given to Aboriginal peoples, and rarely is the exploration of racism placed in a context of ongoing colonization. In anti-racist political groups, Aboriginal issues are placed within a liberal pluralist framework, where they are marginalized and juxtaposed to other, often contradictory struggles, such as that of Quebec sovereignty.

These practices reflect the theoretical segregation that underpins them. Within anti-racism scholarship, the widespread practice of ignoring Indigenous presence at every stage of Canadian history fundamentally flaws our understandings of Canada and Canadian history. In this view, Canadian history is replete with white settler racism against immigrants of colour. If Aboriginal peoples are mentioned at all, it is at the point of contact, and then only as generic 'First Nations', a term bearing exactly the degree of specificity and historical meaning as 'people of colour'. The 'vanishing Indian' is as alive in anti-racism scholarship as it is in mainstream Canada.

A classic example is James Walker's 1997 text, 'Race', Rights and the Law in the Supreme Court of Canada, which considers four historic Supreme Court rulings that were instrumental in maintaining racial discrimination and anti-Semitism in Canada. Disturbingly, legal decisions affecting Native peoples are ignored in this text. By comparison, Constance Backhouse's 1999 work, Colour-coded: A Legal History of Racism in Canada, 1900–1950, goes a long way toward filling this gap. In this text, Backhouse addresses crucial cases such as the legal prohibition of Aboriginal dance; Re: Eskimos, which ruled on whether 'Eskimos' were legally 'Indians'; as well as other instances of colonial and racial discrimination in the law against Aboriginal peoples and people of colour. Backhouse's approach reveals a more in-depth view of the embeddedness of racism in a colonial regime. Unfortunately, this kind of inclusive perspective is rare.

These practices of exclusion and segregation reflect the contradictory ways in which peoples of colour are situated within the nation-state. Marginalized by a white settler nationalist project, as citizens they are nonetheless invited to take part in ongoing colonialism. The relationship of people of colour to Indigeneity is thus complex. . . .

Recently, people of colour have been implicated as citizens in colonial actions. For example, those with citizenship rights participated in constitutional reform that denied efforts on the part of Aboriginal peoples to fundamentally reshape Canada's approach to decolonization. The Charlottetown Accord proposed constitutional changes that contained important features for Aboriginal peoples: recognition of Aboriginal governments as a third order of government in Canada; a definition of self-government in relation to land, the environment, language, and culture; as well as representation in the Senate. Although the Accord was the result of years of negotiations between Aboriginal leaders and the Canadian government, the government proposed that it be ratified through a national referendum. In essence, all Canadian citizens, including people of colour, were invited to decide on whether the Canadian government should honour its commitments to Aboriginal peoples.[8] We do not know how, or even whether, people of colour voted with respect to the Accord. However, this illustrates the complexities for people of colour living in a settler society. Those with citizenship rights in Canada were in a position to make decisions on Aboriginal sovereignty, which should have been made by Aboriginal peoples. Anti-racist groups failed to note this contradiction.

Perhaps the most difficult and contentious area in which Aboriginal realities conflict with the interests of people of colour regards immigration and multiculturalism. Aboriginal theorists and activists, particularly in Canada, have largely been silent on these issues. This reflects the discomfort and ambivalence of many Aboriginal people when official policies and discourses of multiculturalism and immigration obscure Native presence and divert attention from their realities, and when communities of colour resist their marginalization in ways that render Aboriginal communities invisible. Canadian language policy is a classic example. Multiculturalism policy overrides the redressing of assaults on Indigenous languages, with funding provided first for 'official' languages and then for 'heritage' languages. Only then are the dregs divided up among the 50-odd Indigenous languages in Canada currently at risk of extinction given ongoing cultural genocide.

Ongoing settlement of Indigenous lands, whether by white people or people of colour, remains part of Canada's nation-building project and is premised on displacing Indigenous peoples. Regarding immigration, Aboriginal peoples are caught between a rock and a hard place. Either they are implicated in the anti-immigrant racism of white Canadians, or they support struggles of people of colour that fail to take seriously the reality of ongoing colonization. Often overlooked by anti-racist activists is that the *Delgamuuk'w* decision clearly set out instances in which Aboriginal title could be infringed (i.e., limited or invalidated) by continuing immigration (Persky 1998: 20). Canada's immigration goals, then, can be used to restrict Aboriginal rights. Anti-racist activists need to think through how their campaigns can pre-empt the ability of Aboriginal communities to establish title to their traditional lands. Recent tendencies to advocate for open borders make this particularly important. Borders in the Americas are European fictions, restricting Native peoples' passage and that of peoples of colour. However, to speak of opening borders without addressing Indigenous land loss and ongoing struggles to reclaim territories is to divide communities that are already marginalized from one another. The question that must be asked is how opening borders would affect Indigenous struggles aimed at reclaiming land and nationhood.

Scholarship is needed on ending segregation practices and on the complex histories of inter-actions between peoples of colour and Aboriginal peoples. How did passage of the Multiculturalism Act in 1969 connect with Canada's attempt, in the same year, to pass the White Paper to eliminate 'Indian' status and Canada's fiduciary responsibility to status Indians? To what extent did black–Mi'kmaq in-termarriage in Nova Scotia represent resistance to extermination policies against Mi'kmaw peo-ple and the marginalization of black Loyalists? How did Chinese men and Native communities interact during the building of the Canadian rail-road? Is there a connection at the policy level between the denial of West Coast Native fishing rights and the confiscation of Japanese fishing boats during the internment? In what ways did people of colour support or challenge policies used to colonize Aboriginal peoples? What were the moments of conflict and of collaboration?

With these questions, we are asking anti-racism [theorists] to examine how people of colour have contributed to the settler formation. We are not asking every anti-racism writer to become an 'Indian expert'. This is not desirable. Nor should histories of blacks, South Asians, or East Asians in Canada focus extensively on Aboriginal peoples. Yet, when speaking of histor-ies of settlement, an explicit awareness and artic-ulation of the intersection of specific settlement policies with policies controlling 'Indians' is needed. This requires recognition of ongoing col-onization as foundational. Such a clear rendition of the bigger picture naturally sacrifices any notion of the innocence of people of colour in projects of settlement and colonial relations.

Summary: Taking on Decolonization

This article has addressed the multiple ways in which post-colonial and anti-racist theory has maintained a colonial framework. We would like to suggest the following areas as topics to be taken up:

1. Aboriginal sovereignty is a reality that is on the table. Anti-racist theorists must begin to talk about how they are going to place anti-racist agendas within the context of sover-eignty and restoration of land.
2. Taking colonization seriously changes anti-racism in powerful ways. Within academia, anti-racist theorists need to begin to make ongoing colonization central to the con-struction of knowledge about race and racism. They must learn how to write, research, and teach in ways that account for Indigenous realities as foundational.
3. This article has focused on anti-racism the-ory, but the failure of anti-racist activists to make the ongoing colonization of Indigen-ous peoples foundational to their agendas is also important. Most anti-racist groups have not included Indigenous concerns; when they do, they employ a pluralist framework. There is a strong need to begin discussions between anti-racist and Aboriginal activists on how to frame claims for anti-racism in ways that do not disempower Aboriginal peoples.

The aim of this article was to facilitate dialogue between anti-racism theorists and activists and Indigenous scholars and communities. We chose to write it in one voice, rather than coming from our different perspectives (with Bonita Lawrence rooted in Indigenous perspectives, and Ena Dua in anti-racism and post-colonial theory) because we sought to go beyond a pluralistic method of presenting diverse views without attempting a synthesis. For Ena, working in a collective voice meant attempting to take on Indigenous episte-mological frameworks and values, a process that was difficult and incomplete. For Bonita, work-ing in a collective voice meant viewing Indigen-ous concerns from within anti-racism, instead of attempting to critique it from the outside. However, because our dialogue was a critique of existing trends in post-colonial and anti-racism theory, a centering of issues within Indigenous frameworks was sacrificed. As we worked within the framework of anti-racism and post-colonial theory, we continually struggled over the fact that Indigenous ontological approaches to anti-racism, and the relationship between Indigenous epistemologies and post-colonial theory, could not be addressed.

We have learned that dialogue between anti-racism theorists/activists and Indigenous scholars/communities requires talking on Indigenous terms. Aboriginal people may find little relevance in debating anti-racism and post-colonial theory, which excludes them and lacks relevance to the ongoing crises facing Aboriginal communities. They may prefer to speak to the realities of contemporary colonization and resistance. The conversation they may wish for would take place within Indigenous epistemological frameworks and values—addressing culture, traditional values, and spirituality—as central to any real sharing of concerns. For true dialogue to occur, anti-racist theorists cannot privilege or insist on the primacy of post-colonial or critical race theory as ultimate 'truths'.

A final word must be said about anti-racism *within* Native communities. Aboriginal peoples have long and bitterly resisted the racism shaping Canada's colonial project, yet colonial legislation on Native identity has profound implications in terms of racialization, and the forms that racism can take, within Native communities. This article has focused on the need to decolonize anti-racism as we now know it. Aboriginal peoples may also wish to ask how their communities would shape an anti-racism project to address the violence colonization has inflicted on Indigenous identity. The legacy of cultural genocide and legal classification by 'blood' and descent means that Aboriginal peoples must find their way through a morass of 'racial thinking' about basic issues relating to Native identity and nationhood. Their ways of doing this may move between re-traditionalization and deconstruction, between Indigenous and Western ways of addressing how Indigenous identity has been reduced to biology. Most of all, it means finding ways of working 'with a good heart'.

Wel'alieq!—Thank you.

Notes

1. This project represents an equal collaboration by both authors. The choice to put Bonita Lawrence's name first was explicitly political. Because anti-racism is named here as part of a colonial project, and the positioning of peoples of colour as innocent of colonizing relationships is challenged, both authors struggled with a sense that Bonita Lawrence would face greater criticism and marginalization from anti-racism circles if her name came first than Enakshi Dua would, as a woman of colour with a long history of anti-racism theory and activism. We decided to challenge these practices by situating the Aboriginal person first in the byline.

2. The spectre of 'Native unrest' appears to have haunted the Canadian government since the 1885 uprising, so that the military is usually on the alert whenever Native activism appears to be spreading. As Sherene Razack has noted, the Canadian government, in sending the Airborne Regiment to Somalia in 1993, was highly aware that they might not have enough military power left at home in the event that the country was faced with another Oka (Razack 2004: 147).

3. The meaning of the term 'genocide', as coined by Raphael Lemkin in 1944 during the discus-

sions leading to the United Nations Genocide Convention, was given as follows:

> Generally speaking, genocide does not necessarily mean the immediate destruction of a nation, *except when* accomplished by mass killing of all the members of a nation. It is intended rather to signify a coordinated plan of different actions aimed at destruction of the essential foundations of the life of national groups, with the aim of annihilating the groups themselves. The objective of such a plan would be disintegration of the political and social institutions, of culture, language, national feelings, religion, and the economic existence of national groups, and the destruction of personal security, liberty, health, dignity, and the lives of individuals belonging to such groups. . . . Genocide has two phases: one, destruction of the national pattern of the oppressed group; the other, the imposition of the national pattern of the oppressor.' (Lemkin 1944, quoted in Churchill 1994: 12–13)

4. In the 1999 *Marshall* decision, for example, concerning the rights of Mi'kmaw people in the Maritimes to fish, the courts upheld the integrity of eighteenth-century treaties between Britain and the Mi'kmaw nation (Coates 2000: 7) as superseding the authority that Canada had vested in institutions such as the Department of Fisheries and Oceans.

5. The *St Catharines Milling and Lumber* case involved a dispute between Canada and the province of Ontario over timber revenues. Canada, in its defence, invoked the federal government's relationship to Aboriginal peoples; however, the decision, in Ontario's favour, defined Aboriginal rights virtually out of existence, stating that Indigenous people merely had a right to use their land, and that legally

this right was no more than a 'burden' on absolute Crown title, like a lien that must be discharged before land can be legally acquired. For over a century after this case, every Native litigator was forced to argue against this ruling, drastically limiting the possibilities for asserting Indigenous peoples' rights to their territories.

6. The combined acreage of all existing Indian reserves in Canada is less than one half the amount in the Navajo reservation in Arizona (St Germain 2001).

7. Sherene Razack (2004: 10, 14) states that a critical way in which power relations can be ignored is when individuals assume that they can stand outside hierarchical social relations, and therefore are innocent of complicity in structures of domination. Individuals are often involved in a 'race to innocence', in which they emphasize only their own subordination and disregard how they may simultaneously be complicit in other systems of domination. When we disregard how systems of oppression interlock, it is relatively easy to focus on our own oppression and disregard how we are privileged over others.

8. The Accord was subject to intense debate, particularly the sections on Aboriginal self-government. These sections were questioned first by Aboriginal women's organizations and then by national feminist groups, as they were seen to potentially prevent gender rights within Aboriginal communities because the Accord might allow Aboriginal governments to opt out of the Charter of Rights and Freedoms. Since the Charter was seen as a protector of Aboriginal women's rights, granting government powers to Aboriginal communities could potentially threaten Aboriginal women (NWAC n.d.: 2–7). It was argued that self-government in the Accord was presented as a new right, rather than as a recognition and affirmation of an existing right, and therefore should be challenged. The platform of the national feminist organization, the National Action Committee,

therefore stated that the 'Charlottetown Accord is a bad deal for Aboriginal women' (NAC n.d.). Notably, NAC failed to address the significance of the Accord with respect to Aboriginal decolonization. Rather, gender rights were seen as paramount, even in relation to Aboriginal self-government. In 1992, Canadians voted against the Accord. Nationally, 54 per cent of the votes cast opposed the Accord.

Chapter 23

Speaking Race: Silence, Salience, and the Politics of Anti-racist Scholarship

George J. Sefa Dei

The Salience of Race

This chapter outlines the relationship between race as an illusory Eurocentric scientific concept and race as a function of, and for, inequity and oppression in the Canadian and international contexts. I examine the socio-political underpinnings of the ways in which we speak and do not speak about race, both currently and historically. The idea of the scientific racial category is investigated with an eye for how such definitive scholarship conflates the social and the scientific. Critical anti-racist discourse is posited as a framework that works with the salience of race and that offers an intellectual basis for understanding, researching, and developing positive action-oriented solutions to oppression. I argue that silence around race is far from neutral and that the anti-racist discourse, despite those who blame it for bringing race to the table, is a necessary strategic perspective for addressing that which by all means already exists.

In writing a chapter on the sociological concept of race, I feel it is important to state from the outset where I am coming from and why an anti-racist lens offers a more fruitful entry point for me to engage this discussion. In fact, we cannot honestly discuss the sociological concept of race as a lived reality without addressing the denial and silences around race as a valid concept of analysis. An anti-racist lens requires that we not

only speak of the salience and centrality of race but that we also point to some of the subtle ways that even progressive scholarship can silence race through supposedly acknowledging racism (and not race) as the problem. Omi and Winant (1993: 5) once opined that race is 'a fundamental principle of social organization and identity formation. . . . Our society is so thoroughly racialized that to be without a racial identity is to be in danger of having no identity at all. To be raceless is akin to being genderless.' In a later work, the same authors also argued that race is, in fact, present in every individual social relationship and institution. We must critically evaluate our perceptions and understandings of our personal and collective lived experiences to see how we are constantly compelled to think racially and to use racial codes, categories, meaning systems, and signifiers (Omi and Winant 1994).

In reflecting on these ideas, it is puzzling that denials and silences around race persist. Given the ways we have been socialized to think and act, it is neither possible nor desirable to remain 'colour-blind'. Unfortunately, and understandably, there is a discomfort in speaking race, but this must not be confused with the urgency of addressing racial problems. I say this because of the ways in which the analytical validity, or lack thereof, of the race concept continues to be privileged in our understanding of race and racism. In my anti-racist scholarship, one of the intellectual frustrations I encounter stems from attempts by well-meaning progressive scholars to argue that the notion/idea of race is 'conceptually bankrupt'. This is personally frustrating, largely because anti-racism has some particular non-negotiable principles. One such principle is the salience or centrality of race in the axis of difference for understanding social oppressions. In the analysis of asymmetrical power relations, the utility of social categories in understanding social oppressions (e.g., race, gender, class, sexuality, etc.) is critical.

The concept of race has always been a part of modern human history, although our understandings of it have shifted over the years. From some of the early writings of Banton (1977a; 1977b), for example, we learn how social Darwinism conceived of original races as pure and biologically determined. In fact, the sociologist Ludwig Gumplowicz (1838–1909) argued that societies were socially constructed dialogues between inferior and superior races. In his many writings, Gumplowicz also advanced notions of ethnocentrism in which he argued that all peoples seek dominance—a sort of eat or be eaten philosophy—which lends itself to a notion that is still with us: 'everyone is racist if given the chance, and it's all just a matter of who is on top' (see Gumplowicz 1875; 1881; 1883, cited in Banton 1977a). In later scientific scholarship on race, physical as well as social anthropological approaches attempted to find physical explanations and justifications for racial differentiation and thus inequality. These approaches used phenotypical variation such as head, nose, and body size/shape as measurements of racial differences among groups. Racial antagonism was often understood as innate in these frameworks (Banton 1967; 1977a; 1977b), and, in fact, modern science must be understood as having shaped modern understandings of race.

In this chapter, I conceptualize race as a social relational category defined by socially selected physical and cultural characteristics (see also Li 1990). I do not think that the discomfort of speaking race is merely due to the fact that race lacks analytical significance or conceptual clarity as a 'real' attribute of human beings. After all, race is already on the table, and our discomfort in acknowledging it does not make it go away. Unfortunately, the significance of race is repeatedly denied and masked by other forms of difference. I find it hard to believe that one can take a stand that denies race and simultaneously can challenge racism effectively. Denying race is both theoretically and politically suspect. This stance merely privileges a form of Western scientific knowledge to the exclusion of other epistemic realities. How, for instance, does science account for the power of an illusion? Do we simply dismiss race because it is an illusion? Within this dominant perspective, action-oriented questions become muddled. Where, for example, does one place the call for keeping race-based statistics to understand institutional racism (see Dei and Kempf 2005)? How do we call for representation of diverse faculty in our schools, colleges, and universities? Are white identities and whiteness not both racial and racialized categories? How do we render visible the racialized relationships that we often take for granted (see also Duncan 2002; 2005)? In the face of black and Aboriginal youth disengagement from school, racist profiling of black and Asian bodies, and the dominant propensity to encode black and racial minority bodies with criminality, how far can a critic go in transformative praxis with an unending zeal to complicate racial identities? For far too long, liberal ideologies have rendered the colour line, as well as race, invisible. Any critical anti-racist writing must challenge these silences.

The intellectual gymnastics around the race concept have taken many forms. Even in early, so-called progressive scholarship, we can point to works by Cox (1948; 1976), Miles (1989; 1993), Miles and Torres (1996), Solomos (1986), and Solomos and Back (1995) that have attempted to reduce or subsume race under class. I contend that it is dangerous to subsume race under class, especially in anti-racist work (Dei 1996; see also Gabriel and Ben-Tovim 1978; 1979). If we do not speak of race as the central entry point to anti-racist practice, we cannot address the problem of racism. It is a delusion to think otherwise. While I share the desire to bring a historical–materialist lens to understanding anti-racist work, we must be careful not to simply locate race and racism in material conditions/existence. Race and class are inextricably linked, perhaps more so today than ever before, but the functions of a phenomenon do not adequately explain its origins. No doubt, class may be a more relevant formal analytical category than race, but to argue that class is the most important perspective for analyzing social oppression negates the utility of race as a social organizing principle. In other words, although linked, racism does not always substitute for race and vice versa. Scholarly attempts to offer a class/materialist-based analysis of race run the risk of failing to engage with the non-material dimensions of social existence, as captured through the lens of Indigenous knowings or knowledges such as equity/anti-racist work as flowing from spirituality. It is legitimate to query the limitations of a strictly class-based, historical–materialist analysis of racism. For example, is there a form of subtle racism inherent in class-based analysis? What is being denied and why? How do we account for the intellectual agency of raced subjects who resist the amputation of race as a significant part of their identity, one that makes them whole alongside other identities? Is there not intellectual purpose in working with the power of illusion?

In this vein, it is highly problematic for scholars to place race in commas, either figuratively or literally. Similar arguments can be advanced in support for other social categories of identification (e.g., gender, sexuality, and class). Anti-racism is a political engagement and not merely an intellectual/discursive undertaking. The issue is not merely deciding whether or not a concept

has an analytical status or validity. For example, how do we understand the process of racialization in the absence of the race concept? How is race situated and refracted in our understanding of the historical processes of racialization? Racialization also works with other categories such as class, gender, and sexuality. The power of dominant consciousness is so deeply rooted that it is not simply the product of material conditions or forces.

The denial of race and racial difference is at the heart of the failure to acknowledge racism (see also Winant 1994). The existence of races and racial differences do not themselves constitute the problem of racism in the first place. There is an important understanding of difference beyond the hegemonic and often Eurocentric understanding of difference as hierarchical. It is more than just the way(s) in which such categories are evoked or constructed. A critical reading of race brings a political, ideological, and spiritual reality to the understanding of our myriad identities. The non-recognition of identities is as problematic as the misrecognition of our identities (May 1999). Understanding race as a social construct can only go so far without negating the material consequences of evoking language. Put bluntly, there are times when we must separate the metaphor from the real. Working with the race concept does not translate a priori into an objectification and reification of the concept, particularly when most anti-racists point to the historically fluid, contested, and contextualized nature of our concepts. While race is not a fixed or static concept, it works in 'broadly predictable ways and through well-rehearsed narratives to position whites as superior to non-whites' (Howard 2004: 4). This is the underlying power of white supremacy. Furthermore, and specifically, African anti-racism offers a powerful way of knowing that black bodies experience race differently than other non-white bodies.

When we fail to acknowledge the power of white racial identity, whiteness, white supremacy, and their critical linkages, we also fail to uncover how race plays out beyond racism. For example, apartheid, the system of institutional racism in South Africa, was not based exclusively on material or economic interests. It was also based on an ideology of black inferiority and hatred. If the roles had been reversed, I do not believe it would have been tolerated for any length of time by the major European superpowers, even if the hypothetical black minority controlled the political, material, and economic forces in the interest of global capital. Unfortunately, some may want to dismiss this.

At one level, it could be argued that racism produces race(s) and not vice versa. This may be a powerful thought. However, since social practices and constructs are inextricably linked, where does this proposition lead us? Constructs themselves are constitutive of social practices. We can, similarly, argue that classism and sexism produce social classes and sexes/genders, respectively. An acknowledgement of this should not translate to abandoning the social categories of race, class, and gender. Sure, there is a connection between racism and race, but the link cannot simply be understood as unidirectional. Can there be racial designations without imbuing/encoding negative racist meanings to difference? Can there be race without the existence of racism? The answer is both yes and no. History indicates that this is what happened because of Eurocentric understandings of 'difference'. Race is about difference. Racial differences per se are not the problem. In fact, they are sources of potential opportunities. There are Indigenous communities that bring varied, positive (as in solution-oriented) meanings to difference. At the same time, the existence of perceived racial differences has also fostered differential and unequal treatment. It is precisely because of this connection (perhaps conundrum) that we cannot choose discursively to separate race and racism. We thus instead argue that, analytically and discursively, the focus must be on racism and not on race. When race is ignored, however, racism is further reproduced.

The power of naming race and privilege is an important act in decolonization projects. Similarly, the power to self-define is also a form of resistance. In order to deal with race and difference positively, we must be able to speak about race in different ways. Silence and avoidance is unproductive. We cannot separate the 'politics of difference' from the 'politics of race' because this practice merely helps dominant bodies to deny and refuse to interrogate white privilege and power. We need to be acutely aware of how anti-essentialism can serve white power and privilege, bringing them to the centre of supposedly critical political pursuits (see also Doyle-Wood 2002). In other words, the emphasis on individual and dispersed myriad identities can be paralyzing to the extent that it can deny the ways centralized dominant systems of power work to establish and sustain particular advantages. The articulation of white hegemonic power can also deny and silence the experiential realities of bodies of colour.

In making these assertions, I do not mean to suggest that we should ignore the fact that gender, ethnicity, and social class demarcate whiteness or that it is unproblematic to generalize white privilege. A critical approach to understanding the questions of power and difference from an anti-racist lens requires, however, that we speak of the salience of race, even as we recognize the intersections of race with other forms of difference. What is notable is that whiteness is often rendered invisible through a process of normalization. Johal (2005: 273) is particularly instructive when he declares that 'as much as white folks across differences of class, gender, sexuality, ethnicity, or religion may be oppressed in relation to the dominant white middle-class heterosexual male subject, they hold a pigmentary passport of privilege that allows sanctity as a result of the racial polity of whiteness'. This is a luxury bodies of colour across all our differences do not enjoy.

Race as an Experiential Reality

To better understand the sociological concept of race as a contemporary lived or experiential reality, I focus briefly on what Kempf (2006) has termed five conversations of the current race discourse. It is important to recognize that race occupies more than one space at a time. What this means is that there is no monolithic discourse within which, or from which, race can be understood. It is taken up in different historical, social, and geopolitical contexts, with each of these factors affecting discourses of race. The following 'five conversations' bring together the well-established fields of anti-racism discourse and multiculturalism, and they contextualize anti-racism and multiculturalism within historical and social contexts. What follows is a brief 'state of the union' summary of five key discourses on race.

The first conversation identified by Kempf is 'The Old Debate'. Despite overwhelming scientific proof that scientific conceptualizations of race conceal more than they reveal, the debate about the biological underpinnings of race persists through the efforts of numerous scholars and funding agencies whose research and efforts advance a social agenda wrapped in a (Eurocentric) scientific package. Inherent to the argument that there is credible evidence supporting a biological division of the human population by race is the notion of different racial intelligences. Arguments of this nature can be found in works such as Rushton (1994; 2001) and Murray and Herrnstein (1994). They demonstrate how the 'old debate' continually resurfaces as part of the lived reality of raced bodies. For example, there is a hypervisibility to peoples of African descent that is not accorded to any other community of colour (Deliovsky 2005). Almost everyone else is designated by his or her established ethnic/geographic location. This conflation of colour and racial/ethnic origins has applied only to Africans and Europeans. To a large extent, the use of a colour descriptor has fed, and has fed on, a black/white binary. It has been a source of contention even among black groups. The politics of racial/ethnic categorization has led to a black/white Manichaeism that shapes aesthetic and moral valuations and which is operative in the determination of power and privilege in North American society (Deliovsky 2005: 9). Such Manichean moral frameworks have symbolized positional tensions between racialized groups (see also Hoch 1979), and they have served as the raison d'être for the primordial conflict between light/darkness, good/bad, and goodness/evil dualisms. In such dualism, European or whiteness is mythologized as goodness and blackness is mythologized as devilish and evil (see also Deliovsky 2005: 9).

The question, then, is what to do with these racial terms and their ideological and political baggage without re-inscribing their concomitant ideological heaviness? As I have already argued, the answer lies in avoiding the reification of these terms by putting them in inverted commas or in contexts that might lead to dismissing or disregarding them. We need to find a way to come to grips with the problematic and socially constructed nature of these terms as they speak to and for lived reality.

The second conversation that is taking place in the contemporary context is about 'Multiculturalism'. As, perhaps, the dominant paradigm in minority and, increasingly, in majority world contexts, multiculturalism works with principles of symbolic equality at the expense of material and cultural equity. Taking a top-down approach, the multicultural idea works with acts of tolerance in place of acts of valuing difference. Characterized by the 'Samosas and Saris' version of understanding difference, multiculturalism fits tightly into a capitalist paradigm of rights in place of responsibilities, and it relies on myths pertaining to social mobility. It focuses on recognition of the positive contributions of different groups in society, and it problematizes issues as resulting from misunderstandings and miscommunications among segments of a population. Multiculturalism celebrates cultures and their diversity without necessarily responding to power issues of difference. Its emphasis is on rooting out intolerance, discrimination, and a lack of goodwill.

The third conversation about race is unfolding under the auspices of the 'Binary Conceptions within the Current State of the Empire'. This colonial framework has characterized all Euro-American colonial encounters; its current metaphorical articulation pits Islamophobia against Americanism. This is not simply 'good' versus 'bad', but rather 'safety' versus 'insecurity'. While Eurocentric science has taken pre-emptive strikes in defining and pathologizing non-white bodies, imperialist military strategy invades and occupies the 'other' under the not-so-hidden guise of a civilizing mission. Indeed, this is a pre-emptive strike on otherness! In this context, race is seemingly conflated with the rise of religious fundamentalism guiding policy in various contexts. Class, gender, and sexuality intersect with race as contestations arise around identity, power, and self-definition. This has implications on micro and macro levels as, globally, Euro-American colonialism moulds trade and migration, and, locally, people struggle for voice against an increasingly smaller number of dominant bodies acting as custodians of knowledge. The implications for endangered cultures are particularly grave.

In the 'local' context of Canadian consciousness, we see the emerging question of youth violence and the subsequent representation of black cultures today. Apart from the fact that the pejorative term 'black on black violence' stereotypes a whole community as violent, the identities of black and African peoples are scripted in very limited ways by institutional forces, particularly the media and police. There is a constant juxtaposing of whiteness and blackness, and it is one that achieves its full effects and intended impact when the evils/transgressions/criminality of other black bodies are served simply to sanctify the benevolence/goodness/morality and humanity of white bodies. Again, we can see some analogies in the local contexts of the lived realities of the racialized identities of so-called immigrant and other minority populations in Canada. Such identities are paired with punishment and repulsion. Consider, for instance, current discussions regarding racist profiling, testimonies of the Ontario Human Rights Commission, and how brown/Asian bodies and Muslim identities were, and continue to be, branded as 'terrorists'.

The fourth conversation about race is found within the 'Critical Anti-racism Discourse'. Anti-racism has become an action-oriented political strategy to confront the problem of race and myriad forms of racism, as well as their intersections with other forms of oppressions that reproduce and sustain white dominance, power, and privilege (Dei 2000; Dei and Kempf 2005). There is a crucial link between the 'Critical Anti-racist Discourse' and the 'Multiculturalism' and 'Binary Conceptions within the Current State of the Empire' discourses. Working with the anti-colonial framework, critical anti-racism resists the hegemony of multiculturalism and imperialism. It seeks to connect broader questions about structural racism to social oppression, domination, and the marginalization of peoples in society. It interrogates the underlying assumptions of empathy, commonality, and goodwill, and shifts the discourse to challenging and changing values, structures, and behaviours that perpetuate *systemic* racism and other forms of oppression. The entrenched inequities and power imbalance among social groups are addressed. Critical anti-racism also works with the idea of situational and contextual variations in intensities of oppressions, alongside recognition of the relative saliencies of different identities. There is the severity of issues for certain bodies. In Euro-American society, race demarcates life chances in very profound ways (see Dei 1996).

Finally, the fifth conversation of the current race discourse identified by Kempf is 'Minority Bodies React: Resistant Dialogues'. In 2005, a number of important events brought race to the forefront of mainstream media attention. Internationally, Hurricane Katrina, the uprising of minoritized French youth, and the Sydney race riots at the very least stimulated numerous conversations about race that would not otherwise have occurred. Gun violence in Toronto has also produced a highly racialized response from the popular press. These events are not to be celebrated or championed. They have, however, forced dialogue on race, and they have exposed structural and individual forms of racism in at least four dominant nations (i.e., the US, France, Canada, and Australia). It also tells those who did not know it before that people understand their oppression and that they are much closer to doing something about it than many might otherwise think. In the US, Jon Bon Jovi and Oprah Winfrey debated class and race on television, while President George W. Bush patted colleagues on the back for the swift response that left thousands dead. In France, youth took up whatever arms they could against the state—and this uprising spread to neighbouring countries as quickly as it had begun. Using the latest technology, white youth in Australia organized lynch mobs. Women were assaulted and used as racial currency in the ensuing battles between dominant and non-dominant bodies. The responses to these crises are most informative about the state of race and racism in our world. As thousands of poor black citizens remain unaccounted for in the US after the hurricane, a number matched only by the death toll, authorities continue to deny the role of race in the response to the aid effort. In France, official representatives re-enacted 50-year-old laws first implemented to quell the Algerian revolution. Colonialism has never ceded! As a response to the uprising, French authorities are deporting dozens of protestors on shaky legal ground. Indeed, rights run thin when power is threatened. In Australia, the prime minister, like many white Australians, continues to deny that Australia is a racist country.

What are the implications of these events for understanding the lived realities of raced subjects? Despite pretensions to the contrary, there persists pointed discursive and political pursuits aimed to preserve a racial hierarchy in the absence of slavery. Racial minorities continue to experience a process of historical, ideological, and symbolic signification in the white imagination alongside a subordinate positioning in contemporary social formation. This process has been referred to as racialization. It is a process that attributes a racial consciousness/awareness to even a previously unclassified racial relation and which entails the notion of biological determinism—the concept of particular human traits as biologically determined and thus as consistent both for individuals and for the group to which those individuals may belong. The most important point here is that racialization is a historical construction, one that allows for white supremacist systems of power to suppress racial minority resistance.

In looking at racialization today, we see how certain historical and contemporary processes and trajectories have allowed dominant groups to call upon culture, ethnicity, language, religion, and, of course, race and skin colour as a way of distinguishing groups for differential and unequal treatment. Closely aligned with the processes of racialization is the production of racialized subjects. As Lawson (2004) argues, we must call upon the notion of 'racialize' as a verb, that is, the act of doing something to the body based on its phenotypical features. In the broader sense, the production of racialized subjects refers to how bodies are read or scripted according to skin colour and other features. For example, when we associate black skin with dishonesty or when we associate brown skin with terrorism, we are engaged in the process of racialization. In framing the issue in terms of the 'racialized subject', we place the gaze on the people doing the 'racializing' rather than on the people being 'racialized'. The process of racializing is thus external and strategic, and it is not the responsibility of the person who is targeted. This distinction is important because of the tendency for some to argue that those who do anti-racist work actually create the problem by engaging with race. Anti-racist workers do not speak of race to create it but rather to acknowledge what already exists.

Biologically determined (and thus racist) ideas of behaviour, values, beliefs, cultural practices, etc., are grafted onto particular social relations and issues such as immigration, education, and crime. In this sense, dominant systems of racialized power construct ideas of criminality. For example, some see crime and 'gang violence' largely through (and in terms of) black and brown bodies and communities because they believe it is these bodies who have been invested with a biological propensity toward violence and crime.

As mentioned, particular bodies are now invested with the notion of terrorists—they are viewed as a group possessing certain biological traits that lead to the nurturing of suicide bombers, fanatical hatred of the West, sexist oppression, etc. The process of racialization and the making of racialized subjects are indicative of larger cultural and social forces. We need to ask, for example, why is it that Canadian families largely constitute themselves as white? What does this practice tell us about race and racism in Canadian history and contemporary politics and culture?

The Politics of Anti-racist Scholarship

Again the racialized context of everyday non-material and discursive realities, and challenges to the positivists' goals of value-free detachment and objectivity, is not merely impossible but undesirable. Research must start with personal implication in the subject of inquiry and draw connections between personal experiences and the larger social mechanisms that organize society. It must subvert dominant/taken-for-granted knowledge. For example, race is not the exclusive property and epistemic knowledge of bodies that the dominant group has marked with racial difference. Consequently, a basic principle of anti-racist research is also to subvert the idea that the dominant group is an unnamed, unmarked racial category. We work with the understanding that all groups are raced and that they are raced differently.

The racial identity of the researcher is as significant as her class, gender, and sexual identifications. Both the researcher and the research subjects have the power to influence the direction of research. This speaks to a complex power dynamic in the field, the question of how power is negotiated. Also, both the researcher and the researched bring situated knowledges to the research process. As situated knowers, we must be critical and self-reflective. For example, the location of the research may influence the data-gathering process or the site of data gathering. These of course have a bearing on the content of the information.

In discussing race as a lived reality, I have allowed myself to be informed by 'embodied knowing'. I have worked with the relationship between questions of embodiment and subjectivity as separate but related concerns. Although there is an epistemic significance of the body, 'embodiment' largely works with the understanding of the self, the inner environment, and one's aspirations, desires, and anxieties. There is a relationship between bodies and embodied selves, but it is also important to know that the racialized body may not necessarily be working with embodied knowing. 'Embodied knowing' is crucial to understanding 'the ontological nature of racism (particularly white racism) because of the danger that comes with ignoring or denying the embodied nature of racial ideologies

(Howard 2005). The 'sociology of embodiment' addresses ways we come to know, through our social and individual interactions, practices, experiences, histories, and bodies. We can speak of moral agency and how certain understandings of our bodily-ness simultaneously help produce and resist hegemonic knowledge. I allude to embodiment in order to challenge the certainties of knowing, particularly, but not exclusively, binary thinking.

What, then, to do with race? There is the 'mythology of racelessness' that has been a hallmark of Canadian historical tradition (see Backhouse 1999). Canada has cultivated a national persona (ostensibly free from systemic racial exploitation) as a 'raceless' society (Deliovsky 2005: 29). The Canadian refusal to see what is there is more than complacency. It speaks of our desire to avoid complicities while claiming innocence. We need to subvert the constant juxtaposition of the US when racial issues emerge in Canadian contexts. For example, in dealing with silences around race, we must 'return the gaze' and problematize how Canadians can see race and class at play in the aftermath of Hurricane Katrina in New Orleans yet fail to acknowledge any systemic neglect of our own communities.

All social identities morph into complex configurations. Racial identities are historically contingent/specific, calling into focus the history and context of their evocations. But while identities are transient we must also recognize the 'permanence' of skin colour as a salient marker of identity through human history. The significance of colour in the mind of the racist cannot be dismissed. This has served to perpetuate not only the material but also the psychic injury of invisibility and insignificance of an important reality—the racial identity of the minoritized. We must also be aware of the structural dynamics of whiteness, that is, the socio-economic forces and the institutional aspects of structure/society that work alongside everyday discursive practices and social scripts/texts to place whites in a 'positional superiority' (Said 1979) over 'others'. The positional superiority of whites is also fed constantly by the ideological system of white supremacy. Relations of domination are not shaped by history, politics, culture, and materiality alone. They are also shaped by local actions and daily discursive practices (see also Deliovsky 2005: 12; Hall 1997).

Chapter 24

Acts of Resistance: Black Men and Women Engage Slavery in Upper Canada, 1793–1803

Afua Cooper

The year 2007 marks the bicentenary of British abolition of the Atlantic slave trade. The study on which this paper is based is part of my ongoing research into the role black people played in the history of early Canada; their slave status; issues of race and gender; and, of course, the early North American anti-slavery movement. By particularizing the issue of slavery and resistance, this larger analysis centres black people, particularly the enslaved, as historical subjects and agents in the making of their own, and thus a significant part of Canada's, history. I dedicate this paper to the numerous enslaved African men and women in Upper Canada and British North America who, through their own actions, helped to end slavery in these places.

In the past few decades, historians of slavery, in exploring the lives of the enslaved, have attempted to put them at the centre of historical inquiry by showing that they were not the atomized victims of slavery that previous historians have shown them to be, but active agents in their own emancipation. One way that the enslaved tried to rise above their victimization was to resist as best as they could the degradation and brutalization of slavery. Historian David Barry Gaspar has defined resistance within the context of New World slavery as a concept that is used to apply to slave behaviour that cannot be equated

with co-operation with slavery. He also notes that resistance was 'an important organizing principle of slave life'.[1]

Resistance 'spans a continuum that takes into account important qualitative differences between individual acts and those that were collective or had collective potential'.[2] Individual acts, often placed in the category of everyday resistance, involve such actions such as breaking of tools, destruction of livestock and other moveable property, work stoppage, talking back to their owners, malingering, temporary *marronnage* (absenting oneself temporarily), and so forth. Though this type of resistance 'incrementally hampered' the slave system, it posed no long-term danger to it. At the other end of this conceptual spectrum is collective resistance, which is more radical in its orientation and outlook, and thus has a long-term impact on the slave system. Examples of long-term resistance are arson, permanent *marronnage* (permanent self-emancipation), armed rebellions and revolts, and homicide. However, the cataloguing of resistance in such a dichotomous manner suggests that everyday resistance and long-term resistance stand in contradistinction to each other, and that the two poles never meet. Not so. Both types often shade into each other. For example, everyday acts of resistance 'added up and constituted the foundation upon which slaves built more ambitious schemes of subversion that matured into collective political resistance or insurrection'.[3]

And if we think of resistance running as a continuum, then surely there were responses that occur somewhere between these two extreme poles. And there were. For example, arson as employed by the enslaved could either be an individual or a collective act. Moreover, Bernard Moitt has argued for a gender-specific understanding of resistance, and notes that there were multiple forms of enslaved women's resistance. He notes that 'gender made it possible for women to restrict fertility and control reproduction through abortions and other techniques . . .' [like infanticide and abstinence].[4] Poisoning was also associated with females because of their close links to domestic and household work. Sometimes resistance could be subtle and fleeting, a scream, a cut eye, or the sucking of teeth. These could often help restore the self-esteem of the enslaved, if only fleetingly.

Why Did Slaves Resist?

Slavery was an inhuman system in which one group of persons permanently owned the life and labour of another group, and had the power of life and death over them. The raison d'être of the enslaved group was to serve the enslaving group. Moreover, the benefits accrued from the labour of the enslaved belonged not to them but to their enslavers.

Slavery in the New World, in addition to being an economic and labour arrangement, was also a racialized system that 'created a white over black hierarchy' where enslaved blacks experienced the stigma of racial slavery. And whites, whether or not they were slaveholders, promoted and benefited from an all-encompassing system of white racial supremacy.

African scholar Joseph Ki-Zerbo remarked that as a result of the slave trade and slavery Africans

were ousted from humanity.[5] These institutions, plus the legal codes that they spawned, defined and treated enslaved Africans as chattel or property that was bought, sold, and traded. Moreover, slavery in the New World was a permanent condition; one was a slave for life. Another cruel feature of the slave system was that it was hereditary. Slave masters ensured that slavery would reproduce itself by making it legal that slave children inherited their mothers' status. Women in particular, given how gender impacted the experience of enslavement, faced particular kinds of abuse such as sexual assaults from the enslaver group. Even when slave masters accepted the humanity of the slave, as in the case of holding them legally responsible for crimes they might have committed, enslaved people had little or no social status. Orlando Patterson, sociologist of slavery, notes that given the marginal status of the enslaved, they experienced and endured what he terms 'social death'.[6]

On the other hand, enslaved Africans never saw themselves as chattel. It was a status imposed on them by their owners and white society as a whole. And it was a status they rejected. In so doing, they refused in significant ways to cooperate with slavery. Enslaved Africans who resisted, whether in everyday acts or in more spectacular forms, were asserting their personhood and dignity. Through their actions they articulated their protest at the system that degraded them.

Slave Control in Early Canada

Slave resistance was only one side of the master–slave dialectic. It is not possible to understand the resistance of the enslaved without paying due attention to the masters' control of slave behaviour because, as Gaspar notes, 'slave resistance and masters' control . . . were important interlocking dimensions of the overall workings of the slave system'.[7]

A variety of legal codes were used to regulate slavery in New World slave societies, including

Canada. During the *ancient regime* in early Canada, aspects of the French slave code, the *code noir*, were applied with respect to the enslaved and their owners. Further, English legal codes brought by British immigrants after the Conquest and the Revolutionary War strengthened existing legislation. Both French and English laws defined slaves as chattel, and under the full authority of their owners. Colonial laws and ordinances applied to the everyday life of colonists also covered the lives of the enslaved. Masters thus used the full arsenal of the legal apparatus to control their slaves. They had them arrested, thrown in prison, taken before the courts, whipped, branded, placed in the stocks, and legally murdered (for example, hanged).[8]

Slaveholders also exercised tremendous personal power in their ownership of, and rule over, their human property. The employment and deployment of power was a constant in any master–slave relation. However, as I hope I have made clear by now, the enslaved was not totally deprived of power. Power as defined by Michel Foucault is diffused and unstable. From a Foucauldian point of view, even the most downtrodden and marginalized person has some modicum of power. And scholars of slavery have indeed shown that enslaved peoples within the Americas exercised different degrees of power in their relations with each other and with slaveholding society. Yet, it would be irresponsible and perhaps even racist to say that slave people 'were powerful' and could engage in an equal fight with masters and owners. The enslaved had some agency but they were also severely victimized. Slavery, as this paper will show, was not a game played by equals. Yet 'unco-operative' behaviour by the enslaved revealed that slavery was not a system of absolute power and authority on the part of the enslaver or a system of total powerlessness and victimization on the part of the enslaved.

The question, 'can the subaltern speak?' has been asked in a different context.[9] This paper looks at how Upper Canadian slaves, in their condition of subalternity, protested and resisted their enslavement in diverse ways. It also challenges the temporary/permanent binary of acts of resistance, and shows that, as in the case of Upper Canadian slave Chloe Cooley, her sole act of courage led to a collective and permanent protest movement called the Underground Railroad, in which tens of thousands of enslaved people resisted bondage by running away from it.

The Case of Chloe Cooley

On 21 March 1793, at the Upper Canadian legislature, then in Niagara-on-the-Lake, Peter Martin, a black man, appeared at a meeting of the Executive Council of the Upper Canadian legislature. Members of the council present were Governor John Graves Simcoe, Chief Justice William Osgoode, and Peter Russell. Martin had appeared before these men to bring them news that he thought was vital. He told them

> of a violent outrage committed by one [Vrooman] . . . residing near Queens Town . . . on the person of Chloe Cooley, a Negro girl in his service, by binding her, and violently and forcibly transporting her across the [Niagara] River, and delivering her against her will to persons unknown.[10]

Peter Martin had come to Government House to relate the violent removal of slave woman Chloe Cooley from Upper Canada across the international boundary to the state of New York. Because Martin was a black man and a former slave, he knew that the powerful white men before whom he stood could doubt the veracity of his words. Thus taking precaution he brought with him an eyewitness, whom he produced 'to prove the truth of his allegation'. That witness was a white man named William Grisley, who it seemed worked for Vrooman, and he did indeed back up Martin's report about the violent removal and sale of the slave woman, Chloe Cooley, by her master, William Vrooman. Grisley notes:

> That on Wednesday evening last he was at work at Mr Frooman's [Vrooman] near Queens Town, who was in conversation told him he was going to sell his Negro wench to some persons in the States, that in the evening he saw the said Negro girl, tied with a rope, that afterwards a boat was brought, and the said Frooman with his brother and one Van Every, forced the said Negro girl into it . . . and carried the boat across the river; that the said Negro girl was then taken and delivered to a man upon the bank of the river by [Vrooman], that she screamed violently and made resistance, but was tied in the same manner. . . . Wm Grisley farther says that he saw a Negro at a distance, he believes to be tied in the same manner, and has heard that many other people mean to do the same by their Negroes.[11]

This document provides illumination on slaves, their owners, gender and slavery, an example of how enslaved and free black people resisted enslavement, the fluidity of the frontier, and the treatment of enslaved people in the then-frontier province of Upper Canada. But most of all, it tells in startling details the fight that Cooley put up against her enslaver and master William Vrooman. Perhaps because William Grisley was white Vrooman confided in him and told him that he was going to sell his slave woman to persons in New York. Grisley also told Simcoe and the council that many of the slaveholders in the region intend to sell off their enslaved property.

It took a week after the forced removal of Cooley from Niagara-on-the-Lake to New York before Martin appeared before the House. Why was this? And what did he hope to accomplish? It could be that the black community, free and enslaved, met and discussed the removal of Cooley, then decided to inform the government about it, and chose Martin, because he had witnessed the offence, to report the matter at Government House. But Martin was more than an eyewitness.

Martin had gained prestige as an American Revolutionary War veteran. As a member of the guerilla unit Butler's Rangers, he had fought in the war on the side of the British, along the Canadian/American frontier in the eastern Great Lakes region. In fact, his then-master John Butler led the unit. After the war ended, Martin and the survivors of his unit, plus thousands of other British supporters, were evacuated to Canada. Though now free, he continued working for his former master Colonel John Butler, who still owned Martin's daughter. As a war vet, Martin was deemed a natural leader of the black community, and Governor Simcoe, himself a Revolutionary War veteran, must have also known about Martin's military credentials.

Martin most likely knew Cooley. They could have been related or in a love relationship. What was he doing at the Vrooman farm at the very moment Cooley was being removed from her home? Did Cooley send for him? But perhaps the more important question is what did Martin hope to gain by reporting the incident? The enslavement of black people was perfectly legal in Upper Canada and other parts of the British Empire. Vrooman, with the law on his side, had every legal right to do what he did with Chloe Cooley.

What Martin and the rest of the black population might have heard when Simcoe arrived in the colony just a few months earlier was that he meant to abolish slavery there.[12] If that was what Martin believed, then when he went to Government House he could have entertained the hope that Simcoe could somehow move against Vrooman, and perhaps retrieve Cooley.

William Grisley is also important here. Clearly knowing about 'the performance of race' in the colony, Martin brought Grisley as a 'second eye'. It was the general belief at the time that blacks and the enslaved were untruthful and thus their words could not be trusted. Did the men at Government House believe Martin because Grisley backed him up? In any event, Grisley supported Martin's statement.

Martin (and Grisley) must have been gratified that after hearing their story, the council took action. Simcoe directed his attorney general, John White, to prosecute Vrooman, not for selling Cooley but for disturbing the peace by his actions. However John White knew that the government had no case since English civil law regarded slaves as mere property. Under this law the slave 'was [also] deprived of all rights, marital, parental, proprietary, even the right to live'. William Renwick Riddell, jurist and historian wryly noted that 'Chloe Cooley had no rights which Vrooman was bound to respect, and it was no more a breach of peace than if he had been dealing with his heifer'.[13] Attorney General White knew that Vrooman was well within his rights and did not move to prosecute him.

Since nothing could be done to penalize Vrooman, Simcoe ordered his chief justice, William Osgoode, to draft a bill prohibiting the importation of slaves into the colony. Why was Simcoe so concerned about the plight of enslaved Africans in his colony? Upon his arrival in Upper Canada in 1792, Simcoe was surprised to learn that so many of the colonists owned slaves. In fact, he seemed to have been under the impression that there was no slavery in Upper Canada. More surprising was his discovery that many of the legislators in both chambers in the House were slaveholders. Apparently, once Simcoe got to Upper Canada and saw the state of race relations, he made the assertion that he would make no distinction between the natives of Europe, Africa, and America. Soon the rumour became rife that Simcoe was going 'to free all the slaves'.[14]

In his former life, Simcoe was a Member of Parliament in Britain and was well acquainted with the struggles in the British House regarding the abolition of the slave trade. He would also have been aware of the cases of Jonathan Strong and James Somersett, two slaves who ran away from their masters in London, and who were freed by the courts, and the support given to these two fugitive slaves by the anti-slavery society in London.[15] Moreover, Simcoe was himself a colonel on the British side during the Revolutionary War, and led a very fearsome regiment called the Queen's Rangers. He would have known that Lord Clinton and Sir Henry Dunsmore, in the Thirteen Colonies, had called upon enslaved Americans to join the British standard, and such calls resulted in what can seriously be called the 'first emancipation' in the New World. Because, at the close of the war, at least 5,000 Africans who had served the British found freedom in various British colonies, but mainly in eastern Canada. Simcoe would have been aware of the sacrifices blacks, both enslaved and free, made for the British during the late war, and took offence to them being enslaved in his colony. Thus, if he wanted to bring about the demise of slavery in Upper Canada, and he did, the removal of Cooley was the opportunity he was waiting for.[16]

After several amendments, on 9 July 1793, at the second sitting of Parliament, the bill that Osgoode had drafted to prohibit the importation of slaves in Upper Canada was made law. It was called 'An Act to Prevent the Further Introduction of Slaves and to Limit the Terms of Contract for Servitude within this Province'. The preamble reads:

> Whereas it is unjust that a people who enjoy freedom by law should encourage the introduction of slaves; and whereas it is highly expedient to abolish slavery in this province so far as the same may gradually be done without violating private property. . . .[17]

The new law, though it aimed to limit slavery, was very much concerned that private property (that is the slaves) was protected. This bill, which became known as Simcoe's Act, was passed 'with much opposition' from the slaveholding interests in the House who insisted that slave labour was necessary in an agricultural economy. What did this new legislation accomplish? First it secured the property rights of those who held slaves before 9 July 1793 and confirmed the status of those who were already enslaved. It did not free one slave. The slaveholders within and outside of Parliament clamoured for their property rights and told Simcoe in no uncertain terms that they would not give up their rights in their slaves. Simcoe and his chief justice buckled under the pressure. As Nancy Butler and Michael Power note, most of the slaveholders were of the Loyalist establishment.

> Its members, recent immigrants to the province, were naturally jealous of their property rights as British citizens, having forfeited practically everything in their defence of the Crown in the late Revolutionary War. They were in no rush to deprive themselves of valuable property they regarded as essential to their economic viability in the colony.[18]

However, the Act provided for children born to slave mothers after 1793; they would become free on their 25th birthday, and their children would earn their freedom at birth, though, and this is important, it did not prohibit the buying and selling of slaves within the colony or exportation across international lines. Though slavery was 'unable to expand, it continued to function openly after 1793', what did the legislation achieve in regards to the emancipation of enslaved Africans? First, the stated objective of the Act was to prohibit the importation of slaves into the colony as the first clause outlined. In doing so it repealed the 1790 Imperial Act that allowed white settlers to bring in enslaved Africans to work the colony. Second, and of great import was the fact that embedded also in the first clause was the idea that any slave arriving on Upper Canadian soil from another country would immediately be free. In other words, touching the soil of Upper Canada guaranteed the freedom of an enslaved person. And this was where the Act was most potent. I will elaborate on this point later.

The new law was a disappointment to Simcoe. He and Osgoode wanted outright abolition; instead the bill was a compromise that would bring about abolition . . . but gradually. If enslaved people in Upper Canada were waiting on the Act to free them, it would take 50 years before that would happen. Nonetheless, Simcoe's emancipation bill would have a definite effect on the fate of black people in the colony, on the continent, and on race relations in the colony.

The Act had two immediate and paradoxical outcomes. Perhaps the first and most immediate was that many Upper Canadian slaves, realizing that the Act would not free them, took matters in their own hands and escaped the colony to such places like the Old Northwest Territories (Michigan, Ohio, Indiana, Minnesota, and parts of Wisconsin) and New York, places that had either prohibited slavery [or] were passing legislation to do so. So numerous were black Upper Canadians in some American towns that, in Detroit, for example, [a] group of former Upper Canadian slaves formed a militia in 1806 for the defence of that city against Canadians. So widespread was the flight of Upper Canadian slaves into Michigan territory that in 1807 Upper Canadian slaveholders petitioned the government of the United States to help them retrieve their former slaves from American soil. 'I regret equally with yourself the inconveniences which his Majesty's subjects in Upper Canada experience from the desertion of their slaves into the territory of the United States . . .' reads a portion of the letter that D.M. Erskine, the British representative in the United States, wrote to Upper Canada's lieutenant governor, Sir Francis Gore. The American government expressed its regret but refused to act on behalf of the slaveholders.[19]

Henry Lewis was one fugitive slave who came to our attention because he fled Canadian slavery and then wrote a letter to his former master. The letter is dated 3 May 1798 and was sent from Schenectady, New York.

My desire to support myself as a free man and enjoy all the benefits which may result from being free in a country where a black man is defended by the laws as much as a white man is induces me to make you an offer of purchasing myself. I am a black man and am not able to pay you all the money down which you may ask for me but upon these conditions I will purchase myself. Ten pounds this years and every year after 16 pounds until the whole sum is payed. I should wish to pay the money to Joseph Yates the Mare [mayor] of this sitty because he is the most proper man that I can think of at present. The reason I left your house is this your women vexed me to so high a degree that it was far beyond the power of man to support it, it is true and I will say in all company that I always lived as well in your house as I should wish. Please write to Joseph Yates what you will take in cash for me and let him be the man to whom I shall pay the money yearly. In a supplicant manner I beg your pardon ten thousand times and beg that you would be so kind as to permit me to purchase myself and at as low a rate as any other person. My mistress I also wish a long life and good health and pleas tell her I beg her pardon then thousand times. My mistress I shall always remember on account of her great kindness to me.

I remain your affectionate servant, Henry Lewis.[20]

The man to whom Lewis writes is none other than William Jarvis, secretary of the province, a member of the Upper Canadian legislature, and of the Executive Council. In other words, he was one of the province's political elite. It was his wife Hannah Jarvis who went into a tirade when Simcoe pushed the abolition bill through Parliament, that Simcoe 'had freed all the Negroes', which was not true at all.[21] Now five years after the bill, one of the Jarvis's slaves had fled to New York. The letter has an ironic, almost mocking, tone; it is as if Lewis is laughing to himself as he writes it. (I am here, you are there, catch me if you can.) Lewis, fully aware that while he had been in a state of bondage others had benefited from the fruits of his labour, which underscores this as a central reason for his flight—he wants his labour to benefit himself, and so did not want to remain in the state of enslavement any longer. And he was doing the very noble thing of buying himself. However, he set the conditions of his sale, and Jarvis, away in Upper Canada and probably believing that he had lost all his investment in Lewis, must have been somewhat gratified at the offer. Why did Lewis decide to buy himself? Perhaps he heard that Jarvis was hunting for him. Maybe he feared arrest and decided to put his mind at ease. Or could it be that Lewis had internalized the concept of the sacredness of private property? Lewis had well-connected friends. He knew the Mayor of Schenectady and had found a ready support in him. Lewis might have been originally from New York, and probably came from there as a slave with the Loyalist migration to Upper Canada.

The reason Lewis gave for leaving the Jarvis household is contradictory. He said the women of the house made his life unbearable, yet his closing remark is about the great goodness and kindness of his mistress Hannah Jarvis, of whose pardon he begs ten thousand times. Perhaps Lewis [was] just being political when he wrote this about Mrs Jarvis, and could have been laughing as he wrote the letter. For he must have known that Hannah Jarvis was pro-slavery and did not wish any Upper Canadian slave to be free.

In this letter to Jarvis, Lewis voiced his protest against slavery. He rebelled against that condition by running away. He too, like Cooley, went across the international boundary. But in contrast to her, he 'stole himself' while she was sold away by her owner. A year after Lewis wrote the letter, the state of New York, where he was domiciled, began the process of gradual emancipation. Ensconced in New York, and away from the authority of his master, Lewis realized that he was holding the metaphorical handle, and Jarvis the blade. And so he used the power he had to negotiate the terms of his freedom.

Lewis and the enslaved Africans of the Western District of Upper Canada who gave grief to their owners were not the only ones who resisted bondage by taking flight. There are numerous examples of Upper Canadian slaves and other enslaved persons in other parts of British North America fleeing across the border to places in the Old Northwest and such states as New York and Vermont.[22]

The second outcome of Simcoe's Act, with which we are more familiar, is the creation of Upper Canada as a haven for foreign slaves. News travelled to the United States, especially after the War of 1812, that if any foreign slaves made it to Upper Canada they would find freedom. Those who were enslaved in the United States, on 'learning that they would not be enslaved north of the American border, soon began the trek to freedom and a greater measure of security in Upper Canada'. This was the beginning of the legendary Underground Railroad. The supreme irony is that the railroad came about because of the brutalization and selling of a black Upper Canadian slave woman to an American slaveholder. It must also be noted that the same year the Upper Canadian legislature passed its Abolition Act, the United States Congress passed its first Fugitive Slave Law. Undoubtedly, this was a coincidence but the passing of both pieces of legislation naturally made Upper Canada more attractive to fugitive American slaves.

History has dealt kindly with Simcoe. White, powerful, and male we know his role in the drama of the early anti-slavery movement in early Canada. It is he who emerges as the hero of the moment. But what of the woman, Chloe Cooley, the woman whose fate brought about the anti-slavery legislation and made Upper Canada a refuge for oppressed American blacks, and further gave the young colony the distinction of being the first jurisdiction within the British Empire to enact a piece of anti-slavery legislation?

We do not know Cooley's age, or if she had children, or even if she was married. We assume she was young because she was called a 'wench'. As a young woman of child-bearing age, she more than likely would fetch a good price. Her owner, William Vrooman, of Dutch ancestry, was a Loyalist from New York's Hudson Valley region. Like most of his compatriots he would have arrived in Upper Canada after the close of the war in 1783. It is likely that Cooley made the trek with him and his family from New York to Upper Canada.

Cooley's removal from Upper Canada to the United States mirrors that of the removal of captured slaves from Africa. She was tied up, thrown in a boat, and sold away.[23] The fact that Vrooman bound Cooley with a rope showed how much black women were thought of as brute, unfeminine, and unworthy of masculine protection.[24] This happened at a time when the 'frailty' of woman was articulated in the patriarchal gender discourse gaining ground at that time in Europe and Euro-dominated societies. Hilary Beckles, in discussing how New World slavery re-gendered black women by denying them 'feminine' characteristics, notes:

The colonial gender discourse confronted and assaulted traditional concepts of womanhood in both Europe and Africa, and sought to redefine notions of black feminine identity. The black woman was ideologically constructed as essentially 'non-feminine' insofar as primacy was placed upon her alleged muscular capabilities, physical strength, aggressive carriage, and sturdiness. Pro-slavery writers presented her as devoid of feminine tenderness and graciousness in which the white woman was tightly wrapped.[25]

Cooley was outraged at the treatment she received from Vrooman. As a slave woman, she occupied the margins of society. She might have lived in Canada for most of her life, and saw it as home. Perhaps she even had family here from whom she was loath to part. Vrooman clearly was a brutal master, and might have decided to sell Cooley because he could not 'control' her, or because he had heard that Simcoe meant to abolish slavery and wanted to get something from his investment in Cooley before he lost everything. Slaves tried in everyday acts to assert their personhood. Black women as enslaved persons in the Americas have been beaten, overworked, raped, hanged, murdered, and brutalized in many forms. By manhandling Cooley, tying her up, and forcing her into a boat, Vrooman, as slave owner, continued the slaveholder's and white man's engagement with 'killing the black body'.

Cooley was unable to protect herself but she had one thing at her disposal that she could use to express her anger, outrage, and fear—her voice. And so she screamed—a heart-rending scream that echoed beyond the boundaries of Vrooman's farm, and summoned Martin and Grisley to witness. Because the two men also related that she 'made resistance', we can only imagine Cooley screaming, crying, cursing, and straining her limbs against the rope with which her master tied her. In spite of Cooley's low social status, which conspired to deny her a

place in history, she nonetheless enters the historical record as a resisting and freedom-seeking woman.

And what of Peter Martin, the black man who went to Government House to report the matter? Peter Martin, former slave, former soldier, now British subject and pioneer, sought to bring about more freedom for black people. Martin was outraged that he had fought for what he believed would have ensured freedom for his people only to discover that many were still enslaved, beaten, abused, and sold away as if they were cattle. By going to Government House to report Cooley's abuse, he protested the treatment of black people in general in the province.

Can the subaltern speak? Cooley was clearly a victim but she exercised what little agency she could muster. Martin literally spoke out in a loud and clear voice to the most powerful people in the land. As a Revolutionary soldier he had fought to preserve 'British freedom'. As a war veteran and colonial pioneer he had helped found the new province of Upper Canada, and had preserved it for the British Crown. In going to Simcoe and his council he acted as an empowered person, one who refused to watch the mistreatment and abuse meted out to his people. By going to the council, he signalled his intention to work for black liberation. Cooley and Martin by their acts of resistance created for themselves new status as historical subjects.

Resistance as a conceptual tool is useful in the construction of historical knowledge about enslaved Africans in British North America and their quest for freedom. Cooley and Martin resisted slavery on an individual basis, but their actions eventually led to a freedom movement with vast collective outcomes. Many of the runaway slaves of the Western District of Upper Canada regrouped as a collectivity in a foreign country. And Henry Lewis, likewise, made a small dent in the institution of slavery when he emancipated his own self.

In 1807 and 1808, the British and Americans abolished their respective transatlantic slave trades. The countless number of black men and women in Upper Canada and the wider BNA who rebelled against slavery had set the stage for this milestone in Canadian, African, Atlantic, and world history.

Notes

1. David Barry Gaspar, 'From "The Sense of Their Slavery": Slave Women and Resistance in Antigua, 1632–1763', in *More than Chattel, Black Women and Slavery in the Americas*, eds D.B. Gaspar and D.C. Hine (Indiana University Press, 1996), 220.
2. Ibid.
3. Ibid.
4. Bernard Moitt, *Women and Slavery in the French Antilles, 1635–1848* (Indiana University Press, 2001), 125.
5. J. Ki-Zerbo, 'The Mental Route of the Slave: A Few Thoughts Inspired by the Present-day Situation of the Black Peoples', in *From Chains to Bonds: The Slave Trade Revisited*, ed. Doudou Diene (Paris: UNESCO Publishing, 2001), 122.
6. Orlando Patterson, *Slavery and Social Death: A Comparative Study* (Cambridge, MA: Harvard University Press, 1982).
7. Gaspar, 'Slave Women and Resistance'.
8. On the legality of slavery in Canada see Maureen Elgersman, *Unyielding Spirits: Black Women and Slavery in Early Canada and Jamaica* (New York: Garland Publishing, 1999), 10–16. Also, Robin Winks, *The Blacks in Canada* (Montreal: McGill-Queen's University Press, 1997), 51, describes master abuse of slaves.
9. Gayatri Spivak, 'Can the Subaltern Speak?', in *Marxism and the Interpretation of Culture*, eds C. Nelson and L. Grossberg (Urbana and Chicago: University of Illinois Press, 1988).
10. William Riddell, 'The Slave in Upper Canada', *JNH* 4 (1919): 377.
11. Ibid., 333–78.
12. Michael Power and Nancy Butler, *Slavery and Freedom in Niagara* (Niagara Historical Society, 2000).
13. Riddell, 'Slave in Upper Canada', 380.
14. Winks, *Blacks in Canada*, 98.
15. On the Somersett case see Adam Hochschild, *Bury the Chains: Prophets and Rebels in the Fight to Free an Empire's Slaves* (Boston: Houghton and Mifflin, 2005), 49–51.
16. James Walker has documented the story of the black Loyalists in his seminal work *The Black Loyalists: The Search for a Promised Land in Nova Scotia and Sierra Leone, 1783–1870* (Toronto: University of Toronto Press, 1992).
17. 'An Act to Prevent the Further Introduction of Slaves and to Limit the Term of Contracts for Servitude within this Province', 33 George IV, c. 7, 9 July 1793, The Provincial Statutes of Upper Canada, Revised, Corrected, and Republished by Authority (York: R.C. Horne, 1816).
18. Power and Butler, *Slavery and Freedom*, 9.
19. For information of the flight of Upper Canadian slaves into Michigan and other American territories, and the letter sent by Erskine to Gore, see William Riddell, 'Additional Notes on Slavery', *Journal of Negro History* 17 (1932): 368–73.
20. Letter from Henry Lewis to his former master, William Jarvis, at Niagara-on-the-Lake (Toronto Public Library, Baldwin Room).
21. Power and Butler, *Slavery and Freedom*, 29.
22. Winks, *Blacks in Canada*, 99. For examples of advertisements giving notice of runaways in colonial newspapers see the *Quebec Gazette*, 19 Oct. 1769, and the *Upper Canada Gazette*, 19 Aug. 1795. Further, Peggy Pompadour, [a] slave woman of Upper Canadian political leader Peter

Russell, constantly ran away from the Russell household. Russell confined her to jail after recapturing her after one of her flight attempts. See Edith Firth, *The Town of York, 1793–1815* (Champlain Society, 1962), 243.

23. Elgersman, *Unyielding Spirits*, 29.

24. The three men, William Grisley, Peter Martin, and definitely John Graves Simcoe, could be seen as trying to 'protect' Cooley. And even though Simcoe failed as her knight in shining armour, his actions can be interpreted as chivalrous.

25. Hilary Beckles, *Centering Woman, Gender Discourses in Caribbean Slave Society* (Kingston, JA: Ian Randle, 1999), 10.

Part IV

Questions

1. How did the use of critical race theories and methodologies, specifically through the *R.D.S.* case cited in Aylward's article, effectively challenge one aspect of systemic racism in Canada?
2. What does it mean to 'decolonize anti-racism'?
3. Instead of analyzing 'race', George J. Sefa Dei calls for a focus on the 'racialized subject'. Why?
4. Resistances exist on a continuum between individual acts and collective potential. What are some examples Afua Cooper provides of these resistances? Identify some similarities in today's resistances to racial exclusionary practices in Canada.

Websites

African Canadian Online: http://www.yorku.ca/aconline/culture/pioneers.html
Amnesty International Canada—A Human Rights Agenda for Canada—No Security Without Human Rights: http://www.amnesty.ca/themes/canada_no_security.php
Assembly of First Nations: http://www.afn.ca
Caribbean and Mexican Migrant Workers in Canada: http://www.justicia4migrantworkers.org

Suggested Readings

Arat-Koc, Sedef. 2001. *Caregivers Break the Silence: A Participatory Action Research on the Abuse and Violence, Including the Impact of Family Separation, Experienced by Women in the Live-in Caregiver Program* (Toronto: Intercede).

Backhouse, Constance. 1999. *Colour-coded: A Legal History of Racism in Canada 1900–1950* (Toronto: University of Toronto Press for The Osgoode Society for Canadian Legal History).

Frideres, James. 1974. *Canada's Indians: Contemporary Conflicts* (Scarborough, ON: Prentice-Hall).

Jain, Harish. 1981. *Equal Employment Issues: Race and Sex Discrimination in the United States, Canada, and Britain* (New York, NY: Praeger).

Jakubowski, Lisa M. 1997. *Immigration and the Legalization of Racism* (Halifax, NS: Fernwood).

Reitz, Jeffrey G. 2003. *Host Societies and the Reception of Immigrants* (La Jolla, CA: Center for Comparative Immigration Studies, University of California, San Diego).

Sharma, Nandita R. 2006. *Home Economics: Nationalism and the Making of 'Migrant Workers' in Canada* (Toronto: University of Toronto Press).

Winks, Robin. 1997. *The Blacks in Canada* (Montreal: McGill-Queen's University Press).

Conclusion

Theorizing Race in Canada: Future Possibilities

That race matters when we should know better is indisputable; what is more important is how and why. That race continues to matter as a central organizing principle in society is also both alarming and disarming, yet indicative of the distance that must be travelled to adequately theorize race. On one side, the depth of racial injustice can be gauged from studies that demonstrate how race still influences where people live, where they work, and what they can expect from life. In this context, the common assumption of Canada as a raceless society is simply a hegemonic lie to continue dominating and exploiting people, and to perpetuate a system of internal colonization based on race, class, and gender. On the other side, however, the race dynamic is transformative in its process and outcome. Racialized minorities rely on race as identity construction, to challenge Eurocentric constructs, as grounds for recognition and equality as per equity programs, and as a basis for anti-racism politics.

Academics who debate issues of race and its consequences tend to disagree over its importance. Does one abandon race and examine instead relationships and activities that become racialized by those in positions of power (Miles 1982)? Or, do we keep race in focus as a biologically infused social construction that has proven politically significant in shaping identities, experiences, relationships, opportunities, and outcomes (Dei 2007)? Whatever strategy is used, the key fact is irrefutable: race profoundly shapes a person's life and life chances—not because race is objectively real but because people believe it to be real, and think and act accordingly. In keeping with this theme of race as a racialized construction, *The Politics of Race in Canada* focuses on how race remains both (mis)understood and (under)theorized in Canada. Particular attention is devoted to identifying the transition of perspectives for studying race in Canada, in part by demonstrating how shifts in race discourse have influenced public policy and vice versa.

Race Discourses/Racial Politics: Past, Present, Future

Race has proven a discursive and material force in shaping society and social life for nearly two centuries (Anderson 2007). Until the 1930s, few in the West questioned the reality of race or the universality of moral claims to race doctrines and white supremacy. Imperialism, colonialism, and the expansion of Western powers were couched as positive contributors to human evolution and civilization. In white settler societies, the idea of race profoundly influenced public perceptions of social differences and the workings of institutions, laws, and everyday life. As smartly put by Omi and Winant (1994: xi):

To study race in the United States is to enter a world of paradox, irony, and danger. In this world, arbitrarily chosen attributes shape politics and policies, love and hate, life and death. All the powers of the intellect—artistic, religious, scientific, political—are pressed into service to explain racial distinctions and suggest how they may be maintained, changed, or abolished.

To the dismay or amazement of many, race continues to matter. Race remains as resilient as ever in shaping identities and institutions, as well as an exclusionary device, notwithstanding the growing prominence of colour-blind discourses that purport to do otherwise. In contrast with an openly racialized past, references to race are more muted or denied altogether by those who see themselves as beyond race. Yet race is discursively real and persists as a fundamental dimension of social organization and cultural meaning, despite a tendency to diminish its significance as a variable among many, an anomaly within the social structure, a socially constructed illusion, or an epiphenomenal manifestation of more important social relations like class or ethnicity (Omi and Winant 1994). But race is this and more, and much remains at stake in theorizing this most 'daring' and 'contested' of categories in defining the dynamics of racialized relations.

The theorizing of race has led to a rethinking of racialization and racism (see Hier and Bolaria 2007). Consider the paradigm-busting publication of *The Racial Contract* in 1997 by Charles Mills (also Pateman 1988). For Mills, references to race must go beyond its status as a discursive construct or explanatory variable. Rather, race has reflected the discourse of white supremacy as a global system of domination for the last 500 years. According to Mills (1997) race is the quintessential project involving a global theoretical framework to explain a commitment to dominate displaced Indigenous peoples and exploited minorities. Or as W.E.B. DuBois wrote in 1940,

the history of the modern world is 'epitomized in one word—Empire; the domination of white Europe over black Africa and yellow Asia through political power built on the economic control of labour, income, and ideas' (96). To be sure, Mills writes, whites at present are not necessarily personally responsible for a white supremacist society. Nor is it a case that a cabal of whites conspired to make a historical pact (contract) to dominate the world. Nevertheless, whites in positions of power have embarked on a mission to maintain and expand their power and privilege through the exploitation of the global 'south'. The conclusion seems inescapable: in framing race as a global historical occurrence, race harmony will never exist until both whites and racialized minorities acknowledge the hegemonic system in which they operate, the degree to which whiteness permeates every issue and institution in society, and how white privilege defines who gets what and why (Thomas 2007; also Omi and Winant 1994; McIntosh 1988). That kind of complicity puts the onus on abolishing the privileges of whiteness, according to the authors of *Race Traitor* (Garvey and Ignatiev 1996), especially if justice and equality are to prevail.

The persistence of race raises a central question: Will race continue to matter in the future? Or will moves in Canada (and the United States) endorse a race-neutral society in which race will no longer matter in defining who gets what and why? Some would argue that we are just about there (Foster 2005; but see Doane 2006; 2007). An ideology of colour-blindness ('race-neutrality') has emerged involving a series of claims about the current state of race relations in Canada and the United States. According to the tenets of colour-blind ideology and liberal universalism, race no longer matters because people are fundamentally the same under the skin and equal before the law. Furthermore, the combination of civil rights, human rights safeguards, and multiculturalism has not only discredited racial prejudice and discriminatory barriers but also dislodged structural and ideological barriers that block success. To the extent that race and racism persist, proponents of the colour-blind doctrine argue it is largely a survival from the past, restricted to isolated hate crimes and expressed by prejudicial individuals (Doane 2007). To the extent that inequality persists, the fault lies with dysfunctional individuals and social pathologies implicit within minority communities.

The implications of this position are far-reaching. In a so-called colour-blind society where race allegedly no longer matters, taking race into consideration for policy-making cannot be justified, even if the goal is to ameliorate inequality or redress past injustices (Bonilla-Silva 1996; Doane 2006). Race policies for amelioration of racial segregation and racial equality are themselves deemed racist, unfair to whites, and a violation of core values pertaining to liberal universalism, with its espousal that our commonalities as individuals are far more important than what divides us as members of racialized groups. But doubts prevail: Are Canada and the United States as race-neutral and colour-blind as advocates seem to say? If yes, is this neutrality reflective of reality or rhetoric? At surface levels or in the deep structures of society? Is a race-neutral and colour-blind society humanly possible? Evidence suggests no, and it appears that race will remain a factor in defining who gets what. Consider the following indicators in confirming the centrality of race to society:

- Moves to create a more inclusive, equitable society cannot paper over the inevitable. Race is deeply embedded in the core values, institutional arrangements, and Eurocentric constitutional order of Canadian and American societies. No amount of denial over race-neutrality can dislodge an entrenched structural whiteness.
- Despite laws outlawing discrimination at individual and institutional levels, structural barriers and systemic biases continue to favour white interests rather than those of non-whites (Fleras and Elliot 2007). Not surprisingly, critics argue, by doing nothing and justifying it on principled grounds, a commitment to colour-blindness does little more than provide a thinly veiled defence of dominant ideology and white supremacy.
- Laws cannot possibly eradicate deep-seated prejudices or subliminal biases that continue to racialize people's identities, experiences, and outcomes. Yes, laws may alter people's behaviour but they are largely ineffective in challenging the conventions and foundational principles upon which the law is constructed.
- Formal equality before the law sounds good in theory. In practice, without special treatment, racialized groups that are disadvantaged because of structural barriers will continue to fall further behind. That is, in contexts of inequality, applying similar standards to unequal situations has the effect of freezing the status quo, in addition to the prevailing distribution of power and resources.
- If the problems of inequality and marginalization are the result of race, it stands to reason that race-conscious initiatives must be part of the solution. The discrediting of race as solution thus becomes commensurate with securing white privilege behind a facade of formal fairness (Doane 2006).

In short, the embeddedness of race in constructing the modern state (or society) cannot be ignored or underestimated (Vickers 2002; Goldberg 2002). Contrary to popular opinion, race is not simply a psychological disorder or a consequence of excessive immigration (forced or voluntary). Rather, it is foundational to the origin, character, and functioning of the modern state (and colonial settlers who saw themselves as white countries), including its manifestations in justice and law enforcement, and politics, legislation, and bureaucracy. For Goldberg, the modern state is tantamount to a racial state not only because the state is implicated in the reproduction of local conditions of racist exclusion, but because the modern state conceived of itself as racially configured throughout its emergence, formation, and development. While the apartheid regime in South Africa and the colour bar in the United States are the most egregious examples of race regimes on behalf of white supremacist interests, the settler societies of Canada and Australia were no less racialized but were more subtle and systemic. Put bluntly, rather than something incidental to the functioning of the state both then and now, race is fundamental in establishing and maintaining a system of racial domination that espouses colour-blind principles but tolerates colour-conscious discrimination. Race underlies political systems of power and privilege, and that alone should disabuse anyone of any notions of simple or simplistic solutions (Vickers 2002).

The Canadian Context: The Politics of Race, Theorizing Race

Historically, the concept of race was used explicitly to organize the creation of Canada. First Nation peoples were viewed as in need of salvation, and the 'others'—the Irish at first, then Italians and so on—were to be part of the 'white man's burden'. The articles in Part I document how 'common sense' perspectives of white superiority and the moral panic generated concerns over the purity of the Anglo-Saxon race.

The aftermath of World War II, and the global transformations brought on by various independence achievements, subjected the concept of race to intense scrutiny. In Canada, as elsewhere, the term 'race' became taboo and the word 'ethnicity' was substituted. This was more than a shift in terminology. A focus on ethnicity

made it easier to associate issues of 'the other' with issues of integration and settlement. Heavily influenced by the work of American sociologists such as Robert Park (1864–1944) and his conceptualization of the cycle of competition, conflict, accommodation, and assimilation when ethnic groups merged, Canadian sociologists studied—among other issues—ethnic identification and retention.

This perspective was challenged by the seminal work of B. Singh Bolaria and Peter Li in 1988—*Racial Oppression in Canada*. The cultural dimension of race was seen as obscuring the practices of social institutions. Individual based explanations were seen as justifying the 'few bad apples' perspective. An institutional and systemic lens highlighted issues of power, privilege, and exploitation. This approach led to the search for the tools, including concepts, to identify how the adverse impacts of such racial exclusionary practices were occurring.

The sophisticated, modern ways of coding race, then, both in Canada and internationally, shifted the theorizing of race to the process of racialization. Yet, as Murji and Solomos (2005) argue, 'the mere use of the term "racialization" has become a rather glib tag, which is sometimes made to stand as an explanation itself rather than being applied rigorously' (2005: 2). The strength and benefit of the concept of racialization is the space to discuss power relations without validating the concept of a biological race.

The persistence and entrenchment of racial exclusion, while it is being simultaneously denied in Canada, is the rocky terrain for current resistances. The battle over ideas, the power to name, and the audacity of resistances, despite official denial and silence, continues in Canada today. Will race exist in our future? The answer will have to emerge from contested terrains.

The Politics of Race in Canada tracks one of the fundamental organizing principles in Canadian society. In Part I, the articles provide a glimpse of Canada's 'white settler' mentality at a time when race was more explicit than it is today. Discourses of racial purity were rampant and, as Walker (1997) and Backhouse (1999) demonstrate, often legitimized by the judiciary and legislation. Winks documents the existence of slavery in Canada (1969: 164–9), a narrative so often eliminated from today's high-school textbooks. Education segregation was accepted even though the 'majority of Negroes paid taxes for common school' to which they had no access (Winks 1969: 171). Woodsworth proclaimed the absence of a 'Negro problem' in 1909, yet warned readers of the dangers of 'incompatible elements' and of pauperism and crime, and their consequences, for 'lowering the average standard of citizenship' (217–18, 227). Backhouse highlights the Supreme Court decision that 'Eskimos' were Indians (1999: 18–29). Such race definitions reveal the glaring white supremacist attitudes and actions that were explicit and 'common sense' in Canada, as they were in the rest of North America and Europe. The other articles highlight the politics involved in demarcating a 'white' population from groups which today are considered 'African, Asian, or Aboriginal' (Boyd et al. 2000: 36). This history of a 'white settler' mentality saw the end of the last segregated school in Ontario in 1965, and the elimination of explicit references to race in Canadian immigration policies in the late 1960s, which is relatively recent given our nation's historical development.

In Part II we see a shift in Canadian theorizing of race as a response to issues of 'difference' after the atrocities of World War II. After the War, the United Nations made a strong denunciation of the concept of race. In 1945, the United Nations Educational, Scientific, and Cultural Organization (UNESCO) declared 'Wars begin in the minds of men' and went on to state that World War II had been 'made possible by the denial of the democratic principles of the dignity, equality, and mutual respect of men, and by the propagation, in their place, through ignorance and prejudice,

of the doctrine of the inequality of men and race' (Banton 2002: 1).

In Canada, we saw the emergence of 'ethnicity' as a conceptual focus after the UN denunciation of the concept of race. John Porter's landmark work in 1965, *The Vertical Mosaic: An Analysis of Social Class and Power in Canada*, made a major observation about the articulation of ethnicity in Canadian society. Porter set out to challenge the idea of a classless society. According to Porter, 'One of the most persistent images that Canadians have of their society is that it has no classes' (1965: 3). His study demonstrated a hierarchical relationship between Canada's cultural groups and issues of class and power in Canadian society—the vertical mosaic. Other studies (Kalbach and McVey 1971; Driedger 1978) attempted to map out Canada's ethnic origins given the diversity of immigrants coming into Canada, and to track issues of ethnic identification and/or assimilation. Wilson Head (1975) and Frances Henry (1978) were among the first to document discrimination and racism in Canada. In 1975, Head wrote,

> This study evolved from a concern by the author that Metropolitan Toronto is beginning to experience increasing discrimination and tension between the various racial groups constituting the population of this city. Aside from a few studies on the subject, and reports of incidents by the mass media, there has been little solid documentation of the situation as it actually exists. (1975: 1)

Similarly, in 1978, in a study on individual, or personal, racism in the city of Toronto, Henry reported: 'According to the results of this study, 16 per cent of the population can be considered to be extremely racist; 35 per cent incline toward some degree of racism; 19 per cent are extremely tolerant; and 30 per cent incline toward tolerance' (1978: 1). However, other sociologists at the time continued to examine issues of assimilation, acculturation, and ethnic identification.

Major challenges to this focus on ethnicity came in 1988 with the publication of two seminal works: *Racial Oppression in Canada* by B. Singh Bolaria and Peter Li and *The Politics of Community Services* by Roxana Ng. In *Racial Oppression*, racial categorizations are linked to labour reproduction. Critiquing the discipline's focus on issues of adaptation and assimilation, Bolaria and Li write: 'Racial contacts are not cultural encounters, but confrontations between the dominant group and the subordinate group in an unequal power relationship' (1988: 7). Similarly, in Ng's work (edited in Part II) the role of the state is examined as 'relations of ruling' in the social construction of 'immigrant women' that resulted in marginalized social locations in the Canadian labour force. The conceptual focus began to shift from an individual analysis to systemic or structural analysis of racism in Canada. Courts were urged to look beyond 'intent to discriminate' and to look instead for adverse outcomes on the basis of race.

In the early 1990s, some scholars began asking questions about the absence of a race analysis in feminist research in Canada. The primacy of gender over race oppression to unify all women was soundly rejected. In 1991 Bannerji wrote of her 'deepest disappointment' (1991: 70) when she discovered that 'racism was not even mentioned as a real issue by the Canadian women's movement' (1991: 71). In 1999 and 2000, sociologists began publishing texts on anti-racist feminism—*Scratching the Surface: Canadian Anti-racist, Feminist Thought* by Enakshi Dua and Angela Robertson (1999) and *Anti-racist Feminism: Critical Race and Gender Studies* by Agnes Calliste and George Dei (2000). Dua and Robertson's collection of articles point to 'the importance of discourses of race for how women of colour are positioned within Canadian society', while Calliste and Dei view their collection of articles as making important contributions to the anti-racism discourse and practice (2000: 16).

The social production of racial inequality has been called racialization (UK), racial formation (US), and systemic racism (Canada). The critical element being suggested is political processes that transcend more than one institution and that result in racial inequality. Howard Winant writes of how race issues are integrated in the major issues of the twentieth century:

> Race is situated at the crossroads of identity and social structure, where difference framed inequality, and where political processes operate with a comprehensiveness that ranges from the world historical to the intrapsychic. (2004: ix)

This concept has been highlighted in the articles in Part II on the social construction of immigrant women (Ng), on analyzing race through the intersection of class and gender (Stasiulis), on democratic racism (Henry et. al.), and on post-9/11 (Razack). The range of systemic racism stretches from local and domestic issues to international and transnational ones. As a result, Winant writes:

> I consider race to be a key organizational and ideological component of both state and civil society. Race shapes both public and personal life, historical and contemporary experience. (2004: x)

Any analysis of race, specifically systemic racism, requires a focus on resistance too. People have fought, and continue to fight, for their very humanity. The final section in this book, as a result, focuses on anti-racism and resistance (a topic we return to later).

In Part III we see how race analysis shifts from an explicit focus on race to that of racialization. Li and Mahtani point to explicit processes of racialization—policies of the institutional exclusion of Chinese Canadians and the discourse of identity-naming mixed-race women, respectively. In Tanovich's article on racial profiling, however, we see subtle racialization processes that are denied. While the concept of racialization can signify power relations without validating race, it simultaneously helps in the analysis of power and privilege and the consequences of exclusion and marginalization. Although this approach is useful, questions are asked of the possibilities of the depoliticization of race (Murji and Solomos 2005: 22). Racial inequality is of course interconnected with issues of gender, class, sexuality, disability, age, religion, language, etc. The specific ways racial issues still preoccupy Western social imaginaries make this specific form of social inequality a continuing issue in the twenty-first century.

Scholarship on race and racialization in Canada grew with unprecedented richness and diversity in the 1990s. There is no question of race being a fundamental organizing force in Canadian society. In 2000, there was a new urgency: A. Kazemipur and S.S. Halli published *The New Poverty in Canada: Ethnic Groups and Ghetto Neighbourhoods*. This urgency was given a new name by community activists and taken up in the 2006 publication of Grace-Edward Galabuzi's *Canada's Economic Apartheid: The Social Exclusion of Racialized Groups in the New Century*, and in the 2008 publication of Maria Wallis and Siu-ming Kwok's *Daily Struggles: The Deepening Racialization and Feminization of Poverty in Canada*. Racialized communities, organized collectively in Toronto, gave birth to this name for social reality at the beginning of the twenty-first century—economic apartheid. In such a political reality, in 2005, Jo-Anne Lee and John Lutz in *Situating 'Race' and Racisms in Space, Time, and Theory: Critical Essays for Activists and Scholars* called for critical self-reflection:

> Changing concepts of 'race', different manifestations of racisms, and intricate complexities of racializations require activists and scholars to develop a broad range of tools to analyze racial formations as they exist and change across space, time, and theory.

Critical self-reflection becomes crucial in assessing where we have come from and where we are heading. (2005: 10)

On one level, *The Politics of Race in Canada* is conceptualized to provide a general overview of where we have come from, where we are now, and to provide some direction forward. What is clear as we do step forward is our collective desire to respond and, through our response, to create a critical anti-racism discourse and practice that will challenge and undermine the racial hegemony in Canada.

The four articles in Part IV demonstrate some of the strategies being utilized by Canadian scholars to address racial inequality. Aylward documents the use of critical race theory and perspectives to challenge the racial bias of the 'reasonable person' standard. Lawrence and Dua call for an alliance between anti-racism and Indigenous scholars and activists by taking Indigenous decolonization seriously. Dei makes problematic the silence around race in official Canadian circles. 'To examine the racializing gaze', Dei writes, 'is to be politically engaged in anti-racism work and to expose the structural ways white supremacy and privilege continue to exist in Canada' (Dei in Hier and Bolaria 2007: 59). Finally, Afua Cooper reveals how the resistances to slavery in 1793–1803 created black men and women as active agents in their own emancipation. All the articles in this section, in their own way, call for active resistance. Despite the diversity of approaches to anti-racism and resistance, all of the above authors acknowledge the centrality of race as an organizing social force in Canadian society and the Canadian state.

Anti-Racism as Political Engagement and Critical Reflection

Anti-racism in the twenty-first century includes several other strategies, some of which we shall discuss briefly as a way to critically self-reflect on future anti-racist political engagement. In the tradition of William DuBois and Frantz Fanon is the documentation and analysis of the internalization of racial inequality and its consequences. Both authors show how the racially marginalized and oppressed are psychologically wounded as they negotiate the violence of racism. These studies can be strategic for establishing racial self-worth. The documentation of the pain and suffering of racism can also validate people's individual suffering as that of a collective experience. This strategy clearly aims to empower the racialized individual and communities by aiming to liberate the colonized mind and consciousness.

Given contemporary society's influences of globalization and international migration, scholars have used the lenses of diaspora and transnationalism to analyze global racial inequality. The transcendence of national boundaries creates the opportunity to reject essentialized subjectivities and, as Paul Gilroy writes in *The Black Atlantic*, 'to create identities of resistance' (Gilroy in Anthias and Lloyd 2002: 29). According to Floya Anthias, 'Gilroy suggests that diasporic positionality produces a form of consciousness that crosses the borders of given national, or ethnic, tunnel visions, constituting a double consciousness' (2002: 35). International anti-racism has a solid tradition in the struggles against colonialism, the apartheid in South Africa, and the achievement after World War II of the rejection of the scientific scaffolding of 'race' and the establishment of the grounds of 'crimes against humanity'.

Gilroy, in *Against Race: Imagining Political Culture beyond the Colour Line* (2000b), suggests a radical strategy of anti-racism. He calls for transcending race to aim for 'the goal of authentic democracy' (2000b: 12). Such a strategy he suggests would liberate people from the hierarchies of raciology (2000b: 13). This approach, in fact, would serve to liberate *all* people: 'Dr Martin Luther King, Jr, . . . was fond of pointing out that

race thinking has the capacity to make its beneficiaries inhuman even as it deprives its victims of their humanity' (2000b: 13). Toward the end of his book, however, Gilroy seems to call not for the transcendence of race but for a linking and a re-articulation:

> We had to show how 'race' could be articulated together with other dimensions of power and to demonstrate the formative force of imperial and colonial relations in shaping metropolitan social life. (2000b: 334–5)

This re-articulated perspective would enable 'a different inventory of political tasks' that would meet the challenge of powerful visions, or, as Robin Kelley (2002) calls it, 'freedom dreams', by being connected to 'democratic and cosmopolitan traditions' (Gilroy 2000b: 335–6).

This call to connect the work against racism to the general struggle for social justice and democracy is echoed in Howard Winant's work. He writes: 'I suggest that the future of democracy itself depends on the outcomes of racial politics and policies, as they develop both in various national societies and in the world at large' (2002: 100). Given that slavery, colonization, and the world economic order shaped the world's social, economic, and political institutions, Winant argues that 'race defines and organizes the world's future, as it has done for centuries' (2002: 100). He sees race issues as central to movements for social justice and democracy. Resistance to slavery, for example, eventually resulted in the focus on the human and political rights of other subordinated groups such as women and the working class. Winant writes, 'race has become a trope for the unfinished agendas of egalitarianism, democratization, and cultural pluralism' (2004: ix).

After World War II, the United Nations drew on international expertise to delegitimize any doctrine of racial superiority. On 10 December

1948, the United Nations General Assembly adopted the Universal Declaration of Human Rights to ensure that the 'barbarous acts which have outraged the conscience of mankind' during World War II would never occur again (Banton 2002: 39). Winant identifies this historical moment as a 'racial break':

Starting after the Second World War and culminating in the 1960s, there was a global shift, a break in the worldwide racial order that had endured for centuries. The shift occurred because many challenges to the old forms of racial hierarchy converged after the war: anti-colonialism, anti-apartheid, worldwide revulsion at fascism, and perhaps most important, the US civil rights movement, and US–USSR competition in the world's 'south' all called white supremacy into question to an extent unparalled in modern history. These events and conflicts linked antiracism to democratic political development more strongly than ever before. (2002: 100)

In Canada these international developments were definitely an important influence on domestic policies. Both international and domestic pressures resulted in the removal of any mention of race in immigration policies with the late-1960s introduction of the point system. In the field of sociology, ethnic identity, retention, and transformations were focused on in ethnic studies. The identification of increasing incidents of racism and discrimination were initially addressed with equal opportunity policies and eventually focused on human rights.

Worldwide, nations were being pressured by human rights and anti-racist movements to create racial reform initiatives. In Canada, the Universal Declaration of Human Rights was signed in 1948. In 1960, Parliament passed the Canadian Bill of Rights and made discrimination illegal in Canada. Then in 1977, Parliament adopted the Canadian Human Rights Act to address human rights violations in Canada. In 1982, the Canadian Charter of Rights and Freedoms made equality rights part of the Canadian Constitution. Canada's diversity was formally recognized with the establishment of the Canadian Multiculturalism Act in 1988.

Yet there are signs that these rights are formal and not substantive. A 1984 report titled *Equality Now!*, published by the federal Special Committee on Participation of Visible Minorities in Canadian Society, documents the persistence of pervasive racial discrimination in Canada. As a result, a Royal Commission on equality in employment was set up in 1984 with Judge Rosalie Abella at the helm. Abella's recommendations reflect the conceptual shift from individual rights to collective rights being advocated by anti-racist activists and scholars. To address systemic, structural racism in Canadian institutions by way of proactive initiatives, the federal employment equity legislation was passed in 1986. However, the increasing racial inequality in Canada, combined with a strong domestic anti-racism movement, pressured the Canadian government in Durban at the United Nation's Conference against Racism (2001) to address this social inequity. As a result, in March 2005, the federal government established a new initiative publicized in a document titled *A Canada for All: Canada's Action Plan against Racism* (Dewing 2006: 19–21).

The official commitments to racial equality reflected the hope of racialized individuals and communities, including all advocates for social justice in Canada. However, along with the widening gap both internationally and nationally, there was documentation of the increasing racialization and feminization of poverty in Canada (Wallis and Kwok 2008; Galabuzi 2006). The denial and subsequent lack of political response and leadership to address these current social injustices validates what Howard Winant calls a 'new racial hegemony' (2004: 18).

In Canada, it takes many years for human rights commissions to resolve human rights complaints. The onus on the individual combined with long delays give rise to the understanding that justice delayed is basically justice denied. Employment equity legislation penalizes companies for not filing employment equity reports, not for failing to achieve equitable representation in their entire workforce. As a result, so much of Canada's equality measures are public relations that simply reinforce the illusion of racial equality in a multicultural Canada. The public relations facade is utilized to argue against any substantive measures that would hold individuals and institutions accountable for racial equality in Canada. Howard Winant writes,

> [T]here is also a widespread recognition that the reforms undertaken in the 1950s and 1960s have ossified, that they have not gone far enough, that indeed they may be providing a kind of cover for a reassertion of white privilege, white rule, northern cultural norms, all under the banner of post-racial societies, now officially colour-blind and pluralist. (2002: 101)

The 'white settler' mentality explicit in the past still exists, albeit in modern transformations, and, as Frances Henry argues, coexists with democratic and egalitarian principles of a liberal society. The most explicit example of this coexistence is Canada's Indian Act, defining Indian status in Canada as, Bonita Lawrence notes, 'a legacy of legal restrictions and racial apartheid . . .' (2004: 227).

There are other ways systemic racism and racialization processes continue to exist in Canada today. Phrases such as 'playing the race card' and 'being politically correct', for example, are used in ways that seem neutral, yet they are simultaneously denigrating and trivializing a deeply serious issue—racism. By suggesting social manipulation ('playing the race card') and censorship ('being politically correct'), what is in fact 'done' *is* manipulation and censorship of the critical

consequences of racism. Speaking about race and racism is to argue for equality, equity, and social justice. No one needs to 'trump' anyone to have equal access to justice.

Race is re-introduced, too, in more sophisticated discussions around the Human Genome Project, which has as its objective, the search for ways to improve health (Duster 2006: 428). According to Duster,

> In the last five years, there has been a peculiar and fateful irony in the convergence of the desire (and pressure) to use genetics to improve our health, and the decision by the US Congress to require that the National Institute of Health record data and engage in research to lessen the health disparities between racial and ethnic groups. (2006: 428)

The slippery slope is in the next step that sees scientists and clinicians attempt to make conclusions that focus on genetic differences without any social context, such as gender, social class, unemployment, etc. These developments bring echoes of the eugenics movement and the Nazi period to mind (Duster 2006).

Race also emerges in current discussions of national security, the 'war on terror', immigration, Africentric schools, and the use of so-called 'neutral' social processes such as the exclusive use of anonymous student evaluations to judge quality of teaching in white-dominated universities, and the height restrictions of firefighters. In addition, any discussion of cutbacks to services, such as raising recreation centre fees, because of the adverse effect on the working class and the poor who are increasingly people from racialized communities, become racialized.

Given current sophisticated and ubiquitous forms of systemic racism, connecting anti-racist resistance and scholarship to democratic and social justice traditions will, as Paul Gilroy writes, 'make a different inventory of political tasks around "race" and to undertake them in a new spirit' (2000b: 335). The coercive, hostile, and undemocratic measures undertaken in the name of 'the war on terror' are currently reinforcing racial divides and attempting to justify infringements of human rights and social justice. Denial of racial injustice in Canada, and within Canadian institutions, includes the tactic of erasing the focus on racial inequality by reifying and abstracting the central issues under topics such as diversity, transnationalism, and global studies. Domestic racial inequality is made invisible, perpetuating the illusion of a liberal state that prides itself on formal multiculturalism and tolerance. In 2008, the new racial hegemony, internationally and nationally, presents new challenges. Collectively, as anti-racist activists and scholars, we can challenge the contradictions and hypocracies of liberal societies, including Canadian society, while maintaining our focus on the exploited, the homeless, and the devalued and marginalized.

In creating a Canada that *is safe for race, safe from race,* the challenge is twofold. First, we must acknowledge the continuing salience of race in an ostensibly race-neutral society. As long as racism and racialized inequality persist in a society where people are rewarded or penalized without justifiable cause (Cose 1997), race matters in privileging some, disempowering others (Morris and Cowlishaw 1997). Second, we must deconstruct the coded concepts and subtextual discourses by which people continue to attribute social significance to race in everyday life, despite laws and norms that discourage its use to differentiate, deny, or exclude (Li 2007). The combination of contested terrains and the concerted efforts to theorize race will continue to be fuelled by our 'freedom dreams'. Our 'freedom dreams', our principles of equality, democracy, and social justice, and our vision of human dignity, will continue to guide us. Theorizing race is critical for the very future of democracy. We will continue, in the twenty-first century, to reinvent resistance to racial inequality, and all forms of social injustice, and to build the hope for a just society.

Appendix A

Universal Declaration of Human Rights[1]

Preamble

Whereas recognition of the inherent dignity and of the equal and inalienable rights of all members of the human family is the foundation of freedom, justice and peace in the world,

Whereas disregard and contempt for human rights have resulted in barbarous acts which have outraged the conscience of mankind, and the advent of a world in which human beings shall enjoy freedom of speech and belief and freedom from fear and want has been proclaimed as the highest aspiration of the common people,

Whereas it is essential, if man is not to be compelled to have recourse, as a last resort, to rebellion against tyranny and oppression, that human rights should be protected by the rule of law,

Whereas it is essential to promote the development of friendly relations between nations,

Whereas the peoples of the United Nations have in the Charter reaffirmed their faith in fundamental human rights, in the dignity and worth of the human person and in the equal rights of men and women and have determined to promote social progress and better standards of life in larger freedom,

Whereas Member States have pledged themselves to achieve, in co-operation with the United Nations, the promotion of universal respect for and observance of human rights and fundamental freedoms,

Whereas a common understanding of these rights and freedoms is of the greatest importance for the full realization of this pledge,

Now, Therefore THE GENERAL ASSEMBLY proclaims THIS UNIVERSAL DECLARATION OF HUMAN RIGHTS as a common standard of achievement for all peoples and all nations, to the end that every individual and every organ of society, keeping this Declaration constantly in mind, shall strive by teaching and education to promote respect for these rights and freedoms and by progressive measures, national and international, to secure their universal and effective recognition and observance, both among the peoples of Member States themselves and among the peoples of territories under their jurisdiction.

Note

1. This selection is taken from the Universal Declaration of Human Rights, © 1948, United Nations, available at <http://www.un.org/Overview/rights.html>. Reprinted with the permission of the United Nations..

Appendix B

UNESCO and Its Programme: The Race Question[1]

The importance which the problem of race has acquired in the modern world scarcely needs to be pointed out. Mankind will not soon forget the injustices and crimes which give such tragic overtones to the word 'race'. It was inevitable that UNESCO should take a position in a controversy so closely linked not only with its goals but also with its very nature. For, like war, the problem of race which directly affects millions of human lives and causes countless conflicts has its roots 'in the minds of men'. The preamble of UNESCO's Constitution, adopted in 1945, specifically named racism as one of the social evils which the new Organization was called upon to combat. Moreover, the Constitution declares that 'the great and terrible war which has now ended was a war made possible by the denial of the democratic principles of the dignity, equality and mutual respect of men, and by the propagation, in their place, through ignorance and prejudice, of the doctrine of the *inequality* of men and races'.

The vigorous action which UNESCO is about to undertake in support of the struggle against race prejudice was evolved in response to a resolution adopted by the United Nations Social and Economic Council at its sixth session in 1948. By that resolution UNESCO was called upon to consider the timeliness 'of proposing and recommending the general adoption of a programme of dissemination of scientific facts designed to bring about the disappearance of that which is commonly called race prejudice'.

The General Conference of UNESCO in 1949 adopted three resolutions which committed the Organization 'to study and collect scientific materials concerning questions of race', 'to give wide diffusion to the scientific material collected', and 'to prepare an educational campaign based on this information'.

There is great confusion on the notion of race, so great that no campaign designed to remove prejudices can be effectively undertaken without careful preparation. Such groundwork must include a clarification of the present scientific position in the controversy on the subject; indeed, it must first of all provide a definition of race on which the different scientific circles concerned can agree.

It was with this in view that UNESCO invited a number of anthropologists and sociologists from various countries to meet as a committee of experts in UNESCO House in December 1949. They discussed all aspects of the problem at great length and finally drew up a declaration, the text of which is presented further on. Every word of this declaration was carefully weighed. Nothing was neglected in the effort to present to the public in a simple and clear manner the conclusions which science has reached on the subject.

Nor was the declaration in the form decided upon in Paris the end of the effort to make the statement fully authoritative. It was submitted to many leading scientists in various countries. They examined it in detail and a number of them suggested additions and amendments. The competence and objectivity of the scientists who signed the document in its final form cannot be questioned.

In organizing the meeting of experts which produced this authoritative declaration on the race problem, UNESCO took up again, after a lapse of fifteen years, a project which the International Institute of Intellectual Co-operation has wished to carry through but which it had to abandon in deference to the appeasement policy of the pre-war period. The race question had become one of the pivots of Nazi ideology and policy. Mazaryk and Benes took the initiative in calling for a conference to re-establish in the minds and consciences of men everywhere the truth about race. Scientists were unanimous in wishing to have the opportunity of denouncing before world opinion the absurdity of the racist dogma. But they were not given such an opportunity. Nazi propaganda was able to continue its baleful work unopposed by the authority of an international organization.

Knowledge of the truth does not always help change emotional attitudes that draw their real strength from the subconscious or from factors beside the real issue. Knowledge of the truth can, however, prevent rationalizations of reprehensible acts or behaviour prompted by feelings that men will not easily avow openly. UNESCO has the will and the means to make available to everyone the achievements of science, if those achievements can help to lessen the hatreds that separate human groups from one another. But UNESCO can really succeed in this task only if it is careful to present the facts in all their complexity without trying to hide ignorances and doubts.

Science was faced with the problem of race at the beginning of the nineteenth century when the great evolutionary theories were being formulated. Unfortunately, the problem soon shifted from the purely scientific field to the field of politics. As a result, the discussions which it has provoked have rarely been free from the passions and prejudices of the moment.

But psychology, biology, and cultural anthropology, which have developed so remarkably during the last fifty years, have made possible extensive inquiries and experimental research studies into the problem. The results of this important work are presented in general terms in the declaration of the experts assembled by UNESCO. It should not be forgotten, however, that new methods and techniques of appraising results are being put into practice every day. At the present moment, it is impossible to demonstrate that there exist between 'races' differences of intelligence and temperament other than those produced by cultural environment. If, tomorrow, more accurate tests or more thorough studies should prove that 'races' as such do, in fact, have different innate faculties or aptitudes, UNESCO's moral position on the race question would not be changed.

Racism is a particularly vicious and mean expression of the caste spirit. It involves belief in the innate and absolute superiority of an arbitrarily defined human group over other equally arbitrarily defined groups. Instead of being based on scientific facts, it is generally maintained in defiance of the scientific method. As an ideology and feeling, racism is by its nature aggressive. It threatens the essential moral values by satisfying the taste for domination and by exalting the contempt for man. Concern for human dignity demands that all citizens be equal before the law, and that they share equally in the advantages assured them by law, no matter what their physical or intellectual differences may be. The law sees in each person only a human being who has the right to the same consideration and to equal respect. The conscience of all mankind demands that this be true for all the peoples of the earth. It matters little, therefore, whether the diversity of men's gifts be the result of biological or of cultural factors.

Thus, the problem of race must be approached not only on the biological and social levels but also on the moral level. And, in view of the growing interrelation of the sciences affecting man and society, it can be solved only by the joint action of different scientific disciplines. UNESCO will undertake to make known to a vast public the results of the researches obtained in all these various fields. It will, for example, publish pamphlets prepared by eminent specialists.

Many inquiries have already been undertaken into interracial conflicts and the factors that produce them. The time has now come for us to consider the societies which have in large measure succeeded in resolving antagonisms by overriding racial differences. Thus, the General Conference of UNESCO in Florence recommended for the 1951 programme of the Organization a study of racial relations in Brazil. This great republic has a civilization which has been developed by the direct contributions of different races. And it suffers less than other nations from the effects of those prejudices which are at the root of so many vexatious and cruel measures in countries of similar ethnic composition. We are as yet ill-informed about the factors which brought about such a favourable and, in many ways, exemplary situation. But in the present state of the social sciences, general speculations no longer suffice. We must have specialists make searching inquiries in the field. We must learn from them exactly why and how social, psychological, and economic factors have contributed in varying degrees to make possible the harmony which exists in Brazil. Then the results of their inquiries can be set forth in publications in order to stimulate those who are still struggling elsewhere to introduce more peaceable and happier interracial relations.

Yet, no matter how great an effort UNESCO may make in this field, it cannot by itself bring to an end the most tenacious and the most widely spread of human prejudices. It must be able to count on the support of groups and organizations formed in many countries to achieve the same purpose. To these fighters, indeed to all those who rebel against the idea that millions of human beings are condemned by the mere fact of their birth to humiliation and misery, UNESCO brings its co-operation. It brings too the hope that the struggle against the misdeeds of racism will become a crusade to be carried out in common by all the peoples of the earth.

Text of the Statement Issued 18 July 1950

1. Scientists have reached general agreements in recognizing that mankind is one: that all men belong to the same species, *Homo sapiens*. It is further generally agreed among scientists that all men are probably derived from the same common stock; and that such differences as exist between different groups of mankind are due to the operation of evolutionary factors of differentiation such as isolation, the drift and random fixation of the material particles which control heredity (the genes), changes in the structure of these particles, hybridization, and natural selection. In these ways groups have arisen of varying stability and degree of differentiation which have been classified in different ways for different purposes.

2. From the biological standpoint, the species *Homo sapiens* is made up of a number of populations, each one of which differs from the others in the frequency of one or more genes. Such genes, responsible for the hereditary differences between men, are always few when compared to the whole genetic constitution of man and to the vast number of genes common to all human beings regardless of the population to which they belong. This means that the likenesses among men are far greater than their differences.

3. A race, from the biological standpoint, may therefore be defined as one of the group of populations constituting the species *Homo sapiens*. These populations are capable of interbreeding with one another but, by virtue of the isolating barriers which in the past kept them more or less separated, exhibit certain physical differences as a result of their somewhat different biological histories. These represent variations, as it were, on a common theme.

4. In short, the term 'race' designates a group or population characterized by some concentrations, relative as to frequency and distribution, of hereditary particles (genes) or physical characters, which appear, fluctuate, and often disappear in the course of time by reason of geographic and/or cultural isolation. The varying manifestations of these traits in different populations are perceived in different ways by each group. What is perceived is largely preconceived, so that each group arbitrarily tends to misinterpret the variability which occurs as a fundamental difference which separates that group from all others.

5. These are the scientific facts. Unfortunately, however, when most people use the term 'race' they do not do so in the sense above defined. To most people, a race is any group of people whom they choose to describe as a race. Thus, many national, religious, geographic, linguistic, or cultural groups have, in such loose usage, been called 'race', when obviously Americans are not a race, nor are Englishmen, nor Frenchmen, nor any other national group. Catholics, Protestants, Moslems, and Jews are not races, nor are groups who speak English or any other language thereby definable as a race; people who live in Iceland or England or India are not races; nor are people who are culturally Turkish or Chinese or the like thereby describable as races.

6. National, religious, geographic, linguistic, and cultural groups do not necessarily coincide with racial groups: and the cultural traits of such groups have no demonstrated genetic connexion with racial traits. Because serious errors of this kind are habitually committed when the term 'race' is used in popular parlance, it would be better when speaking of human races to drop the term 'race' altogether and speak of *ethnic groups*.

7. Now what has the scientist to say about the groups of mankind which may be recognized at the present time? Human races can be and have been differently classified by different anthropologists, but at the present time most anthropologists agree on classifying the greater part of present-day mankind into three major divisions, as follows:

> The Mongoloid Division
> The Negroid Division
> The Caucasoid Division

The biological processes which the classifier has here embalmed, as it were, are dynamic, not static. These divisions were not the same in the past as they are at present, and there is every reason to believe that they will change in the future.

8. Many sub-groups or ethnic groups within these divisions have been described. There is no general agreement upon their number, and in any event most ethnic groups have not yet been either studied or described by the physical anthropologists.

9. Whatever classification the anthropologist makes of man, he never includes mental characteristics as part of those classifications. It is now generally recognized that intelligence tests do not in themselves enable us to differentiate safely between what is due to innate capacity and what is the result of environmental influences, training, and education. Wherever it has been

possible to make allowances for differences in environmental opportunities, the tests have shown essential similarity in mental characters among all human groups. In short, given similar degrees of cultural opportunity to realize their potentialities, the average achievement of the members of each ethnic group is about the same. The scientific investigations of recent years fully support the dictum of Confucius (551–478 BC): 'Men's natures are alike; it is their habits that carry them far apart.'

10. The scientific material available to us at present does not justify the conclusion that inherited genetic differences are a major factor in producing the differences between the cultures and cultural achievements of different peoples or groups. It does indicate, however, that the history of the cultural experience which each group has undergone is the major factor in explaining such differences. The one trait which above all others has been at a premium in the evolution of men's mental characters has been educability, plasticity. This is a trait which all human beings possess. It is indeed, a species character of *Homo sapiens*.

11. So far as temperament is concerned, there is no definite evidence that there exist inborn differences between human groups. There is evidence that whatever group differences of the kind there might be are greatly over-ridden by the individual differences, and by the differences springing from environmental factors.

12. As for personality and character, these may be considered raceless. In every human group a rich variety of personality and character types will be found, and there is no reason for believing that any human group is richer tha[n] any other in these respects.

13. With respect to race mixture, the evidence points unequivocally to the fact that this has been going on from the earliest times.

Indeed, one of the chief processes of race formation and race extinction or absorption is by means of hybridization between races or ethnic groups. Furthermore, no convincing evidence has been adduced that race mixture of itself produces biologically bad effects. Statements that human hybrids frequently show undesirable traits, both physically and mentally, physical disharmonies and mental degeneracies, are not supported by the facts. There is, therefore, no *biological* justification for prohibiting intermarriage between persons of different ethnic groups.

14. The biological fact of race and the myth of 'race' should be distinguished. For all practical social purposes 'race' is not so much a biological phenomenon as a social myth. The myth 'race' has created an enormous amount of human and social damage. In recent years it has taken a heavy toll in human lives and caused untold suffering. It still prevents the normal development of millions of human beings and deprives civilization of the effective co-operation of productive minds. The biological differences between ethnic groups should be disregarded from the standpoint of social acceptance and social action. The unity of mankind from both the biological and social viewpoints is the main thing. To recognize this and to act accordingly is the first requirement of modern man. It is but to recognize what a great biologist wrote in 1875: 'As man advances in civilization, and small tribes are united into larger communities, the simplest reason would tell each individual that he ought to extend his social instincts and sympathies to all the members of the same nation, though personally unknown to him. This point being on[c]e reached, there is only an artificial barrier to prevent his sympathies extending to the men of all nations and races.' These are the words of Charles Darwin in *The Descent of*

Man (2nd ed., 1875, pp. 187–8). And, indeed, the whole of human history shows that a co-operative spirit is not only natural to men, but more deeply rooted than any self-seeking tendencies. If this were not so we should not see the growth of integration and organization of his communities which the centuries and the millennia plainly exhibit.

15. We now have to consider the bearing of these statements on the problem of human equality. It must be asserted with the utmost emphasis that equality as an ethical principle in no way depends upon the assertion that human beings are in fact equal in endowment. Obviously individuals in all ethnic groups vary greatly among themselves in endowment. Nevertheless, the characteristics in which human groups differ from one another are often exaggerated and used as a basis for questioning the validity of equality in the ethical sense. For this purpose we have thought it worthwhile to set out in a formal manner what is at present scientifically established concerning individual and group differences.

(1) In matters of race, the only characteristics which anthropologists can effectively use as a basis for classifications are physical and physiological.

(2) According to present knowledge there is no proof that the groups of mankind differ in their innate mental characteristics, whether in respect of intelligence or temperament. The scientific evidence indicates that the range of mental capacities in all ethnic groups is much the same.

(3) Historical and sociological studies support the view that genetic differences are not of importance in determining the social and cultural differences between different groups of *Homo sapiens*, and that the social and cultural *changes* in different groups, have, in the main, been independent of *changes* in inborn constitution. Vast social changes have occurred which were not in any way connected with changes in racial type.

(4) There is no evidence that race mixture as such produces bad results from the biological point of view. The social results of race mixture whether for good or ill are to be traced to social factors.

(5) All normal human beings are capable of learning to share in a common life, to understand the nature of mutual service and reciprocity, and to respect social obligations and contracts. Such biological differences as exist between members of different ethnic groups have no relevance to problems of social and political organization, moral life, and communication between human beings.

Lastly, biological studies lend support to the ethic of universal brotherhood; for man is born with drives toward co-operation, and unless these drives are satisfied, men and nations alike fall ill. Man is born a social being who can reach his fullest development only through interaction with his fellows. The denial at any point of this social bond between man and man brings with it disintegration. In this sense, every man is his brother's keeper. For every man is a piece of the continent, a part of the main, because he is involved in mankind.

Note

1. The original statement was drafted at UNESCO House, Paris, by the following experts:

    Professor Ernest Beaglehole, New Zealand
    Professor Juan Comas, Mexico
    Professor L.A. Costa Pinto, Brazil
    Professor Franklin Frazier, United States
    Professor Morris Ginsberg, United Kingdom
    Dr Humayun Kabir, India
    Professor Claude Levi-Strauss, France
    Professor Ashley Montagu, United States (Rapporteur)

    The text was revised by Professor Ashley Montagu, after criticism submitted by Professors Hadley Cantril, E.G. Conklin, Gunnar Dahlberg, Theodosius Dobzhansky, L.C. Dunn, Donald Hager, Julian S. Huxley, Otto Klineberg, Wilbert Moore, H.J. Muller, Gunnar Myrdal, Joseph Needham, and Curt Stern.

Appendix C

The Canadian Charter of Rights and Freedoms[1]

Guarantee of Rights and Freedoms
Section 1

The Canadian Charter of Rights and Freedoms guarantees the rights and freedoms set out in it subject only to such reasonable limits prescribed by law as can be demonstrably justified in a free and democratic society.

Equality Rights
Section 15(1)

Every individual is equal before and under the law and has the right to the equal protection and equal benefit of the law without discrimination and, in particular, without discrimination based on race, national or ethnic origin, colour, religion, sex, age, or mental or physical disability.

Section 15(2)

Subsection (1) does not preclude any law, program or activity that has as its object the amelioration of conditions of disadvantaged individuals or groups including those that are disadvantaged because of race, national or ethnic origin, colour, religion, sex, age, or mental or physical disability.

Note

1. For the full text, see <http://laws.justice.gc.ca/en/charter>.

References

Abdel-Shehid, G. 2000. 'Writing Hockey through Race: Rethinking Black Hockey in Canada', in *Rude: Contemporary Black Canadian Cultural Criticism*, ed. R. Walcott (Toronto: Insomniac Press), 69–86.

———. 2003. 'In Place of "Race", Space: "Basketball in Canada" and the Absence of Racism', in *Sporting Dystopias: The Making and Meanings of Urban Sport Cultures*, eds R.C. Wilcox, D.L. Andrews, R. Pitter, and R.L. Irwin (Albany: State University of New York Press), 247–63.

Abele, F., and D. Stasiulis. 1989. 'Canada as a "White Settler Colony": What about Natives and Immigrants?', in *The New Canadian Political Economy*, eds W. Clement and G. Williams (Montreal: McGill-Queen's University Press).

Abella, I., and H. Tropper. 1982. *None Is too Many* (Toronto: Lester & Orpen Dennys).

Abella, R.S. 1984. *Equality in Employment: A Royal Commission Report* (Ottawa: Supply and Services Canada).

Abu-Lughod, L. 2003. 'Saving Muslim Women or Standing with Them? On Images, Ethics, and War in Our Times', *Insaniyaat* 1, 1 (spring), available at <http://www.aucegypt.edu/academic/insanyat/Issue%20I/I-article.htm>. Accessed 15 Nov. 2003.

Adamson, N., L. Briskin, and M. McPhail. 1988. *Feminist Organizing for Change: The Contemporary Women's Movement in Canada* (Don Mills, ON: Oxford University Press).

Adilman, T. 1984. 'A Preliminary Sketch of Chinese Women and Work in British Columbia, 1858–1950', in *Not Just Pin Money: Selected Essays on the History of Women's Work in British Columbia*, eds B.K. Latham and R.J. Padro (Victoria, BC: Camosun College).

Agnew, V., ed. 2007. 'Introduction', in *Interrogating Race and Racism* (Toronto: University of Toronto Press), 3–36.

Agocs, C., and M. Boyd. 1993. 'The Canadian Ethnic Mosaic Recast for the 1990s', in *Social Stratification in Canada*, 3rd edn, eds J.E. Curtis, E. Grabb, and N. Guppy (Scarborough, ON: Prentice Hall).

Ahmad, A. 1992. *In Theory: Classes, Nations, Literatures* (London: Verso).

Alexander, C. 1996. *The Art of Being Black: The Creation of Black British Youth Identities* (New York: Oxford University Press).

Alfred, T. 2005. *Wasase: Indigenous Pathways to Action and Freedom* (Peterborough, ON: Broadview Press).

Ali, T. 2002. *The Clash of Fundamentalisms: Crusades, Jihads, and Modernity* (London: Verso).

Althusser, L. 1971. 'Ideology and Ideological State: Philos Apparatuses', in *Lenin and Philosophy and Other Essays* (London: Monthly Review Press).

Amin, N.A., and G. Dei. 2006. *The Poetics of Anti-racism* (Halifax: Fernwood).

Amos, V., and P. Parmar. 1984. 'Challenging Imperial Feminism', *Feminist Review* 17 (July): 3–19.

Anderson, B. 1983. *Imagined Communities* (London: Verso).

———. 1991. *Imagined Communities: Reflections on the Origin and Spread of Nationalism* (London and New York: Verso).

————. 2003. 'Nationalism and Cultural Survival in Our Time: A Sketch', in *At the Risk of Being Heard: Identity, Indigenous Rights, and Postcolonial States*, eds B. Dean and J.M. Levi (Ann Arbor: University of Michigan Press), 165–90.

Anderson, K. 2007. *Race and the Crisis of Humanism* (New York: Routledge).

Anisef, P., P. Axelrod, E. Baichman, C. James, and A. Turrittin. 2000. *Opportunities and Uncertainty: Life Course Experiences of the Class of '73* (Toronto: University of Toronto Press).

Anthias, F. 1988. 'Race and Class Revisited: Conceptualizing Race and Racism', paper presented at the International Sociological Association's Research Committee for Race, Ethnic and Minority Studies, Amsterdam, Dec.

————, and C. Lloyd. 2002. *Rethinking Anti-racisms: From Theory to Practice* (New York: Routledge).

Anzaldua, G. 1987. *Borderlands: The New Mestiza: La Frontera* (San Francisco: Spinsters/Aunt Lute).

Apple, M. 1993. 'Constructing the "Other": Rightist Reconstructions of Common Sense', in *Race, Identity and Representation in Education*, eds C. McCarthy and W. Crichlow (New York and London: Routledge).

Armstrong, J., ed. 1998. 'Land Speaking', in *Speaking for the Generations: Native Writers on Writing*, ed. S.J. Ortiz (Tucson: University of Arizona Press), 174–95.

Armstrong, P., and H. Armstrong. 1978. *The Double Ghetto: Canadian Women and Their Segregated Work* (Toronto: McClelland & Stewart).

————. 1986. 'Beyond Sexless Class and Classless Sex: Towards Feminist Marxism' and 'More on Marxism and Feminism: A Response to Patricia Connelly', in *The Politics of Diversity: Feminism, Marxism and Nationalism*, eds R. Hamilton and M. Barrett (Montreal: Book Center), 208–40, 249–54.

Arnopoulous, S.M. 1979. 'The Settlement of Immigrants: The Need for a Policy', unpublished ms., Faculty of Education, University of British Columbia.

Austin, J. 1955. *How to Do Things with Words* (Cambridge, MA: Harvard University Press).

Avery, D. 1979. *'Dangerous Foreigners': European Immigrant Workers and Labour Radicalism in Canada, 1896–1936* (Toronto: McClelland & Stewart).

Aylward, C.A. 1999. 'Canadian Critical Race Litigation: Wedding Theory and Practice', in *Canadian Critical Race Theory: Racism and the Law* (Halifax: Fernwood).

————. 2002. *Critical Race Theory and Praxis* (Toronto: Faculty of Law, University of Toronto).

Azoulay, K. 1997. *Black, Jewish and Interracial: It's Not the Colour of Your Skin, but the Race of Your Kin, and Other Myths of Identity* (Durham, NC: Duke University Press).

Back, L. 1996. *New Ethnicities and Urban Culture* (London: UCL Press).

Backhouse, C. 1999. *Colour-coded: A Legal History of Racism in Canada, 1900–1950* (Toronto: University of Toronto Press for The Osgoode Society for Canadian Legal History).

Ball, W., and J. Solomos. 1990. *Race and Local Politics* (London: Macmillan).

Bannerji, H. 2000. *The Dark Side of the Nation: Essays on Multiculturalism, Nationalism and Gender* (Toronto: Canadian Scholars' Press).

————, et al. 1991. *Unsettling Relations: The University as a Site of Feminist Struggles* (Toronto: Women's Press).

Banton, M. 1967. *Race Relations* (New York: Basic Books).

————, ed. 1977a. 'Social Darwinism', in *The Idea of Race* (London: Tavistock), 89–100.

————, ed. 1977b. 'The Intellectual Inheritance', in *The Idea of Race* (London: Tavistock).

————. 1987. *Racial Theories* (Cambridge: Cambridge University Press), vii.

————. 2002. *The International Politics of Race* (Cambridge: Polity Press).

Baptiste, M.J. 1988. 'The Implications of the New Immigration Bill', *Critical Social Policy* 23: 62–9.

Barrett, M. 1980. *Women's Oppression Today* (London: Verso).

————. 1989. 'Some Different Meanings of the Concept of "Difference": Feminist Theory and the Concept of Ideology', in *The Difference Within:*

Feminism and Critical Theory, eds E. Meese and A. Parker (Amsterdam: John Benjamins), 37–48.

Basran, G.S. 1983. 'Canadian Immigration Policy and Theories of Racism', in *Racial Minorities in Multicultural Canada*, eds P.S. Li and B.S. Bolaria (Toronto: Garamond Press).

BBC News. 2001. 'Playing the Race Card: Trump or Joker?' (24 Apr.), available at <http://www.news.bbc.co.uk>.

Beckett, C., and M. Macey. 2001. 'Race, Gender, and Sexuality: The Oppression of Multiculturalism', *Women's Studies International Forum* 24, 3, 4 (May–Aug.): 309–19.

Bell, D., and G. Valentine. 1995. 'The Sexed Self: Strategies of Performance, Sites of Resistance', in *Mapping the Subject*, eds S. Pile and N. Thrift (London: Routledge), 143–58.

Berardi, D. 2008. *The Persistence of Whiteness: Race and Contemporary Hollywood Cinema* (New York: Routledge).

Bhabha, H. 1994. *The Location of Culture* (London: Routledge).

Bhavnani, K. 1989. 'Complexity, Activism, Optimism: An Interview with Angela Davis', *Feminist Review* 31 (spring): 66–83.

———. and M. Coulson. 1986. 'Transforming Socialist-Feminism: The Challenge of Racism', *Feminist Review* 23 (June).

Biddiss, M.D., ed. 1979. *Images of Race* (New York: Holmes & Meier).

Billig, M., et al. 1988. *Ideological Dilemmas: A Social Psychology of Everyday Thinking* (London: Sage).

Billings, A., B. Denham, and K. Halone. 2002. 'Differential Accounts of Race in Broadcast Commentary of the 2000 NCAA Men's and Women's Final Four Basketball Tournaments', *Sociology of Sport Journal* 19: 315–32.

Bishop, A. 2005. *Beyond Token Change: Breaking the Cycle of Oppression in Institutions* (Halifax: Fernwood).

Blank, R.M., M. Dabady, and C. Citro, eds. 2004. *Measuring Racial Discrimination* (Washington: The National Academies Press).

Blauner, R. 1991. 'Racism, Race and Ethnicity: Some Reflections on the Language of Race', paper pre-

sented at the Annual Meeting of the American Sociological Association, thematic session: Re-examining the Commonly Used Concepts in Race–Ethnic Relations, Cincinnati, Aug.

Bogle, M.T. 1988. 'Brixton Black Women's Centre: Organizing on Child Sexual Abuse', *Feminist Review* 28 (Jan.): 132–5.

Bolaria, B.S., and P.S. Li. 1988. *Racial Oppression in Canada*, 2nd edn (Toronto: Garamond).

BondGraham, D. 2007. 'The New Orleans that Race Built: Racism, Disaster, and Urban Spatial Relationships', *Souls* 9, 1: 4–18.

Bondi, L. 1993. 'Locating Identity Politics', in *Place and the Politics of Identity*, eds M. Keith and S. Pile (London: Routledge), 84–102.

Bonilla-Silva, E. 1996. 'Rethinking Racism: Toward a Structural Interpretation', *American Sociological Review*.

Bonnett, A. 2000. *Anti-racism* (London: Routledge).

Booth, D., and C. Tatz. 2000. *One Eyed: A View of Australian Sport* (Sydney: Allen & Unwin).

Boyd, M. 1975. 'The Status of Immigrant Women in Canada', *Canadian Review of Sociology and Anthropology* 12: 406–16.

———. 1984. 'At a Disadvantage: The Occupational Attainments of Foreign Born Women in Canada', *International Migration Review* 18 (winter).

———. 1986. 'Immigrant Women in Canada', in *International Migration*, eds R.J. Simon and C. Bretell (Towota, NJ: Rowman & Allenhed), 47–75.

———. 1989. 'Immigration and Income Security Policies in Canada: Implications for Elderly Immigrant Women', *Population Research and Policy Review* 8: 5–24.

———. 1993a. 'Measuring Ethnicity in the Future: Population, Policies, Politics, and Social Science Research', in *Challenges of Measuring an Ethnic World: Science, Politics and Reality*, eds G. Goldmann and N. McKenney (Ottawa and Washington: Statistics Canada and the United States Bureau of the Census).

———. 1993b. 'Measuring Ethnicity', paper presented at the lecture series, Robert F. Harney Professorship and Program in Ethnic, Immigration and Pluralism Studies, Department of Sociology, University of Toronto, Feb.

———. 1996. 'Constructing Ethnic Responses: Socioeconomic and Media Effects', Working Paper 96-133, Center for the Study of Population and Demography, Florida State University, Tallahassee.

———, G. Goldmann, and P. White. 2000. 'Race in the Canadian Census', in *Visible Minorities in Canada*, eds L. Driedger and S. Halli (Montreal and Toronto: McGill-Queen's University Press), 33–54.

Brace, C.L. 2005. *'Race' Is a Four-letter Word* (New York: Oxford University Press).

Brand, D. 1984. 'A Working Paper on Black Women in Toronto: Gender, Race and Class', *Fireweed* 19 (summer/fall): 26–43.

Brandt, G. 1986. *The Realization of Anti-racist Education* (London: Falmer Press).

Brathwaite, K., and C. James. 1996. *Educating African Canadians* (Toronto: James Lorimer & Company).

Brattain, M. 2007. 'Race, Racism, and Antiracism: UNESCO and the Politics of Presenting Science to the Postwar Public', *American Historical Review* 112, 5: 1–53.

Breedon Research Inc. 1988. 'Report on Focus Groups to Study Reactions to Ethnicity/Race Questions for the 1991 Census', prepared for the Housing, Family and Social Statistics Division, Statistics Canada (Ottawa: Supply and Services).

Breton, R. 1988. 'From Ethnic to Civic Nationalism: English Canada and Quebec', *Ethnic and Racial Studies* 11: 1–10.

Broom, D. 1987. 'Gender and Inequality: An Overview: Another Tribe', in *Three Worlds of Inequality: Race, Class and Gender*, eds C. Jennet and R.G. Stewart (Melbourne: Macmillan), 264–81.

Brown, R., and C. Brown. 1996. 'Comments: Reflections on Racism', in *Perspective on Racism and the Human Services Sector: A Case for Change*, ed. C.E. James (Toronto: University of Toronto Press).

Bruegel, I. 1989. 'Sex and Race in the Labour Market', *Feminist Review* 32 (summer): 49–68.

Buchanan, P. 2001. 'Endlessly Playing the Race Card', available at <http://www.theamericancause.org>.

Butler, J. 1990. *Gender Trouble* (London: Routledge).

———. 1993. *Bodies that Matter* (London: Routledge).

Calliste, A., and G. Dei, eds. 2000. *Anti-racist Feminism: Critical Race and Gender Studies* (Halifax: Fernwood).

Callister, P., et al. 2007. 'Measuring Ethnicity in New Zealand: Developing Tools for Health Outcomes Analysis', *Ethnicity & Health* 12, 4: 299–320.

Campbell, M. 2003. 'Stewart's Tough Journey to the NHL', *Toronto Star* (22 June): E8.

Campbell, M.L. 1980. 'Sexism in British Columbia Trade Unions, 1900–1920', in *In Her Own Right: Selected Essays on Women in BC History*, eds B. Latham and C. Kess (Victoria, BC: Camosun College).

Carby, H. 1982. 'White Women Listen! Black Feminism and the Boundaries of Sisterhood', in *The Empire Strikes Back: Race and Racism in 70s Britain*, ed. CCCS (London: Hutchinson), 212–35.

———. 1987. *Reconstructing Womanhood: The Emergence of the Afro-American Woman Novelist* (New York: Oxford University Press).

Cardozo, A. 1996. *The Ottawa Citizen* (14 May).

Carpay, J. 2007. 'Hooked by the Fight for a Race-free BC Fishery', *Globe and Mail* (4 Oct.).

———. 2008. 'Dividing the Catch', *National Post* (22 July).

Carter, R. 2007. 'Genes, Genomes, and Geneologies: The Return of Scientific Racism?', *Ethnic and Racial Studies* 30, 4: 546–56.

Cashmore, E., and J. Jennings, eds. 2001. *Racism: Essential Readings* (Thousand Oaks, CA: Sage).

Centre for Contemporary Cultural Studies (CCCS), ed. 1982. 'The Organic Crisis of British Capitalism and Race', in *The Empire Strikes Back* (London: Hutchinson).

Chambers, I., and L. Curti, eds. 1996. *The Post-colonial Question* (London: Routledge).

Chan, W., and K. Mirchandani, eds. 2002. 'From Race and Crime to Racialization and Criminalization', in *Crimes of Colour: Racialization in the Criminal Justice System in Canada* (Peterborough, ON: Broadview Press).

Chesler, P. 2003. *The New Anti-Semitism and What We Must Do about It* (New York: Jossey-Bass).

Churchill, W. 1992. *Struggle for the Land: Indigenous Resistance to Genocide, Ecocide, and Expropriation in Contemporary North America* (Toronto: Between the Lines Press).

———. 1994. *Indians Are Us? Culture and Genocide in Native North America* (Toronto: Between the Lines Press).

Coates, K. 2000. *The Marshall Decision and Native Rights* (Montreal: McGill-Queen's University Press).

Cockburn, C. 1983. *Brothers: Male Dominance and Technological Change* (London: Pluto Press).

Collier, P., and D. Horowitz. 2004. *The Race Card: White Guilt, Black Resentment, and the Assault on Truth and Justice*. Commission on Systemic Racism in the Ontario Criminal Justice System. 1995. Report (Ontario: Queen's Printer).

Connelly, P. 1979. *Last Hired, First Fired: Women and the Canadian Work Force* (Toronto: Women's Press).

———. 1986. 'On Marxism and Feminism', in *The Politics of Diversity*, eds R. Hamilton and M. Barrett (Montreal: Book Center), 241–8.

Cook-Lynn, E. 1996. *Why I Can't Read Wallace Stegner and Other Essays: A Tribal Voice* (Madison: University of Wisconsin Press).

Cooper, A. 2007. 'Acts of Resistance: Black Men and Women Engage Slavery in Upper Canada, 1793–1803', *Ontario History* 99, 1: 5–17.

Corrigan, P., and D. Sayer. 1985. *The Great Arch: English State Formation as Cultural Revolution* (New York: Blackwell).

Cose, E. 1997. *Color-blind: Seeing beyond Race in a Race Obsessed World* (New York: HarperCollins).

Cox, O. 1948. *Caste, Class and Race: A Study in Social Dynamics* (New York: Monthly Review Press).

———. 1976. *Race Relations: Elements and Social Dynamics* (Detroit, MI: Wayne State University Press).

Crang, P. 1994. 'It's Showtime: On the Workplace Geographies of Display in a Restaurant in Southeast England', *Environment and Planning D: Society and Space* 12: 675–704.

Cream, J. 1995. 'Women on Trial: A Private Pillory?', in *Mapping the Subject: Geographies of Cultural Transformation*, eds S. Pile and N. Thrift (London:

Routledge), 158–70.

Crenshaw, K. 1997. 'Color-blind Dreams and Racial Nghtmares: Reconfiguring Racism in the Post–Civil Rights Era', in *Birth of a Nationhood: Gaze, Script, and Spectacle in the O.J. Simpson Case*, eds T. Morrison and C.B. Lacour (New York: Pantheon Books), 97–168.

Cresswell, T. 1996. *In Place/Out of Place* (Minneapolis: University of Minnesota Press).

Crissman, L. 1967. 'The Segmentary Structure of Urban Overseas Chinese Communities', *Man* 2: 185–204.

Das Gupta, T. 1986. *Learning from Our History: Community Development with Immigrant Women, 1958–86, a Tool for Action* (Toronto: University of Toronto Press).

———. 1996. *Racism and Paid Work* (Toronto: Garamond Press).

———, et al. 2007. *Race and Racialization: Essential Readings* (Toronto: Canadian Scholars' Press).

Davenport, C. 1917. 'The Effects of Race Intermingling', *Proceedings of the American Philosophical Society* 56: 364–8.

Davis, A. 1971. 'Reflections on the Black Women's Role in the Community of Slaves', *Black Scholar* 3, 4: 2–15.

———. 1983. *Women, Race and Class* (New York: Women's Press).

Davis, J.F. 1991. *Who is Black: One Country's Definition* (University Park: Pennsylvania State University Press).

Dawson, C.A. 1936. *Group Settlement: Ethnic Communities in Western Canada* (Toronto: Macmillan).

Dehli, K. 1984. 'Women in the Community: Reform of Schooling and Motherhood in Toronto', paper presented at the 1984 CSAA Annual Meeting.

Dei, G. 1996. *Anti-racism Education: Theory and Practice* (Halifax: Fernwood).

———. 1997. *Reconstructing 'Dropout': A Critical Ethnography of the Dynamics of Black Students' Disengagement from School* (Toronto: The Osgoode Society for Canadian Legal History and Wilfrid Laurier University Press).

———. 2000. 'Towards an Anti-racist Discursive

Framework', in *Power, Knowledge and Anti-racism Education*, eds G. Dei and A. Calliste (Halifax: Fernwood), 23–40.

————. 2007. 'Speaking Race: Silence, Salience, and the Politics of Anti-racist Scholarship', in *Race and Racism in 21st Century Canada: Continuity, Complexity, and Change,* eds S.P. Hier and B.S. Bolaria (Peterborough, ON: Broadview Press), 53–60.

————, and A. Kempf. 2005. 'The Application and Impact of Race-based Statistics to Effect Systemic Change and Eliminate Institutional Racism', paper presented at the Canadian Race Relations Foundation Policy Dialogue, Novotel Hotel, North York, ON, 21 Oct.

de Lepervanche, M. 1989. 'Women, Nation and the State in Australia', in *Woman–Nation–State*, eds N. Yuval-Davis and F. Anthias (London: Macmillan), 36–57.

Deliovsky, K. 2005. 'Elsewhere from Here: Remapping the Territories of White Femininity', PhD diss., Department of Sociology, McMaster University, Hamilton.

Dershowitz, A. 2003. *The Case for Israel* (New Jersey: John Wiley & Sons).

Dewing, M. 2006. *Canadian Multiculturalism* (Ottawa: Library of Parliament, Parliamentary Research Service, on-line).

Didion, J. 2003. 'Mr Bush and the Divine', *New York Review of Books* 17 (6 Nov.): 81–6.

di Leonardo, M. 1984. *The Varieties of Ethnic Experience* (Ithaca, NY: Cornell University Press).

Dill, B.T. 1983. 'Race, Class and Gender: Prospects for an All-inclusive Sisterhood', *Feminist Studies* 9, 1: 131–50.

DiManno, R. 1993. *Toronto Star* (6 Sept.).

Dixson, A.D., and C.K. Rousseau, eds. 2006. *Critical Race Theory in Education: All God's Children Got a Song* (New York: Routledge).

Doane, A. 2006. 'What Is Racism?', *Racial Discourse and Racial Politics* 32, 2–3: 255–75.

————. 2007. 'The Changing Politics of Color-blind Racism', in *The New Black: Alternative Paradigms and Strategies for the 21st Century (Research in Race and Ethnic Relations)* 14: 159–74.

Dolha, L. 2006. 'Judicial Inquiry into Fraser River Fishery "Racist"', *First Nations Drum* (Nov.): 13.

Donnelly, P. 2003. 'October 2 Muslim Writer Challenges Her Faith', *The Gazette* (2 Oct.), available at <http://www.muslim-refusenik.com/news/mtl gazette-oct02-03.html>. Accessed 14 Apr. 2004.

Downey, D. 1992. 'Rowlands Calls for Healing, Chretien Sees Unrest as "Wake-up Call", Blacks Fear Troubled Summer', *Globe and Mail* (6 May): A1.

Doyle-Wood, S. 2002. Personal communication, Department of Sociology and Equity Studies in Education, OISE/University of Toronto.

Driedger, L., ed. 1978. *The Canadian Ethnic Mosaic: A Quest for Identity* (Toronto: Canadian Ethnic Studies Association, McClelland & Stewart).

Dua, E., and A. Robertson. 1999. *Scratching the Surface: Canadian Anti-racist, Feminist Thought* (Toronto: Women's Press).

DuBois, W.E.B. 1940. *Dusk of Dawn: An Essay toward an Autobiography of a Race Concept* (New York: Harcourt Brace).

Dumont, M., et al. 1987. *Quebec Women: A History* (Toronto: Women's Press).

Duncan, G.A. 2002. 'Critical Race Theory and Method: Rendering Race in Urban Ethnographic Research', *Qualitative Inquiry* 8, 1: 85–104.

————. 2005. 'Critical Race Ethnography in Education: Narrative, Inequality and the Problem of Epistemology', *Race, Ethnicity & Education* 8, 1: 93–114.

Duster, T. 2006. 'The Molecular Re-inscription of Race: Unanticipated Issues in Biotechnology and Forensic Science', in *Patterns of Prejudice* 40, 4, 5 (Sept.): 427–41.

Economist, The. 2007. 'Darwin's Children' (13 Dec.).

Eisenstein, Z. 2007. *Sexual Decoys: Gender, Race, and War in Imperial Democracy* (New York: Zed Books).

Employment and Immigration Canada (EIC). 1986. *Annual Report: Employment Equity Act* (Ottawa: Supply and Services Canada).

Engel, R.S. 2008. 'A Critique of the "Outcome Test" in Racial Profiling Research', *Justice Quarterly* 25, 1: 1–36.

Eracism. 2006. '*Survivor* Draws Fire for Playing the Race Card', available at <http://www.eracismblog.com>.

Essed, P. 1990. *Everyday Racism: Reports from Women of Two Cultures* (Alameda, CA: Hunter House).

Estable, A. 1986. 'Immigrant Women in Canada—Current Issues', a background paper for the Canadian Advisory Council on the Status of Women.

Ewan, E., and S. Ewan. 2006. *Typecasting: On the Arts and Sciences of Human Inequality* (New York: Seven Stories Press).

Fallaci, O. 2002. *The Rage and the Pride* (New York: Rizzoli International Publications Inc.).

Fanon, F. 1968. *Wretched of the Earth* (New York: Grove Press).

Fernández-Balboa, J.-M. 2000. 'Discrimination: What Do We Know and What Can We Do about It?', in *Sociology of Sport: Theory and Practice*, eds R.L. Jones and K.M. Armour (Essex: Longman), 134–44.

Fernando, S. 2006. *Race and the City: Chinese Canadian and Chinese American Political Mobilization* (Vancouver: University of British Columbia Press).

Ferreira da Silva, D. 2001. 'Towards a Critique of the Socio-logos of Justice: The Analytics of Raciality and the Production of Universality', *Social Identities* 7, 3: 421–54.

Fireweed. 1986. Special Issue by Native Women (winter).

First Annual Chutzpah Awards, The. 2004. *Oprah Magazine* 234 (May): 240.

Fiske, J. 1994. *Media Matters: Everyday Culture and Political Change* (Minneapolis: University of Minnesota Press).

Fiss, T. 2004. *Apartheid: Canada's Ugly Secret* (Calgary: Centre for Aboriginal Policy Change, Canadian Taxpayer Federation).

Flanagan, T. 2000. *First Nations? Second Thoughts* (Montreal and Kingston: McGill-Queen's University Press).

Fleras, A. 2002. *Engaging Diversity: Multiculturalism in Canada* (Scarborough, ON: Nelson).

———. 2003. *Mass Media Communication in Canada* (Scarborough, ON: Nelson).

———. 2008. 'The Politics of Re/Naming', paper commissioned by the Department of Justice and delivered at the 9th National Metropolis Conference, Halifax, 6 Apr.

———, and J. Elliott. 1992. *Multiculturalism in Canada* (Scarborough, ON: Nelson).

———. 2007. *Unequal Relations*, 5th edn (Toronto: Pearson).

Ford, R.T. 2008. *The Race Card: How Bluffing about Bias Makes Race Relations Worse* (New York: Farrar, Strauss and Giroux).

Foster, C. 2005. *Where Race Does Not Matter: The New Spirit of Modernity* (Toronto: Penguin).

Foxman, A. 2003. *Never Again? The Threat of the New Anti-Semitism* (San Francisco: Harper).

Frankenberg, R. 1993. *White Women, Race Matters: The Social Construction of Whiteness* (Minneapolis: University of Minnesota Press).

———, and L. Mani. 1992. 'Cross-currents, Cross-talk: Race, "Post-coloniality" and the Politics of Location', *Cultural Studies* 7, 2.

Freedman, M. 1958. 'Lineage Organization in Southeastern China', *L.S.E. Monographs on Social Anthropology* 18 (London: Athlete Press).

———. 1961–62. 'The Family in China, Past and Present', *Pacific Affairs* 24 (1962): 323–36.

Frey, D. 1994. *The Last Shot: City Streets, Basketball Dreams* (New York: Houghton Mifflin).

Gabor, P., S. Thibodeau, and S. Manychief. 1996. 'Taking Flight? The Transition Experiences of Native Youth', in *Youth in Transition: Perspectives on Research and Policy*, eds B. Galaway and J. Hudson (Toronto: Thompson Educational Publishing), 79–89.

Gabriel, J., and G. Ben-Tovim. 1978. 'Marxism and the Concept of Racism', *Economy and Society* 7, 2: 118–54.

———, and ———. 1979. 'The Conceptualization of Race Relations in Sociological Theory', *Ethnic and Racial Studies* 2, 2: 190–212.

Gaertner, S.L. 1976. 'Non-reactive Measures in Racial Attitude Research: A Focus on Liberals', in *Towards the Elimination of Racism*, ed. P. Katz (New York: Pergamon Press).

———, and J.F. Dovidio. 1981. 'Racism among the Well Intentioned', in *Pluralism, Racism and Public Policy*, eds E.G. Clausen and J. Bermingham (Boston: G.K. Hall).

———, and ———, eds. 1986. 'The Aversive Forms of Racism', in *Prejudice, Discrimination and Racism* (New York: Academic Press).

Galabuzi, G.-E. 2006. *Canada's Economic Apartheid: The Social Exclusion of Racialized Groups in the New Century* (Toronto: Canadian Scholars' Press).

Gallagher, C.A. 2007. *Rethinking the Color Line: Readings in Race and Ethnicity*, 3rd edn (New York: McGraw-Hill).

Gannage, C. 1986. *Double Day, Double Bind: Women Garment Workers* (Toronto: Women's Press).

———. 1987. 'A World of Difference: The Case of Women Workers in a Canadian Garment Factory', in *Feminism and Political Economy*, eds H.J. Maroney and M. Luxton (Toronto: Methuen), 213–28.

Garcia, A.M. 1989. 'The Development of Chicana Feminist Discourse, 1970–1980', *Gender & Society* 3, 2 (June): 217–38.

Gardner, D. 1995. *Globe and Mail* (21 Oct).

Garfinkel, H. 1967. *Studies in Ethnomethodology* (Englewood Cliffs, NJ: Prentice Hall).

Garvey J., and N. Ignatiev, eds. 1996. *Race Traitor* (New York: Routledge).

George, R.M. 1993–94. 'Winter Homes in the Empire, Empire in the Home', *Cultural Critique* 26: 95–129.

Gibbon, J.M. 1938. *Canadian Mosaic: The Making of a Northern Nation* (Toronto: McClelland & Stewart).

Gilbert, M. 2007. *Churchill and the Jews* (Toronto: McClelland & Stewart), reviewed by M. Marrus, *Globe and Mail* (14 July).

Gilroy, P. 1987. *There Ain't no Black in the Union Jack* (Chicago: University of Chicago Press/London: Hutchinson).

———. 2000a. *Between Camps: Nations, Cultures, and the Allure of Race* (London: Allen Lane).

———. 2000b. *Against Race: Imagining Political Culture beyond the Colour Line* (Cambridge, MA: Harvard University Press).

Glenn, E.N. 1980. 'The Dialectics of Wage Work: Japanese-American Women and Domestic Service, 1905–1940', *Feminist Studies* 3 (fall): 432–71.

Goffman, E. 1959. *The Presentation of Self in Everyday Life* (New York: Doubleday Anchor).

Goldberg, D.T., ed. 1990. *The Anatomy of Racism* (Min-neapolis: University of Minnesota Press).

———. 1993. *Racist Culture: Philosophy and the Politics of Meaning* (Oxford: Blackwell).

———. 2002. *The Racial State* (Oxford: Blackwell).

Goldmann, G., and N. McKenney. 1993. *Challenges of Measuring an Ethnic World: Science, Politics and Reality* (Ottawa and Washington: Statistics Canada and the United States Bureau of the Census).

Gould, S.J. 1994. 'The Geometer of Race', *Discover* (Nov.).

Greenfield, N. 1996. *Ottawa Citizen* (2 May).

Gregson, N., and G. Rose. 2000. 'Taking Butler Elsewhere: Performativities, Spatialities and Subjectivities', *Environment and Planning D: Society and Space* 18: 433–52.

Grewal, I., and C. Kaplan. 1994. *Scattered Hegemonies: Postmodernity and Transnational Feminist Practices* (Minneapolis: University of Minnesota Press).

Guess, T.J. 2006. 'The Social Construction of Whiteness: Racism by Intent, Racism by Consequence', *Critical Sociology* 32, 1, available at <http://www.ingentaconnect.com/content/brill/crs>.

Gumplowicz, L. 1875. *Rasse und Staat: Eine Untersuchung Uber Das Gesetz Der Staatenbilding* (Vienna: Verlag Der Manzschen Buchhandlung).

———. 1881. *Rechtsstaat und Socialismus* (Innsbruck: Verlag Der Wagner Schen Universtaets-Buchhandlung).

———. 1883. *Der Rassenkampf: Sociologische Untersuchungen* (Innsbruck: Verlag Der Wagner Schen Universtaets-Buchhandlung).

Gunter, H. 1996. *Edmonton Journal* (6 May).

Gwyn, R. 1993. *Toronto Star* (18 July).

———. 1996. *Toronto Star* (19 May).

Hall, A.J. 2000. 'Racial Discrimination in Legislation, Litigation, Legend, and Lore', *Canadian Ethnic Studies* 32, 2: 119–37.

Hall, P.F. 1906. *Immigration and Its Effects upon the United States* (New York: Henry Holt and Company).

Hall, S. 1978. 'Racism and Reaction', in *Five Views of Multi-racial Britain* (London: Commission for Racial Equality).

———. 1983. 'The Great Moving Show', in *The Politics of Thatcherism*, eds S. Hall and M. Jacques

(London: Lawrence & Wishart).

———. 1986. 'Variants of Liberalism', in *Politics and Ideology*, eds J. Donald and S. Hall (Milton Keynes: Open University Press).

———. 1992a. 'The Question of Cultural Identity', in *Modernity and Its Futures*, eds S. Hall, D. Held, and T. McGrew (Cambridge: Polity Press in association with Blackwell and Open University Press), 273–326.

———. 1992b. 'Cultural Studies and Its Theoretical Legacies', in *Cultural Studies*, eds L. Grossberg, C. Nelson, and P. Treichler (London: Routledge), 328–45.

———. 1994. 'Cultural Identity and Diaspora', in *Colonial Discourse and Postcolonial Theory*, eds P. Williams and L. Chrisman (New York: Columbia University Press), 392–403.

———. 1996a. 'The West and the Rest: Discourse and Power', in *Modernity: An Introduction to Modern Societies*, eds S. Hall, D. Held, D. Hubert, and K. Thompson (Milton Keynes: Open University Press), 184–224.

———. 1996b. 'When Was "the Post-colonial"? Thinking at the Limit', in *The Post-colonial Question: Common Skies, Divided Horizons*, eds I. Chambers and L. Curti (London: Routledge), 242–60.

———. 1997. *Representations: Cultural Representations and Signifying Practices* (London: Sage).

———, et al. 1978. *Policing the Crisis* (London: Macmillan).

Harding, S. 2002. 'Science, Race, Culture, Empire', in *Companion to Racial and Ethnic Studies*, eds D.T. Goldberg and J. Solomos (Oxford: Blackwell), 217–28.

Harney, R.F. 1988. 'So Great a Heritage as Ours: Immigration and the Survival of the Canadian Polity', *Daedalus* 117: 51–97.

Harrison Jr, L., L. Azzarito, and J. Burden Jr. 2004. 'Perceptions of Athletic Superiority: A View from the Other Side', *Race, Ethnicity & Education* 7, 2: 149–66.

Harriss, K. 1989. 'New Alliances: Socialist-Feminism in the Eighties', *Feminist Review* 31 (spring): 34–53.

Hatchell, H. 2004. 'Privilege of Whiteness: Adolescent Male Students' Resistance to Racism in an Australian Classroom', *Race, Ethnicity & Education* 7, 2: 99–114.

Haug, F. 1989. 'Lessons from the Women's Movement in Europe', *Feminist Review* 31 (spring): 107–18.

Hawkins, F. 1972. *Canada and Immigration* (Kingston: McGill-Queen's University Press).

Hayward, V. 1922. *Romantic Canada* (Toronto: Macmillan & Company).

Head, W.A. 1975. *The Black Presence in the Canadian Mosaic: A Study of Perception and the Practice of Discrimination against Blacks in Metropolitan Toronto* (Toronto: Ontario Human Rights Commission).

Hebridge, D. 1993. 'From Culture to Hegemony', in *The Cultural Studies Reader*, ed. S. During (London: Routledge).

Henderson, J. (Sakej) Youngblood. 1997. *The Mi'kmaw Concordat* (Halifax: Fernwood).

Henry, F. 1978. *Dynamics of Racism in Toronto* (North York, ON: York University).

———, et al. 1995. *The Colour of Democracy: Racism in Canadian Society* (Toronto: Harcourt Brace).

———. 2000. *The Colour of Democracy: Racism in Canadian Society*, 2nd edn (Toronto: Harcourt Brace).

Hernandez, C.R. 1988. 'The Coalition of Visible Minority Women', in *Social Movements/Social Change*, eds F. Cunningham et al. (Toronto: Between the Lines).

Herring, C., V.M. Keith, and H.D. Horton, eds. 2004. *Skin Deep: How Race and Complexion Matter in the 'Color-blind' Era* (Chicago: University of Illinois Press).

Herrnstein, R.J., and C. Murray. 1994. *The Bell Curve: Intelligence and Class Structure in American Life* (Glencoe, IL: Free Press).

Hier, P.S. 2007. 'Studying Race and Racism in 21st Century Canada', in *Race and Racism in 21st Century Canada: Continuity, Complexity, and Change*, eds S.P. Hier and B.S. Bolaria (Peterborough, ON: Broadview Press), 19–34.

———, and B.S. Bolaria, eds. 2007. *Race and Racism in 21st Century Canada: Continuity, Complexity, and Change* (Peterborough, ON: Broadview Press).

Hill, H. 1987. 'The Gender Variable in Development Policies: Was Nairobi a Turning Point?', in *Three Worlds of Inequality: Race, Class and Gender*, eds C. Jennett and R.G. Stewart (Melbourne: Macmillan), 340–60.

Hinton, E.L. 2007. 'Derek Jeter's Not Black Enough? Joe Torre Discriminates? What's the Truth?', *DiversityInc* (16 July).

Hoch, P. 1979. *White Hero Black Beast: Racism, Sexism and the Mask of Masculinity* (London: Pluto Press).

Holdaway, S. 1996. *The Racialisation of British Policing* (New York: St Martin's Press).

———, and M. O'Neill. 2007. 'Where Has All the Racism Gone? Views of Racism within Constabularies after McPherson', *Ethnic and Racial Studies* 30, 3: 397–415.

hooks, b. 1981. *Ain't I a Woman? Black Women and Feminism* (Boston: South End Press).

———. 1984. *Feminist Theory: From Margins to Centre* (Boston: South End Press).

Howard, P. 2004. 'Reflections on a Reading Course: Interrogating Whiteness in Critical/Anti-racist and Other Ostensibly Equitable Spaces', unpublished paper, Department of Sociology and Equity Studies in Education, OISE/University of Toronto.

———. 2005. PhD comprehensive examination, unpublished paper, Department of Sociology and Equity Studies in Education, OISE/University of Toronto.

Hull, G., P.B. Scott, and B. Smith, eds. 1982. *All the Women Are White, All the Blacks Are Men, but Some of Us Are Brave* (New York: Basic Books).

Huntington, S.P. 1997. *The Clash of Civilizations and the Remaking of World Order* (New York: Touchstone Press).

Hussain, A. 2007. 'Nike Pays up $7.6 Million in Class-action Race-discrimination Suit', *DiversityInc* (31 July), available at <http://www.diversityinc.com/public/2237.cfm>.

Hyde, A.A. 1888. In *Popular Science Monthly* 52: 388.

Iacovetta, F. 1986. 'From Contadina to Worker: Southern Italian Immigrant Working Women in Toronto, 1947–62', in *Looking into My Sister's Eyes*, ed. J. Burnet (Toronto: Multicultural History Society of Ontario), 195–222.

Ifekwunigwe, J. 1999. *Scattered Belongings: Cultural Paradoxes of 'Race', Nation and Gender* (London: Routledge).

Iganski, P., and B. Kosmin. 2003. *A New Anti-Semitism? Debating Judeophobia in 21st Century Britain* (London: Institute for Jewish Policy Research).

Ignatieff, M. 1998. 'Identity Parades', *Prospect* (Apr.): 19–23. Immigrant Women of Saskatchewan (IWS). 1985. *Doubly Disadvantaged: The Women Who Immigrate to Canada* (Saskatoon: IWS).

Inglehart, R., and P. Norris. 2003a. 'The True Clash of Civilizations', *Foreign Policy* (Mar./Apr.): 67–74.

———, and ———. 2003b. *Rising Tide: Gender Equality and Cultural Change around the World* (Cambridge: Cambridge University Press).

Jackson, N.S. 1980. 'Class Relations and Bureaucratic Practice', paper presented at the CSAA Annual Meeting, Montreal, June.

Jackson, P., and J. Penrose, eds. 1993. *Constructions of Race, Place and Nation* (London: UCL Press).

James, C.E. 1990. *Making It: Black Youth Racism and Career Aspirations* (Oakville, ON: Mosaic Press).

———. 1995. 'Negotiating School through Sports: African Canadian Youth Strive for Academic Success', *Avante* 1, 1: 20–36.

———. 2003. *Seeing Ourselves: Exploring Race, Ethnicity, and Culture* (Toronto: Thompson Educational Publishing).

———. 2005. *Race in Play* (Toronto: Canadian Scholars' Press).

Jenke, B., and R. Yaron. 1979. 'A Report on Conditions in the Labour Market and Training Opportunities for Non-English Speaking Immigrant Women in Metro Toronto', Oct. (Toronto: Working Women Community Centre).

Jenson, J. 1986. 'Gender and Reproduction, or Babies and the State', *Studies in Political Economy* 20: 9–46.

Jessop, B. 1982. *The Capitalist State: Marxist Theories and Methods* (New York: New York University Press).

Jiwani, Y. 2006. *Discourses of Denial: Mediations of Race, Gender, and Violence* (Vancouver: University of British Columbia Press).

Johal, G. 2005. 'Order in KOS: On Race, Rage and Method', in *Critical Issues in Anti-racist Research Methodology*, eds G. Dei and G. Johal (New York: Peter Lang), 269–93.

Johal, R. 2003. *The World Is Ours: Second Generation South Asian Youths Reconcile Conflicting Expectations* (Toronto: Faculty of Education, York University). Reprinted by permission of the author.

Johnson, L. 1982. *The Seam Allowance: Industrial Home Sewing in Canada* (Toronto: Women's Press).

Jones, J. 1985. *Labor of Love, Labor of Sorrow* (New York: Basic Books).

Jones, R.L., and K.M. Armour, eds. 2000. 'The Practical Heart Within: The Value of a Sociology of Sport', in *Sociology of Sport* (Essex: Longman), 3–12.

Kalbach, W.E., and W.W. McVey. 1971. *The Demographic Bases of Canadian Society* (Toronto: McGraw-Hill Ryerson).

Kalman, M. 2004. 'A Muslim Calling for Reform—and She's a Lesbian', *San Francisco Chronicle* (19 Jan.), available at <http://www.muslim-refusenik.com/news/sfchronicle20040119.html>. Accessed 14 Apr. 2004.

Kaplan, C. 1995. '"Getting to Know You": Travel, Gender, and the Politics of Representation in *Anna and the King of Siam* and *The King and I*', in *Late Imperial Culture*, eds R. de la Campa, E.A. Kaplan, and M. Sprinkler (London: Verso), 33–52.

Kazemipur, A., and S. Halli. 2000. *The New Poverty in Canada: Ethnic Groups and Ghetto Neighbourhoods* (Toronto: Thompson Educational Publishing).

Kearns, G. 1997. 'The Imperial Subject: Geography and Travel in the Work of Mary Kingsley and Halford Mackinder', *Transactions of the Institute of British Geographers, New Series* 22: 450–72.

Keith, M. 1991. 'Knowing Your Place: The Imagined Geographies of Racial Subordination', in *New Words, New Worlds: Reconceptualizing Social and Cultural Geography*, ed. C. Philo (Lampeter: Social and Cultural Geography Study Group of the Institute of British Geographers, University of Lampeter), 178–93.

Kell, P. 2000. *Good Sports: Australian Sport and the Myth of the Fair Go* (Annandale: Pluto Press).

Kelley, R. 2002. *Freedom Dreams: The Black Radical Imagination* (Boston: Beacon Press).

Kempf, A. 2006. Unpublished paper (untitled), Department of Sociology and Equity Studies in Education, OISE/University of Toronto.

Keung, N. 2007. 'Forums to Focus on Link between Poverty, Race', *Toronto Star* (6 Sept.).

King, D. 1988. 'Multiple Jeopardy, Multiple Consciousness: The Context of a Black Feminist Ideology', *Signs* 14, 1.

Klug, F. 1989. '"Oh to Be in England": The British Case Study', in *Woman–Nation–State*, eds N. Yuval-Davis and F. Anthias (London: Macmillan), 16–35.

Kobayashi, A., and G.F. Johnson. 2007. 'Introduction', in *Race, Racialization, and Anti-racism in Canada and Beyond*, eds G.F. Johnson and R. Enomoto (Toronto: University of Toronto Press), 3–16.

———, and L. Peake. 1994. 'Un-natural Discourse: "Race" and Gender in Geography', *Gender, Place & Culture* 1: 225–43.

Kovel, J. 1970. *White Racism: A Psychohistory* (New York: Pantheon).

LaChapelle, C. 1982. 'Beyond Barriers: Native Women and the Women's Movement', in *Still Ain't Satisfied!*, eds M. Fitzgerald, C. Guberman, and M. Wolfe (Toronto: Women's Press), 257–64.

Lamoureux, D. 1987. 'Nationalism and Feminism in Quebec: An Impossible Attraction', in *Feminism and Political Economy*, eds H.J. Maroney and M. Luxton (Toronto: Methuen), 51–68.

Langton, M. 1981. 'Urbanizing Aborigines: The Social Scientists' Great Deception', *Social Alternatives* 2, 2: 16–22.

Lapchick, R. 2001. *Smashing Barriers: Race and Sport in the New Millennium* (Boston: Madison Books).

LaPrairie, C. 1987. 'Native Women and Crime in Canada: A Theoretical Model', in *Too Few to Count: Canadian Women in Conflict with the Law*, eds E. Adelberg and C. Currie (Vancouver: Press Gang), 103–12.

Lawrence, B. 2004. *'Real' Indians and Others: Mixedblood Urban Native Peoples and Indigenous Nationhood* (Vancouver: University of British Columbia Press).

———, and E. Dua. 2005. 'Decolonizing Anti-racism',

Social Justice 32, 4: 120–43.

Lawrence, C.R. 1987. 'The Id, the Ego, and Equal Protection: Reckoning with Unconscious Racism', *Stanford Law Review* 39: 317.

Lawrence, E. 1982. 'Just Plain Common Sense: The "Roots" of Racism', in *The Empire Strikes Back*, ed. CCCS (London: Hutchinson).

Lawson, E. 2004. 'Notes on Racialization and Racialized Subjects', Department of Sociology and Equity Studies in Education, OISE/University of Toronto.

Lay, J. 1980. 'To Columbia on the Tynemouth: The Emigration of Single Women and Girls in 1862', in *In Her Own Right: Selected Essays in Women's History in BC*, eds B. Latham and C. Kess (Victoria, BC: Camosun College).

Le Camp, L. 1998. 'Terra Nullius/Theoria Nullius— Empty Lands/Empty Theory: A Literature Review of Critical Theory from an Aboriginal Perspective', unpublished ms., Department of Sociology and Equity Studies in Education, OISE/University of Toronto.

Lee, J., and J.S. Lutz. 2005. *Situating 'Race' and Racisms in Space, Time, and Theory: Critical Essays for Activists and Scholars* (Montreal: McGill-Queen's University Press).

Lee, S. 2003. 'Model Minorities and Perpetual Foreigners', in *Adolescents at School: Perspectives on Youth, Identity and Education*, ed. M. Sadowski (Cambridge, MA: Harvard University Press), 41–9.

Lerner, G. 1997. *Why History Matters: Life and Thought* (New York: Oxford University Press).

Lewis, C., and S. Pile. 1996. 'Woman, Body, Space: Rio Carnival and the Politics of Performance', *Gender, Place & Culture* 3: 23–46.

Li, P.S. 1988. *The Chinese in Canada* (Don Mills, ON: Oxford University Press).

———, ed. 1990. 'Race and Ethnicity', in *Race and Ethnic Relations in Canada* (Don Mills, ON: Oxford University Press).

———. 2007. 'Contradictions of "Racial" Discourse', in *Interrogating Race and Racism*, ed. V. Agnew (Toronto: University of Toronto Press), 37–54.

Lipsig-Mumme, C. 1987. 'Organizing Women in the Sewing Trades: Homework and the 1983 Garment Strike in Canada', *Studies in Political Economy* 22 (spring): 41–72.

London-Edinburgh Weekend Return Group. 1979. *In and against the State* (London: Pluto Press).

Loney, M. 1995. *Toronto Star* (16 Nov.).

Longhurst, R. 2000. '"Corporeographies" of Pregnancy: "Bikini Babes"', *Environment and Planning D: Society and Space* 18: 453–72.

Lopez, I.F.H. 2006. 'Colorblind to the Reality of Race in America', *Chronicle of Higher Education* (3 Nov.): B6–9.

Maaka, R., and A. Fleras. 2005. *The Politics of Indigeneity: Indigenous Peoples–State Relations in Canada and New Zealand* (Dunedin, NZ: University of Otago Press).

McCalla, A., and V. Satzewich. 2002. 'Settler Capitalism and the Construction of Immigrants and "Indians" as Racialized Others', in *Crimes of Colour*, eds W. Chan and K. Mirchandani (Peterborough, ON: Broadview Press).

McClintock, A. 1997. '"No Longer in a Future Heaven": Gender, Race, and Nationalism', in *Dangerous Liaisons: Gender, Nation, and Postcolonial Perspectives*, eds A. McClintock, A. Mufti, and E. Shohat (Minneapolis: University of Minnesota Press), 89–112.

McConahay, J.B., and J.C. Hough Jr. 1976. 'Symbolic Racism', *Journal of Social Issues* 32, 2: 23–45.

McDowell, L., and G. Court. 1994. 'Performing Work: Bodily Representations in Merchant Banks', *Environment and Planning D: Society and Space* 12: 727–50.

Macedo, D., and P. Gounari. 2006. *The Globalization of Racism* (Boulder, CO: Paradigm Publishers).

McIntosh, M. 1978. 'The State and the Oppression of Women', in *Feminism and Materialism*, eds A. Kuhn and A. Wolpe (London: Routledge & Kegan Paul), 254–90.

McIntosh, P. 1988. 'White Privilege and Male Privilege: A Personal Account of Coming to See Correspondence through Work in Women's Studies', Working Paper No. 189, Wellesley College Centre for Research on Women, Wellesley, MA.

Mackey, E. 1996. 'Managing and Imagining Diversity: Multiculturalism and the Construction of National

Identity in Canada', PhD diss., Department of Social Anthropology, University of Sussex.

McKittrick, K. 2000. 'Black and "Cause I'm Black I'm Blue": Transverse Racial Geographies in Toni Morrison's *The Bluest Eye*', *Gender, Place & Culture* 7: 125–42.

Mahtani, M. 1996. 'Sketching beyond the Site-lines: A Geographer's Topography of the Politics of Negotiation for Mixed "Race" Women', *absinthe* 9: 15–20.

———. 2001. 'Racial Remappings: The Potential of Paradoxical Space', *Gender, Place & Culture* 8: 299–305.

———. 2002. 'Tricking the Border Guards: Performing Race', *Environment and Planning D: Society and Space* 20: 425–40.

Malarek, V. 1987. *Haven's Gate: Canada's Immigration Fiasco* (Toronto: Macmillan).

Mama, A. 1989. 'Violence against Black Women: Gender, Race and State Responses', *Feminist Review* 32 (summer): 30–47.

Manji, I. 2003. *The Trouble with Islam: A Wake-up Call for Honesty and Change* (Toronto: Random House).

Marin, L. 1996. 'Bringing It on Home: Teaching/Mothering Antiracism', in *Everyday Acts against Racism: Raising Children in a Multiracial World*, ed. M. Reddy (Seattle: Seal Press), 110–32.

Marshall, B. 1988. 'Feminist Theory and Critical Theory', *Canadian Review of Sociology and Anthropology* 25, 2.

Martin, J.G., and C.W. Franklin. 1973. *Minority Group Relations* (Columbus, OH: Charles E. Merrill Publishing Co.).

Marx, K. 1954. *Capital*, Vol. I (Moscow: Progress Publishers).

———, and F. Engels. 1967. *The Communist Manifesto* (Middlesex: Penguin).

———. 1970. *The German Ideology* (New York: International Publishers).

May, S., ed. 1999. *Critical Multiculturalism: Rethinking Multicultural and Anti-racist Education* (London: Falmer Press).

Mendes, E., ed. 1995. *'Racial Discrimination': Law and Practice* (Toronto: Carswell, in co-operation with Justice Canada and the Canada Communications Group, Supply and Services Canada).

Michaels, A. 1996. *Fugitive Pieces* (Toronto: McClelland & Stewart).

Miles, R. 1982. *Racism and Migrant Labour* (London: Routledge & Kegan Paul).

———. 1988. 'Racism, Marxism and British Politics', *Economy and Society* 17, 3: 428–60.

———. 1989. *Racism* (London: Routledge/Tavistock).

———. 1992. 'Migration, Racism and the Nation State in Contemporary Europe', in *Deconstructing a Nation: Immigration, Multiculturalism and Racism in 1990s Canada*, ed. V. Satzewich (Halifax: Fernwood).

———. 1993. *Racism after 'Race Relations'* (London: Routledge).

———, and M. Brown. 2003. *Racism*, 2nd edn (London: Routledge).

———, and R. Torres. 1996. 'Does Race Matter? Transatlantic Perspectives on Racism after Race Relations', in *Re-situating Identities: The Politics of Race, Ethnicity and Culture*, eds V. Amit-Talai and C. Knowles (Peterborough, ON: Broadview Press), 24–46.

Miliband, R. 1969. *The State in Capitalist Society* (London: Quartet Books).

Mills, C.W. 1997. *The Racial Contract* (Ithaca, NY: Cornell University Press).

Minh-ha, T.T. 1989. *Women, Native, Other* (Bloomington: Indiana University Press).

Mirchandani, K., and E. Tastsoglou. 1998. 'Toward a Diversity beyond Tolerance', ms. submitted to the *Journal of Status in Political Economy*.

Mitchell, A. 1995. *Globe and Mail* (12 Sept.).

Modood, T. 2007. *Multiculturalism* (Cambridge: Polity Press).

Mohanty, T.C. 1993. *Beyond a Dream: Deferred Multicultural Education and the Politics of Excellence* (Minneapolis: University of Minnesota Press).

Moore, D. 1997. 'Remapping Resistance', in *Geographies of Resistance*, eds S. Pile and M. Keith (London: Routledge), 87–107.

Morris, B., and G. Cowlishaw, eds. 1997. *Race Matters: Indigenous Australians and 'Our' Society* (Canberra: Aboriginal Studies Press).

Mosse, G.L. [1978] 1985. *Toward the Final Solution: A History of European Racism* (Madison, WI: University of Wisconsin Press).

Murji, K., and J. Solomos, eds. 2005. *Racialization—Studies in Theory and Practice* (New York: Oxford University Press).

Murphy, L., and J. Livingstone. 1985. 'Racism and the Limits of Radical Feminism', *Race & Class* 36, 4: 61–70.

Murray, C., and R. Herrnstein. 1994. *The Bell Curve* (New York: The Free Press).

Nakamura, Y. 2003. 'Finding a Way, Finding the Self: The Journeys of Nine Physical Educational Students Pursuing "Non-traditional" Paths', Graduate Department of Exercise Science, University of Toronto.

National Action Committee on the Status of Women (NAC). n.d. 'NAC Says NO' (Toronto: NAC).

National Post. 2004. 'If That's Not Racist, What Is?', editorial (14 July).

Native Women's Association of Canada (NWAC). 1988. 'The Implementation of Bill C-31 (Amendments of the Indian Act)', *Resources for Feminist Research* 17, 3: 125–8.

———. n.d. *Aboriginal Women, Self-government, and the Canadian Charter of Rights and Freedoms* (Ottawa: NWAC).

Nelson, L. 1999. 'Bodies (and Spaces) Do Matter: The Limits of Performativity', *Gender, Place & Culture* 6: 331–53.

Ng, R. 1986. 'The Social Construction of Immigrant Women in Canada', in *The Politics of Diversity*, eds R. Hamilton and M. Barrett (Montreal: Book Center).

———. 1988. *The Politics of Community Services: Immigrant Women, Class and State* (Toronto: Garamond).

———, and J. Ramirez. 1981. *Immigrant Housewives in Canada* (Toronto: Immigrant Women's Centre).

———, and T. Das Gupta. 1981. 'Nation Builders? The Captive Labour Force of Non-English Speaking Immigrant Women', *Canadian Women's Studies* 3, 1.

Nixon, R. 1997. 'Of Balkans and Bantustans: Ethnic Cleansing and the Crisis in National Legitimation', in *Dangerous Liaisons: Gender, Nation, and Post-colonial Perspectives*, eds A. McClintock, A. Mufti,

and E. Shohat (Minneapolis: University of Minnesota Press), 69–88.

Nova Scotia Barristers' Society (NSBS). 1990, consolidated May 1998. *Legal Ethics and Professional Conduct: A Handbook for Lawyers in Nova Scotia* (Halifax: NSBS).

O'Connell, K. 2007. '"We Who Are Not Here": Law, Whiteness, and Indigenous Peoples and the Promise of Genetic Identification', *International Journal of Law in Context* 3, 1: 35–58.

Omi, M., and H. Winant. 1993. 'On the Theoretical Concept of Race', in *Race, Identity, and Representation in Education*, eds C. McCarthy and W. Critchlow (New York: Routledge).

———, and ———. 1994. *Racial Formation in the United States: From the 1960s to the 1990s* (London and New York: Routledge).

Palmer, H. 1982. Patterns of Prejudice: A History of Nativism in Alberta (Toronto: McClelland & Stewart).

Paraschak, V. 2000. 'Knowing Ourselves through the "Other": Indigenous Peoples in Sport in Canada', in *Sociology of Sport*, eds R.L. Jones and K.M. Armour (Essex: Longman), 153–216.

Parekh, B. 1986. 'The "New Right" and the Politics of Nationhood', in *The New Right: Image and Reality* (London: Runnymede Trust).

Parker, D., and M. Song, eds. 2001. *Rethinking 'Mixed Race'* (London: Pluto Press).

Parmar, P. 1982. 'Gender, Race and Class: Asian Women in Resistance', in *The Empire Strikes Back*, ed. CCCS (London: Routledge), 236–75.

———. 1989. 'Other Kinds of Dreams', *Feminist Review* 31 (spring): 55–65.

Parry, B. 1987. 'Problems in Current Theories of Colonial Discourse', *Oxford Literary Review* 9, 1–2: 27–58.

Pascal, J. 2006. 'What's in a Name?', *Catalyst* (20 Nov.), available at <http://83.137.212.42/siteArchive/catalystmagazine/Default.aspx.LocID-0hgnew0n5.RefLocID-0hg01b00100k.Lang-EN.htm>.

Pascale, C.-M. 2007. *Making Sense of Race, Class, and Gender: Common-sense, Power, and Privilege in the United States* (New York: Routledge).

Pateman, C. 1988. *Sexual Contract* (Cambridge: Polity Press).

PBS. 1970. *Frontline: A Class Divided*, available at <http://www.pbs.org>.

Pendakur, K. 2005. 'Visible Minorities in Canada's Workplace: A Perspective on the 2017 Projection', RIIM Paper No. 05-11, Metropolis Project, Vancouver.

————, and R. Pendakur. 1996. *Earning Differentials among Ethnic Groups in Canada*, Strategic Research and Analysis, SRA-34b (Ottawa: Heritage Canada, Supply and Services Canada).

Penrose, J. 1993. 'Reification in the Name of Change: The Impact of Nationalism on Social Constructions of Nation, People and Place in Scotland and the United Kingdom', in *Constructions of Race, Place and Nation*, eds P. Jackson and J. Penrose (London: UCL Press), 27–49.

Persky, S. 1998. *Delgamuuk'w: The Supreme Court of Canada Decision on Aboriginal Title*, commentary (Vancouver and Toronto: Greystone Books).

Pettman, J. 1989. '"All the Women Are White, All the Blacks Are Men" . . . Racism, Sexism and the Representation of Black Women', Peach Research Centre, Australian National University, Canberra, mimeo.

Phillips, A. 2007. *Multiculturalism without Culture* (London: Palgrave Macmillan).

Pile, S. 1997. 'Introduction: Opposition, Political Identities, and Spaces of Resistance', in *Geographies of Resistance*, eds S. Pile and M. Keith (London: Routledge), 1–32.

Pipes, D. 2003. '(Moderate) Voices of Islam', *New York Post* (23 Sept.), available at <http://www.danielpipes.org/article/1255>. Accessed 1 Mar. 2004.

Podur, J. 2003. 'A Multifaceted Fraud—Review of the Book *The Trouble with Islam*', *Znet* (5 Dec.), available at <http://www.zmag.org/content/showarticle.cfm?ItemID=4624>. Accessed 14 Apr. 2004.

Pollitt, K. 2002. 'Introduction', in *Nothing Sacred: Women Respond to Religious Fundamentalism and Terror*, ed. B. Reed (New York: Thunder's Mouth Press/Nation Books), ix.

Pon, G. 2000. 'Beamers, Cells, Malls and Cantopop:

Thinking through the Geographies of Chineseness', in *Experiencing Difference*, ed. C.E. James (Halifax: Fernwood), 222–34.

Porter, J. 1965. *The Vertical Mosaic: An Analysis of Social Class and Power in Canada* (Toronto: University of Toronto Press).

Posner, M. 2003. 'Rousing Islam', *Globe and Mail* (16 Sept.), available at <http://www.muslim-refusenik.com/news/globeseptl6–03.html>. Accessed 14 Apr. 2004.

Poston Jr, D.L., M.X. Mao, and M.-Y. Yu. 1992. 'Patterns of Chinese Global Migration', paper delivered to Luo Di Sheng Gen International Conference on Overseas Chinese, San Francisco.

Poulantzas, N. [1974] 1978. *Classes in Contemporary Capitalism* (London: Verso).

————. [1978] 1980. *State, Power, Socialism* (London: Verso).

Pratt, G. 2000. 'Research Performances', *Environment and Planning D: Society and Space* 18: 639–51.

Price, S.L. 1997. 'Whatever Happened to the White Athlete?', *Sports Illustrated* (8 Dec.) 23, 12: 30–51.

Priest, G. 1990. 'Ethnicity in the Canadian Census', Department of Sociology, University of Toronto.

Pryor, E.T., et al. 1992. 'Is "Canadian" an Evolving Indigenous Ethnic Group?', *Ethnic and Racial Studies* 15: 214–35.

Radhakrishnan, R. 1996. *Diasporic Mediations* (Minneapolis: University of Minnesota Press).

Rahier, J., ed. 1999. *Representations of Blackness and the Performance of Identities* (Westport, CT: Greenwood).

Ramazanoglu, C. 1989. *Feminism and the Contradictions of Oppression* (London: Routledge & Kegan Paul).

Razack, S. 2002. *Dark Threats and White Knights: The Somalia Affair, Peacekeeping, and the New Imperialism* (Toronto: University of Toronto Press).

————. 2004. *Dark Threats and White Knights* (Toronto: University of Toronto Press).

————. 2005. 'Geopolitics, Culture Clash, and Gender after September 11', *Social Justice* 32, 4: 11–31.

Reed, J. 2003. 'Extreme Makeover', *Vogue* (Nov.):

465–72, 510.

Reitz, J., and R. Banerjee. 2007. 'Racial Inequality, Social Cohesion, and Policy Issues', in *Belonging?*, eds K. Banting et al. (Montreal: IRPP), 489–546.

Remsen, J. 2004. 'Stirring up Fellow Muslims', *Philadelphia Inquirer* (11 Jan.), available at <http://www.philly.com/mld/inquirer/living/religion/7679655.htm?lc>. Accessed 14 Apr. 2004.

Renaud, V. 1994a. *Report No. 16. National Census Test: Ethnic Origin* (Ottawa: Statistics Canada, Supply and Services Canada).

———. 1994b. *Report No. 18. National Census Test: Population Groups* (Ottawa: Statistics Canada, Supply and Services Canada).

Rich, P.B. 1986. *Race and Empire in British Politics* (Cambridge: Cambridge University Press).

Roediger, D. 1991. *The Wages of Whiteness: Race and the Making of the American Working Class* (London: Verso).

Root, M. 1996. *The Multiracial Experience* (London: Sage).

———. 1997. 'Mixed-race Women', in *Race/Sex*, ed. N. Zack (London: Routledge), 157–75.

Roscigno, V.J., et al. 2007. 'Racial Discrimination at Work: Its Occurrence, Dimensions, and Consequences', in *The New Black: Alternative Paradigms and Strategies for the 21st Century (Research in Race and Ethnic Relations)* 14: 111–35.

Rose, G. 1993. *Feminism and Geography* (Minneapolis: University of Minnesota Press).

———. 1995a. 'Geography and Gender: Cartographies and Corporealities', *Progress in Human Geography* 19: 544–8.

———. 1995b. 'The Interstitial Perspective: A Review Essay on Homi Bhabha's *The Location of Culture*', *Environment and Planning D: Society and Space* 13: 365–73.

———. 1996. 'As if the Mirrors Had Bled: Masculine Dwelling, Masculinist Theory and Feminist Masquerade', in *Body Space*, ed. N. Duncan (London: Routledge), 56–74.

Rosen, J. 1996. 'The Bloods and the Crits', *New Republic* (9 Dec.).

Rowbotham, S., L. Segal, and H. Wainwright. 1979. *Beyond the Fragments: Feminism and the Making of Socialism* (London: Merlin).

Ruddick, S. 1997. 'Constructing Difference in Public Space: Race, Class and Gender as Interlocking Systems', *Urban Geography* 17: 131–51.

Rushton, P. 1994. *Race, Evolution, and Behavior: A Life History Perspective* (New Brunswick, NJ: Transactions Publishers).

———. 2001. 'Is Race a Valid Taxonomic Construct?', Internet essay (14 Dec.), available at <http://www.charlesdarwinresearch.org/TaxonomicConstruct.pdf>.

Said, E. 1979. *Orientalism* (New York: Vintage Books).

———. 1992. *The Question of Palestine* (New York: Vintage Books).

———. 2001. 'The Clash of Ignorance', *Media Monitors Network* (11 Oct.), available at <http://www.mediamonitors.net/edward40.html>. Accessed 13 Aug. 2003.

Sailes, G.A. 1991. 'The Myth of Black Sports Supremacy', *Journal of Black Studies* 21, 4: 480–7.

St Germain, J. 2001. *Indian Treaty-making Policy in the United States and Canada, 1867–1877* (Toronto: University of Toronto Press).

Sarich, V., and F. Miele. 2004. *Race: The Reality of Human Differences* (Boulder, CO: Westview Press).

Sassen-Koob, S. 1981. 'Toward a Conceptualization of Immigrant Labour', *Social Problems* 29, 1: 65–85.

Satzewich, V. 2007. 'Whiteness Studies: Race, Diversity, and the New Essentialism', in *Race and Racism in 21st Century Canada*, eds S.P. Hier and B.S. Bolaria (Peterborough, ON: Broadview Press), 67–84.

———, and T. Wotherspoon. 1992. *First Nations: Race, Class and Gender Relations* (Scarborough, ON: Nelson).

Saxton, A. 1971. *The Indispensable Enemy: Labor and Anti-Chinese Movement in California* (Berkeley and Los Angeles: University of California Press).

Sayer, D. 1979. *Marx's Method: Ideology, Science and Critique in Capital* (Sussex: Harvester Press).

Scales-Trent, J. 1995. *Notes of a White Black Woman: Race, Color, Community* (University Park: Pennsylvania State University Press).

Schempp, P.G., and K.L. Oliver. 2000. 'Issues of

Equity and Understanding in Sport and Physical Education: A North American Perspective', in *Sociology of Sport*, eds R.L. Jones and K.M. Armour (Essex: Longman), 145–52.

Schroer, T. 2007. *Recasting Race after World War II: German and African Americans in American Occupied Germany* (Boulder: University Press of Colorado).

Sears, D., and J. McConahay Jr. 1973. *The Politics of Violence: The New Urban Blacks and the Watts Riot* (Boston: Houghton Mifflin).

Seuffert, N. 2006. *Jurisprudence of National Identity* (Burlington, VT: Ashgate Publishing).

Sharp, J., P. Routledge, C. Philo, and R. Paddison, eds. 2000. *Entanglements of Power: Geographies of Domination/Resistance* (London: Routledge).

Sheridan, W., and A. Saouab. 1992. *Canadian Multiculturalism*, Current Issue Review (Ottawa: Library of Parliament, Research Branch), Cat. No. 87-10E.

Silman, J. 1987. *Enough Is Enough: Aboriginal Women Speak Out* (Toronto: Women's Press).

Smedley, A. 2007. *Race in North America: Origin and Evolution of a World View*, 3rd edn (Boulder, CO: Westview Press).

Smith, C.C. 2007. *Conflict, Crisis, and Accountability: Racial Profiling and Law Enforcement in Canada* (Ottawa: Canadian Centre for Policy Alternatives), available at <http://www.policyalternatives.ca>.

Smith, David E. 1989. 'Canadian Political Parties and National Integration', in *Canadian Parties in Transition: Discourse, Organization and Representation*, eds A. Gagnon and B. Tanguay (Scarborough, ON: Nelson).

Smith, Dorothy E. 1974. 'The Social Construction of Documentary Reality', *Sociological Inquiry* 44, 4: 257–68.

———. 1981a. 'On Sociological Description: A Method from Marx', *Human Studies*, No. 4: 313–37.

———. 1981b. 'Institutional Ethnography: A Feminist Method', paper presented at the conference on the Political Economy of Gender Relations, OISE/University of Toronto (an abbreviated version of the paper is published in *Resources for Feminist Research* 16, 1 [1986]).

———. 1981c. 'The Experienced World as Problematic: A Feminist Method', Sorokin Lectures, No. 12, University of Saskatchewan.

———. 1983. 'Women, Class and Family', in *The Socialist Register, 1983*, eds R. Miliband and J. Saville (London: Merlin).

———. 1984. 'Textually Mediated Organizations', in *International Social Science Quarterly* 36, 1: 59–75.

Solomon, R.P. 1992. *Black Resistance in High School: Forging a Separatist Culture* (Albany: State University of New York Press).

Solomos, J. 1986. 'Varieties of Marxist Conceptions of "Race", Class and the State: A Critical Analysis', in *Theories of Race and Ethnic Relations*, eds J. Rex and D. Mason (Cambridge: Cambridge University Press), 84–109.

———, and L. Back. 1995. 'Marxism, Racism and Ethnicity', in *Theories of Ethnicity*, ed. J. Stanfield (Thousand Oaks, CA: Sage), 407–20.

Sondhi, R. 1987. *Divided Families: British Immigration Control in the Indian Subcontinent* (London: Runnymede).

Spicer, K. 1991. *Citizens' Forum on Canada's Future* (Ottawa: Canadian Government Publishing Centre).

Spivak, G. 1994. Presentation at the University of Toronto, May.

Stam, R. 1993. 'From Stereotype to Discourse', *Cine-Action* 23 (fall): 12–29.

Stasiulis, D.K. 1987. 'Rainbow Feminism: Perspectives on Minority Women in Canada', *Resources for Feminist Research* 16, 1: 5–9.

———. 1990. 'Theorizing Connections: Gender, Race, Ethnicity, and Class', in *Race and Ethnic Relations in Canada*, ed. P.S. Li (Don Mills, ON: Oxford University Press).

———. 1991. 'Symbolic Representation and the Numbers Game: Tory Policies on "Race" and Visible Minorities', in *How Ottawa Spends: 1988–1989*, ed. K.A. Graham (Ottawa: Carleton University Press).

Statistics Canada. 1976. *1971 Census of Canada, Population: General Characteristics*, Vol. I, Pt. II, Bulletin 1.3–2 (Ottawa: Department of Industry, Trade and Commerce).

———. 1984. *Census of Canada*, public use sample tape, individual file (Ottawa).

————. 1994a. *Report of the November 1993 National Census Test Results* (Ottawa).

————. 1994b. *1996 Census Consultation Report* (Ottawa).

————. 1994c. *Census of Canada,* public use microdata file for individuals (Ottawa). Stepan, N. 1982. *The Idea of Race in Science: Great Britain, 1800–1960* (London: Macmillan).

Stocking Jr, G. 1968. *History of Anthropological Theory* (New York: Free Press).

Stolcke, V. 1993. 'Is Sex to Gender as Race Is to Ethnicity?', in *Gendered Anthropology,* ed. T. del Valle (London: Routledge), 17–38.

Sullivan, A. 2004. '"The Trouble with Islam": Reform from Within', *New York Times* (25 Jan.), available at <http://www.muslim-refusenik.com/news/nytimes-04-1-5ptl.html>. Accessed 14 Apr. 2004.

Sunseri, M. 2005. 'Theorizing Nationalisms: Intersections of Gender, Nation, Culture, and Colonization in the Case of Oneida's Decolonizing Nationalist Movement', unpublished PhD diss., Department of Sociology, York University, June.

Tanovich, D.M. 2006. 'What Is It?', in *The Colour of Justice: Policing Race in Canada* (Toronto: Irwin Law), 9–30.

Tator, C., and F. Henry. 2006. *Racial Profiling in Canada* (Toronto: University of Toronto Press).

Taylor, L., C. James, and R. Saul. 2007. 'Who Belongs? Exploring Race and Racialization in Canada', in *Race, Racialization, and Anti-racism in Canada and Beyond,* eds G.F. Johnson and R. Enomoto (Toronto: University of Toronto Press), 151–78.

Teelucksingh, C., and G.-E. Galabuzi. 2005. 'Working Precariously: The Impact of Race and Immigrant Status on Employment Opportunities and Outcomes in Canada', report for the Canadian Race Relations Foundation, Toronto.

Therborn, G. 1980. *What Does the Ruling Class Do When It Rules? State Apparatuses and State Power under Feudalism, Capitalism and Socialism* (London: Verso).

Thobani, S. 2007. *Exalted Subjects* (Toronto: University of Toronto Press).

Thomas, J.M. 2007. 'Re-upping the Contract with Sociology: Charles Mill's *Racial Contract* Revisited a Decade Later', *Sociology Compass* 1, 1: 255–64.

Thompson, E.P. 1963. *The Making of the English Working Class* (Middlesex: Penguin).

Thrift, N., and J.-D. Dewsbury. 2000. 'Dead Geographies—and How to Make Them Live', *Environment and Planning D: Society and Space* 18: 411–32.

Trinh, T. 1992. *The Framer Framed* (London: Routledge).

Turner, D.A. 2006. *This Is Not a Peace Pipe: Towards a Critical Indigenous Philosophy* (Toronto: University of Toronto Press).

Twine, F. 1998. *Racism in a Racial Democracy* (New Brunswick, NJ: Rutgers University Press).

Tyner, J., and D. Houston. 2000. 'Controlling Bodies: The Punishment of Multiracialized Sexual Relations', *Antipode* 32: 387–409.

Ugwu, C. 1995. *Let's Get It On: The Politics of Black Performance* (London: Institute of Contemporary Arts and Bay Press).

Varpalotai, A. 1996. 'Canadian Girls in Transitions to Womanhood', in *Youth in Transition: Perspectives on Research and Policy,* eds B. Galaway and J. Hudson (Toronto: Thompson Educational Publishing).

Venne, S. 1998. *Our Elders Understand Our Rights: Evolving International Law Regarding Indigenous Rights* (Penticton, BC: Theytus Books).

Vickers, J. 2002. *The Politics of 'Race': Canada, Australia, and the United States* (Ottawa: Golden Dog Press).

Walker, B. 2002. 'The Canary Is Choking', *The Social Contract* (fall), available at <http://www.thesocialcontract.com/pdf/thirteenone/xiii-1-60.pdf> Accessed 15 Nov. 2003.

Walker, J. 1985. *The Black Identity in Nova Scotia: Community and Institutions in Historical Perspectives* (Dartmouth: Black Cultural Centre for Nova Scotia).

————. 1997. *'Race', Rights and the Law in the Supreme Court of Canada* (Waterloo, ON: Wilfrid Laurier University Press for The Osgoode Society for Canadian Legal History).

Wallace, P.A. 1980. *Black Women in the Labor Force* (Cambridge, MA: MIT Press).

Wallis, M.A., and S. Kwok, eds. 2008. *Daily Struggles:*

The Deepening Racialization and Feminization of Poverty in Canada (Toronto: Canadian Scholars' Press).

———, W. Giles, and C. Hernandez. 1988. 'Defining the Issues on Our Terms: Gender, Race and the State', *Resources for Feminist Research* 17, 3 (Sept.): 43–8.

Wargon, S. 2000. 'Historical and Political Reflections on Race', in *Race and Racism: Canada's Challenge*, eds L. Driedger and S. Halli (Montreal and Kingston: McGill-Queen's University Press), 20–32.

Warren, K. 1992. 'Transforming Memories and Histories: The Meanings of Ethnic Resurgence for Mayan Indians', in *Americas: New Interpretive Essays*, ed. A. Stepan (New York: Oxford University Press), 189–219.

Weaver, J., ed. 1998. 'From I-Hermeneutics to We-Hermeneutics: Native Americans and the Post-colonial', in *Native American Religious Identity: Unforgotten Gods* (Maryknoll, NY: Orbis Books): 1–25.

Webster, C. 2007. *Understanding Race and Crime* (Milton Keynes: Open University Press).

Wellman, D. 1977. *Portraits of White Racism* (Cambridge: Cambridge University Press).

Wetherell, M., and J. Potter. 1992. *Mapping the Language of Racism* (New York: Columbia University Press).

Wheeler, S., ed. 1969. *On Record: Files and Dossiers in American Life* (New York: Russell Sage Foundation).

White, E.F. 1984. 'Listening to the Voices of Black Feminism', *Radical America* 18, 2, 3: 7–26.

White, P.M. 1988. 'Testing 1991 Ethnic Ancestry, Ethnic Identity and Race Questions', paper presented at the Annual Meeting of the Canadian Population Society, Statistics Canada, mimeo, Windsor, ON.

———. 1992. 'Challenges in Measuring Canada's Ethnic Diversity', in *Twenty Years of Multiculturalism: Successes and Failures*, ed. S. Hryniuk (Winnipeg: St Johns College Press).

———, J. Badets, and V. Renaud. 1993. 'Measuring Ethnicity in Canadian Censuses', in *Challenges of Measuring an Ethnic World: Science, Politics and Reality*, eds G. Goldmann and N. McKenney (Ottawa and Washington: Statistics Canada and the United States Bureau of the Census).

Williams, L. 2002. *Playing the Race Card: Melodramas of Black and White from Uncle Tom to O.J. Simpson* (Princeton, NJ: Princeton University Press).

Winant, H. 1994. 'Racial Formation and Hegemony: Global and Local Implications', in *Racism, Modernity and Identity*, eds A. Rattansi and S. Westwood (Cambridge: Polity Press), 266–89.

———. 1997. 'Behind Blue Eyes: Whiteness and Contemporary US Racial Politics', in *Off White: Readings on Race, Power and Society*, eds M. Fine et al. (New York and London: Routledge), 40–56.

———. 1998. 'Racism Today: Continuity and Change in the Post–Civil Rights Era', *Ethnic and Racial Studies* 21, 4: 89–97.

———. 2002. 'Race in the Twenty-first Century', *Tikkun* 17, 1: 33–40.

———. 2004. *The New Politics of Race: Globalism, Difference, Justice* (Minneapolis: University of Minnesota Press).

Winks, R.W. 1969. 'Negro School Segregation in Ontario and Nova Scotia', *Canadian Historical Review* 52, 2: 164–91.

Wise, T. 2006. 'What Kind of Card Is Race?', available at <http://www.counterpunch.org>.

Wiwa, K. 2001. 'Black, White, and Colourful', *Globe and Mail* (15 Sept).

Women, Immigration and Nationality Group (WING). 1985. *Worlds Apart: Women Under Immigration and Nationality Law* (London: Pluto Press).

Woodsworth, J.S. 1909. *Strangers within Our Gates, or Coming Canadians* (Toronto: F.C. Stephenson/ Missionary Society of the Methodist Church).

Wortley, S. 2005. *Bias Free Policing: The Kingston Data Collection Project, Preliminary Results* (University of Toronto and the Centre for Excellence for Research on Immigration and Settlement).

Yegenoglu, M. 1998. *Colonial Fantasies: Towards a Feminist Reading of Orientalism* (Cambridge: Cambridge University Press).

Yon, D. 1995. 'Unstable Terrain: Explorations in Identity, Race and Culture in a Toronto High School', PhD diss., Department of Anthropology, York University.

Young, J., and J.E. Braziel, eds. 2006. *Race and the Foundation of Knowledge: Cultural Amnesia in the Academy* (Champaign: University of Illinois Press).

Yuval-Davis, N., and F. Anthias. 1989. *Woman–Nation–State* (London: Macmillan).

Zeitlin, I.M. 1990. *Ideology and the Development of Sociological Theory* (Englewood Cliffs, NJ: Prentice Hall).

Index